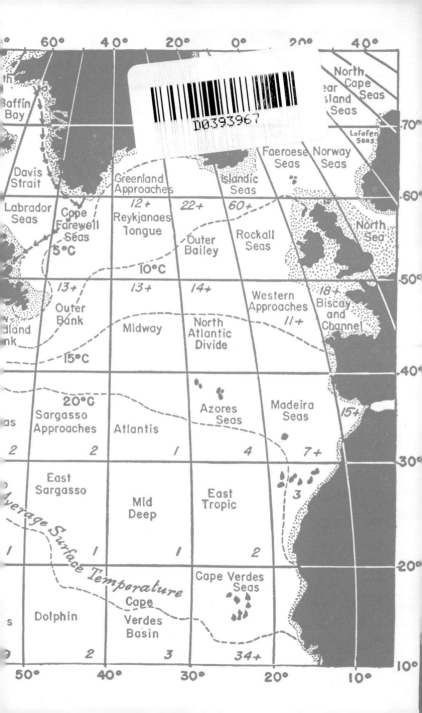

AUDUBON WATER BIRD GUIDE

The map reproduced on the front end paper of this book has been designed to provide helpful data for the student of waterfowl and pelagic birds. The major flyways along which the ducks and geese of eastern North America travel on their annual migrations are shown by arrows. The coastal shelf waters into which truly pelagic birds seldom wander are shown as dotted areas. The average surface temperature of the various parts of the North Atlantic is indicated by isothermic lines at 5-degree Centigrade intervals. For convenience in recording bird observations on the high seas, E. M. Nicholson has suggested assigning a name to each 10-degree square area of the Atlantic Ocean, as indicated. Some years ago Poul Jespersen published a map giving the average number of sea birds that he recorded per day in various parts of the Atlantic, and these have been inserted in each square. In order to develop really significant averages for various parts of the Atlantic many more such daily counts should be made and published even if the observer cannot always identify every one of the birds seen.

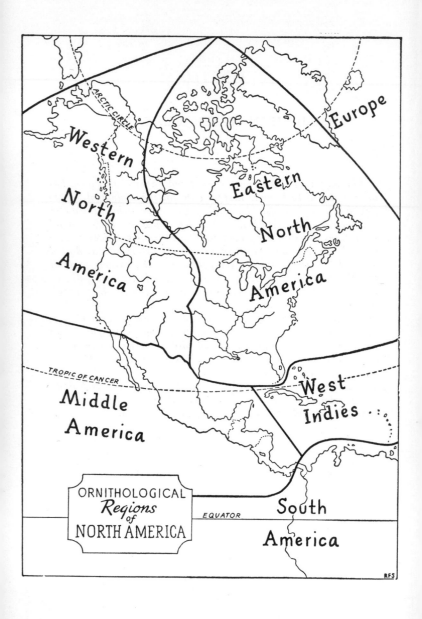

Western North America

Eastern North America

Europe

ARCTIC CIRCLE

Middle America

TROPIC OF CANCER

West Indies

ORNITHOLOGICAL
Regions
of
NORTH AMERICA

EQUATOR

South America

RFS

DOUBLEDAY NATURE GUIDES SERIES

AUDUBON
WATER BIRD GUIDE

WATER, GAME AND LARGE LAND BIRDS

Eastern and Central North America
from Southern Texas to
Central Greenland

BY RICHARD H. POUGH

•

Color illustrations by Don Eckelberry
Line drawings by Earl L. Poole

•

SPONSORED BY

NATIONAL AUDUBON SOCIETY

•

Doubleday & Company, Inc., Garden City, N.Y.

To all who find joy and recreation in a better understanding of the many forms of life with which we share the earth.

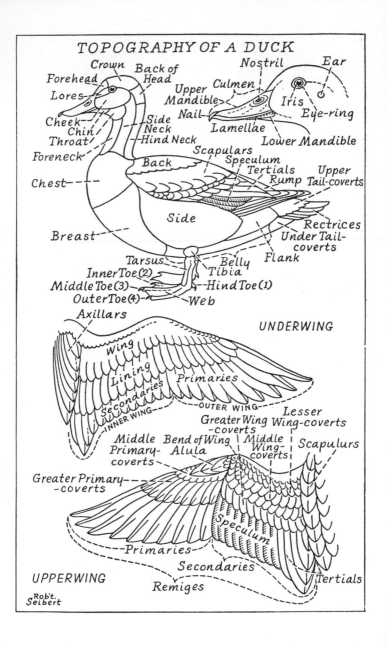

Foreword

To get the most out of this book you should know certain things about the region and the birds it covers. These will be covered in the Foreword and not repeated again in the text.

AREA: The area covered (some five million square miles) is eastern North America north of Mexico, excluding East Greenland. The line dividing eastern from western North America is taken as the eastern edge of the semi-arid Great Plains, where the tall-grass prairie country meets the drier, short-grass plains. In the United States it corresponds approximately with the one hundredth meridian running north through central Texas, western Oklahoma and Kansas, central Nebraska, and the Dakotas. In the Prairie Provinces of Canada, where the Great Plains end at the edge of the Hudsonian Forest, it swings sharply west and closely parallels the eastern side of the Rocky Mountain system almost to Alaska. The line roughly marks the westward range limit of many of the most typical birds of the humid East, but is far enough east to exclude most of the distinctly western birds, except for species that roam far out across the grass-covered lowlands in winter.

SCOPE: All birds are classified in a systematic series. The position of any bird in the general scheme is determined by its degree of specialization. Fossil remains show that birds were originally less highly specialized than they are now. Some water birds are still relatively simple, but most land birds are exceedingly complex. The standard classification begins with the more primitive birds like loons and grebes and ends with the most highly specialized—the sparrows.

The first and broadest of the groupings are called orders. Within the orders, closer relationship is expressed by the term family. Families are divided into genera and genera into species. The species describes the individual bird. It is a natural biological unit. It reproduces its own kind and, no matter how much two birds may look alike, they are not of the same species if they live in the same area and do not interbreed. This book follows the sequence of orders, families, genera, and species established by the American Ornithologists Union in their check-list.

The birds (estimated as between twelve and fifteen billion) that regularly spend at least part of the year on the American continent north of Mexico, frequent its coastal waters, or appear as occasional visitors are currently divided into 708 species, of which 533 occur more or less regularly in eastern North America. Many of these also occur in western North America, in addition to the 175 species confined to that area. The 258 species covered in this book are the more primitive birds of eastern North America; i.e., those that comprise the first half of the A.O.U. check-list.

BIRD NAMES: Every bird has a scientific name formed of Latin and Greek terms. The name of a species consists of two words. The first, which is capitalized, is its generic or group name and is the same for all species in a genus. The second, which is not capitalized, is the bird's specific name; each species has its own.

Every species is also given an official English name in the A.O.U. check-list. In some cases this name as it appears in the latest edition differs from that in the preceding edition. In other cases we have been in the habit of using the English name of our local race rather than a name applicable to the species as a whole. In order to avoid confusion these other names are given in parentheses under the present official A.O.U. name. Currently an effort is being made to bring the British and American names of species that occur in both countries into agreement, but where this has not yet been accomplished the official British Ornithologists Union (B.O.U.) name is given in parentheses. Many additional names are in widespread local use and will be found in the Index with a reference to the A.O.U. name.

Since this book is concerned only with species, it is unnecessary to do more than point out in passing that many species are now being subdivided geographically into subspecies or races. In most cases the differences are so minute as to have no significance in the field, and in some instances the question of whether to regard two similar but geographically separated bird populations as races or distinct species becomes a matter of judgment.

VARIATIONS IN APPEARANCE: It is important to remember that a bird may not look the same the year round and that male and female may not look alike. Where sexes have virtually the same appearance, the bird's name is followed by an asterisk (*). A young bird may not look like either parent, but if there is a difference between the sexes it usually resembles the female.

Newly hatched birds are usually covered with down or soon acquire a downy covering. As the bird grows this is soon replaced by the first true feathers which give it its *juvenile* plumage. Generally within a few months a molt starts which may take a short or long time to complete. As a result the *first winter* plumage may in some cases be subject to continuous change until sometime in the spring, and in a few cases there is little change until the *first prenuptial* molt in the spring. When in these subadult plumages birds are spoken of as *immature,* and in some species it takes several years of gradual change at each molt for an individual to become fully mature or adult.

Most birds regularly molt their body plumage twice a year and their flight feathers only once. These molts commonly occur in the late winter or early spring (i.e., the prenuptial molt which produces the breeding plumage) and again in late summer (i.e., the postnuptial molt which produces the fall and winter plumage). The flight-feather molt takes place in late summer, and in the waterfowl these feathers are all shed at one time, rendering the bird flightless for some weeks. In the drakes of the highly colored ducks this molt is preceded by a body-feather molt which produces a dull plumage rather like that of a female or juvenile. This is known as the *eclipse* plumage and is usually shed again as soon as the flight feathers have been replaced, the bird returning to its bright plumage, which is then worn for the next eleven months. In the duller geese and swan there is but one molt a year—the postnuptial—which is complete.

While this is a brief, generalized summary, the variations from family to family and species to species are infinite and give rise to many often puzzling plumages during the periods of change. This is especially true of juveniles and immatures, the very individuals most likely to wander out of their normal range and, therefore, to puzzle the bird student.

Freak birds with white or paler-than-usual feathers are not uncommon, and complete albinos are occasionally found. Another variation is *melanism,* in which darker feathers replace those of normal color. A few birds, like the jaegers, occur in two colors or phases, irrespective of age or sex. Hybrids between species, while rare, are another possibility, especially among waterfowl.

COLOR PLATES: The color plates in this book are a key to the birds. An attempt has been made to illustrate every plumage except the downy and juvenile stages. During the short period when these are worn the birds are best identified by their close association with their parents. Usually the plumage extremes of any species are represented by the adult breeding male and the immature female. If other plumages are so close to one of these as to be unmistakable, they are not shown. Figures not labeled as to season may be assumed to be in breeding plumage. If not labeled as to sex, adults may be assumed to be virtually alike. If there is a marked difference between sexes in immature plumage, the duller female is usually shown and so labeled. All birds on a plate are drawn to the same scale.

Familiarity with the color plates will greatly increase the usefulness of this book. To add further value, it is suggested that you go over it species by species, checking the ranges as you go along, and mark in some way the birds apt to be in your locality. A convenient way is to underline the birds you may expect, using a distinctive color for each seasonal group: red for permanent local resident; green for summer resident; blue for migrant; brown for winter visitor; and some other color for accidental visitors that might occur occasionally after a storm or other disturbance.

The beginner will usually find that a detailed, annotated list of the birds that occur within his state or more local area is available for further guidance. These range from short summaries that have appeared in some ornithological journals to books like A. D. Cruickshank's *Birds around New York City.* They are commonly called "check-list" or "annotated lists," and the best ones give details on the local status, migration dates, and local habitats of each species.

MEASUREMENTS: In making an identification it is important to note the bird's general size. Size is very important in differentiating between closely similar birds, and tables have been prepared to facilitate size comparisons. They are, however, based on averages, and it should be kept in mind that an occasional individual may deviate considerably from the average for the species as a whole. Nevertheless, it is a great help to have the sizes of a few of the most common local birds well fixed in your mind so that they can be used as a yardstick in estimating the size of unknown species. In the text the average length from tip of bill to end of tail (L.) is given. Where the ratio of tail length to over-all length has a decided effect upon the bird's appearance, the tail length in inches (T.) is given, and (B.) indicates the over-all length of the bill. If a bird is most commonly seen in the air the spread from wing tip to wing tip (W.) is given. Egg measurements are in inches, the maximum long diameter or axis by the maximum short diameter or thickness. All dimensions are average.

VOICE AND COURTSHIP: Unlike the passerine birds covered in the *Audubon Bird Guide to Small Land Birds,* most of the birds in this volume hardly have what could be called a song. They are often quite noisy, however, although the sounds they make are extremely difficult to describe satisfactorily. On the other hand, these larger birds generally have very distinctive and interesting courtship performances that are a fascinating field for study. A fuller understanding of the significance of the various sounds made by birds and the various posturings they go through in connection with each stage of their daily and annual routine is something toward which every amateur can contribute. Dr. Edward A. Armstrong's book, *Bird Display and Behavior,* provides an essential introduction to the subject and should be in every amateur ornithologist's library.

AGE: With the increased banding of wild birds by co-operators of the United States Fish and Wildlife Service, Washington, D.C., we are each year learning more about the migrations, mortality, sex ratios and longevity of birds. To date all the data indicate an extremely heavy mortality among juvenile and immature individuals and a greatly lessened rate once maturity is reached. The turnover in any population is, however, fairly high, a necessary concomitant of the high breeding rate most birds possess. In view of the low average age reached by the members of any species, it is interesting to note how long certain lucky individuals have been able to survive. Such a figure is given in this volume for the species for which data are available. It probably represents the maximum potential life span in only a few cases.

RESEARCH PROJECTS FOR AMATEURS: Throughout this book numerous gaps in the data on average weight, wingspread, incubation period, and other aspects of the reproductive cycle of many species will be noted. In general it can be said that this indicates a lack in the ornithological literature of any but the most fragmentary and unreliable information on these points. This amazingly frequent lack of such basic data for even the most common species offers the amateur bird student a wonderful opportunity to make valuable contributions to science.

Although the data from a single individual or nesting pair are useful in the absence of any data at all, it is best to try to obtain the same material from a series of individuals or pairs. This not only insures against the error that is always possible in the recording of a single instance, but it makes possible the establishment of a more significant average figure.

Once obtained, such data, to be of any value to science, must be placed on record, where all interested ornithologists will have easy access to it. This can best be accomplished by submitting it for publication to one of the state or regional ornithological journals, of which some 25 are now appearing in the United States. These can be easily located through any public library or natural history museum.

RANGE AND SEASONAL MOVEMENTS: Some birds remain in one locality throughout their lives. Others migrate in winter to areas far south (north in the Southern Hemisphere) of their breeding grounds. The first are generally spoken of as residents, noted in this book by (R.), the second as migrants (M.). Many species fail to give such clean-cut examples. Migrants may be summer or winter residents, depending upon the observer's location. Often a bird appears to be a migrant only in the northern part of its range and a more or less permanent resident farther south. Often it is difficult to know whether this indicates a southward shift of the whole population or whether there are two population groups, one migratory, one sedentary. At any rate, wintering birds appear south of the breeding range, and there are species where the most northerly breeders are the ones that winter farthest south. Such species are referred to in this book as partially migratory (P.M.).

A few species wander erratically except during the breeding season, pausing wherever they find suitable food. As the majority of these erratic wanderers (E.W.) belong to the North, most of us see them only in winter. Because of their irregularity in any given locality they are often called winter visitors rather than winter residents. Another group of erratic wanderers are southern species, chiefly herons, which breed early and come north during the summer in numbers that vary greatly from year to year.

In the section on range, if a bird is a permanent resident, its over-all range is given. If it is a migrant, its breeding range is given first, followed by its winter range, in which case it can be assumed that it is a migrant between the two. Only where breeding and wintering ranges are widely separated and the birds follow a rather well-defined route between the two is the route specified. For dates of arrival and departure, one should consult a local check-list or make one's own.

Although oceans are sharply divided into shallow and deep areas, cold and warm areas, those rich in nutrients and plankton life and those that are virtually lifeless, each with its characteristic birds, powerful storms often carry these birds far from their normal haunts. As a result, this volume includes many birds that wander occasionally to our shores or coastal waters although their normal range lies far away. To avoid confusion it is best to mark their pictures, as they are not something to be looked for every day but only when a puzzling newcomer fails to fit any of the plumages of the local residents.

FIELD STUDY: As many of these birds will be observed at some distance over water, the use of powerful binoculars or telescopes is a great help in their study. Hand-held (with or without a rest) binoculars up to 16- or 18-power are a great help. Excellent telescopes or tripod binoculars are also available at even higher powers and often open up such an extensive water area to observation that an entire day's birding can be done from one spot.

At other times extremely close observation of these birds is possible if you can station yourself near a nest or favorite feeding ground. For this a blind is a great help and will often permit the taking of excellent still and motion pictures of such activities as courtship. A blind can be made of local vegetation or burlap fastened to a permanent frame or need be no more than an old fish net draped over your head and body to break your outline as you sit on the ground.

CONSERVATION: Active steps for their conservation are needed more by the birds in this volume than by most of the smaller birds. Some are game birds that can easily be overshot if hunting regulations are too liberal or are not conscientiously observed. Many are so large that they offer tempting targets to the thoughtless. Others, like the hawks and some of the fish eaters, are frequently killed by farmers, ranchers, and fishermen even though science has demonstrated their intrinsic value as components of a healthy, balanced wildlife community.

For many the most critical factor is the highly specialized nature of the habitat that they require either for nesting or for year-round residence. This, added to the intolerance of disturbance that is shown by so many species, makes it essential for us to plan to keep certain areas free from the influences of civilization—influences that if not subject to conscious checks seem destined to reach into every corner of our once seemingly spacious continent as population pressure increases year after year. A start has been made in our National Parks, our National Forest Primitive Areas and our Wildlife Refuges, but more needs to be done and the time left to do it is none too long.

Especially serious is the plight of many of the colonial nesting water birds. Even where their habitat and feeding grounds remain relatively unimpaired, many species are finding it harder and harder each year to find nest sites. Islands are being occupied by summer resorts, or visited daily by picnickers, and secluded swamp woodlands are either being cut or made increasingly accessible to the public by roads. Yet often the sanctuary or reservation that would be necessary to preserve a breeding colony that could enliven the countryside for miles around with attractive birds need not be more than a few acres.

In the main, these are not projects for the Federal Government or even for state governments; they are projects for public-spirited individuals who appreciate what the presence of bird life can mean to a community both economically and aesthetically. Others can be handled by small local groups banded together by a common interest in birds and a desire to do something to insure their preservation for the enjoyment of future generations; generations that may, as civilization becomes ever more omnipresent, value bird life and the chance to study and enjoy it even more than we do.

Acknowledgments

In preparing this book I have drawn freely upon the literature on North American birds which has been accumulating for more than two hundred years. I myself have had the privilege of studying birds in every state of the Union, but I have made full use of the recorded observations of others. Only in this way would it be possible to present a well-rounded picture of each species throughout its range.

I owe an especial debt to Arthur C. Bent, whose *Life Histories of North American Birds,* published in many volumes by the United States National Museum, provide a thorough abstract of the extensive and widely scattered literature on birds. I have also found the published works of such outstanding naturalists as Arthur A. Allen, Frank M. Chapman, A. K. Fisher, Francis H. Kortright, W. L. McAtee, Robert C. Murphy, Roger T. Peterson, Thomas S. Roberts, and Witmer Stone of special help. V. C. Wynne-Edwards's summary of his own field work and that of others in his report, "On the Habits and Distribution of Birds in the North Atlantic," and Warren F. Eaton's "List of Birds Recorded from the Bermudas" provided much helpful data on the birds of the vast and ornithologically little-known Atlantic. For data on food habits I have had to lean heavily on the many published studies of the Food Habits Research Division of the United States Fish and Wildlife Service and its predecessor, the Biological Survey. My range paragraphs are an abbreviation of the data in the fourth edition and more recent supplements of the American Ornithologists Union's *Check-list of North American Birds.*

Don Eckelberry, in my opinion, has made an outstanding contribution to ornithology in his illustrations for these books. On his behalf and my own I wish to thank the American Museum of Natural History and the Cleveland Museum of Natural History for their patience in making available typical skins for use in preparing both the paintings and the identification text. I am also greatly indebted to Earl L. Poole of the Reading Public Museum for taking time from his many other activities to do the fine black-and-white drawings that so enliven the text pages.

To the National Audubon Society and its directors, who have made it possible for me to undertake this book and have honored me by sponsoring it, I owe an especial debt of gratitude.

For the helpful suggestions and other courtesies I am also indebted to the following: Robert P. Allen, Dean Amadon, John H. Baker, James Bond, Charles L. Broley, Donald G. Carter, James P. Chapin, Allan D. Cruickshank, Jean Delacour, Monica de la Salle, Ludlow Griscom, Nella Braddy Henney, Joseph J. Hickey, Eleanor King, John Lynch, Ernst Mayr, Robert C. Murphy, J. T. Nichols, Charles E. O'Brien, Roger T. Peterson, Charles H. Rogers, Robert Seibert, Victor E. Shelford, Alexander Sprunt, Jr., W. E. Clyde Todd, Josselyn Van Tyne, Alexander Wetmore, Edward M. Weyer, John T. Zimmer, to my wife, Moira, who doubled as my secretary throughout the preparation of the manuscript, and to the many members of the staff of Doubleday and Company who have been so helpful, especially Clara Claasen and Sabra Mallett.

RICHARD H. POUGH

Pelham, New York

Contents

CONTENTS

Standard Abbreviations Used in Text

※   Color plate number

*   Sexes similar in appearance

♂   Male

♀   Female

Jv.   Juvenile

Im.   Immature

n.   northern

s.   southern

e.   eastern

w.   western

c.   central (between east and west)

m.   middle (between north and south)

mts.   mountains

L.   Over-all length (tip of bill to end of tail) in inches

W.   Wingspread (tip to tip) in inches

B.   Length of bill in inches

T.   Length of tail in inches

L.L.   Length of legs in inches

Wt.   Weight in pounds and ounces (grams for very small birds)

R.   Resident; i.e., non-migratory

M.   Migratory

P.M.   Partially migratory (found in some areas the year round)

E.W.   Erratic wanderer

Age.   Maximum age known to have been reached by an individual of the species in the wild

B. Age.   Normal age at which individuals first breed

E.   Number of eggs in an average clutch

Br.   Number of broods normally reared in a season

A.   An altricial species; i.e., one in which the young remain in the nest until nearly fully feathered and about ready to fly

P.   A precocial species; i.e., one in which the young leave the nest almost as soon as they are out of the egg

B. Ter.   The average size in acres of the territory defended by a pair when breeding

W. Ter.   The average size in acres of the territory defended by an individual or flock when established in an area for the winter

C.   Average number of days of courtship preceding pair formation

N.C.   Average number of days required for the construction of the nest

E.L.   Days required from the time of the laying of the first egg for the completion of the clutch

I.   Average incubation period in days

(2.8x1.9)   Average egg length and maximum diameter in inches

N.   Number of days that the young birds normally remain in the nest after hatching

D.   Average number of days that the young are dependent on the parents for food, shelter, or care of one sort or another after they leave the nest

F.S.   Average normal flight speed

AUDUBON WATER BIRD GUIDE

Many people ask what they can do to assist in the cause of conservation of birds and other wildlife. One of the best suggestions is that they support the work of the National Audubon Society, 1130 Fifth Avenue, New York 28, N.Y., and local Audubon societies. These and other conservation organizations deserve your aid.

LOONS

Order Gaviiformes

LOONS   Family Gaviidae

Common Loon*   *Gavia immer*—✳ 1
(Great Northern Diver)   L. 28–34; W. 54–58; Wt. 5–9 lbs.

IDENTIFICATION: In breeding plumage the black bill separates
this species from the similar but rarer yellow-billed loon. In
winter it differs from other loons in its greater size, bigger
head (slightly darker than the back), and heavier bill. Until
the spring of their second year, young are like winter adults
but have even paler, almost brown-colored bills, and the pale
edges to the back feathers are more pronounced, giving the
birds an obscurely barred effect. On water loons ride low,
with neck curved and head down. In flight the stout, moderately long neck seems to reach downward a little, giving the
bird a hunchbacked appearance. The small, narrow, pointed
wings are set well back on the body, and the big webbed feet
trail out beyond the short tail.

HABITS: (Age 8 yrs.) This loon breeds both on deep, clear lakes
and small fishless ponds. It will not be crowded, and only a
large lake has room for more than a single pair. The birds
seem to find shallow, marshy bays off big lakes especially
attractive. Most of them winter on salt water along the coast,
but a few stay inland and travel no farther south than forced
to by ice. Loons migrate singly or in small groups up to 5 or
6, but gather in considerable numbers in favorable feeding
areas. Although they eat fish they also take a variety of other
items—crayfish, crabs, amphibians, aquatic insects, shellfish,
and vegetation—and seem able to get along entirely without
fish. They catch fish in underwater dives averaging 30 to 45
seconds in length, during which they normally propel themselves with their feet, though occasionally the wings are also
used. There are numerous records of loons being caught in
fishing nets placed 180 and 200 feet below the surface. The
feet are well adapted for swimming but are so far back on the
body that on land the bird cannot stand upright or take flight
and has to shove itself along on its breast. Even on water it
cannot take off unless it has room for a long run into the
wind.

VOICE: The weird, mournful, and loud, resonant calls vary from a tremulous *ha-ha-ha-ha-ha* to long-drawn-out yodeling howls that rise, then fall and fade away. These can be closely approximated by the human voice.

NEST: (I. 28, P., D. 45) A flat 2-foot mass of vegetation with a slight depression in the center, situated close to the water's edge or anchored in the water near the outer edge of a bed of reeds. Occasionally a muskrat house is used. The 2 olive-brown to olive-green eggs (3.5 x 2.2) are sparingly marked with small brown spots. The white-bellied, dark brown downy young swim within a day or two of hatching.

RANGE: (M.) Breeds from Iceland, c. Greenland, the Arctic Islands, and n.w. Alaska south to Massachusetts, n. Indiana, n. Iowa, Montana, and n. California. Winters from Nova Scotia, the Great Lakes, and s. Alaska south to Florida, the Gulf Coast, n. Mexico, and Lower California, and in Europe from the British Isles south and east to Madeira and the Black Sea.

Yellow-billed Loon*   *Gavia adamsii*—✕1
(White-billed Northern Diver) L. 33–36; W. 60; Wt. 10–12 lbs.

IDENTIFICATION: The large bill, straw-colored with a brownish base, has a distinctive shape—straight along the upper edge and strongly upcurved below. Adults are glossed with purple, not green as in the common loon, and the back pattern is bolder. The distinctive bill is slow in developing, and immatures, with bills dusky at the base and whitish only at the tip, are often hard to separate from those of other loons. The flight is powerful and fast, with head and bill pointed slightly upward.

HABITS: The fresh-water lakes, ponds, and rivers of the tundra are the home of this loon, which clings so close to the Arctic that it has always been a bird of mystery. It is evidently a late nester, as it is often encountered in early summer in areas where there is no sign of nesting activity, and it remains on many inland lakes and rivers until the last open water freezes over in the fall. Like all loons, these winter on salt water along seacoasts. To date there are almost no records of this bird on the East Coast. In winter its food seems to be largely fish.

VOICE: Similar to that of the common loon but said to be louder and harsher with an even more mournful, lonely quality.

NEST: (P.) A flat platform of mud a few inches above water on the edge of a lake or river. The slight hollow that holds the 2 dark-spotted warm brown eggs (3.5 x 2.2) is generally somewhat lined with vegetation. The light brown downy young are buffy above and nearly white below.

RANGE: (M.) Breeds from Foxe Basin west through the arctic regions of Canada (south to Great Slave Lake), Alaska, Siberia, and n. Europe to n. Finland. Winters off the coasts of s. Alaska and British Columbia, Siberia, Japan, and Norway.

Arctic Loon*   *Gavia arctica*—⚡1
(Black-throated Diver)   L. 24; W. 40; Wt. 5 lbs.

IDENTIFICATION: This and the red-throated loon are much smaller than the two preceding birds. The proportionately smaller bill in this species is straight or downcurved. The gray head and nape and striped neck of summer adults are distinctive, and the white on the back is restricted to the scapular area. Winter adults are uniform blackish-gray above (slightly lighter on the head), and the contrast with the white under parts is stronger than in other loons. Young are similar but have a light edging to the back feathers which produces a slightly scaled effect.

HABITS: This is an adaptable, wide-ranging species. It nests on large lakes like other loons and also on small ponds, sloughs, and other patches of shallow water. In many cases the birds

fly back and forth long distances to larger bodies of fresh
water or to the seacoast for food. The main wintering grounds
seem to be well offshore along the coasts of southern and
Lower California. In migration many hundreds may pass but
always in small groups.

VOICE: The loud calls are weird and varied. The commonest is
a harsh *kok, kok, kok.* Others are described as bloodcurdling
howls, screams, and squeals that carry for great distances.
Like all loons, these become comparatively silent after they
leave the breeding grounds.

NEST: (I. 29, P., D. 60) Always close to the water or on a
mound built up in shallow water. The nest varies from a lined
depression on bare ground to a large mass of rotted stems,
roots, and mud that scarcely raises the 2 dark-brown-spotted,
olive-brown eggs (3.0 x 1.85) above the water. The downy
young are brown above and drab below.

RANGE: (M.) Breeds in northern Europe, Asia, and in North
America from the Arctic Islands and coast south to the James
Bay area, n. Manitoba, c. British Columbia, and s.w. Alaska.
Winters from s.e. Alaska to s. Lower California. Occurs
rarely on the Atlantic coast.

Red-throated Loon*
(Red-throated Diver)

Gavia stellata—✳ 1
L. 25; W. 44

IDENTIFICATION: This small loon has a slender bill, slightly
uptilted at the tip, and its head and neck are rather slender.
In summer the back is a uniform brownish-black, faintly
flecked with white. In winter the white spotting is more conspicuous and the head and neck are white below and often
rather light gray above. Young birds are browner and less
spotted on the back, and the white about the head and neck
is not as clear.

HABITS: These birds often nest on small shallow bodies of water
just big enough to permit them to take off and land readily.
In many cases most of their feeding is done elsewhere, frequently on nearby salt water. This active bird is less clumsy
than the large loons and can, with some effort, walk upright.
It is a fast, strong, and usually high flier, covering long
distances with ease. When surprised it will often fly rather
than dive and can practically jump into flight even on a
windless day. Like all loons, red-throateds are curious and
can often be brought close to shore by a fluttering handker-
chief. Their food, while preponderately small fish like cape·

lin, sand launces, and herrings, runs the gamut of aquatic life from shellfish to insects.

VOICE: On breeding grounds this is a noisy bird, but at other times it calls rather infrequently. The commonest call is a prolonged, somewhat gooselike, rolling growl. There are others, a mewing wail, soft mews, and a loud *kark*.

NEST: (I. 26, P., D. 60) The nest is on a low flat area on the water's edge or built up in shallow water. It is never more than a flattened mass of moss and other soft vegetation and often is simply a hollow on bare ground. The 2 olive-brown eggs (2.8 x 1.8) are usually spotted with dark brown. The downy young are dark brown above and drab below.

RANGE: (M.) Arctic and northern areas around the world. In North America it breeds on the Arctic Islands and coast from Greenland to Alaska south to Newfoundland, c. Quebec, n. Manitoba, and the s. British Columbia coast. Winters, chiefly on salt water, from the Gulf of St. Lawrence, the Great Lakes, the coast of British Columbia, and the Aleutian Islands south to Florida and n. Lower California. Rare on the Gulf Coast.

GREBES

Order Colymbiformes

GREBES   Family Colymbidae

Red-necked Grebe*   *Colymbus grisegena*—⚹2
(Holboell's Grebe)   L. 19½; W. 31; Wt. 3 lbs.

IDENTIFICATION: This short-bodied bird has a long slim neck and a triangular head which is carried erect. Winter adults are best told by the yellow base of the bill, the gray neck, and the vertical white area behind the grayish cheeks. The head and cheeks of young birds are striped with black and white and the neck is rufous; the stripes are generally lost in fall, but the neck color may persist. This grebe's flight is loonlike, but the wings have conspicuous white areas on the leading and rear edges of the inner wing.

HABITS: The summer home is a marshy lake or a deep marsh with many channels and pondlike openings. The bird is generally shy. Ordinarily it rides high in the water with its head nodding back and forth as it swims, but it can reduce its buoyancy by compressing its feathers and sink out of sight before it is noticed. Often the downy young scramble to the parent's back, where they can hang on even through a dive. In winter most of these grebes migrate to salt water and feed just outside the breakers or in protected bays. A few stay in large bodies of inland water, leaving only if they freeze over. Like most birds of its group, the red-necked takes a variety of aquatic food. Fish, though eaten, are not essential, and the birds often nest on fishless ponds. In general they eat whatever small aquatic animal life is most abundant and therefore easiest to obtain.

VOICE: The distinctive courtship notes vary from loud piercing brays or wails to vibrant squeaks or whinnies. The call is a nasal *konk,* said to suggest a donkey's bray.

NEST: (I. 23, P.) A floating mass of soft or rotted aquatic vegetation placed in the open on a bed of submerged plants or in a stand of broken-down reeds. The 4 or 5 unmarked whitish eggs (2.3 x 1.4) are soon stained and muddied. The downy young are almost black above, lighter below, with boldly striped heads and necks.

RANGE: (M.) Most of the Northern Hemisphere north to the Arctic Circle. In North America it breeds from n. Ungava,

n. Mackenzie, and n.w. Alaska south to s.w. New Brunswick, s. Ontario, c. Minnesota, n.w. Montana, and c.n. Washington. Winters, chiefly coastwise, from Maine, s. Ontario, s. Wisconsin, and s. British Columbia south to North Carolina, Tennessee, and s. California.

Horned Grebe* *Colymbus auritus*—⚹2
(Slavonian Grebe) L. 13; W. 24; Wt. 1 lb.

IDENTIFICATION: This compact little bird rides high in the water and has a rounded head outline with slightly puffed cheeks. In swimming, the neck is somewhat curved or thrust forward. Summer adults need no description. In winter the clear white of the neck and cheeks, extending almost across the back of the head, is distinctive. This species flies more readily than most grebes, with a strong, direct, loonlike flight, revealing a large white patch at the rear of the inner wing.

HABITS: Small ponds, sloughs, and shallow bays of large lakes are the summer home. Often several pairs are present on a small pond, and in more extensive habitats loose colonies of 4 to 6 pairs are formed. The birds are not shy and sometimes nest with little concealment. When migrating they occur inland on rivers, lakes, and ponds, staying often until these freeze over. The main winter home is on salt water in the open ocean beyond the surf or in sheltered bays and sounds. Like loons, grebes catch their food in long dives under water. The horned starts with a pronounced upward and forward leap and propels itself under water solely with its feet. Its food includes fish, insects, crayfish, tadpoles, shrimp, and some vegetable matter.

VOICE: The commonest call on the breeding grounds is a low, uneven trill. The bird also utters a variety of croaking, chattering, and squealing notes, often with a mournful or plaintive quality.

NEST: (I. 24, P.) A floating mass of mud and vegetation in water up to several feet deep. Nests are generally anchored to, and often well concealed by, emergent vegetation. The 4 greenish-white eggs (1.7 x 1.2) soon become mud-stained. The downy young are black, finely striped and spotted with white.

RANGE: (M.) Occurs over much of the Northern Hemisphere. In North America breeds from s.w. Ungava, n. Manitoba, n. Mackenzie, and c. Alaska south to e. Maine, s. Ontario, s.

Wisconsin, n. Nebraska, n. Wyoming, and s. British Columbia.
Winters from Maine, c. New York, the Great Lakes, and
British Columbia south to Florida, the Gulf Coast, and s.
California.

Eared Grebe*   *Colymbus caspicus*—⚹2
(Black-necked Grebe)   L. 13; W. 22½; Wt. ½ lb.

IDENTIFICATION: The eared grebe has a finer bill with a tip that
appears upturned, a slimmer neck, a more upright carriage,
a more triangular head, and more white on the wing than
the horned grebe. Its short, dumpy body usually seems very
high-sterned. In summer the black crest and neck are distinctive. In winter the white of the cheeks and neck is not so
pure or extensive but is washed, often unevenly, with gray.
In young birds there is little color difference between cheek
and crown.

HABITS: The eared grebe frequently nests in dense colonies in
which several hundred pairs are crowded into a limited area,
but smaller groups or single pairs are also common. Shallow,
marshy lakes or marshy sections of large lakes are its summer
home. The gregariousness of the species continues through
the winter, when it commonly feeds in flocks. The main
migration is southwestward to salt water, but some birds
remain all winter on fresh water. On inland water, aquatic
insects are a staple food—one bird took 1,300 water boatmen
in a single meal. In many areas wind-blown land insects are
important. Small shrimplike crustacea are evidently the bird's
chief food on salt water.

VOICE: This is not a noisy bird and its calls have a soft quality.
A common one is a *poo-eep, poo-eep,* with a rising inflection.
It also utters an emphatic, rapid 3-note call in a wheezy
voice.

NEST: (I. 21, P.) The very small, ill-constructed nests are little
more than a heap of soggy vegetation floating in shallow
water or resting on a bed of submerged aquatic plants or
rubbish. Often, instead of concealing them in reeds, the birds
appear deliberately to seek an open area. The 4 or 5 whitish
eggs (1.7 x 1.2) often lie in a little water and are soon
stained brown. The downy young are black and dusky with
light streaks and spots.

RANGE: (P. M.) Occurs throughout Europe, Asia, s. Africa, and
w. North America. Breeds from n. Iowa, c. Manitoba, s.
Mackenzie, and c. British Columbia south to s. Texas, n.

New Mexico, and s. California. Winters chiefly on the Pacific coast from Washington to Guatemala, appearing only rarely on the Atlantic coast.

Least Grebe* *Colymbus dominicus*—✻2
(Mexican Grebe) L. 9; W. 14

IDENTIFICATION: The diminutive size of this short-necked grebe and its whitish-tipped, small black bill are distinctive, as are the largely white flight feathers of the wing. Winter adults have a white or partly white throat and lack the black crown. Young are similar, but the bill is even smaller and its lower half is pale.

HABITS: Almost any body of fresh water is likely to have a pair or more of these abundant little grebes. When nesting they make little use of protective cover but place the nests in open water. The bird is shy, however, and if disturbed quickly sinks out of sight to come up in the concealment of a clump of reeds.

VOICE: A loud, trumpetlike *clang* note.

NEST: A small floating heap of old vegetation and mud, anchored in an area of fairly deep, open water. The 3 or 4 whitish eggs (1.3 x .92) soon stain brown. The downy young are blackish-brown, striped with white.

RANGE: (R.) Occurs from s.e. Texas and s. Lower California south through tropical South America and in the West Indies.

Western Grebe* *Aechmophorus occidentalis*—✻2
(Swan Grebe) L. 22–29; W. 30–40; Wt. 1½ lbs.

IDENTIFICATION: The very long, slender neck, greenish-yellow, slightly upturned bill, and the gleaming white under parts contrasting strongly with the dark gray above are distinctive. In winter, when the under parts are slightly duller, the contrast is less. In flight the rear half of the wing is extensively white.

HABITS: These grebes nest in well-defined colonies in the marshy borders of large lakes and in wide shallow sloughs filled with tall marsh vegetation. The colonies vary in size from a dozen to hundreds of pairs. All loons and grebes have interesting courtship performances, of which the western's is typical. Paired birds repeatedly throw their heads back almost to their tails, then suddenly rise out of the water and run along the surface side by side, neck up and body almost vertical. The climax is reached when the birds rear up and

circle breast to breast, treading water so rapidly that most of
the body is exposed. When these grebes migrate west to the
coast it is generally in large flocks. On the coastal bays and
lagoons great numbers are found together on favorable feeding grounds. They apparently depend more heavily on fish
than other grebes. For some unaccountable reason all grebes
have the habit of eating and retaining in a ball in their
stomachs large quantities of their own feathers—numbering
331 in the stomach of one western.

VOICE: The common note is a loud, rasping, squeaky whistle
which suggests the note of the osprey. It also utters a low,
rolling croak.

NEST: (I. 23, P.) A large, often floating, mass of both dead
and green marsh vegetation. Although the nests are sometimes in fairly deep water they float high and are always
anchored to, and frequently well hidden in, a growth of
reeds. The 3 or 4 eggs (2.3 x 1.5) are at first bluish-white
but soon stain. The downy young are solid mouse gray above
and pale gray to white below, without stripes.

RANGE: (M.) Breeds from c. Manitoba, n. Alberta, and c.
British Columbia south to c. South Dakota, w. Nebraska, c.
Utah, and s. California. Winters on the Pacific coast in
coastal and adjacent inland waters from s. British Columbia
to s. Mexico. Rare on the Atlantic coast.

Pied-billed Grebe* *Podilymbus podiceps*—♯2
L. 13; W. 23; Wt. 1 lb.

IDENTIFICATION: The thick, blunt bill of the pied-bill is distinctive even in winter, when it is dusky-colored and lacks the
black band. This is the only grebe that does not show a white
patch on the wing in flight and is the brownest in general
appearance. On water it ordinarily holds its tail high enough
to reveal its white under tail coverts.

HABITS: This is the common "helldiver" of the East. Any pond
or sluggish stream with shallow reed-grown banks or other
cover is likely to harbor a nesting pair. They also occur in
extensive marshes if the water is deep or the area is interspersed with openings and channels. One of the shiest of the
grebes, this one manages to keep out of sight so well that its
presence is often unsuspected. If surprised it can slowly sub-
merge until only its bill is visible or swim under water to
the nearest cover where it can emerge unseen. In spring it
goes north very early and often does not leave in the fall

until the ponds freeze. It generally sticks to the same sort of fresh-water habitats throughout the year, but a few work coastwise and turn up in shallow bays and salt-marsh channels when inland habitats freeze over. A variety of aquatic animals, including fish, snails, frogs, tadpoles, and insects, are taken as food.

VOICE: A series of a dozen or more loud, resonant, cuckoo-like *cow-cow-cow* notes is the common springtime call. It also has other wailing and grunting notes.

NEST: (I. 23, P.) A generally well-concealed mound of soft plant material resting on a large floating mass of dead plant remains. It is sometimes in water several feet deep but is always well anchored to growing vegetation. The rim of the nest is of loose material that the bird pulls over the eggs to hide them when it goes away. The 5 to 7 blue or green-white eggs (1.7 x 1.2) are soon stained with brown. The newly hatched young, which are strikingly striped with black and white, are very active.

RANGE: (P. M.) Breeds throughout most of the Western Hemisphere north to Nova Scotia, s. Ontaria, c. Manitoba, s. Mackenzie, and c. British Columbia, and south to s. Argentina. Winters from New York south along the Atlantic coast, in the Southern States, and from s. British Columbia south along the Pacific coast.

ALBATROSSES and ALLIES

Order Procellariiformes

SHEARWATERS and FULMARS
Family Procellariidae

Sooty Shearwater*   *Puffinus griseus*—✹20
L. 17; W. 42

IDENTIFICATION: This slender-billed, narrow-winged shearwater is characterized by its over-all sooty brown-black coloring.

The underwing coverts, however, vary with the individual from white to pale gray and the chin-throat region from dark gray to pale gray.

HABITS: The sooty shearwater is widely dispersed over the oceans of the world during its non-breeding season. It seems more attracted to coastal waters than other species. In the Atlantic the birds work north off our coast in May and June, few appearing on the European side until late summer. They most commonly occur as scattered individuals associated with other shearwaters on favorable feeding grounds such as off-shore fishing banks. Occasionally flocks numbering into the hundreds are encountered. In the eastern Pacific they travel in vast flocks that often take the form of a huge circle around which the individual birds keep moving as they feed. Here they migrate north and south so close to land that hundreds of thousands are sometimes seen from points on the shore. Staple foods seem to be squids, small fish, and crustacea. These are found close to the surface, but the birds to a limited extent can dive and swim under water. Shearwaters and petrels are inordinately fond of oily fish livers and often materialize out of nowhere when chopped liver or fish oil is thrown overboard at sea.

VOICE: A squawk or cackle. On breeding grounds it is very noisy, uttering many weird, guttural, choking sounds.

NEST: (I. 56, A., N. 95) The nest is in an underground chamber lined with plant material at the end of a 3- or 4-foot burrow in open ground. The elongated egg (2.9 x 1.9) is white.

RANGE: (M.) Breeds from November to March in s. New Zealand, Chile, and on many islands of the subantarctic seas. Migrates north over the oceans of the world as far as Labrador, Iceland, Norway, and the Aleutians.

Common Shearwater*   *Puffinus puffinus*—⚹20
(Manx Shearwater)   L. 14

IDENTIFICATION: This medium-sized blackish shearwater resembles the little dusky shearwater, but it flies like its larger relatives, gliding on rigid wings for long periods, interspersed occasionally with a few rapid wingbeats. Its chief points of difference are its shorter tail with long white under tail coverts extending to the tip, and its gray cheeks. Its feet and legs are a gray-tinged pale pink.

HABITS: (Age 12 yrs.) Breeding colonies are generally in grass-covered areas on small coastal islands, though a few nest in rocky areas or on inaccessible mainland cliffs. Around the colonies the birds are active only at night. The incubating bird may not be relieved for as long as 5 days, the feeding member of the pair apparently wandering off as far as 500 or 600 miles. The young are abandoned when about 2 months old, and after an 11- to 15-day fast they venture forth and awkwardly make their way overland to water. This shearwater seems to have an affinity for coastal shelf waters, but, unlike many of its relatives, it pays little attention to boats. Its known foods are small fish and squids, in pursuit of which it sometimes dives and swims under water for short distances with the help of its wings. There are few records of the bird along our coasts.

VOICE: A babel of guttural, half-strangled clucking or cooing notes, heard only at night and chiefly about breeding colonies. There appears to be much individual variation in tone.

NEST: (I. 53, A., N. 72) Underground, often 6 feet or more below the surface, at the end of a burrow which many times is the abandoned home of a rabbit. Also in rock crevices. The single egg (2.4 x 1.6) is white.

RANGE: (M.) Breeds from Iceland to Madeira, east to the islands of the Aegean Sea, and at one time on Bermuda. It migrates south in August to largely unknown wintering grounds that extend at least as far south as the Argentine coast. It returns north in February and March. Rare in the w. North Atlantic.

Dusky Shearwater*　　　　*Puffinus lherminieri*—⚹20
(Audubon's Shearwater)　　　　　　　　　　L. 11½

IDENTIFICATION: This bird is even more sharply black and white than the much larger, heavier common shearwater. Its tail is proportionately longer, the under tail area dark gray, and the cheeks white. The fluttery flight, with short glides and much flapping, is very different from that of the larger shearwaters. The feet are slate-blue, the toes black.

HABITS: This shearwater of the Tropical Zone has a prolonged breeding season and seems to be a permanent resident of the seas near its breeding areas. Offshore the birds are often encountered in flocks, sometimes of considerable size. A common feeding habit is to drop down, with wings held high, to a patch of floating seaweed over which they run with flapping wings. They also swim freely with all the buoyancy of ducks, dipping their heads from time to time to look under water.

Little is known of their feeding habits, but they probably depend largely on small flying fish and squids. They dive readily and often stay under water for considerable periods.

VOICE: About the breeding areas at night they are noisy, uttering mournful, catlike mews and plaintive, liquid, twittering notes.

NEST: (A.) This bird nests in colonies close to the sea. Sometimes the nests are in burrows and at other times in natural cavities and crevices in rock outcrops. The single white egg (2.1 x 1.4) is laid on bare ground or in a loosely constructed nest.

RANGE: (R.) Breeds on Bermuda, the Bahamas, the Virgin Islands, the Lesser Antilles, and many oceanic islands in the equatorial zone all the way around the world. Occasionally wanders north off our coasts as far as New Jersey.

Great Shearwater*   *Puffinus gravis*—✗20
(Greater Shearwater)   L. 19; W. 43

IDENTIFICATION: The dark sooty-brown cap, contrasting strongly with the white cheeks and grayer neck, and the often extensively white-bordered upper tail coverts are distinctive. The under tail coverts are brownish, and the white of the underwing is broken by a series of brown markings where it meets the more or less brown-spotted sides and flanks.

HABITS: During early summer this bird—a lover of cold oceans —is the abundant shearwater off our North Atlantic coast. Occasionally it can be seen from land, but generally it stays 5 or more miles offshore. Like its larger relatives, the albatrosses, one of which has the greatest wingspread of any bird in the world (11 feet 4 inches), it has long, narrow wings, the most efficient sort for gliding or scaling. Flying close to the water, wings stiff and slightly decurved, these shearwaters utilize the updraft created when the wind is deflected from the curved surface of a wave. From time to time, as they slow down, they bank sharply into the full force of the wind, using their inertia to gain altitude for another glide down a wave trough. With this technique they are able to fly for miles on a windy day without once flapping their wings. On calm days they are very inactive and often have difficulty in getting off the water. To the fisherman of the Grand Banks this is the hag or hagdown which formerly was extensively used for bait and occasionally eaten. The birds' normal food is small fish like sand eels and squids, but they follow fishing boats for scraps and, if necessary, dive to get them.

VOICE: Croaking sounds have been noted on breeding grounds. When fighting over food or frightened, the birds utter peculiar grunting and wailing sounds.

NEST: (A.) A single white egg (3.0 x 1.9) is laid in a burrow in grassy ground.

RANGE: (M.) The only known breeding ground is on islands of the Tristan da Cunha group in the c. South Atlantic, but the bird is so abundant that it seems there must be others. It migrates north rapidly, chiefly through the w. Atlantic west of the warm waters of the Sargasso Sea, and is seen off our coasts in greatest numbers in late May and June. After this it scatters over the North Atlantic to Greenland, Iceland, and the Faeroes, concentrating on especially favorable feeding grounds like the Grand Banks. The southward fall movement is less clearly defined than that of spring.

Cinereous Shearwater*   *Puffinus diomedea*—✕ 20
(Cory's Shearwater)   L. 21; W. 45

IDENTIFICATION: The distinctive characteristics of this, our largest shearwater, are the gradual transition from pale sooty-brown on top of the head to the white throat; the uniform and rather pale color of the upper parts from head to tail; the absence or at most the slight suggestion of pale tips to the upper tail coverts; and the uniformly white underwing surfaces, sides, and under tail coverts. It has longer, narrower wings than the great shearwater and its stout, yellowish-brown bill is very different from that of the latter.

HABITS: This warm-water species summers largely south of the cold waters frequented by the great shearwater. It flies with slow, powerful wingbeats and does not hug the water as closely as does the latter. From August to early November, when surface temperatures are at their highest, this is the commonest shearwater off the New England coast, occurring in greatest abundance between Cape Cod and the eastern end of Long Island. When mackerel drive young herrings close inshore in late September and October, numbers of the birds can be seen from such promontories as Montauk Point, Long Island. Their habit of following feeding schools of such predaceous fish or whales often helps fishermen, whose boats they also follow, to locate their quarry.

VOICE: On breeding grounds all through the night the birds

utter both harsh, guttural wails and purring notes.

NEST: (A.) In burrows in the ground or in crevices and holes in rock. When an extensive cave is available it often supports a large colony, every cranny and niche being occupied by a pair of birds. In these cases no nest is constructed and the single white egg (3.0 x 2.0) is laid on bare rock.

RANGE: (M.) Breeds on islands in the Mediterranean and from the Azores to the Cape Verde Islands, also Kerguelen Island in the c. South Indian Ocean. Wanders west and north to the Gulf Stream after breeding, occurring off our coast as far north as Cape Cod, and occasionally off Nova Scotia, from mid-July to December. Winters in the South Atlantic.

Black-capped Petrel* *Pterodroma hasitata*—⩩20
(Diablotin) L. 15; W. 38

IDENTIFICATION: The dark crown of this heavy-billed and heavy-bodied petrel is sharply accented by the pale or almost white neck, nape, and forehead. Its long, white tail coverts reaching nearly to the end of the tail both above and below are characteristic. This species has a dark phase in which it is a uniform sooty-brown except for white upper tail coverts.

HABITS: This once abundant petrel is today a bird of mystery whose present breeding grounds are unknown, although it is still seen occasionally at sea. It is never active about its nesting burrow during the day, but hunters are able to locate the occupied ones with the help of a dog. To secure the bird it is necessary only to insert a long stick, as the bird will grab the end with its bill and allow itself to be dragged out. As other petrels have survived centuries of similar persecution, it seems likely that the recent introduction of such predators as the Norway rat, mongoose, and opossum into its former haunts has been the major factor in its disappearance.

VOICE: The call heard at night around the breeding grounds is described as mournful and owl-like.

NEST: (A.) In burrows which the birds dig in banks high up on mountain cliffs and steep slopes, often among the roots of trees. No specimens of eggs or young exist.

RANGE: (M.) Probably bred at one time on most of the islands of the West Indies, most recently on Dominica, Guadeloupe, Jamaica, and probably Hispaniola. Present extent of breeding range unknown. At other seasons it evidently wanders widely over the South Atlantic, as hurricanes have carried it inland as far as New Hampshire, s. Ontario, and Kentucky.

Bermuda Petrel*
(Cahow)

Pterodroma cahow—✳ 20
L. 15; W. 35

IDENTIFICATION: Closely related to the preceding species, the cahow lacks most of the white markings on the nape and has gray-tipped upper tail coverts that largely hide the white base of the tail.

HABITS: When first visited the Bermuda Islands were the nesting grounds of vast numbers of pelagic birds of at least 3 species —dusky and common shearwaters and the Bermuda petrel. The last named was apparently the most abundant of all, but it was good to eat and so fearless that it was ruthlessly exploited. One early account speaks of a single night's bag of 4,000. As early as 1616 the local governor issued an order designed to save them from extinction, but apparently he was too late. For almost 300 years these petrels dropped out of sight, but incredibly a few survived, and a small breeding population is still present on the outlying islets of the Bermuda group.

Oceanic birds like albatrosses, shearwaters, and petrels range over millions of square miles of water for some 8 months of the year, yet the entire population is dependent upon what often amounts to no more than a few square miles of breeding territory. Many find the essential freedom from mammalian predators on coastal islands, but others nest only on the truly oceanic islands, where they are also free from such avian predators as gulls and skuas. Undoubtedly our offshore waters were once well populated at certain seasons of the year by the oceanic birds that gathered to breed on the Bermudas—the only group of truly oceanic islands off the coast of e. North America. Now with it virtually eliminated as a nesting ground, we can no longer expect to see so many of them on offshore trips. Fortunately other oceanic species are still common, but no one knows what their future is likely to be as oceanic islands the world over come into increased use for air strips, meteorological stations, and naval bases. Seldom does man occupy an island long without bringing in his destructive pets—the cat and dog—and his even more destructive camp follower—the Norway rat.

VOICE: Heard only at night; described as a strange, harsh, hollow-sounding howl, like the word *cahow* or *cowhow*.

NEST: (A.) This bird nests in burrows or holes in rocks and lays a single white egg.

RANGE: Breeds on Bermuda. Range at other seasons unknown.

Fulmar*   *Fulmarus glacialis*—⚡20
(Fulmar Petrel)   L. 18½; W. 41; Wt. 1½ lbs.

IDENTIFICATION: The short neck, stubby yellow bill, and the
narrow, nearly straight wings without black tips separate the
fulmar from any gull. Every color gradation occurs, from
white-bodied birds with gray backs, wings, and tails to birds
that are completely gray, but most individuals are clearly
in either the dark or the light phase, the proportion of each
varying widely from one breeding colony to another.

HABITS: Except when nesting, the fulmar is strictly pelagic,
observable only on the high seas beyond the 100-fathom line,
which is beyond the range of all gulls except the kittiwake.
It is an abundant species (Darwin considered it the most
abundant bird in the world) and in certain areas has greatly
increased in recent years. Prior to 1877 there was only a
single nesting colony in the British Isles, where today there
are more than 200. For some reason (possibly because they
are immature) there are always many non-breeding fulmars
along North Atlantic steamship routes, even during summer.
The maximum concentration off our coasts occurs in early
September, but great numbers stay on the fishing banks until
the spring migration. Most members of this group are not
ship followers, but the fulmar is, and often rides the updrift
close astern or to leeward, thus permitting observation of the
curious nostril tubes on the top of the bill that are characteristic of albatrosses, shearwaters, and petrels. In flight (3 or 4
flaps and a soar) and feeding the fulmar resembles shearwaters, although it flaps more frequently. It feeds on the more
important plankton animals, such as squids, jellyfish, and
crustacea (shrimp, etc.), as well as on small fish, and it
scavenges voraciously for oily fish wastes.

VOICE: A variety of low, guttural chuckling or cackling sounds
and occasionally a nasal grunt.

NEST: (I. 48, A., N. 53) On a steep slope or cliff overlooking
the ocean. There are a few inland colonies, one being 20
miles from the sea on a mountain slope running up to 3,000
feet in elevation. The single white egg (2.9 x 2.0) is laid on
bare rock or in a slight hollow in the earth lined with a little
plant material.

RANGE: (P. M.) Breeds in large colonies on islands off Cumber-
land Peninsula, Baffin Island, the coast of c.w. Greenland,
Iceland, and the British Isles north and east to the c. Siberian
coast, Wrangell Island, and the islands of Bering Sea. It is

a common oceanic species throughout the year, occurring south to the edge of the warm Gulf Stream, where it feeds about the large, floating masses of gulfweed.

STORM PETRELS   Family Hydrobatidae

Leach's Petrel* *Oceanodroma leucorhoa*—✕ 20
(Leach's Forked-tailed Petrel)   L. 8; Wt. 1½ oz.

IDENTIFICATION: Not a ship follower, it is generally seen only at a distance, where it can best be identified by its very distinctive flight, somewhat like that of a nighthawk or a butterfly. The slow, irregular beats of its long wings give it a springy, bounding motion with frequent abrupt changes in direction, interrupted by short glides on stiff, down-flexed wings. When it settles on water for a moment to feed it holds its wings extended high over its back until it springs into the air again. Compared with other petrels, Leach's is larger and paler (lightest on the greater and middle wing coverts, which form a band along the front of the inner wing). The legs are short, the feet black, the tail forked, and the white rump is broken by a dark area in the center.

HABITS: (Age 7 yrs.) These petrels are widely distributed over northern oceans, even during the breeding season. Nesting birds apparently range up to several hundred miles from the colony when off on feeding expeditions, as the members of a pair relieve each other only about once every 4 days during the incubation period. The colonies are always on islands—open, grass-covered, or wooded—as the birds are very vulnerable to predatory mammals like foxes and rats. Many once thriving colonies have been wiped out by lighthouse keepers' cats and fishermen's dogs. Herring gulls and especially great black-backed gulls are potential enemies, which probably explains the petrels' nocturnal habits about the breeding grounds. Even so, the gulls, to whom a petrel is only a mouthful, take a heavy toll on bright moonlight nights.

VOICE: The common call heard at night is a series of 8 strongly enunciated low, guttural cooing or crowing notes. The birds have other softer, more liquid twittering notes, suggesting those of a bluebird, as well as harsh screams and a continuous purr or trill.

NEST: (I. 42, A., N. 50) In a chamber at the end of a shallow burrow from 1 to about 3 feet long which the birds excavate themselves and use year after year. The single egg (1.3 x .95) is white, occasionally finely marked with purple. It is laid in a loose nest of grass and twigs.

RANGE: (M.) Breeds on coastal islands of the North Atlantic and North Pacific from Massachusetts to s. Greenland and the British Isles, and from Lower California to the Aleutians and Kuriles. Ranges south in winter across the equator.

Storm Petrel*   *Hydrobates pelagicus*—✳20
                                                      L. 6

IDENTIFICATION: This tiny, long-winged petrel habitually follows in the wake of ships, fluttering back and forth from one side to the other with an unsteady moth- or batlike flight, broken only by the shortest of glides. The most distinctive marking is a small white area in the middle of the underwing. In fresh plumage a fine line of white can be seen along the inner part of the upper wing surface. The feet and legs are black and do not extend beyond the tail in flight.

HABITS: It has been rumored that this petrel breeds on our side of the Atlantic, but no nest has been found. The storm petrel's close resemblance to Wilson's makes it difficult to get reliable sight records in our waters where it might be expected most often in October or November. Birds seen in June or July would presumably indicate a breeding site in the general vicinity.

VOICE: A sustained, uneven, and rather harsh purring or churring sound. Also a more musical warbled chatter.

NEST: (I. 38, A., N. 61) In a cavity among loose stones or under large boulders, among ruins, and sometimes in burrows dug by the birds in soft ground. The single white egg (1.1 x .85) is often finely marked with brown.

RANGE: (P. M.) Breeds on islands in the e. Atlantic and w. Mediterranean from Iceland and n. Norway south to the Canaries and east to Malta. Ranges west in spring and fall as far as our northeast coast and south on both coasts of Africa to the Cape of Good Hope in winter.

Wilson's Petrel*   *Oceanites oceanicus*—✳20
                                        L. 7; W. 15½; Wt. 1¼ oz.

IDENTIFICATION: Like the Leach's and storm, this is a small, white-rumped petrel, but its wings are shorter and more

rounded and its flight steadier; glides alternating regularly
with swallowlike flutters. It is a ship follower and when feeding has a habit of "walking" on the water with outstretched
wings held high and feet dangling. Its yellow-webbed feet
and long legs project beyond the short, square tail.

HABITS: Only 3 Southern Hemisphere birds migrate north in
large numbers to spend their winters in the Northern Hemisphere, in contrast to the hundreds that go south during our
winters. Of these—the sooty and great shearwaters and the
Wilson's petrel—the petrel is the most abundant and is regarded by some ornithologists as possibly the world's most
abundant bird. It appears off our coasts in numbers in late
May and stays until September. The Gulf Stream seems to
be a favorite habitat; from it the birds move in to fishing
banks and coastal waters. Occasionally great numbers are
seen from shore, and they regularly enter such enclosed
waters as those of New York Harbor.

Not nearly enough is known about the distribution of these
and other pelagic birds, and everyone who is sufficiently
familiar with them to distinguish them with reasonable certainty should keep a detailed log of species encountered
during an ocean voyage.

All small petrel feed heavily on shrimplike crustacea but
seem to take any plankton animals of proper size. They also
take fish and waste matter of all sorts, commonly following
feeding schools of whales and steamers to pick up scraps and
gathering about fishing boats when fish are being cleaned.

VOICE: When feeding at sea they utter a rasping twitter and a
soft peeping note. Croaks, chuckles, and whistles are among
the notes described from breeding grounds.

NEST: (I. 39, A., N. 52) In cavities and crevices among loose
rocks or under boulders or in cliffs. Less commonly in burrows in soft earth or peat. The single egg (1.3 x .95) is white,
speckled with reddish-brown.

RANGE: (M.) Breeds on islands off the southern end of South
America and on most islands in the Antarctic Ocean. Ranges
north in its winter (our summer) to Newfoundland and the
English Channel; i.e., to about Lat. 50° N.

Frigate Petrel*   *Pelagodroma marina*—⚇ 20
(White-faced Petrel)   L. 8

IDENTIFICATION: The white under parts and underwing and the
strikingly marked head are very different from those of any

other small petrel. Its flight is erratic and bounding and its orange toe webs can often be seen as it dangles its long legs while "walking" on water.

HABITS: A recent record of this bird off Cape Cod emphasizes how little we know about the frequency of occurrence of species like this which nest in the e. North Atlantic and may be expected to come into our offshore waters from time to time.

VOICE: Silent except on breeding grounds, where it makes typical petrel sounds.

NEST: The single white egg (1.4 x .85), finely spotted with reds, is laid in a shallow burrow in soft earth.

RANGE: Widely distributed as a breeding bird from the islands off w. Africa to islands in the Australian region. Wanders, at least occasionally, to the w. North Atlantic.

PELICANS and ALLIES

Order Pelecaniformes

TROPIC-BIRDS   Family Phaëthontidae

Yellow-billed Tropic-bird*   *Phaëthon lepturus*—⚡27
(White-tailed Tropic-bird)   L. 16 (immature), 32 (adult);
W. 37; T. 5–21; Wt. 14½ oz.

IDENTIFICATION: This bird looks like a heavy-bodied tern but has a bold black-and-white wing pattern and a rapid pigeon-like wingbeat. Young lack the long central tail feathers but have a finely barred back and a yellow bill instead of the orange-red bill of adults. When the bird is seen from below in flight the dark flanks frame the rear half of the body with a narrow line of black.

HABITS: The tropic-birds are well named, as they all belong to the warm-ocean areas, this species being the most character-istic bird of the Sargasso Sea. Yet even in this area of clear and relatively unproductive water it is never abundant; gen-erally only a single individual is encountered at a time, and

3 or 4 together are a rare sight. Squids and fish, especially flying fish, are staple foods and, near the shore, crabs. As squids rise to the surface only as the light fades and sink again as morning comes, the birds do most of their feeding early and late in the day. They obtain food in dives from considerable heights, usually hovering a moment before closing their wings for the downward plunge and often turning as they fall. On land tropic-birds are almost as awkward as loons and grebes, pushing themselves about on their breasts —a good reason why they always nest on cliffs or steep slopes. On water they float high with their long tail feathers well up in the air.

VOICE: A harsh, squeaky *tick-et-tick-et* is given repeatedly in flight.

NEST: (I. 28, A., N. 63) On a rocky shelf or ledge or in a natural pocket of rock, usually close to the shore, but occasionally some distance inland. Some nests are in extensive caves, others in shallow depressions scooped out on sloping ground under a bush. The single egg (2.1 x 1.5), pinkish, thickly speckled with brown, is laid on a bare rock. Two broods are reared.

RANGE: (P. M.) Breeds in Bermuda (early March to October), the Bahamas, most of the West Indies, and in the islands of the equatorial zones of the South Atlantic, s.w. Pacific, and Indian oceans. In fall it wanders widely over the Sargasso Sea region of the w. Atlantic, regularly coming as far north as Lat. 40°. Stray birds occasionally reach our coast.

PELICANS   Family Pelecanidae

White Pelican*   *Pelecanus erythrorhynchos*—✕19
                                L. 60; W. 100; Wt. 15 lbs.

IDENTIFICATION: This pelican's large size, coupled with its lack of long legs or a long neck, is fairly diagnostic. The black area on the wing includes all the primaries and about half the secondaries, making the outer two thirds of the extended wing black along its rear half. Young differ only in having grayish instead of white lesser wing coverts and a brownish-gray cap on the head.

HABITS: (Age 8 yrs.) This heavy bird is a surprisingly good soarer and seems to enjoy circling in small flocks high in the air, often returning to earth in a spectacular, almost vertical dive that ends in a sharp upturn accompanied by a thunderous roar. When traveling these birds form a V or a straight line and alternately flap and sail—each bird synchronizing its actions with the rest of the group.

In summer the white pelican requires for nesting an isolated island, reasonably close to the type of shallow water that is suited to its highly specialized fishing method. Large and small fish, mostly of non-game species, and other aquatic animals like salamanders and tadpoles are the chief foods. This is one of the few species of birds in which large numbers of individuals engage in what appears to be carefully planned and closely co-ordinated group action leading to the capture of prey that could not be obtained so efficiently in any other way. Having located a school of fish, the birds gather in a line offshore, wing to wing, and then at what seems like a signal from a leader they slowly move shoreward, beating the water with their wings and keeping an almost perfect line. This drives the fish into shallow water, where the pelicans scoop them up into their pouches, drain off the water, and swallow them. With a wingspread that sometimes approaches 10 feet, the white pelican is the most spectacular bird that we have left in anything like its original numbers, but it must be constantly guarded against those who would destroy it for selfish or petty reasons.

VOICE: Silent except for a low croaking or grunting about the breeding grounds.

NEST: (I. 29, A.) In dense colonies on bare ground, more rarely on matted-down marsh vegetation. Earth and debris are drawn up to form a rim around the eggs, the nest occasionally becoming a low mound with a depression in the center. Two chalky-white eggs (3.5 x 2.2) are the normal clutch.

RANGE: (M.) Breeds from c. Manitoba, s. Mackenzie, and c. British Columbia south to c. North Dakota, n. Wyoming, n. Utah, and s. California and on the s. Texas coast. Winters from n. Florida, the Gulf Coast, and s. California south to the Florida Keys and Panama.

Brown Pelican* *Pelecanus occidentalis*—※19
L. 50; W. 80; Wt. 8¼ lbs.

IDENTIFICATION: This is a striking bird in any plumage. The white-striped, rich brown neck characteristic of the breeding plumage is replaced by a solid-white neck during the post-nuptial molt. Young birds have a brownish-gray neck, a browner back, and largely white under parts.

HABITS: (Age 12½ yrs.) The brown pelican is strictly a coastal species, never occurring inland or out of sight of the shore; and as its method of fishing requires clear water, it also avoids river mouths and other turbid areas. The birds commonly travel in small groups close to the water, gliding for long distances with only an occasional flap of their wings on the updraft behind a breaking wave. When fishing they maintain an altitude of 25 or 30 feet. If food is sighted, they turn sharply into a vertical dive, with beak thrust forward and half-closed wings trailing back, that carries them completely under water with a tremendous splash. The fish on which this pelican feeds are usually members of the herring family that occur in dense schools near the surface. Menhaden furnish most of its food along the Atlantic coast and careful studies have shown that the charge that pelicans seriously compete with commercial fishing is without foundation.

These birds are constantly harried by gulls, man-o'-war-birds, and even terns, ever on the alert to steal part of their catch. Around nesting colonies gulls and other predators are always on the watch, ready to pounce on eggs or young left unguarded for even a moment, which is why one should never go near their breeding colonies, even for a short visit, during the early part of the nesting season.

VOICE: Noisy when young, making notes that vary from low grunts and barks to a shrill squeal. Adults seldom utter more than a low cluck.

NEST: (I. 30, A., N. 60) These pelicans seem to prefer to nest in low, brushy trees, but they also commonly nest on the ground. The site is usually on a small island in a shallow bay. The interval between breeding seasons in some colonies is less than a full year, so instead of recurring at the same time each year, the breeding season moves slowly around the calendar over a period of years. The nest varies from a well-built structure of sticks and miscellaneous trash to almost nothing in the case of some ground nests. The 3 eggs (2.9 x 1.8) are a dull, dirty white.

RANGE: (P. M.) Breeds on salt water from South Carolina and c. California south to Venezuela and c. Chile. Wanders north to North Carolina and s. British Columbia and south to the mouth of the Amazon and s. Chile.

BOOBIES and GANNETS   Family Sulidae

Blue-faced Booby*   *Sula dactylatra*—✳19
(White Booby)   L. 32; W. 63; Wt. 4¾ lbs.

IDENTIFICATION: The blackish-brown tail, wing tips, and entire rear edge of the wing are distinctive. The larger females have bills pink at the base while those of the males are bright orange-red. In both the area around the base of the bill is more black than blue. Young are smoky-brown flecked with white above with light areas where the neck joins the back and at the base of the tail. Like adults, they have dark wing and tail feathers and white under parts.

HABITS: Unlike most birds, boobies do not as a rule fly to escape man but stand their ground and defend themselves with their bills. This is evidently how they got their name; and it is true both of birds at the nest and of the occasional individuals that alight on ships. The staple food of the blue-faced is flying fish (of which there are 65 known species), varied with a few squids. Squids are caught in sudden dives from heights of 25 to 30 feet that may carry the birds 10 feet under water. As flying fish live in schools near the surface of clear, warm waters far from land, these boobies often feed 100 miles or more from their nests. At other seasons they often wander even more widely, but never beyond a supply of flying fish. Occasionally they follow a ship to catch the fish they scare into flight. Frigate-birds constantly plague boobies and have been known to grab them by the tail while in flight to make them disgorge their catch.

VOICE: The female makes a quacking sound, the male a hissing whistle.

NEST: These birds nest in loose colonies on islands. An open or grassy slope or cliff top facing the ocean or to windward seems preferred. The 2 chalky, pale blue eggs (2.6 x 1.8) are laid in a shallow scrape on the ground. Although both eggs generally hatch, seldom is more than a single young bird reared.

RANGE: (R.) Breeds in the Atlantic from the Bahamas and islands of the Gulf of Mexico and Caribbean to South Trinidad and from islands off the w. Mexican coast across the Pacific to the Indian Ocean. Wanders to our Gulf Coast and occasionally north over the warm waters of the Sargasso Sea.

Brown Booby*   *Sula leucogaster*—✕19
(White-bellied Booby)   L. 29; W. 57

IDENTIFICATION: In adults the sharp line of separation between the pure white of the under parts and underwing coverts and the dark brown of the rest of the bird is distinctive. Young are rather gray-brown all over, a little paler on the belly and darker on the breast.

HABITS: This is the booby most commonly seen off our southern coast. Immature birds should not be confused with the much lighter young gannets. Brown boobies are active on the wing, flying sometimes close to the water in the troughs of the waves like shearwaters and at other times well up in the air with slow, steady wingbeats. These boobies eat a variety of fish, but in many areas flying fish and halfbeaks are the staple food, plus mullet. When a large school of fish is located the birds dive repeatedly in quick succession from only a few feet up in the air. Ashore they are apt to perch in a tree, shrub, or other elevated point that will facilitate a take-off, which they find difficult in the absence of a strong wind.

VOICE: Hoarse cries, seldom heard except on the breeding grounds.

NEST: A low mound of trash or a hollow scrape in the ground suffices for a nest. It may be in an open, bare area or well covered with low vegetation and sloping to windward or, if flat, close to a sharp drop-off. Two pale blue to chalky eggs (2.4 x 1.6) are laid, but as a rule only a single chick is reared.

RANGE: (R.) Breeds in the Bahamas, West Indies, and on islands off both coasts of Central America and in many other parts of the Tropical Zone of the Atlantic and Pacific oceans. It once nested on the Dry Tortugas and still occurs there. It wanders to our coasts as far north as South Carolina (occasionally Massachusetts) and is the booby most likely to be encountered on the high seas.

Red-footed Booby*

Sula sula—✕ 19
L. 29; W. 60

IDENTIFICATION: This small, long-winged, long-tailed booby occurs in several not very well understood color phases. White adults have only a narrow blackish-brown border on the rear of the wing (and a few spots of gray on the coverts), although the whole end of the wing is dark like a gannet's. Occasionally one of these birds has a brownish tail. Young are uniformly brownish, paler below. Some never develop beyond the stage where the head and neck become a paler brown and the tail and rump white. The feet and legs, however, change from the dull yellowish of the immature to the distinctive bright red of the adult.

HABITS: This is the only American booby that is at home in the branches of a tree and will not nest on the ground. Unfortunately, civilized man or his animals, most commonly goats or hares, have destroyed all the trees and shrubs on many former nesting islands and the red-footed is not as common as it was. Its complete dependence on trees is due to its inability to fly from the ground without first scrambling into a bush or tree. Fish and, to a greater degree than for other boobies, squids are standard foods, which probably explains why the birds have large eyes and are more active early and late in the day and at night. They have a graceful, buoyant flight and are often seen in a line or group of 5 to 20, alternately ascending during a wingbeat period, then coasting to the wave tops in perfect synchronization. Fishing is done by diving from a height of 20 or 30 feet.

VOICE: The common call is a prolonged cackle.

NEST: (I. 45, A., N. 45) A rather loosely constructed flat platform of sticks and twigs in a bush or low tree. The single pale blue egg (2.5 x 1.6) has a rough, chalky covering. As with all boobies, the young are naked when hatched and must be carefully protected from the sun until their long, white down develops.

RANGE: (R.) Breeds in the West Indies and on other islands in tropical seas around the world. Occasionally seen off the Florida coast.

Gannet*   *Moris bassana*—✕19
                              L. 36; W. 72

IDENTIFICATION: The long, tapered tail, long wings, and the big bill that is kept pointed downward in flight are distinctive, as is the wholly black outer end of the wing. The white-flecked, brown-black young birds take 4 years to mature, the head, neck, and under parts becoming white first and the back and wing coverts last, which often gives them a blotched appearance. The head color of adults varies from orange-buff through various shades of yellow to white.

HABITS: (Age 16½ yrs.) The gannet is one of the few birds whose breeding population is at all accurately known. It breeds in 22 colonies which, when censused in 1939, gave a total of 167,000 birds. The 5 American colonies contained a total of approximately 14,000, as follows: Bonaventure, 7,200; Cape St. Mary, 5,036; Bird Rocks, 1,250; Gull Cliff, 496, and Funk Island, 7. This is a bird of coastal waters inside the edge of the continental shelf and is seldom seen more than 300 miles from land, even during winter. It is the young birds that make the longest migration and the old adults that winter farthest north. Although gannets nest in congested colonies and may travel in single file or small flocks, feeding groups are usually small. The birds fly with a rapid wingbeat, sailing at frequent intervals, and can soar to great heights as well as glide over the waves like shearwaters. Fish of all kinds, especially those that travel in schools close to the surface, like menhaden and herring, are almost their sole food. These are caught in spectacular diagonal dives from heights up to 100 feet or more in the air. It appears that with the help of their wings under water they occasionally reach depths of 50 feet or more. Gannets are often seen from shore and can always be identified by their dives and the splash they make when they hit the water.

VOICE: Call at breeding colonies is a loud, hoarse, snoring note.

NEST: (I. 42, A., N. 100) A mound of seaweeds and trash on a cliff edge or on the slope above a cliff. The single egg (3.0 x 1.8) is pale blue with a chalky covering. The newly hatched young is naked and gray in color; its covering of white down is not complete until it is 3 weeks old. Feeding is stopped after 12 or 13 weeks, and the young fasts for about 10 days before it finally launches itself into the air from the edge of the nest ledge and half falls, half flies into the sea. Apparently it floats on water without food for an additional time before it is able to get into the air and start fishing for itself.

RANGE: (P. M.) Breeds on 3 small islands or rocks in the Gulf of St. Lawrence and 2 off Newfoundland; in Iceland, the Faeroes, and the British Isles. Winters from Virginia (rarely Cape Cod) to Cuba and the c. Mexican coast, and from British Isles to c. West Africa.

CORMORANTS   Family Phalacrocoracidae

Cormorant*   *Phalacrocorax carbo*—⚬ 18
(European Cormorant)   L. 36; W. 61

IDENTIFICATION: The white area near the base of the heavy bill and the stocky neck that gives the bird a bitternlike appearance in flight are the only good year-round field marks for adults. From February or March through June they have a white patch on the thigh, a hoary cast to the head and neck, and generally a very yellowish throat pouch. Young can usually be distinguished by their large size and the rear under parts, which are whitish to the tail, but some individuals are no larger than the double-crested and some lack the whitish rear under parts.

HABITS: Years ago this bird was widely domesticated and trained for fishing in England and parts of Europe, a practice, which continues to this day in China. It occurs in abundance over half the world, lives on both salt and fresh water, nests both in trees and on rocks, and the only reasonable explanation for its scarcity in North America seems to be that it

occupies a niche so close to that which is already filled by
the double-crested cormorant that it can make little headway
where the latter is present. The overlap between the two is
small. Shallow waters of coastal bays and river mouths are
preferred feeding grounds. In winter, when the birds come
south of the rocky New England coast, they favor breakwaters. They consume a wide variety of fish.

VOICE: At the breeding colony various deep croakings and other
guttural noises, each of which seems to have a distinct mean-
ing.

NEST: (I. 28, A., N. 30+) Flat, broad ledges near the tops of
cliffs overlooking water seem to be preferred sites for nesting colonies of this species, but the flat tops of rocky islets
are also used, and in some places trees. The nest is a bulky
mound of sticks, seaweed, and other material, built higher
each year. The 3 or 4 eggs (2.5 x 1.6) are pale blue with
a chalky covering.

RANGE: (P. M.) Breeds throughout most of the Eastern Hemisphere and in North America from w. Greenland and Baffin
Island south to the Gulf of St. Lawrence. Winters regularly
from its breeding grounds south to New York and casually
to South Carolina.

Double-crested   *Phalacrocorax auritus*—✕18
Cormorant*   L. 32; W. 51; Wt. 4½ lbs.

IDENTIFICATION: Large black birds with longish tails, flying in
long strings or gooselike formations with outstretched necks
held above the horizontal and with mouths open, are cormorants. The upward tilt of the bill in swimming birds, the
bolt-upright or "spread-eagle" pose when perched, and the
occasional sailing periods in flight are distinctive. Young are
more grayish and brownish and have rather pale under parts.

HABITS: (Age 14 yrs.) The double-crested cormorant is an
abundant and widely distributed species nesting on salt or
fresh water, by itself or with herons and other water birds in
colonies of from a few to many thousands of pairs. In recent
years it has suddenly become abundant along the New England coast, probably because of some not too well understood
change that has increased its food supply. However, the
largest colony of a million or more birds is still on the coast
of n. Lower California. Grotesque courtship posturing by the
male marks the start of breeding activities. When first
hatched, the naked, coal-black young look like rubber toys,

but within 2 weeks they are covered with dense black down. Although they require about 7 weeks to get all their feathers and learn to fly, they wander freely about the colony and after they are about a month old will take to the water if disturbed.

Cormorants obtain their food by diving from the surface and swimming under water with the help of their wings to depths of from 5 to 25 feet. Extensive food-habit studies reveal that on salt water this species is invariably beneficent to the local fishing industry. The bulk of its food consists of trash fish like sculpin, cunner, gunnel, and eel that not only are of no commercial value but often prey upon and compete with valuable species. Perch, bullheads, carp, crappie, stickleback, and similar fish of small value, plus animals like salamanders, make up a large proportion of their fresh-water food.

Cormorants rapidly convert the greater part of what they eat into droppings containing a high percentage of nitrates and phosphates—the fertilizing elements most needed by aquatic plants. Thus the presence of a colony tends to stimulate the growth of diatoms and other algae—the basic support of all underwater life. There is little question that a colony, simply by increasing the over-all productivity of nearby waters, produces more fish, including game and food fish, than its members eat. This, coupled with the fact that the bird feeds preponderately on non-game fish and thus corrects the un-balance caused by highly selective commercial fishing, gives it a vital role in maintaining the yield of many coastal and lake fisheries.

VOICE: A wide variety of harsh, croaking sounds like *awk, hawk, oak,* and *oop,* seldom heard except at a breeding colony.

NEST: (I. 25, A., N. 25, D. 35) Nests are placed on top of rocky islets, on cliff ledges, or in trees. Those in trees are compactly woven out of sticks and weed stems and are lined with leafy twigs and grasses. Those on rocks are often raised on a foundation of seaweeds and trash and are sometimes wholly of such material. Feathers, green fir twigs, and all sorts of odd objects are incorporated in the lining. The 3 or 4 eggs (2.4 x 1.5) are pale blue with a chalky covering.

RANGE: (P. M.) Breeds from Newfoundland, n. Ontario, c. Saskatchewan, and the Alaska Peninsula south to the Bahamas, Isle of Pines, and s. Lower California. Winters along the seacoast from Long Island and s. Alaska and inland from Tennessee south to the West Indies and Panama.

Olivaceous Cormorant* *Phalacrocorax olivaceus*—✗18
(Mexican Cormorant) L. 25; W. 40; Wt. 3¾ lbs.

IDENTIFICATION: Its smaller, slimmer appearance is this bird's best field mark. Its black has a purplish rather than a greenish sheen, and when nesting it has a distinctive white line where the throat and gular sac meet. Young are brownish with pale to whitish under parts.

HABITS: The olivaceous cormorant is a zoneless bird, so tolerant of varying temperatures that it has no habitat requirements beyond water with some form of animal life in it to serve as food. From the humid heat of the equator to the cold stormy seas off Cape Horn and in icy Andean lakes, this species seems equally at home. It occurs on rocky, sandy, or muddy, marshy coasts and inland on rivers and mountain streams and lakes; it nests in deserts, tropical forests, and on coastal islands. One of its notable characteristics in many areas is its fearlessness and its readiness to accept man-made structures for nest sites. Bottom fish caught in rather shallow water seem to be its chief food.

VOICE: A frequently heard guttural, piglike grunt.

NEST: (A.) In colonies in trees, on rocks, or on the ground. The nests vary from substantial platforms of sticks to mounds composed of little more than seaweed. The 4 pale bluish eggs (2.1 x 1.3) are chalky and often nest-stained.

RANGE: (R.) Occurs from the Bahamas, Cuba, s. Louisiana, and n.w. Mexico south to Tierra del Fuego.

DARTERS   Family Anhingidae

Anhinga   *Anhinga anhinga*—❋18
(Snake-bird; Water-turkey)   L. 34; W. 48

IDENTIFICATION: The long fanlike tail, very long snaky neck, and small head, held straight out in flight, are distinctive, as is the habit of alternately flapping and soaring. Often when the bird is in water only the head and neck are visible. When perched it sits upright and frequently holds its wings in a "spread-eagle" position like a cormorant.

HABITS: Small bodies of quiet or sluggishly flowing fresh water are the preferred feeding grounds of the snake-bird, which is generally common about the numerous channels and open ponds of extensive marshlands, where suitable clumps of willow or other trees are available for roosting. Fish and other aquatic life constitute the food supply. The anhinga is an excellent soarer and appears to engage in aerial play in which a group soars up so high that it almost disappears.

VOICE: All one commonly hears are harsh guttural grunts like those of cormorants. During courtship in spring soaring birds often emit a short series of hawklike whistles or squeals.

NEST: (A.) During the breeding season these birds are frequently associated with various herons, their nests being scattered through the trees among those of the other species. They do, however, nest in small groups by themselves or on the outskirts of a big rookery. The nests are bulky structures of sticks and dead leaves used year after year, generally with the addition of a lining of fresh green leaves and moss. The 4 pale blue chalky eggs (2.1 x 1.4) are soon stained brown.

RANGE: (P. M.) Breeds s. North Carolina, s. Missouri, s.c. Texas, n. Mexico south to s. Brazil and n. Argentina. Winters South Carolina, the Gulf States, and s. California south.

MAN-O'-WAR-BIRDS   Family Fregatidae

Magnificent Frigate-bird   *Fregata magnificens*—❋18
(Man-o'-war-bird)   L. 40; W. 90; Wt. 3½ lbs.

IDENTIFICATION: The deeply forked tail and the extremely narrow wings, much longer than those of the swallow-tailed kite, are diagnostic. Sexes are alike during the first year, when the head, neck, and under parts (except the underwing primaries) are largely pure white. Fully adult plumage, in which sexes are different, is not acquired until the end of the second year.

HABITS: This species is common along all tropical seacoasts, but it is not in any sense a pelagic bird and seldom goes far from land. For its weight it has the largest wings of any bird alive; it is able to rise and soar on the gentlest breeze and in the air is the very embodiment of speed and grace. In contrast with the wings, the feet and legs are so weak and small that it can hardly walk and must always take off from an elevated position. It is a sea bird and yet it never goes near the sea; its feathers do not shed water and it is not known that it can take off from water. It has wonderful eyesight and often detects its prey from aloft, after which it descends in a spectacular dive to catch it. It obtains much of its food by following feeding schools of albacores or other large predaceous fish and seizing their quarry as it leaps into the air to escape. Surface swimmers are lifted from the water with hardly a ripple, and flying fish are important in the diet. The stronger the wind and the more turbulent the air, the easier the fishing. On calm days the birds seem to depend more on robbing pelicans, cormorants, and other sea birds of their catches, using rough tactics when necessary. Since their preference is for rather large fish (up to 12 to 14 inches), smaller sea birds like terns are unmolested. All kinds of animal waste are scavenged from the water, and the birds often become quite tame and fearless. During the breeding season the male has a curious way of inflating the gular sac, which at this time is bright crimson instead of the usual pale orange.

VOICE: The only sounds are harsh gurgling notes during courtship.

NEST: (A.) These birds generally nest in colonies by themselves, but occasionally the nests are scattered among those of such birds as pelicans and cormorants. The usual site is on top of low vegetation or, at times, on the ground or in tall trees. The nest is a sparse, loosely built platform of sticks and twigs. The single egg (2.7 x 1.8) is white and thin-shelled.

RANGE: (R.) Breeds in the Bahamas, West Indies, and from Mexico south to n. South America, also to the Cape Verde and Galápagos Islands. Ranging regularly north to Florida and the whole Gulf Coast and south to c. South America.

HERONS and ALLIES
Order Ciconiiformes

Comparison of Average Length and Wingspread of Crane-like Birds

SPECIES	LENGTH	WINGSPREAD
Least Bittern	13	18
Green Heron	18	25
Scarlet Ibis	22	36
Glossy Ibis	22	38
White-faced Glossy Ibis	23	38
Snowy Egret	24	38
Little Blue Heron	24	41
Yellow-crowned Night Heron	24	44
White Ibis	25	40
Night Heron	25	44
Tricolored Heron	26	38
Limpkin	26	42
American Bittern	27	39
Reddish Egret	30	46
Roseate Spoonbill	33	52
Egret	39	55
Wood Ibis	41	65
Sandhill Crane	44	80
Great Blue Heron	46	70
American Flamingo	48	60
Great White Heron	49	75
Whooping Crane	50	90

HERONS and BITTERNS   Family Ardeidae

Great White Heron*   *Ardea occidentalis*—❋14
L. 49; W. 75

IDENTIFICATION: The large size and heavy appearance, together with the broad heavy bill—yellow to greenish at the tip—and the yellow legs that are greenish in front, are distinctive, as are the elongated fore neck and crest feathers of breeding adults.

HABITS: This heron is almost entirely maritime in distribution, typical habitat being the shallow bays and mangrove-covered keys of Florida Bay and adjacent areas. It feeds along the channels among the flats, chiefly by waiting patiently for its prey to come within striking distance. Here it takes fish, shrimp, and probably anything else that comes within range. It seems at all times a slow, sedate bird and flies with a slow, powerful wingbeat. If it were not for its color, short head plumes, and slightly larger average size, this would be just another great blue heron. Many authorities consider it such, but this seems unlikely, as a typical large race of the latter occurs in the same area, and yet the two stay so well isolated in a reproductive sense that they seldom interbreed.

VOICE: A rough, rasping squawk or scold.

NEST: (A.) Small mangrove-covered keys are the usual nest site, and a single key may contain from 1 to a dozen nests. The nests are bulky, well-made platforms of large sticks, with a hollow in the center that is lined with finer materials, and are always placed in the tops of low trees. The 3 eggs (2.4 x 1.7) are pale blue-green.

RANGE: (R.) Occurs in Florida Bay and adjacent areas, the West Indies, and Yucatan.

Würdemann's Heron* ✳14

IDENTIFICATION: This bird is characterized by its pure-white head and crest, otherwise it looks very much like a great blue heron.

HABITS: Nothing specific is known about the habits of this heron that indicates a difference between it and the great white heron or the great blue heron.

RANGE: (R.) Seems to occur throughout the range of the great white heron.

COMMENT: All that is definitely known about these birds is that they occasionally occur in the same brood with pure-white birds and can have at least one white parent. Some ornithologists believe them to be hybrids between the great blue heron and the great white heron, but such a mating has never been authenticated in the field. Another difficulty is that in a cross of this type all offspring of the original cross generally look alike. It seems more reasonable, as has been suggested by Dr. Ernst Mayr, that the plumage we call Würde-mann's is recessive in the great white heron population and crops out only when a bird happens by accident to receive the recessive Würdemann color genes from both parents.

Great Blue Heron*

Ardea herodias—⚔ 14
L. 46; W. 70; Wt. 7 lbs.

IDENTIFICATION: The great size of this 4-foot-high heron, fre-quently called a blue crane, is absolutely distinctive. In flight it folds back its neck and rests its head on its shoulders in typical heron fashion (a true crane flies with its neck out-stretched like a goose).

HABITS: (Age 15 yrs.) This fine big heron that adds such a picturesque touch to the landscape is a versatile and adapt-able bird. It is at home on small streams, upland meadows, and even in crop fields, as well as on the shores of ponds and lakes. Marshes, salt and fresh, are much frequented, as are coastal mud flats, sand bars, and shallow bays. It fishes either by waiting patiently for its prey to come within range or by slowly walking through the shallow water. Occasionally a bird will drop down with outstretched wings on the surface of deeper water and feed as it floats. Wet meadows and pastures are common feeding grounds.

Although completely protected by the Federal Migratory Bird Treaty, no bird is in greater need of friends than the great blue heron. Its large size makes it an easy and tempt-ing target for the thoughtless, and its nesting colonies are easily broken up by intruders. It eats a great many different kinds of small animal life from snakes, insects, mice, and frogs to fish, eels, salamanders, and an occasional rail or other marsh bird. Many thorough researches into this heron's food habits have been made in various parts of the country. They all show that the bird takes very few adult game or food fish. Most of those that are taken are so small that their removal usually constitutes a desirable culling or weeding of a population of growing fish relatively few of which can hope to mature. The bulk of the great blue heron's fish diet is drawn from the ranks of the non-game species, many of which prey on game fish at some stage of their development and, what is far more serious, compete with them for the always very limited supplies of natural fish foods in the water.

The fine fishing so commonly encountered in the waters of wild, remote areas where wild fish eaters like this heron have never been disturbed and therefore still occur in normal numbers suggests that man would profit from a greater abundance of these species in settled areas. Here they are needed even more, as man's highly selective take of game species creates an unbalanced condition that the heron's fishing would tend to correct. Unfortunately the keen senses of these birds enable them quickly to detect the location of fish-hatchery pools crowded with small fish, where they can be very destructive unless the pools have been fenced and screened to exclude them. As this essential feature of a properly built fish hatchery is still lacking at many establishments, these potentially useful birds are still being lured in and destroyed, often by the hundreds, at hatcheries all over the country.

VOICE: In flight a drawn-out, harsh, gooselike *honk;* when startled, a hoarse, guttural squawk.

NEST: (I. 28, A.) These birds nest in colonies of from a few to many pairs, either by themselves or more frequently in association with other herons and water birds. They prefer an isolated patch of woodland or an island. Customarily they nest in the tops of the tallest trees, but they also use the tops of low shrubs or even nest on the ground. The flat nests are made of coarse sticks but are lined with finer materials and are usually placed well out on a tree limb. Many are over 3 feet in diameter and are repaired and used year after year. The 4 eggs (2.5 x 1.8) are pale green.

RANGE: (P. M.) Breeds from Nova Scotia, c. Quebec, n. Ontario, n. Alberta, and the Alaska Peninsula south to the West Indies, s. Mexico, and the Galápagos Islands. Winters from Massachusetts, s. Michigan, Wyoming, and Alaska south to n. South America and east to Bermuda.

Egret*
(Great White Heron B.O.U.)

Casmerodius albus—✕14
L. 39; W. 55

IDENTIFICATION: The yellow bill, only slightly blackish at the tip (more extensively black in young birds), and the blackish legs are outstanding field characters.

HABITS: These tall, slim-necked herons frequent the borders of sluggish streams and ponds as well as salt- and fresh-water marshes. After feeding all day singly and in small groups they fly at sunset to large communal roosts which they share with other herons. The 40 to 50 long nuptial plumes that develop on the backs of both sexes during the breeding season are the "aigrettes" or "ospreys" of the millinery trade. Because of them the bird has been extirpated from many areas by plume hunters. In the United States it was reduced to rarity in the early 1900s and is still hunted for its plumes in many parts of the world. To obtain the "aigrettes" clean and fresh, the birds are usually shot when they have young, which means that the nestlings slowly starve to death. Public sentiment and the militant efforts of Audubon groups have suppressed the trade in the United States, and the birds are now common over most of their original range. Elsewhere they have not been so fortunate, as the plume trade that still thrives in the Latin countries, provides a tempting market for their plumage. Their food includes all types of aquatic animal life and rice farmers consider them valuable allies because of their heavy consumption of crayfish. They take a great number of frogs and snakes as well as fish.

VOICE: A deep, hoarse, rattlelike croak is its only note.

NEST: (I. 23, A.) This egret usually nests in swamp woods or willow thickets near water in a mixed rookery with other herons and such birds as cormorants and anhingas. Where possible the nests are placed well up (at least 20 to 40 feet) in large trees, but at times they may be quite low, especially if over water. The nest is a rather small, loosely made platform of sticks, often quite flat, with little or no lining. The 3 or 4 eggs (2.2 x 1.6) are a pale blue-green.

RANGE: (P. M.) Occurs on every continent in the world. In North America breeds from c. New Jersey, n. Ohio, s. Wisconsin, Utah, and Oregon south. It wanders north after the breeding season, in greater numbers some years than others, as far as Nova Scotia, s. Ontario, s. Manitoba, and Washington. Winters from South Carolina, s. Louisiana, and c. California south.

Snowy Egret*
(Snowy Heron)

Leucophoyx thula—✳14
L. 24; W. 38; Wt. 12 oz.

IDENTIFICATION: The bright yellow feet, contrasting sharply
with the black legs, are distinctive. The backs of the legs of
the young are greenish-yellow, and the feet are often not so
bright a yellow, but the narrow bill is a uniform black at all
ages.

HABITS: In full nuptial plumage this well-proportioned bird
has a delicate, ethereal quality that makes it unquestionably
the most beautiful of our herons. Its lovely recurved back
plumes are the milliners' "cross aigrettes," and it probably
came even closer to extirpation in this country than its larger
relative. Fortunately, it has now gone a long way toward re-
covering its former abundance and reoccupying its original
range. When feeding it is the most active of all our herons,
constantly stirring the bottom ahead of it with a quick vibra-
tion of its foot and running here and there in active pursuit
of its prey, often with partly raised wings. The shallow water
of marshes and ponds and wet meadows and fields are favorite feeding grounds. Salt bays and salt marches are very attractive, and snowies are generally abundant in such places,
occasionally feeding on the open beaches. Crustacea—like
shrimp, crabs, and crayfish—and insects are important in
their diet along with frogs, fish, and other small aquatic life.

VOICE: Although generally quite silent, this heron can utter a
most unpleasant, harsh, grating scold or hiss.

NEST: (I. 18, A., N. 23) These birds nest in mixed colonies
with other small herons and ibis near or over water. Nests
may be 6 to 12 feet up in trees or shrubs but are often only
a foot or two above the water in matted marsh vegetation.
The structure is a frail, sparse platform of sticks lined with
finer material. The 4 or 5 eggs (1.7 x 1.3) are pale blue-green.

RANGE: (P. M.) Breeds from Long Island, s. Missouri, Utah,
and c. California south to Chile and n. Argentina. Occasionally wanders north as far as s. Canada in late summer.
Winters from South Carolina, the Gulf Coast, and California
south.

Reddish Egret*

Dichromanassa rufescens—✳14
L. 30; W. 46

IDENTIFICATION: The heavy, black-tipped, flesh-colored bill, the
bluish legs, and the rough, shaggy appearance of the neck

are distinctive in adults in either of their 2 color phases. Dark-phase young are often almost wholly gray, showing only a little reddish color on the throat and forewing. In both phases the young have uniformly dark grayish-black bills and greenish-black legs.

HABITS: This heron, like the reef heron of the Southwest Pacific, occurs in 2 distinct color phases—one bluish-slate with a rufous-chestnut neck, the other pure white—that bear no relation to the individual's age or sex. The white is the rarer phase, varying geographically from 1 in several hundred to almost 50–50 in some areas. The species is largely a salt-water heron which feeds in the shallow water of coastal bays and on the open beaches.

The accessibility of its island nesting colonies spelled its doom in the plume-hunting days, and it was almost extirpated from our coasts. In Texas, under Audubon warden protection, it has recovered its abundance, but it has only begun to return to s. Florida. The rookeries in which these birds nest seem to be especially vulnerable to the depredations of such egg eaters as boat-tailed grackles and fish crows and occasionally black vultures, which also take young birds. For this reason these colonies should never be visited early in the breeding season, as these predators can do tremendous damage if the herons are kept away from their nests. Nothing specific seems to be known about food preferences, if any, but the birds are conspicuously active when feeding, rushing here and there and maintaining little of the grace and dignity commonly associated with herons.

VOICE: A guttural squawk, somewhat less harsh than that of most herons.

NEST: In colonies with other herons, spoonbills, and cormorants, usually on coastal islands. The well-made nests of sticks and twigs with a lining of finer material are generally placed in the tops of low shrubs, or trees, anywhere from a few to 10 or 15 feet high, but sometimes they are on the ground. The 3 or 4 eggs (2.0 x 1.5) are pale bluish-green.

RANGE: (P. M.) Occurs from s. Florida, the Gulf Coast, and Lower California south to Hispaniola, Jamaica, and Yucatan.

Tricolored Heron*   *Hydranassa tricolor*—✕15
(Louisiana Heron)   L. 26; W. 38

IDENTIFICATION: This heron has a long, almost snakelike neck and a long bill, but its most noticeable characteristics in any plumage are its white under parts and rump. The black-tipped bill varies seasonably from purplish-blue to yellowish and the legs from slate to yellowish-green.

HABITS: (Age 17 yrs.) Today this is probably the most abundant of southern herons. Like the snowy egret, it is a characteristic bird of the vast marshes near the coast, occurring inland only in regions of extensive open marshland. When feeding it usually keeps on the move, crouching or freezing momentarily before darting out unerringly with its long bill. Killifish, minnows, and other small shallow-water fish are probably its chief food, but it takes shrimp and crayfish and in some areas many grasshoppers and other insects.

VOICE: A variety of hoarse, guttural, but not especially loud notes.

NEST: (I. 21, A.) In small colonies by themselves or in large densely crowded ones which they share with other species. Usually nests are in thickets of low trees or shrubs, but occasionally they are in matted canes or other dense vegetation. In trees they may be 10 to 15 feet high, at other times almost on the ground. As a rule they are well-made structures of sticks and twigs, carefully lined with finer materials. The 4 or 5 eggs (1.7 x 1.3) are pale blue-green.

RANGE: (P. M.) Breeds from s. New Jersey, the Gulf States, and Lower California south through the West Indies to n.e. Brazil and n.w. Ecuador. Wanders north of its breeding grounds only rarely and winters from South Carolina, the Gulf Coast, and s. California south.

Little Blue Heron*   *Florida caerulea*— ⚹ 14
L. 24; W. 41

IDENTIFICATION: The uniformly dark body and maroon head and neck of adults, together with their heavy black-tipped bluish bills and dark legs, are distinctive. Young are white, but the broad-based bicolored bill and the uniformly dull greenish feet and legs are very different from those of the snowy egret. Molting young present a curious pied appearance.

HABITS: In inland fresh-water marshes of the South this is generally the commonest heron, but at times it also occurs in considerable numbers in coastal marshes, where it associates with tricolored herons and snowy egrets. After the breeding season it wanders north in greater numbers than any other southern heron except the egret. Most individuals encoun-

tered in the North are the pure-white young of the year;
as a result they are often mistaken for egrets or snowy egrets.
The little blue is a fairly active feeder in shallow water and
on marshlands and upland meadows and seems to take a
higher proportion of crayfish, frogs, and insects and fewer
fish than most herons. At sunset the birds stream in from
their feeding grounds to large communal roosts. It is quite a
sight to watch the flocks come in high in the air, then suddenly break as birds descend almost vertically by means of
a rapid series of "side slips."

VOICE: When alarmed, a hoarse croak; when quarreling, harsh
parrotlike screams.

NEST: (A.) In small groups or large colonies with other herons.
Usually in a dense clump of willows or bushes, but larger
swamp trees, generally those standing in water, are also used.
The normal height is 3 to 8 feet, but they go up to 40 feet
above water. The 4 or 5 pale blue-green eggs (1.7 x 1.3) are
laid in a typical loose, frail heron nest with little or no lining
or hollow for the eggs.

RANGE: (P. M.) Breeds from s. New Jersey, s. Missouri, c.
Texas, and c.w. Mexico south through the West Indies to c.
Argentina and Peru. Wanders north in summer to Nova
Scotia, s. Ontario, Wisconsin, Nebraska, and s. Lower Cali-
fornia. Winters from North Carolina and the Gulf Coast
south.

Green Heron* *Butorides virescens*—⚹ 15
L. 18; W. 25

IDENTIFICATION: This small dark bird does not look much like
a heron as it stands at the water's edge with its neck drawn
in. Its short legs are a fairly bright greenish-yellow, those of
the male turning orange-red in the breeding season.

HABITS: This is the most widely distributed of all our herons.
Usually every brook and pond has a pair, and it is common
in any extensive marsh, whether fresh or salt. When stalking
its prey it often freezes in odd positions and holds them with
great patience. When disturbed it stretches out its neck,
erects its rough crest, and nervously jets its short tail. When
flushed it flies only a short distance with head and neck extended while it utters sharp squawks of alarm. Small fish,
such as killifish, minnows, gobies, and silversides, are the
commonest food, but quantities of crayfish and aquatic and
terrestrial insects, like grasshoppers, are also taken.

VOICE: The most common note is a distinctive, harsh, penetrating *kyow*. The bird also has a number of low clucking and grunting notes.

NEST: (I. 17, A.) Although commonly a solitary nester, this species may nest in colonies up to 30 pairs or occasionally with other herons or grackles. A dense-foliaged tree, often evergreen, is a favorite site, with the nest 15 to 20 feet up. Low shrubs or marsh hummocks may be used, but the site need not be near water. The frail nest is an unlined, rather small, flat platform of loose sticks. The 4 or 5 eggs (1.5 x 1.2) are pale glaucous green.

RANGE: (P. M.) Breeds from Nova Scotia, s. Ontario, North Dakota, and Oregon south throughout the West Indies and to the Canal Zone. Winters from South Carolina, s. Texas, and s. California south.

Night Heron*   *Nycticorax nycticorax*—✻ 15
(Black-crowned Night-heron)   L. 25; W. 44

IDENTIFICATION: The stocky build and predominantly pale gray and white color of adults are distinctive, as is the uniformly gray-brown color of the white-spotted young. Both neck and bill are short and heavy for a heron, and the bird generally sits with its neck contracted, which gives it a hunched-up look. The short legs are normally dull yellow but turn quite red at the height of the breeding season.

HABITS: (Age 15 yrs.) These night herons commonly sleep all day in a treetop roost and stream out at sunset to their feeding grounds, flying with steady deep beats of their heavy broad wings. A few feed by day, especially in dull weather. They are commonest in areas with extensive marshes, either fresh or salt, but after the breeding season they wander widely and may be found on almost any small lake or pond. This is a relatively fearless species, seemingly less bothered by the proximity of civilization than any other heron. There are nesting colonies in or near some of our largest cities. In the North these colonies are always good places to look for the occasional nesting of some of the rarer southern herons and for the great horned owls that begin nesting before the herons and later on are not above feeding nestling herons to their young. The black-crowned eats a variety of animals and is a good enough mouser to subsist on rodents for short periods during the winter when all open water freezes over. Ordinarily fish, chiefly non-game types, make up about half its

diet, with crayfish and other crustacea, aquatic insects, and
frogs constituting the rest.

VOICE: In flight the birds utter a characteristic *quock* or *woc*
that readily identifies them as they fly over at night. In the
breeding colony a variety of other guttural or shrill squawks
are heard.

NEST: (I. 25, A.) Always in crowded colonies and, in the
South, usually with other herons. The site is in a dense grove
of young trees near water, when available, the nests being
at moderate heights (20 to 30 feet). This is an adaptable
species and will nest far from water in tall trees or practically
on the ground in matted reeds or grass. On occasions it
builds a floating nest. Nests vary from fragile to bulky, well-
built structures made of sticks and twigs with a heavy
lining of finer material. The 3 to 5 eggs (2.0 x 1.5) are varying shades of pale blue-green.

RANGE: (P. M.) Occurs over much of Europe, Asia, and Africa
and the whole Western Hemisphere, where it breeds from
Nova Scotia, s. Quebec, n. Manitoba, and n. Oregon south
to Tierra del Fuego. Winters from Massachusetts, s. Illinois,
Utah, and n. California south.

Yellow-crowned Night Heron

Nyctanassa violacea—⚹15
L. 24; W. 44

IDENTIFICATION: The strongly marked head and the uniformly
gray body of adults are distinctive. Young are darker and not
as brown as the night heron and are speckled rather than
spotted. This species has a heavier bill and longer, yellower
legs which, when the bird is seen in silhouette against the sky,
are its best field character, since they project well beyond
the tail while the night heron's do not.

HABITS: This bird is far from strictly nocturnal and often seems
as active by day as any heron. With its slender neck and big
head, which it generally holds high, it is very different in
appearance from the night heron, which contracts its neck
both in flight and on the ground. The key to understanding
this bird's habits lies in its strong preference for crustacea—
crayfish and aquatic insects in fresh water and fiddler and
other crabs in salt water. Its occasional occurrence in dry
uplands can probably be accounted for by its taste for mice
and other small mammals, insects, and land crabs. Frogs,
salamanders, snakes, and some fish enter into its diet at times

Swamp forests of cypress, gum, willow, and other moisture-loving trees and the mangrove swamps of the Florida coast are favorite haunts of these herons.

VOICE: The common call is a short *woc* or *vac,* pleasanter than a night heron's and not so harsh and guttural.

NEST: (A.) These birds usually nest in small groups of 2 to 6 pairs, large colonies being quite rare. They are often attracted to the vicinity of big rookeries of other herons but generally nest by themselves on the outskirts. The nest site may be high up in a cypress tree or in a low tree or shrub or, in some cases, on the ground. The nest is generally a thick, bulky structure of sticks with a substantial lining of finer material. The 3 or 4 eggs (2.0 x 1.5) are pale blue-green.

RANGE: (P. M.) Breeds from e. Massachusetts and Long Island, Indiana, Kansas, s. Texas, and Lower California south through the West Indies and Mexico to s. Brazil and Peru. Winters from c. Florida, the Gulf Coast, and Lower California south.

American Bittern*   *Botaurus lentiginosus*—※15
L. 27; W. 39

IDENTIFICATION: The dark slate-gray outer wing, contrasting with the rich brown of the body and inner wing, and the black stripe down the side of the neck are good field marks. Young differ only in being lighter brown.

HABITS: Marshes, bogs, and wet meadows, salt or fresh, are the home of the American bittern. It seldom leaves the protection afforded by dense beds of cattails or other rank growths and never alights except on the ground. It clings so closely to concealment that one seldom sees it except as a large brown bird that suddenly flushes up with a hoarse croak from almost underfoot. After flapping off low over the marsh for some distance it generally drops back out of sight. Should you see it before it flies but after it has seen you, it will freeze into immobility with its bill pointing straight up, its streaked body blending into its surroundings. When courting the bird erects a pair of fan-shaped white ruffs which seem to spring from the base of the neck and are held up over the back near the shoulders. Frogs seem to be its favorite food, but it takes all small marsh animals, from mice to snakes, crayfish, shellfish, insects, and small fish.

VOICE: Many of the bittern's common names—"stake driver," "thunder pumper," and "dunk-a-doo"—derive from the curious sound it makes, chiefly in spring but to some extent at other seasons. This can best be described as a deep, hollow, rather guttural croaking which the bird makes by gulping in air until its crop is distended; the air is emitted in groups of 3 well-accented syllables, like *pup-er-lunk,* repeated 5 or 6 times; the call carries well and can often be heard half a mile or more, the sharp middle note rising above the others.
NEST: (I. 28, A., N. 14) Usually in a marsh or on the edge of

a wet meadow in a dense growth of tall cattails, grasses, or sedges. The nest itself is a platform of dead plant stems and leaves built up a few inches above the water. The 4 or 5 eggs (1.9 x 1.4) vary from buffy-brown to olive-buff.

RANGE: (P. M.) Breeds from Newfoundland, n. Quebec, s. Mackenzie, and c. British Columbia south to s. New Jersey, the Ohio Valley, Kansas, c. Arizona, and s. California. Winters from Virginia, Illinois, s. Texas, and British Columbia south to Cuba and Panama.

Least Bittern   *Ixobrychus exilis*—✻15
                                    L. 13; W. 18

IDENTIFICATION: This, our smallest heron, displays a bold, distinctive pattern in flight. The inner wing is buffy-yellow forward and rich chestnut behind, and the outer wing is slaty. Upper parts in the male are a glossy greenish-black with a fine white line down the side of the back. Females are dark purplish-brown with a buffy back line, and they and the young (which have a lighter, even more distinctly brown back) have the pale throat and fore neck finely streaked with dark brown.

HABITS: Almost every extensive fresh-water marsh with dense stands of cattails or other reedlike plants generally harbors a few of these elusive little herons. In the South they also occur in salt marshes. Ordinarily they are not colonial in nesting habits, though, like the green heron, they are sometimes attracted to the vicinity of boat-tailed grackle colonies. In behavior and action they are more like rails than herons.

They prefer to escape by running rather than by flying, and they flush with dangling legs just over the vegetation and quickly drop down again out of sight. At times they conceal themselves by freezing with feathers compressed and bill pointed skyward. When the water is too deep for wading they travel through the marsh by clinging to plant stems, a process which does not seem to slow them up appreciably. The many large insects that occur in aquatic habitats are an important food, but small fish and other small animal life of the marsh contribute to their diet.

A melanistic color phase goes by the name of Cory's least bittern. In it the browns are darkened to rufous-chestnut. This phase is rare, and such birds are worthy of close study to detect possible differences in nesting or other behavior.

VOICE: A series of 4 or 5 low, hollow cooing notes that have been likened to those of a coot or gallinule, a cuckoo, dove, frog, or pied-billed grebe. It also utters a harsh cackle when disturbed.

NEST: (I. 17, A.) Usually in a dense clump of cattails, saw grass, or other marsh vegetation growing in a foot or more of water, occasionally in a shrub. The small, flimsy nest is 1 to 3 feet above the water and is generally supported by a mass of bent and broken-down stalks on which are laid twigs and stalks and the finer grasses of the lining. The 4 or 5 eggs (1.2 x .9) are a blue- or green-white.

RANGE: (P. M.) Breeds from New Brunswick, s. Quebec, Wisconsin, North Dakota, and s. Oregon south to Paraguay and Colombia. Winters from s. Georgia, s. Texas, and s. California south.

STORKS   Family Ciconiidae

Wood Ibis*   *Mycteria americana*—✳17
(Wood Stork)   L. 41; W. 65; Wt. 11 lbs.

IDENTIFICATION: This stork differs from any other large white bird in having a black tail and the whole rear part of the outstretched wing black clear to the body. Young birds lack the bare, scaly head and neck of an old "flinthead," and the body plumage is not such a pure white. Unlike a heron, this bird carries its neck and legs fully outstretched in flight.

HABITS: Low, wet country where vast swamps alternate with open marshy meadows and shallow muddy ponds are the home of this gregarious bird—our only native stork. Along the coast flocks feed on the flats and in the shallow water left when the tide is out. When feeding, the wood ibis walks about actively and appears to take every kind of animal life found in shallow water—tadpoles, fish, snakes, insects, etc. After feeding, members of a flock are apt to assemble in the top of a dead tree to sun and to digest their meal, but if the air currents are right, they may soar instead. Circling to stay in a rising column of warm air or thermal, they may go up almost out of sight, frequently only to dive down and repeat the procedure.

VOICE: A hoarse croak when disturbed is all one hears from adults. A nesting colony full of young produces a bedlam of grunts, squeals, and a dozen other sounds that carry for a surprising distance.

NEST: (A.) In colonies of from 20 to 30 pairs to thousands of pairs. The preferred site seems to be a stand of giant swamp trees, the nests being placed in the upper branches. Small colonies are often located in islandlike clumps of such shallow-water trees as mangrove and willow. The nest is a bulky, flat platform of sticks lined with moss. The 3 eggs (2.7 x 1.8) are dull white.

RANGE: (R.) Breeds and winters to some extent from South Carolina, the Gulf Coast, and the Gulf of California south to Argentina and Peru. Wanders north in late summer to North Carolina, s. Illinois, n. Texas, Arizona, and s. California, with occasional stragglers farther north.

IBISES and SPOONBILLS   Family Threskiornithidae

Glossy Ibis*   *Plegadis falcinellus*—✳ 16
                                           L. 22; W. 38

IDENTIFICATION: At a distance this bird looks black. Its legs
are grayish- or greenish-black, and the bare skin of its face
at the base of the bill varies from slaty-blue to white (at the
height of the breeding season). In winter the head and neck
are a duller brownish-black streaked with white. The downy
young are dull black with a white crown patch. The juvenile
plumage is dull gray-brown below and rich metallic green
above, the head and neck becoming streaked like winter
adults in the fall molt.

HABITS: The glossy ibis has a surprisingly restricted North
American range, considering its abundance and wide distribution in the Eastern Hemisphere. Maybe, like the cormorant, it is such a relative newcomer to the Western Hemisphere that by the time it arrived the niche which it is
equipped to fill was already occupied to capacity by other
ibis, especially the closely related white-faced glossy ibis.

   This highly gregarious ibis is at home on mud flats, wet or
inundated fields, and marshes, usually in the vicinity of a
large lake or river. The birds travel in long, often undulating
lines, either in single file, diagonal, or every bird abreast of its
neighbor with outstretched neck and trailing legs. When only
a few are present they associate freely with white ibis and
join their long lines in flight; but when they are abundant,
as around Lake Okeechobee, Florida, they keep to themselves
except when feeding and have their own night roosts and
nesting colonies. Crayfish, grasshoppers, small snakes, insect
grubs, and leeches are among their staple foods.

VOICE: The common call is a grunting sound followed by 4
bleating notes.

NEST: (I. 21, A.) In low trees, shrubs, or beds of reeds growing
in water, either in small groups in colonies of other ibis and
herons or in large colonies by themselves. The nest is a flat,
loosely made platform of sticks placed from a few to 10 or
more feet above the water. The 3 or 4 eggs (2.0 x 1.5) are
pale blue-green.

RANGE: (R.) Widely distributed in the Eastern Hemisphere
from s. Europe south through most of Africa and east through
s. Asia and the Indies to Australia. Occurs in the Western

Hemisphere only in Florida and the Gulf Coast to Mexico, Cuba, and Hispaniola. A few wander north erratically from time to time as far as s. Canada and Colorado, and it has bred in North and South Carolina.

White-faced Glossy Ibis*   *Plegadis mexicana*—✳ 16
L. 23; W. 38

IDENTIFICATION: The white feathers that border the bare skin on the face at the base of the bill are the chief field characters for this bird. The bare area is reddish, as are the legs and bill tip. Young do not differ enough from those of the glossy ibis to be distinguishable in the field.

HABITS: Drainage and reclamation projects have destroyed many of the marsh areas where these ibis were once abundant and, despite full legal protection from hunting, they have diminished in recent years. As they are willing to fly long distances to feed and seem to find plenty to eat in wet fields and irrigated land, the restoration of even a small tule marsh here and there for breeding would probably greatly increase their numbers. Crayfish, earthworms, and many kinds of insects are their chief foods. Occasionally this ibis is found breeding along the coast and feeding in tidal areas, although it generally seems to prefer fresh-water marshes and the shallow open water of inland sloughs.

VOICE: A croaking or grunting note, at times almost piglike.

NEST: (I. 22, A.) In colonies by themselves or in small groups in a heron colony. The site is usually a dense bed of tules or reeds growing in water. The nest is a large well-formed cup made of old reeds and lined with grass and placed on a mat of floating vegetation or supported several feet above water in old or new growth. The 3 or 4 eggs (2.0 x 1.5) are pale blue-green.

RANGE: (P. M.) Breeds from s. Louisiana, n. Utah, and Oregon south to s. Mexico; also from Peru and Brazil south to Argentina and Chile. After the breeding season it wanders (young birds usually) north as far as Minnesota (where it once bred) and s. British Columbia.

White Ibis*   *Guara alba*—✳ 16
L. 25; W. 40

IDENTIFICATION: This ibis shows only a little black on the ends of the 4 outer primaries. Young are white only on the under parts, lower back, and upper tail coverts—the wings being a uniform dark brown. The soft parts vary from dull flesh color in winter to brilliant red during the breeding season.

ᕼABITS: White ibis, thanks to the vigilant protection afforded them in their main Florida rookeries by Audubon wardens, still occur in great numbers. Rookeries of more than half a million birds have been reported in several recent years. Their flocks are a wonderful sight as they wheel high in the air in perfect unison. At a distance they seem alternately to shine out as a cloud of shimmering silver and as suddenly to disappear completely as they bank the other way. Small flocks heading out to feeding grounds or returning to the large roosts in which they spend the night during the non-breeding season travel in single file in long lines close to the marsh, each bird repeating any maneuver executed by the one in front of it.

The quantities of food required by a large colony are so great that the birds must have extensive feeding grounds and must be able to range out for long distances. Drought or other abnormal conditions often necessitate a shifting of the colonies from year to year, and occasionally a sudden failure of the food supply causes the abandonment of a rookery in mid-season. This species is also very sensitive to human disturbance, and rookeries have been abandoned following one or two visits by bird students. The shallow water of marshy areas, wet fields, and tidal flats are favorite feeding grounds. Here they find crayfish, fiddler crabs, snakes, and many kinds of insects.

The fertilizing effect of great rookeries and roosts of ibis and other water birds on nearby lakes and coastal waters, though enormous, is not yet generally appreciated by those most concerned—the local fishermen. Restoration of the bird colonies in Tampa Bay from a population of a few thousand to some 215,000 birds coincided with the recovery of a virtually exhausted crab and mullet fishery that is today worth well over $100,000 annually.

VOICE: On the breeding grounds one hears soft grunting sounds and sometimes hoarse howling notes, but the birds are generally rather quiet.

NEST: (I. 21, A.) These birds nest in dense colonies with herons and other water birds. The site is an area of low trees or shrubs standing in water. The nests vary from small to fairly large and are poorly made of sticks and moss with a lining of leaves. They are generally placed rather low, from 3 to 4 to 15 feet above the water. The 4 eggs (2.3 x 1.5) are greenish- or creamy-white with brown markings.

RANGE: (P. M.) Breeds from South Carolina, s. Louisiana, c. Mexico, and s. Lower California through the Greater Antilles to Venezuela and Peru. Winters from Florida and the Gulf Coast southward.

Scarlet Ibis*   *Guara rubra*—※16
                                       L. 22; W. 36

IDENTIFICATION: Adults are a solid and uniform scarlet except for the black ends of the 4 outer primaries. Young are dull grayish-brown with white under parts and are virtually indistinguishable from young white ibis.

HABITS: The scarlet ibis seems to be a more coastal bird than the white. It does much of its feeding on mud flats and shallow bays, taking crustacea, mollusks, and fish. Many more may come to our shores than we realize, as young birds—the great wanderers in any species—are not likely to be separated from young white ibis. Early writers lead us to believe that the scarlet ibis may have occurred regularly at one time in s. Florida. These beautiful birds would be a great asset to the Everglades if they could ever be established again in this seemingly ideal habitat.

VOICE: Silent except about its nesting colonies, where it makes a variety of grunting, hissing, and gurgling sounds.

NEST: (I. 24, A.) These birds usually nest on dense brush- and mangrove-covered islands near river mouths. The normal clutch is 2 eggs, very similar to those of the white ibis.

RANGE: (R.) Occurs in northern South America from Venezuela to eastern Brazil. Accidental in the West Indies and on the shores of the Gulf of Mexico.

Roseate Spoonbill*   *Ajaia ajaja*—✳16
L. 33; W. 52; Wt. 3½ lbs.

IDENTIFICATION: The adults, with their wholly pink wings and
outstretched heads, are very distinctive in flight. Young are
at first entirely white except for a touch of pink under the
wings and on the tail. They become increasingly pink with
age and are fully adult when 3 years old.

HABITS: The roseate spoonbill, the only pink member of its
family and the only spoonbill of the Western Hemisphere,
frequents areas of shallow water both along the coast and
inland along rivers, ponds, and marsh lagoons. It obtains its
food, which consists of small fish, shrimp and other crustacea,
and aquatic insects, by opening and closing its broad spatu-
late bill as it works it sideways in long arcs through the soft
mud. Gregarious at all seasons, the birds feed in small flocks
and join other water birds in large communal night roosts.
      Once abundant up both sides of the Florida peninsula and
the Texas coast, this magnificent bird had become virtually
extinct in the United States by 1920. Since then, under
Audubon protection, it has made some recovery in Texas,
but only a few dozen pairs still breed in Florida. How stupid
we were not to have encouraged from the first the greatest
possible numbers of large birds like these that add so much
color and beauty to our landscape at no cost save that of
being left alone!
VOICE: Low clucking and grunting sounds about their rookeries are the only notes of this very silent bird.
NEST: (I. 23, A.) In dense rookeries with ibis, herons, and
other water birds, usually on an island. The large, well-built
stick nests are lined with leaves and bark and placed from

5 to 15 feet up in dense low tree or shrub growth. The 3 eggs (2.6 x 1.7) are dull white, well covered with brown markings.
RANGE: (P. M.) Breeds from s. Florida, s. Louisiana, the Texas coast, and n.w. Mexico south through the Bahamas, and from the West Indies and most of South America to n. Argentina and n. Chile. Flocks of non-breeding birds in their second year wander north to c. Florida and other points on the Gulf Coast.

FLAMINGOS   Family Phoenicopteridae

American Flamingo*   *Phoenicopterus ruber*—✳17
(Roseate Flamingo)   L. 48; W. 60; Wt. 7 lbs.

IDENTIFICATION: In the air these great birds fly with legs and neck fully extended and reveal their black flight feathers. These feathers are also largely black in the grayish-brown young birds that show only a tinge of pink on their under parts, tail, and wings.

HABITS: Once fairly abundant in s. Florida, though not known ever to have bred there, this species now occurs in the area only as a rare straggler. Inhabiting the vast open mud flats of shallow bays and lagoons, gregarious and very vigilant, flamingos are hard to approach if they can fly. However, like ducks and geese, the adults molt all their flight feathers simultaneously and are grounded for several weeks in summer. This makes them temporarily almost as vulnerable to hunters as the much-prized tender young birds that leave the nest 3 or 4 days after they hatch.

To date there is no assurance that this spieces, one of the most striking birds in the world, will not follow the passenger pigeon and the great auk into oblivion, and in the not too distant future. One of the important foods of the flamingo in the Florida-Bahama area is the snail-like cerithium mollusks, which are swallowed whole and crushed in the bird's very powerfully muscled stomach. As these animals are so abundant as to nearly pave the bottom along part of the s.w. Florida coast, it seems as though a real effort should be made to restore the flamingo to our avifauna before it is too late.

VOICE: These noisy birds have several loud, gooselike, honking notes, the commonest a *huh-huh-huh* call with the middle note strongly accented. The honks vary in pitch and are supplemented by a henlike cackle.

NEST: (I. 31, P.) Flamingos nest in dense colonies of from several hundreds to thousands on open mud or marl flats that are wet enough to provide mud for their nests. The nests are low, cylindrical mounds varying from an inch or two to a foot in height; they are hollowed out to hold the single rough, chalky-white egg (3.6 x 2.2). The birds seem unable to nest successfully in any area that can be reached by mammalian egg predators.

RANGE: (R.) Breeds in the Bahamas, Cuba, Hispaniola, n.e. South America, Yucatan, and the Galápagos Islands. A few wander from time to time to s. Florida and other points on the Gulf Coast.

WATERFOWL and ALLIES

Order Anseriformes

Comparison of Average Length and Wingspread of Birds Usually Seen on the Water

SPECIES	LENGTH	WINGSPREAD
Dovekie	8	—
Least Grebe	9	—
Puffin	12½	—

SPECIES	LENGTH	WINGSPREAD
Pied-billed Grebe	13	—
Horned Grebe	13	—
Eared Grebe	13	—
Black Guillemot	13	—
Masked Duck	13½	20
Bufflehead	14	22½
Teal	14	23
Green-winged Teal	14	23
Ruddy Duck	15	22½
Blue-winged Teal	15½	24
Cinnamon Teal	15¾	24½
Oldsquaw (female)	16	28½
Murre	16½	30
Harlequin Duck	16¾	25
Razor-billed Auk	17	26
Ring-necked Duck	17	27
Hooded Merganser	17½	25
Lesser Scaup Duck	17½	27½
Scaup Duck	17¾	30½
Thick-billed Murre	18	—
Wood Duck	18	24
Barrow's Goldeneye	18	28½
Goldeneye	18	28½
Widgeon	18½	31
White-cheeked Pintail	19	—
Shoveler	19	31
Surf Scoter	19	32
Black Scoter	19	32½
Fulvous Tree Duck	19	36
Red-necked Grebe	19½	—
Redhead	19½	32
American Widgeon	19½	32½
Gadwall	20	34
Oldsquaw (male)	21	28½
Mottled Duck	21	—
Canvasback	21	33
Black-bellied Tree Duck	21	37
White-winged Scoter	21	37½
Pintail (female)	21½	34
Red-breasted Merganser	22	32
King Eider	22	36
Canada Goose (small)	22	43½

SPECIES	LENGTH	WINGSPREAD
Mallard	22½	36
Black Duck	23	36
Brant	24	45
Arctic Loon	24	—
Merganser	24	36
Eider	24	41
Ross' Goose	24	50
Red-throated Loon	25	—
Olivaceous Cormorant	25	40
Barnacle Goose	25	52
Western Grebe	26	—
Pintail (male)	27	34
Blue Goose	27½	54
Snow Goose	29	58
White-fronted Goose	29	58
Common Loon	29	—
Double-crested Cormorant	32	51
Anhinga	34	48
Yellow-billed Loon	35	—
Cormorant	36	61
Canada Goose (large)	39½	76
Brown Pelican	50	80
Whistling Swan	52	83
Mute Swan	58	—
White Pelican	60	100
Trumpeter Swan	65	100

WATERFOWL Family Anatidae

Mute Swan*

Cygnus olor—#3
L. 58; Wt. 27

IDENTIFICATION: The pinkish-orange bill and the black knob on the forehead—larger on the cob (male) than on the pen (female)—are distinctive. At a distance the sweeping curve of the neck, the downward tilt of the bill, and the habit of arching the secondaries over the back (the attitude of agression) are good field characters. The brownish young have a dusky-pink bill, dark at the base, with only a suggestion of a knob.

HABITS: The shallow, well-sheltered bays of Long Island and New Jersey and the many ponds that have been created by damming the heads of marsh creeks are apparently ideal habitats. Captivity seems to have had no effect on the ability of subsequent generations to return to the wild state, and a thriving and steadily growing population seems to be well established. These swans generally prefer to nest in fresh water, but with freezing weather they migrate to nearby salt water that remains open all winter. They feed exclusively on underwater vegetation, tipping up like ducks, but with their long necks reaching greater depths than those of any dabbling duck or goose. As a result, swans generally do not compete seriously with ducks but instead often make food available to them by loosening it from the bottom. It is in fact a common sight to see a flock of baldpates in attendance on a group of feeding swans.

VOICE: This is a rather silent bird, its only calls hissing and snorting notes and a peeping note from young birds. In flight this swan's wings make a loud, rather musical throbbing sound that can be heard for a long distance.

NEST: (I. 35, P.) Generally a pair exercise complete territorial dominance over a considerable area—often the whole of a pond or small lake; only rarely is anything like a colony formed. The nest is a large pile of sticks, roots, and other trash on a small islet in the shallow marshy margin of a pond or on the bank near the water. The 5 to 7 eggs (4.5 x 2.9) are tinged with gray- or blue-green.

RANGE: (P. M.) Breeds from Great Britain, s. Sweden, and n. Germany east to e. Siberia and south to Iran. Winters south to n. Africa, n.w. India, and Korea. Introduced by man in many other areas. In North America, well established on Long Island and the lower Hudson Valley. Wanders along the coast to c. New Jersey and s. Massachusetts.

Whistling Swan* $\qquad$ *Cygnus columbianus*—✻3
L. 52; W. 83; Wt. 16 lbs.

IDENTIFICATION: The small yellow area in front of the eye is distinctive, but it is often absent. The bird, however, has a very characteristic call. Young are washed with sooty-brown, and the bills are mottled with pink instead of being wholly black as in adults.

HABITS: A wedge of these great birds migrating high in the air, calling as they go, is a thrilling sight. They make only a few stops between their breeding grounds and their winter home; generally these are at the same place year after year and the bird is a rare straggler elsewhere. Swans have to run over the water quite a distance to build up speed for a take-off. This means that they cannot escape danger quickly by flying and makes their stop on the Niagara River above the Falls very hazardous. In some years the swift current sweeps many to their death before they realize they are in danger.

In the North the Eskimos use the eggs and flesh for food, and the down for clothing. Elsewhere this bird has enjoyed full protection for many years, and it seems likely that in the future the hunting of this and other species that breed in the Far North will be limited to Eskimos and northern Indians. In their economy an ample supply of such waterfowl is a necessity and no substitute is available. With us, on the contrary, waterfowl hunting is a sport.

Like all swans, this bird is a vegetarian, feeding largely on underwater plants. Its vigorous rooting loosens the bottoms on which they grow and seems to have an invigorating effect on the beds, the ultimate effect being the production in subsequent years of even more food for themselves and other waterfowl.

VOICE: The babble of a flock varies considerably in volume and generally suggests that of a flock of Canada geese, although higher-pitched and more musical. There is a curious quavering quality to the sound despite its clamorousness. The whoop of a single bird is of 3 notes with a strong accent on the middle.

NEST: A bulky pile of grass, moss, and roots on an island or bank of a small pond. The 4 or 5 eggs (4.1 x 2.7) are creamy-white.

RANGE: (M.) Breeds from about Lat. 74° N. on the Arctic Islands from Baffin Island west, n. Alaska, and n.e. Siberia south to Southampton Island, n. Mackenzie, and the Alaska Peninsula. Winters mainly on coastal bays from Chesapeake Bay to Currituck Sound and from s. Alaska to the n. San Joaquin Valley. Rarely south to n. Florida, the Gulf Coast to Texas, and s. California.

Trumpeter Swan* *Cygnus buccinator*—⚹3
L. 65; W. 100; Wt. 30 lbs.

IDENTIFICATION: The trumpeter's best field character is its voice. Adults always have a solid black bill which in the young is clouded with crimson. The mustard-yellow feet and legs of the young are distinctive, although their dirty gray-brown plumage looks like that of other young swans.

HABITS: The trumpeter swan once bred over a vast area from James Bay, n. Mackenzie, and Alaska south to Indiana, Missouri, and Nebraska and migrated in winter as far as the Gulf Coast and s. California. It would have been too much to expect a fairly tame bird affording such a wonderful target to long survive the settlement of most of its breeding and wintering range. We are fortunate that a few survive in that great sanctuary for wildlife—Yellowstone Park—and in the wild parts of n. Canada. The some 400 birds in the Yellowstone area are virtually non-migratory, and because of the limited amount of natural food available in the few hot springs that stay open all winter the area can never carry many more. For this reason some of the young are captured each year and moved to other suitable areas in an attempt to repopulate some of its original range. The Canadian birds, estimated at 900, are more migratory. They winter on lake outlets and rapids in interior British Columbia and similar areas, as well as on small forest ponds and river-mouth tide flats on the Pacific coast. The food of this big swan seems to be the leaves, roots, and seed of sedges and other aquatic vegetation. Their feeding habits make them very vulnerable to lead poisoning, and several wintering populations have been almost wiped out by it.

VOICE: A distinctive, short, low-pitched, resonant *beep* that suggests an old-fashioned French taxicab horn and carries surprisingly well.

NEST: (I. 38, P.) In an old muskrat or beaver house or on a small islet in a shallow pond or marshy slough. The nest is a broad platform of organic debris lined with down. The 7 to 8 eggs (4.3 x 2.8) are dull white.

RANGE: (P. M.) Breeds in n. British Columbia, n. Alberta, and the Yellowstone Park region. Winters in the coast region of s. Alaska, British Columbia. and on warm springs in the Yellowstone area.

Canada Goose*   *Branta canadensis*—✕3
L. 22–39½; W. 43½–76; Wt. 2½–14 lbs.

IDENTIFICATION: The conspicuous white sides of the head and the solid black neck are distinctive.

HABITS: (Age 9 yrs.) To the average person this is the wild goose whose great V-shaped flocks foretell the coming of fall or the return of spring as they pass noisily overhead night and day. Some are huge birds while others from the Far North are no larger than mallards. On the basis of size as well as differences in general color and habits, various attempts have been made to divide them into races or even species. These geese are so clannish in their habits and so firmly attached to certain breeding areas that close inbreeding is probably the rule. They mate for life, and the family unit stays together until after they return north. The rapid evolution of local races, varying greatly in size and habitat preferences, is undoubtedly favored by these facts. In effect each little colony or regional group is reproductively isolated from the rest of the population, a situation which in time leads to the accumulation of sufficient genetic differences to produce distinct local species.

During the breeding season these geese are found on small ponds and along rivers, in wooded regions as well as in the extensive marshes of the West. In the Far North they nest inland and along the coast among the ponds and lakes of the open tundra. During fall and winter they occur on fresh and salt water, feeding in the shallows and adjacent marshes. Grainfields are often favorite feeding grounds, but the feeding habits of these and other geese vary erratically from region to region. Here they glean waste grain in the fall; there they graze on new shoots of spring and winter crops. They like the grass that springs up after a grass or marsh fire, and they can feed under water like swans, obtaining seeds, leaves, tubers, and roots of aquatic plants, including those of such species as eelgrass and sea lettuce. Little animal food is taken except along the coasts, where certain distinct races frequent tidal flats and appear to depend heavily on marine invertebrates.

Geese usually feed twice a day—early morning and late afternoon—repairing at other times to a safe resting place on a sand bar or out in open water. Jack Miner demonstrated years ago that even a small farm pond near a house would fulfill their need for a resting place once the geese realized they were safe on it. As a result many similar "sanctuaries" have been established. Although those who create them invariably do so with the best of intentions, some of these concentrations draw hunters to their outskirts in such numbers that the geese are virtually slaughtered as they move in and out in loose low-flying groups to nearby feeding areas.

VOICE: Varies in different races from a deep, resonant double honk to a high-pitched, almost cackling call.

NEST: (I. 26, P.) Generally on the ground but occasionally in a tree in the abandoned nest of a large bird like an osprey. The larger races build up a flat mound of grasses, often on a foundation of sticks. These are usually placed on high ground near water or on a small islet in a pond, muskrat and beaver houses being common sites. Smaller races seem more inclined to use a depression sparingly lined with grass and the customary blanket of down. The normal clutch is 5 creamy-white eggs (2.4–3.9 x 1.5–2.5).

RANGE: (P. M.) Breeds through Arctic America from Labrador, s. Baffin Island, Victoria Island, n. Alaska, and n.e. Siberia south to Newfoundland, James Bay, South Dakota, n. Colorado, and n. California. Winters from Nova Scotia, s. Ontario, South Dakota, and s.e. Alaska south to c. Florida, the Gulf Coast of Mexico, n. Mexico, and Japan. This species domesticates readily, and when captive birds are allowed to go wild again they build up small local and relatively non-migratory populations.

Brant*   *Branta bernicla*—✸3
(Brent Goose)   L. 24; W. 45; Wt. 3 lbs.

IDENTIFICATION: The small size, short neck, black chest, pale flanks, and very long white tail coverts are distinctive. The race that winters chiefly in the Pacific has a slaty-brown breast while the common Atlantic race has a pale gray breast that contrasts sharply with the dark chest. Young are similar except for light edgings on the back and wing-covert feathers and a poorly developed neck patch.

HABITS: During the non-breeding season this small sea goose is a bird of shallow coastal bays, where it feeds at low tide on beds of aquatic plants growing in shallow water. It also seems to require large quantities of sand, which it gets from nearby sand bars to which it moves as the tide rises. The roots and succulent white bases of eelgrass are a favorite food, and great concentrations occur on beds of this plant. On water the brant ride high with upturned tails, often tipping up to feed and continually pivoting as they pick up food from the surface. These little geese are fast fliers with long pointed wings and a rapid wingbeat. They are strongly gregarious, moving about in long undulating lines of 20 to 50 birds abreast, generally low and invariably over water, as they have a curious aversion to crossing even a narrow strip of land. In the North on their breeding grounds, however, they appear to feed on land to some extent, taking the leaves and buds of some of the commoner flowering plants of the tundra.

The brant is an example of a dangerously overspecialized bird, too dependent on a single plant species for food. Eelgrass became so important to it that a die-off of the plant virtually all over the world, which started in 1931, greatly reduced its numbers. On the Atlantic coast only a small percentage of the original population survived by turning for food to the algae known as sea lettuce (*Ulva*) and the roots of marsh sedges. As eelgrass is now slowly returning, the brant can probably become abundant again, provided the small breeding stock that survives is carefully protected.

VOICE: A drawn-out, rolling, and guttural honking note as well as various grunting and hissing sounds. When the birds are in a flock these sounds blend into a babble of noise that carries a long distance.

NEST: (P.) Islets along the coast or in nearby inland ponds are favorite sites. At times the nests are bunched in loose colonies. Nests vary from little more than a mass of down in a hollow to a substantial pile of moss and lichens lined with down. The 4 or 5 eggs (2.8 x 1.9) are a dull cream color.

RANGE: (M.) Breeds on the islands and coasts of the entire Arctic Ocean south to Bering Strait and the Greenland coasts to Lat. 70° N. Winters on the northern coasts of the Atlantic and Pacific oceans. In North America from New Jersey to North Carolina and Vancouver Island to Lower California.

Barnacle Goose*

Branta leucopsis—✕3
L. 25; W. 52; Wt. 4 lbs.

IDENTIFICATION: The extensively white face is distinctive. In the browner-backed young birds this is tinged with dusky and the flanks are more strongly barred.

HABITS: This brantlike bird of the Far North is one of the most fearless of geese. Although generally found close to the seacoasts, where it feeds to some extent on exposed mud flats, the barnacle's chief food is the grass in nearby pastures and croplands. Like so many birds that nest in Greenland, its normal wintering grounds are wholly European.

VOICE: A rapid series of short, shrill yelps. A flock sounds like a pack of terriers.

NEST: (I. 25, P.) In colonies on rock ledges, cliffs or mountainsides, occasionally on a rocky island. The 4 grayish eggs (3.0 x 2.0) are laid in a hollow and surrounded with down.

RANGE: (M.) Breeds in n.e. Greenland, Spitsbergen, and Novaya Zemlya. Winters south to Great Britain and the shores of the Baltic Sea. There are occasional records for the Atlantic coast south to North Carolina.

White-fronted Goose*   *Anser albifrons*—✕4
L. 29; W. 58; Wt. 5½ lbs.

IDENTIFICATION: The uniformly brownish fore parts and dark-blotched pale breast of adults are distinctive. Young have yellowish bills, legs, and feet but otherwise closely resemble young blue geese.

HABITS: No other goose has equal speed and agility on the wing. When necessary the bird can rise almost vertically into the air. The "specklebelly" commonly occurs in large, noisy, V-shaped flocks during migration, and vast numbers used to gather on some of its wintering grounds. Shallow ponds and marsh sloughs are its usual resting and loafing places. In some areas the geese feed heavily on aquatic plants and marsh grasses; in others their favorite foods appear to be waste grain from stubble fields and, later, the young leaf growth in newly planted grainfields. Pasture lands attract them, especially if recently burned over or heavily enough grazed to stimulate an abundant fresh growth. In the Arctic these geese eat many of the common tundra plants and a great many berries from the low-growing plants of wet or boggy areas.

VOICE: A laughlike series of rapidly repeated, high-pitched paired notes with a melancholy tone.

NEST: (I. 25, P.) Located in open tundra, often in groups near small bodies of water; also on upland and mountain slopes. The nest is a cup of moss and grasses lined with down and well concealed in a natural hollow. The 5 or 6 eggs (3.1 x 2.1) are light buff or cream color.

RANGE: (M.) Breeds on various islands and points on the mainland shores of the Arctic Ocean. In North America on the w. coast of Greenland from Lat. 72° N. to 66° N., and from Coronation Gulf west to the Yukon delta. Winters south to the Mediterranean, n. India, and Japan, and in North America on the Gulf Coast of Louisiana and Texas, the central valleys of the Pacific States, and c.w. Mexico.

Snow Goose*   *Chen hyperborea*—✳4
                                           L. 29; W. 58; Wt. 6 lbs.

IDENTIFICATION: The black primaries are not conspicuous except in a flying bird, but on water the short neck and the tail carried high distinguish this goose from a swan. Young birds are irregularly marked with various tones of ashy-gray. Rust stains are common on the face and head and sometimes on the breast.

HABITS: These geese migrate in great flocks that move across the sky in curved diagonal lines and broad V's. Away from their regular and somewhat restricted routes of travel and a few concentration areas, they are rather uncommon. Usually they keep to themselves, seldom mixing freely with any geese except their close relative, the blue goose, and the rare Ross'

goose. They visit stubble fields for waste grain and browse on pasture grasses and young grain shoots, but in most areas they are grubbers and eaters of roots. Their favorite foods in the North and on their coastal marsh wintering grounds are the roots and bases of various rushes, sedges, and marsh grasses. Here they seem to prefer areas that are covered with a few inches of water. Often they so concentrate their feeding that they turn the area into a wallow of loose mud, floating plant debris, droppings, and feathers that produces an odor which sometimes carries for miles.

In many parts of the North "wavies," as they are called, are an important part of the food supply of Eskimos and Indians. Early in the season Eskimos gather the eggs by the thousands, and later, when the birds are molting and cannot fly, both adults and young are driven into crude corrals and killed for food and down. Farther south in early fall Indians take heavy toll by shooting them at some of their local concentration points. Despite all this and the threat from hunting farther south, this bird continues to be the most abundant goose in North America.

VOICE: A high-pitched falsetto honking that produces a sustained, somewhat musical clamor when uttered simultaneously by a flock.

NEST: (I. 22, P.) In flat marshy grass tundra near the coast. The nest, which is generally near a pond, is a substantial cup-shaped mass of moss lined with fine grasses and down. The 6 eggs (3.1 x 2.1) are dull white.

RANGE: (M.) Breeds from n.w. Greenland, the Arctic Islands and coast west to n.e. Siberia. Winters on the Atlantic coast from s. New Jersey to North Carolina, on the Gulf Coast from Louisiana to n. Mexico, the Central Valley of California, and the Asiatic coast south to Japan. The East Coast birds were once separated from the rest under the name "greater snow goose."

Blue Goose*   *Chen caerulescens*—✕4
                        L. 27½; W. 54; Wt. 5¼ lbs.

IDENTIFICATION: Adults vary in the amount of rust stain about the head and the extent of the dark color on the under parts. Young have blackish secondaries as well as primaries and dusky to slightly pinkish bills, legs, and feet. The curious so-called "grinning patch" on the side of the bill is present only in blue and snow geese.

HABITS: Almost anywhere an occasional blue goose may turn up among snow geese, but the main population is always concentrated within a relatively small area. Flocks of more than several hundred thousand birds are not uncommon along the 200-mile stretch of Louisiana coastal marsh, where they winter. In spring large flocks stop at various points in the n. Great Plains to feed on the newly sprouted grain, but with this exception the geese have a strong affinity for salt water and are never found much more than 10 miles inland. Like snow geese, blues live chiefly on the roots, tubers, and bases of salt and brackish marsh plants.

The status of the blue goose as a distinct species is questioned by many ornithologists. The fact that blue and snow geese differ only in color leads many to believe them to be dark and light phases of a single species. They readily interbreed in the wild (the whiter-bellied blues are supposed to be hybrids), but they do not appear to do so as freely as they would if the birds were unconscious of difference and mated at random. The marked clannishness of geese and the tendency of family units to stay together might, however, account for this.

VOICE: Indistinguishable from that of the snow goose.

NEST: (I. 24, P.) The nesting habits of the blue goose are in no way different from those of the snow geese that nest with them in the same area of coastal grass tundra.

RANGE: (M.) Breeds in s.w. Baffin Island and Southampton Island. Migrates south to the east side of Hudson Bay, then to

the southern end of James Bay and from there, in a largely
non-stop flight, direct to the wintering ground on the coast of
Louisiana. In the more leisurely spring flight, goes north as
far as Manitoba, east to James Bay, and on to the breeding
grounds.

Ross' Goose*
Chen rossi—✗4
L. 24; W. 50; Wt. 2¾ lbs.

IDENTIFICATION: Its size (little larger than a mallard) and
warty-based, rather stubby bill without a "grinning patch"
on the side are distinctive. Young birds have pinker bills,
legs, and feet and are generally paler than young snow geese.

HABITS: This once abundant and tame little goose has been so
dangerously reduced in numbers that the remnant needs to
be carefully protected. Unfortunately it is closely associated
in winter with the very similar snow goose, from which the
average hunter usually cannot distinguish it. It feeds on waste
grain and fresh young growth in grasslands and grainfields.

VOICE: A rather weak double gruntlike note—quite different
from that of a snow goose—is the only call.

NEST: (I. 21, P.) In loose colonies on islands in lakes in low
tundra country. The nests are grass- and down-lined cavities
with 4 creamy-white eggs (2.7 x 1.9).

RANGE: (M.) Breeds on the Canadian mainland south of King
William Island. Migrates west via Great Slave Lake and w.
Montana to its wintering grounds in the Central Valley of
California.

Black-bellied Tree Duck*
Dendrocygna autumnalis—✗6
(Black-bellied Whistling Duck)   L. 21; W. 37; Wt. 2 lbs.

IDENTIFICATION: The long neck and the white wing patch, which
in flight covers the whole central area of the upper wing
surface, are distinctive.

HABITS: This largely nocturnal duck frequents the banks and
shallow borders of rivers and ponds but seldom seems to
alight on, or swim in, deep water. The birds fly about from
tree to tree with ease and usually resort to a woodland when
disturbed. They do much of their feeding in shallow water
and are fond of corn, visiting the fields as soon as it starts to
ripen.

VOICE: A peculiar and characteristic shrill, chattering whistle,
which it utters constantly on the wing.

NEST: (P.) In cavities in trees in open woodland, often some
distance from water. Twelve creamy-white eggs (2.1 x 1.5)
are a normal clutch.

RANGE: (P. M.) Breeds from s.e. Texas and w.c. Mexico south
to s. Brazil and Ecuador. Winters from c. Mexico south.

Fulvous Tree Duck*   *Dendrocygna bicolor*—✕6
(Fulvous Whistling Duck)   L. 19; W. 36; Wt. 1½ lbs.

IDENTIFICATION: Long legs, long neck, and upright carriage
characterize tree ducks. In flight this species shows a line of
white between the dark undersurface of the wing and the
body, and a white tail base. The wing beat is slow and the
bird thrusts head and feet downward when alighting.

HABITS: Densely grown-up marshy areas adjacent to open croplands—especially low-lying, frequently flooded areas like rice
fields—attract this species, which is so nocturnal that it is
seldom seen. The birds appear to do most of their feeding
while walking about on land. Wild seeds, waste grain, corn,
acorns, and green vegetation like grass and alfalfa are their
chief foods.

    The curious, discontinuous distribution of this bird suggests
either a decadent species of which only a few relics survive
or an aggressive species which is spreading and colonizing
new areas. The former appears more likely, although the bird
seems to have found certain types of recently created man-

made habitats so much to its liking that it has increased markedly in some of these localities.

VOICE: A thin, high-pitched, almost ploverlike double whistle uttered on the wing.

NEST: (P.) In the tall rank grass of a wet meadow or in a dense bed of cattails or other marsh vegetation. Very rarely in a tree hollow. The nest varies from a grass-lined hollow on high ground to a basket woven of the surrounding vegetation that holds the eggs well above the water. A normal clutch is about a dozen eggs, but now and then 2 or more females dump eggs into a nest until 30 or more have accumulated, only to be abandoned. The eggs (2.1 x 1.6) are creamy- or buffy-white.

RANGE: (P. M.) This duck now occurs in 5 widely separated parts of the world: coastal Louisiana and Texas; c. California south to c. Mexico; n. South America; s. Brazil and n. Argentina; e. Africa; and India.

Mallard   *Anas platyrhynchos*—⚡7
                           L. 22½; W. 36; Wt. 2½ lbs.

IDENTIFICATION: In the air the 2 white borders of the violet-blue speculum, clear white underwing linings, and largely white tail (not clear white in the female) are distinctive. This commonly domesticated duck should be memorized as a standard for comparison with other ducks.

HABITS: (Age 15 yrs.) The mallard is a hardy, adaptable bird that domesticates readily. It is the most abundant wild duck in the world. Many go only as far south in winter as they must to find open water, and in spring they push north as fast as the ice melts. In general mallards seem to avoid salt water, but almost any body of shallow fresh water may harbor a few pairs. They are typical river- and pond- or surface-feeding ducks and prefer water that does not exceed 12 to 16 inches in depth—the maximum they can reach when "tipped up." Like other "puddle ducks," mallards can launch themselves into flight with a single, almost vertical leap from the surface of the water.

The mallard is primarily a seedeater. Seeds of sedges, grasses, and smartweeds are its staple food. It eats the leaves and stems as well as the seeds of such plants as pondweeds, duckweed, and coontail. At times the seeds of bottom-land trees like water elm, hackberry, oak, and hickory are taken in great quantities, and in recent years mallards have learned to visit dry stubble fields for waste grain. Their animal food consists chiefly of fresh-water mollusks, especially snails and aquatic insects, but they are opportunists and will eat fish eggs and grasshoppers and will even scavenge on dead fish.

Crosses between mallards and other ducks, like the pintail (Plate #7), that breed in the same region are not uncommon. With the introduction of domestic mallards and the release of hand-raised wild birds into the breeding range of the black duck, crosses between these closely related species have become quite frequent (Plate #7). Usually the parentage of duck hybrids is not difficult to guess, as the birds are a patchwork of the characters of each parent species. There is seldom much blending of characters.

VOICE: Female, a loud, resonant *quack*. Male, a softer, higher-pitched note that carries well.

NEST: (I. 26, P.) Normally in dense reeds or grass close to a body of fresh water. Occasionally a long distance from water in a brush pile or under a fallen log. Rarely in hollows in trees or up in a thick cluster of branches. The nest is usually a hollow lined with dead grass or reeds and filled with down. The 10 eggs (2.3 x 1.6) are light greenish-buff to nearly white.

RANGE: (P. M.) Circumpolar, breeding south from the Arctic Ocean to the Mediterranean, Persia, Tibet, c. China, and n. Japan; in North America from Nova Scotia, s. Ontario, w. Hudson Bay, n. Mackenzie, and n. Alaska south to n. Virginia, s. Illinois, n. Kansas, s. New Mexico, and n. Lower California. Winters along the coast from Nova Scotia and inland from Maryland, n. Indiana, Nebraska, w. Montana, c. Alaska, and the Aleutian Islands south to the West Indies and s. Mexico.

Black Duck*

Anas rubripes— #7
L. 23; W. 36; Wt. 2¾ lbs.

IDENTIFICATION: This is a uniformly dark sooty-black bird with a lighter head and neck showing fine dark streaks. The purplish speculum is black-bordered but may be tipped with white. The gleaming white underwing surfaces are the best field marks in flight. Only fully adult winter males seem to have clear yellow bills and bright red feet. The bills of females are always flecked with dusky.

HABITS: (Age 10 yrs.) The black is probably the wariest, quickest, and most alert of all ducks. Although it is one of the most sought after, it has remained abundant as a breeder in some of the most densely settled parts of the United States. It is the common duck of the salt marshes of the Atlantic coast, nesting in small groups and gathering in great flocks in the fall. During the non-breeding season black ducks spend the day in rafts far out in open water or sitting on the ice of a frozen lake and do most of their feeding at night. They eat more submerged plants than do mallards. Pondweeds, eel-grass, and wild celery are taken in about equal quantity with seeds of sedges, grasses, and grains. When ice and deep snow lock up these foods the birds live on animal food, which they seem to have no trouble finding. Most of it comes from the shallow flats exposed at low tide, where blue mussels, peri-winkles (650 in one stomach), and other shellfish abound. Shrimp, sand fleas, sow bugs, and other crustacea and insects are often important. Occasionally they take small fish.

Nearly every winter the presence of ducks dying of disease, or more often of lead poisoning, leads to false reports that the local black duck population is starving. Any healthy duck can fly farther south if food gets scarce, but the black duck's ability to utilize marine life seldom makes this necessary. Unfortunately, lead poisoning is taking an ever-increasing toll as the quantity of lead shot into our marshes increases with each hunting season. A few pellets sifted from the mud with seeds and other food and held in the duck's gizzard, to be slowly ground away, seem to be enough to paralyze the stomach muscles and cause apparent starvation and death.

VOICE: Females quack like mallards. Males have a short, weak, reedy note.

NEST: (I. 27, P.) On the ground on an isolated islet or other high ground near a marsh or open water, generally well hid-den in a tangle of tall grass or shrubs. Occasionally a nest is built in an old crow or hawk nest high in a tree or off in a woodland near a small stream. The nest is an often bulky cup of grasses and leaves with a lining of down that is added to as incubation progresses. The 9 eggs (2.3 x 1.7) vary from creamy-white to greenish-buff.

RANGE: (P. M.) Breeds from Ungava, n. Ontario, and e. Manitoba south to e. North Carolina, Pennsylvania, n. Indiana, and n.w. Iowa. Winters from Nova Scotia, c. New York, n. Ohio, and e. Nebraska south to s. Florida and the Gulf Coast west to s.c. Texas.

Mottled Duck*
(Florida Duck)

Anas fulvigula—⚵7
L. 21

IDENTIFICATION: These ducks closely resemble female mallards except for their clear yellow or orange bills (bills of females have a few small black spots), dark tails, and black-bordered speculum, which may be white-tipped.

HABITS: The mottled duck occurs in a wild region of vast fresh or brackish marshes that are relatively difficult to penetrate. Usually they are encountered in pairs or small family groups up to a dozen. Of all puddle ducks, these are the most carnivorous. They take quantities of snails and other mollusks and small numbers of crayfish, aquatic insects, and fish. The plant portion of their diet is seeds, tubers, and underwater vegetation.

VOICE: Like the mallard's.

NEST: (I. 27, P.) On the ground, on a high place in or near a marsh or on an island; well concealed in a dense clump of grass or under a bush. The down-filled grass nest usually holds about 9 creamy- to greenish-white eggs (2.2 x 1.6).

RANGE: (R.) Occurs in s. Florida north along the coasts to the middle of the state and inland to Orange Lake, and in the coastal regions of Louisiana and Texas.

Gadwall

Anas strepera—⚵7
L. 20; W. 34; Wt. 2 lbs.

IDENTIFICATION: In flight the speculum, which is white near the body, then black and gray, and the reddish-brown forewing (less noticeable in females) are diagnostic. The male's uniform lead-gray color, black stern, and paler, browner head and neck help identify it on water. Aside from yellowish-orange feet and a touch of orange-yellow on the side of the bill, the female is quite like the larger female mallard and pintail when on the water.

HABITS: This rather shy, early-fall and late-spring migrant normally occurs in small flocks and seldom seems very abundant. It does, however, have the widest range of any duck in the world. Shallow streams, ponds, and lakes, especially when bordered by a dense fringe of tall reeds, are favorite haunts. Occasionally the birds are seen in brackish, but seldom in salt, marshes. Like all ducks, the gadwall has an interesting courtship ritual, rival males displaying before the female in flight. Gadwalls are almost wholly vegetarian. Leaves, stems, and tubers of various pondweeds are their chief foods. Others are coontail, widgeon grass, algae, and the seeds of sedges and grasses. If necessary, they dive for food and at times leave the water to feed on waste grain in stubble fields and on acorns and other mast in the woods.

VOICE: The female has a rather subdued quack, but the male has quite a repertoire of croaks, whistles, rattles, and trills.

NEST: (I. 27, P.) Sites vary from islands in lakes to uplands some distance from water. The nest, which is always well hidden in a dense tangle of tall grass, weeds, or shrubs, is just a hollow in the ground lined with plant material and down. The 11 eggs (2.2 x 1.6) are creamy-white.

RANGE: (P. M.) Breeds over much of the Northern Hemisphere between Lat. 40° N. and 60° N. In North America from c. Manitoba, n. Saskatchewan, and s. British Columbia south to s. Wisconsin, s. Kansas, n. New Mexico, and c. California. It now seems to be reclaiming former range in the East, nesting sparingly in w. Pennsylvania and on the Atlantic coast from Long Island to North Carolina. Winters from Maryland, s. Illinois, c. Texas, and Oregon south to c. Florida, the Gulf Coast, and s.c. Mexico.

Pintail

Anas acuta—✳6
L. ♂ 27; ♀ 21½; W. 34; Wt. 2 lbs.

IDENTIFICATION: Even in the female the long neck and pointed tail are good field characters. The dark blue-gray bill and feet and, in flight, the pointed wings with white along the rear edge of the iridescent brown speculum are diagnostic.

HABITS: (Age 13 yrs.) The hardy pintail is one of our most widely distributed and abundant ducks. Although the birds migrate early in the fall, they push north as fast as the ponds and marshes open up. Shallow fresh-water areas are the usual habitat, but many pintails winter along the coast, where they are not uncommon in brackish marshes or resting by day in rafts on open bays. In very cold weather, when other feeding grounds are frozen, they visit uplands for waste grain or acorns or go to the tidal flats for marine animals. They are chiefly seedeaters and take little other vegetable material. Seeds of pondweeds, sedges, grasses, and smartweeds are staple. At times they eat considerable animal material in the form of snails and other shellfish, crabs and aquatic insects.

There is no stronger, faster, or more dexterous flier among ducks. Even so, the regular migration of such ducks as these and shovelers to the Hawaiian Islands in winter is an extraordinary feat, although occasionally some of the birds miss the way. A flock of 22 very tired pintails turned up on Palmyra Island, 1,100 miles south of Hawaii, in 1942, and one wore a band placed on it in Utah 82 days earlier, after it had been cured of botulism poisoning.

VOICE: The male has a seldom-heard low double whistle, the female a low quack.

NEST: (I. 23, P.) The down-lined nest in a hollow in dry ground may be near water but is often a long distance from it. Sometimes the nest is well concealed under rank grass or a bush, but quite often it is out in open prairie with little to hide it. The 8 eggs (2.1 x 1.5) in an average clutch are buff-green.

RANGE: (P. M.) Circumpolar. Breeds from n. Europe and Asia south to n. Great Britain, s. Russia, and s. Siberia. In North America breeds from n. Mackenzie and n.w. Alaska east to Hudson Bay and south to Iowa, n. Colorado, and s. California; casually east to New Brunswick. Winters from s. New England, s. Ohio, c. Missouri, New Mexico, and s. British Columbia south to the West Indies and Panama, also west to the Hawaiian Islands.

White-cheeked Pintail*   *Anas bahamensis*—⚹6
(Bahama Pintail)   L. 19

IDENTIFICATION: The clear white face and throat, red bill base, and, in flight, the narrow green speculum broadly bordered with buff and the very pale buffy tail are distinctive.

HABITS: This largely coastal duck seems to be quite at home on vast shallow tidal flats. Frequently a pair or family group is flushed from the saline ponds that occupy the centers of the small mangrove islands. Much of the bird's feeding is done in the marshes just back of the coast. It is largely vegetarian and is known to feed on the seeds and leaves of widgeon and musk grass, both plants of brackish areas.

The s. Florida coast seems to have many ideal habitats for this duck, which occurs in the Bahamas as far north as Abaco Island off Palm Beach, yet there is to date only a single recent record—a bird shot near Cape Canaveral. It has been suggested that these ducks may have once been resident in Florida but proved so vulnerable to hunting that they were wiped out in the early settlement days. Certainly its wide range and abundance in South America indicate that it is a prolific and vigorous species that could probably be readily re-established in s. Florida.

VOICE: The male of this very silent bird is said to have a low, squeaky call, the female a high-pitched quack.

NEST: (I. 25, P.) A rough mat of grasses on the ground, hidden in the dense vegetation of a swamp border or among the stiltlike roots of the mangrove trees. The 8 eggs (2.0 x 1.4) are pale reddish-buff.

RANGE: (R.) Occurs in the Bahamas, Greater Antilles, and n. Lesser Antilles; in South America from the Guianas south to c. Argentina and west to n. Chile.

Teal
Anas crecca—※5
L. 14; W. 23; Wt. 12 oz.

IDENTIFICATION: Males of this species and the green-winged teal differ only in the position of their one white streak— horizontal and above the wing in the European bird. Females are indistinguishable.

HABITS: Many ornithologists regard this and our green-winged teal as races of a single world-wide species. They seem alike except for the already noted plumage difference in males. They are usually found together, and males of both species have been observed courting the same female.

RANGE: (P. M.) Breeds from Iceland east across Europe and Asia (north to Lat. 70°) to the Aleutian Islands and south to the Mediterranean, Turkestan, Mongolia, and Hokkaido. Winters south to Nigeria, Kenya, Ceylon, and the Philippines. Rare but regular winter visitor to the Atlantic coast south to North Carolina.

Green-winged Teal
Anas carolinensis—※5
L. 14; W. 23; Wt. 12 oz.

IDENTIFICATION: The size, short wings and neck, and small bill of this compact duck are fair field marks. In poor light only the males' buffy-yellow under tail coverts are conspicuous. In flight the wings look dark, as the iridescent green patch and brown edge of the speculum show up only in sunlight. The dull female is quite colorless except for the speculum.

HABITS: This tiny, hardy duck is a late-fall and early-spring migrant. It is commonly encountered in flocks of considerable size, the evolutions of which are truly remarkable. In tight formation and at high speed the birds twist, turn, and bank with miraculous precision. The shallow ponds and channels of fresh-water marshes are favorite haunts, but in cold weather salt and brackish areas are often visited. This teal is primarily a seedeater but takes some leaves and stems of aquatic plants and, in salt water especially, shellfish and crustacea. Sedges, pondweeds, grasses, and smartweeds supply the bulk of its food. Quite at home and agile on land, it often visits grainfields as well as woodlands, where acorns and other nuts and wild fruits are obtained. These are among the birds that visit the shallow spawning grounds of the salmon in the western rivers and feed heavily on salmon eggs and the rotting flesh of spent salmon that have died after spawning.

VOICE: The call of the male is a short, abrupt whistle or similar trilled note; that of the female, a weak quack.

NEST: (I. 22, P.) A hollow in a grass clump or other cover, lined with grass and feathers and situated at varying distances from water. The 11 eggs (1.8 x 1.35) run from cream to pale olive-buff.

RANGE: (P. M.) Breeds from Quebec, James Bay, Great Slave Lake, n. Mackenzie, and c. Alaska south to the Gulf of St. Lawrence, s. Quebec, s. Ontario, n. Michigan, s. Minnesota, Nebraska, n. New Mexico, and c. California. Winters from s. New England, the Great Lakes, c. Montana, and s. Alaska south to the West Indies and Honduras.

Blue-winged Teal

Anas discors—※5
L. 15½; W. 24; Wt. 14 oz.

IDENTIFICATION: The pale blue inner wing coverts and the iridescent green speculum are characters this species shares with the next two. The uniformly pale pinkish-brown body color, white flank patch, and facial crescent of the breeding male are distinctive. In this species many males are slow in molting the femalelike "eclipse" body plumage which they assume in summer before shedding their wing feathers and becoming temporarily flightless. Blue-wings do not take on full normal body plumage until December, while the drakes of most species have attained it by the end of September. On the water the female is virtually indistinguishable from a green-wing female, but she has a longer body and neck and a larger head and bill.

HABITS: Fresh-water marshes, small ponds, mud flats, and sluggish creeks are favorite haunts. Only rarely do blue-wings visit salt or brackish areas. Unless badly persecuted they are inclined to be tame and unsuspicious. As a result they tolerate civilization and nest in close proximity to man. Their unsuspiciousness and their habit of flying in compact flocks make them easier to shoot than most. As they are very early migrants in fall and equally late in spring, the breeding cycle is compressed into a short period and the young develop rapidly. With short hunting seasons the blue-wing's early migration often carries the bulk of the species south before shooting starts. Ninety-five per cent of the population is estimated to winter south of our borders, which means that the future of the species depends largely on the conservation practices of our West Indian and Latin-American neighbors. The 4 staple food items of the seed-eating ducks—sedges, pondweeds, grasses, and smartweeds—make up about three fourths of the fall and winter diet of these birds in the United States. Musk grass, pondweed leaves, duckweed, and considerable quantities of snails and aquatic insects and crustacea are eaten.

VOICE: The male has a sibilant peeplike whistle, the female a weak quack.

NEST: (I. 22, P., N. 42) On the ground, well concealed in long grass and as a rule near water, but occasionally on a sedge tussock or muskrat house surrounded by water. The well-made nest is built of soft grasses and the eggs are covered with a heavy blanket of down from the female's breast. The 9 eggs (1.8 x 1.3) in an average clutch are dull white.

RANGE: (P. M.) Breeds from New Brunswick, s. Ontario, c. Manitoba, n. Saskatchewan, and s. Yukon south to Florida, the Gulf Coast, s. New Mexico, and s. California. Winters from e. Maryland, s. Illinois, New Mexico, and s. California south to n. Brazil and c. Chile.

Cinnamon Teal
Anas cyanoptera—⅗5
L. 15¾; W. 24½; Wt. 12 oz.

IDENTIFICATION: The uniform dark cinnamon-red head and body color, patches of which show even before the fall molt is complete, readily identify the male. Females cannot be distinguished with certainty from blue-wings.

HABITS: This close relative of the blue-winged teal largely replaces it in most of our Far West, where it is an abundant species. Wherever shallow bodies of water or sluggish streams are bordered with tules or other marsh plants this duck makes itself at home. The small reservoirs and irrigation ditches of western agricultural developments are readily accepted, even when close to civilization, by this remarkably tame and unsuspicious duck. It is seldom encountered

in large flocks and migrates early—factors that may account
for its continuing abundance. The average diet is almost
identical with the blue-wing's and, in general, the two species
seem to occupy identical places in the wildlife communities
in which they occur.

VOICE: Seldom more than a squeaky chatter from the male and
a weak quack from the female.

NEST: Commonly in dense grass or weedy cover, often some
distance from water, at times in dense beds of cattails. Upland nests are in hollows lined with grass and feathers, but
in wet sites a woven cup of grass and leaves is fastened above
the water to plant stems. The 11 or so eggs (1.9 x 1.4) vary
from white to pale pinkish-buff.

RANGE: (P. M.) Breeds from s. British Columbia, w. Saskatchewan, e. Wyoming, s.w. Kansas, and w. Texas west to the
Pacific States and south to c. Mexico; also in South America
from c. Argentina and c. Peru south to the Strait of Magellan.
North American birds winter south from c. New Mexico and
c. California to Panama, occasionally on the coast of Texas
and Louisiana.

Widgeon   *Mareca penelope*—✕6
(Wigeon)   L. 18½; W. 31; Wt. 1½ lbs.

IDENTIFICATION: The pale gray back and darker reddish head
and neck of the male are distinctive, as is the female's cin-
namon-buff head. In flight this species shows no clear white
area under the wing, although the upper surface is like an
American widgeon's.

HABITS: It seems reasonable to suppose that this duck breeds
sparingly in North America, as it occurs as a rare but regular
migrant on both our coasts and in the Mississippi Valley. In
Europe it breeds in the wild open marshes and grasslands of
the North and farther south in more settled areas where
woodlands alternate with cultivated fields. Within the past
100 years it has become established as a breeding bird in
Great Britain and is still increasing and spreading. In contrast with most other ducks, this one, it seems, is favored by
civilization. Widgeon are largely vegetarians. Pondweeds and
widgeon grass are staple foods, but apparently the favorite
fall food along the coast is eelgrass. European observers
report that a good place to look for them is with flocks of
brant that are pulling eelgrass to the surface, where they can
get at it more readily.

VOICE: The noisy male has a prolonged rolling whistle, *whee-oo,* and a shorter sparrowlike chirp; the female, a rough growling sound and, when alarmed, a harsh quack.

NEST: (I. 25, P.) The grass-and-down nest is on the ground, generally well hidden in tall rank grass or other vegetation, either near water or some distance away in a meadow. The 7 or 8 eggs (2.1 x 1.5) are creamy or buff.

RANGE: (P. M.) Breeds across all n. Europe and Asia from Lat. 71° N. south to Great Britain, Germany, Transcaucasia, Turkestan, and Manchuria. Winters south to tropical Africa, India, and the Marshall Islands. Occurs regularly in fall, winter, and spring in North America from s. Canada to Florida, the Gulf Coast, and s. California.

American Widgeon *Mareca americana*—⚡6
(Baldpate) L. 19½; W. 32½; Wt. 1¾ lbs.

IDENTIFICATION: The male, with its white crown and flanks, is quite distinctive. The female is best known by the grayish head contrasting markedly with the pinkish-brown of the body. In flight the whole fore part of the inner wing is white above (grayish-white in female). This sometimes shows when the bird is on water.

HABITS: The American widgeon is an alert duck. On the water feeding birds ride high and pivot rapidly as they pick here and there at floating food. In the air dense flocks wheel and turn in perfect unison almost like teal. Shallow fresh or

brackish ponds are favorite habitats, but the birds also visit
shallow coastal bays at times and feed on eelgrass. Almost
wholly vegetarian except for a few snails, they take relatively
few seeds but depend largely on leaves, stems, and buds of
such plants as pondweed and widgeon grass, the two staple
foods. They appear to like wild celery and are found steal-
ing bits of this deep-water plant from canvasbacks, scaups,
and coots, which can dive down and uproot it. Baldpates are
at home on land and in spring have the gooselike habit of
grazing on tender shoots of grass or grain.

voice: The male has a pleasant, mellow whistled note uttered
in groups of 3. The female has only a weak, guttural quack.

nest: (P.) A hollow in dry ground, lined with leaves, grass,
and down, and in many cases hardly concealed. The site may
be on an island in a lake or near water, or far away in open
grassland or in the shelter of a woodland. The average clutch
is 10 white to cream-colored eggs (2.1 x 1.5).

range: (M.) Breeds from c. Alaska south, east of the coast
ranges, to n. New Mexico and Arizona; east to Hudson Bay,
Minnesota, and Nebraska, and sporadically to w. Pennsylvania. Winters from s. New England, the Ohio Valley, c.
Utah, and s.e. Alaska south to the West Indies and Panama.

Shoveler   *Spatula clypeata*—⚹5
                          L. 19; W. 31; Wt. 1⅓ lbs.

identification: The huge, long bill merging imperceptibly
with the forehead and held below the horizontal is the female's best character, plus the short-necked appearance and
tendency to ride low in front. The colorful male is distinctive
and in the air shows a lot of white on the body. Both sexes
have light tails and a wing pattern like the blue-wing's.

habits: The shoveler is closely related to blue-winged and
cinnamon teals and as a migrant is almost as early in fall
and as late in spring. It is a curious, rather bold duck, which
in recent years has been occupying new breeding territory
in well-settled areas. In flight, shovelers, like teal, are fast,
rather erratic, and as a flock prone to sudden downward
plunges. Shallow and often stagnant fresh-water ponds and
marshy areas or mud flats are normal haunts, but the birds
are often found in brackish marshes where widgeon grass
grows. Shovelers commonly feed in small groups that mill
around in a circle and churn up the mud. Since their food is
strained from near the surface, they seldom have to "tip up."

An enormous development of the comblike teeth along the sides of the mandibles makes this whalelike manner of feeding possible. This is one of the most carnivorous of the dabbling ducks, taking large numbers of snails, aquatic insects, fish, and crustacea, many of them minute forms like ostracods. The rest of the diet consists of seeds and plants of the type preferred by teal.

VOICE: The male occasionally makes a deep, guttural, croaking sound, the female a weak quack.

NEST: (I. 22, P.) A slight hollow where the nest is concealed by dense grass is the usual site. Distance from water does not seem important. The nest has a lining of grass and a generous blanket of down that is slowly increased as incubation progresses. In all ducks incubation, which is carried on solely by the female, does not start until the last egg has been laid. Thus all young hatch and are ready to leave the nest at the same time. The average clutch is 11 olive-buff or grayish-green eggs (2.0 x 1.5).

RANGE: (P. M.) A large part of the Northern Hemisphere. In Europe and Asia, breeds from the Arctic Circle south to France, Turkey, Turkestan, n. Mongolia, and Japan and migrates to tropical Africa, Ceylon, and the Philippines. In North America from w. Alaska and n. Mackenzie east to Hudson Bay and w. Ontario and south to n. Illinois, Okla-

homa, and s. California. Breeds irregularly east to the Atlantic coast from Long Island to North Carolina and south
to Texas. Winters from Long Island, s. Illinois, Arizona, and
s. British Columbia south to the n. West Indies and Colombia and west to the Hawaiian Islands.

Wood Duck
Aix sponsa—✳5
L. 18; W. 28; Wt. 1½ lbs.

IDENTIFICATION: The male's iridescent colors are not apparent
at a distance, but the white lines on the face and sides are
distinctive. The crest that gives it a big-headed appearance
is absent in the summer eclipse plumage, but the small highly
colored bill is a good character, as is the white eye patch of
the female. In flight the white belly and long dark tail show
up well and the bird keeps its head back and held high with
bill pointed downward.

HABITS: This delicately proportioned and exquisitely colored
duck is at home wherever there are trees and quiet fresh
water. If not disturbed it is remarkably tame and fearless,
even nesting in city parks. Were this species allowed to increase to the maximum number that the available habitat
can accommodate it could undoubtedly become a common
sight on almost every pond, stream, and swamp in the wooded
sections of the country. Unfortunately, the 2 millions or so
of our citizens who hunt ducks have not been willing to
exempt from hunting even this one rather small species so
that the 150 million of us who do not hunt can have it around
in abundance where we can enjoy its beauty.

The wood duck is largely vegetarian. Only about 10 per

cent of its food consists of animal life, chiefly aquatic insects. The tiny floating plants, commonly known as duckweeds, that frequently cover a still woodland pond with a sheet of pale green are a favorite food. These ducks also eat seeds of trees and shrubs and often come out of water into the woods to get them. Acorns, hickory and beechnuts, and in the South cone scales of bald cypress are important foods. These they swallow whole and crush with ease in their powerful stomachs. Other foods are seeds of sedges, pond-weeds, and grasses, especially wild rice, a favorite with all ducks.

VOICE: This noisy bird utters a variety of whistled notes that often sound like squeaks or squeals. A distinctive drawn-out squeal of alarm is usually given when the birds are flushed.

NEST: (I. 29, P.) The nest is generally located in a natural hollow in the trunk or rotted-out limb of an old tree. Less frequently an old woodpecker nest is utilized. Distance from water is not important, and the bird often seems to prefer the center to the edge of a patch of woods. Broken-down old apple trees are a favorite in some areas, and an old shade tree close to a house is not an uncommon site. The entrance is generally large, but a hole as small as that made by a flicker can be entered. The nest may be anywhere from a few feet to 50 feet above the ground, but in all cases the young apparently jump to earth without injury. There is no evidence that the female ever carries them down. An old nail keg or regular bird box measuring about 10 x 10 x 24 inches deep, with an entrance hole about 4 inches in diameter and 6 inches of sawdust and a drainage hole in the bottom, is often accepted when nest sites are scarce. The safest location is on a pole standing in water. Twelve white to buff-white eggs (2.0 x 1.5) are a normal clutch.

RANGE: (P. M.) Breeds from s. Nova Scotia, s.e. Ontario, s. Manitoba, and s. British Columbia south to Cuba, s. Texas, and s. California. Winters from s. Virginia, s. Illinois, and s. British Columbia south to Jamaica and c. Mexico.

Redhead   *Aythya americana*—⚹8
(American Pochard)   L. 19½; W. 32; Wt. 2½ lbs.

IDENTIFICATION: The short, pale bluish bill, high forehead, compact build, black lower neck, and gray back of the male are distinctive. The uniformly brown female lacks positive characters besides those of shape, size, and bill. In flight the speculum shows up as distinctly paler and grayer than the rest of the wing, especially in the female.

HABITS: (Age 12 yrs.) Few ducks have suffered such a decline in numbers as this, once the commonest of all diving ducks. The region where it formerly nested most abundantly is now the great wheat belt of the United States and Canada. It is also far too unsuspecting and inquisitive and its flocks too prone to return to their fallen companions. A late migrant,

it generally flies in irregular flocks by itself, though on water it associates with other diving ducks. During the day redheads gather in large rafts far out on lakes or coastal bays. Here, although they may seem to be resting quietly, small groups will suddenly take to the air and as suddenly settle back again. Much of their feeding is done in early morning or late evening, when they fly to shallows where they dive for food in water ranging up to 10 or 12 feet in depth. Along the coast their favorite haunts are the shallow fresh-water ponds that lie just back of the beaches. Insects and shellfish are taken, but the birds are essentially vegetarian. Leaves, stems, and seeds of pondweeds, musk grasses, shoal grasses, and smaller quantities of grass and sedge seeds are staple foods. Some of the best of the original feeding grounds of these and other diving ducks have been destroyed by the introduction of carp from Europe and the opening up of our coastal bays to salt tides through the cutting of canals and the establishment of permanent inlets. Carp are very destructive to underwater plants like wild celery, which they uproot and eat, at the same time rilling the water so that sunlight cannot reach them to promote new growth. The best duck food plants of the shallow coastal bays grow most luxuriantly in brackish water and are killed when too much sea water is allowed to enter the bays.

VOICE: The male has a curious deep, vibrant note which has been likened to a cat's *meow* or a violin tone. The female has only a quacklike note.

NEST: (I. 24, P.) The usual nest site is in a dense bed of cattails or other reedlike growth in shallow water near open water. Occasionally it may be in a bed of phragmites on dry land near water. The nest is attached to reeds and built up out of the water on a base of matted vegetation. It is a well-made, often deep cup consisting of bits of reeds with a blanket of white down. The 12 eggs (2.4 x 1.7) in a normal clutch are pale creamy-buff.

RANGE: (P. M.) Breeds from s. Manitoba, c. Alberta, and s. British Columbia south to s. Wisconsin (occasionally east to w. Pennsylvania), c. Nebraska, n.w. New Mexico, and s. California. Winters from s. New England, the s. Great Lakes, s.e. Arizona, and s. British Columbia south to the West Indies and c.w. Mexico.

Ring-necked Duck
(American Tufted Duck)

Aythya collaris—♀8
L. 17; W. 27; Wt. 1¾ lbs.

IDENTIFICATION: The dark back, puffy head, and vertical white wedge on the side just forward of the wing are the best field marks for the male, and the white eye ring for the brown female. In both sexes the bill has a distinctive light ring behind the black tip and another at the base. In flight the forward half of the wing appears dark like the back, in contrast to the paler grayish secondaries and brownish primaries.

HABITS: (Age 10 yrs.) Among hunters this duck is more commonly known as ring-bill. Once rare in the East, it is now increasing both as breeder and migrant. A mid-fall migrant, it frequents small swamp-bordered ponds and streams, often feeding along their shallow margins with coots and dabbling ducks and roosting out of the water in the branches of fallen treetops. Only in the South where shoal grass occurs do they frequent salt coastal waters. Ring-necks travel in small loose flocks of a dozen or so that alight in open water and later

swim into the shallows. They dive well and if necessary
obtain food in deep water. Essentially vegetarian, they are
fond of the seeds of water shield and other water lilies. Seeds
and leaves of pondweeds and seeds of sedges, grasses, and
smartweeds are eaten and, in small quantities, insects and
snails.

VOICE: A seldom-heard purring note.

NEST: In the low marshy border of a pond or marsh slough; a
bulky mass of vegetation that holds the eggs, in many cases,
only a few inches above water. The average clutch is about
10 olive-buff eggs (2.2 x 1.6).

RANGE: (P. M.) Breeds in New Brunswick, n. Maine, w. Penn-
sylvania, and from w. Ontario, n. Saskatchewan, and c. British
Columbia south to s. Wisconsin, n. Nebraska, and c. Arizona.
Winters from s. New England, the Ohio Valley, n. Arkansas,
and s. British Columbia south to the n. West Indies and
Guatemala.

Canvasback   *Aythya valisineria*—⚹8
                                        L. 21; W. 33; Wt. 3 lbs.

IDENTIFICATION: The long, broad-based bill that blends into the
elongated head without a distinct break and, in flight, the
long bill, head, neck, and the long pointed wings are distinctive. The pale, almost white back, the darkening on the face,
and a neck that is reddish for its full length are the male's
best field marks. The female has a back that is lighter and
grayer than its uniformly dull brown head and neck.

HABITS: The canvasback is a big, fast-flying, wary duck that frequently winters as far north as fresh water stays open and returns in distinctive V̇-shaped flocks early in the spring. Although its breeding grounds extend somewhat farther north than the redhead's, it has suffered almost as severely from the drainage of the marshes and sloughs of the n. Great Plains. The most remarkable feature of its migration is the large number of birds that move almost due east to the Atlantic coast, the greatest winter concentrations occurring in the coastal bays of Virginia and North Carolina. Here they gather in enormous rafts far out from shore, carefully avoiding land areas even in flight, and often feeding in water 20 to 30 feet deep. Roots, tubers, and the basal portions of underwater plants are their chief foods, although they can live on shrimp and other shellfish and fish. Pondweeds and wild celery (*Vallisneria*), where it occurs, are staple items of diet. Tubers of such plants as Sagittaria and water lilies are also favorites. Many seeds of sedges and grasses, especially wild rice, are strained out of the bottom mud, which makes this species very vulnerable to lead poisoning. In heavily shot-over areas 10 per cent of the ducks may carry shot in their gizzards, as many as 96 shot having been found in a single bird.

VOICE: The male has a grunting note, also one that sounds like a *coo* or *moo*. The female has a quack.

NEST: (I. 24, P.) In a bed of cattail or rushes growing in shallow water, generally not far from a deep-water opening. The nest of plant debris rests on the bottom or floats and is anchored to nearby stems. The 10 eggs (2.5 x 1.8) are gray-green.

RANGE: (M.) Breeds from s. Wisconsin, c. Manitoba, Great
Slave Lake, n. Mackenzie, and c. Alaska south to c.w. Nebraska, n. New Mexico, w. Nevada, and c. Oregon. Winters
from c. New York, s. Illinois, n. Colorado, n.w. Montana,
and s. British Columbia south to the n. West Indies and
Guatemala.

Scaup Duck   *Aythya marila*—#8
(Big Bluebill)   L. 17¾; W. 30½; Wt. 2 lbs.

IDENTIFICATION: The uniformly pale bluish bill, solid dark head
and neck of the male, and the sharply defined clear white
area at the base of the bill of the female are good field characters. The male, besides being larger than the lesser scaup,
has a thick neck and a squarish head with a green sheen,
clearer white sides, and the white wing stripe extends well
out beyond the speculum onto the inner primaries.

HABITS: (Age 13 yrs.) This hardy bird, one of the raft ducks,
is commonly encountered in dense flocks well out from shore
on large bodies of fresh water until winter, when the majority
migrate to salt water. Here they gather in harbors, bays, and
estuaries, traveling back and forth from one feeding ground
to another in loosely bunched groups with one or more lines
of stragglers trailing behind. Rafts of 50,000 or more have
been reported from favorable feeding grounds. The birds dive
to depths of at least 20 feet for food and, like all this group,
use only their feet in swimming under water. Sewage outlets
often draw them in large numbers, along with gulls and other
scavengers.

The scaup is omnivorous, making out as well on vegetable as animal food. Commonly it fills up on any single readily available item. Inland its staples are pondweeds, musk grass, mare's-tail, and clams. Coastwise it takes wild celery, widgeon grass, and sea lettuce, but here its mainstay is shellfish of many kinds, and crabs, barnacles, and other crustacea.

VOICE: This usually silent duck utters a variety of low, purring notes when courting. Occasionally a flock breaks into a chorus of discordant *scaup* calls.

NEST: (I. 27, P.) In low moist tundra, generally near a small lake or pond. Often a definite colony is formed on an especially favorable island site. The nest of matted grasses is concealed in a clump of dense vegetation and may at times be well out in a marshy area. The 8 or 9 eggs (2.5 x 1.7) in a normal clutch vary from light to dark olive-buff.

RANGE: (M.) This circumpolar species breeds in both hemispheres from the Arctic Ocean south to about Lat. 60° N., but in North America it is absent from the region east of Hudson Bay, although there are casual breeding records east to the Magdalen Islands and south to s.e. Michigan, n. Iowa, and c. British Columbia. Winters from Maine, the Great Lakes, Colorado, and the Aleutians south to Florida, the Gulf Coast, and n. Lower California and in Eurasia.

Lesser Scaup Duck   *Aythya affinis*—※8
(Little Bluebill)   L. 17½; W. 27½; Wt. 1¾ lbs.

IDENTIFICATION: This duck can be distinguished from the scaup only under ideal conditions. The head of the male is higher-crowned and more elongated, the neck smaller, and the head coloring usually glossed with purple, although traces of green are not uncommon. The sides are grayer, and in both sexes the white in the wing is restricted to the speculum.

HABITS: (Age 10 yrs.) The lesser scaup or bluebill is the common diving duck of small lakes, ponds, and marshes. Here the birds are found in great rafts during migrations, and many winter in such areas. Large numbers, however, reach our southern coasts and become abundant on brackish bays and protected harbors and sounds. When traveling they move in fast-flying mass formations. If protected and fed, they become among the tamest of ducks. Most feeding is done in water not more than 5 or 6 feet deep, but the birds can dive at least 20 feet. Plant foods like pondweeds, widgeon grass, and the seeds of grasses and sedges and animal food in the form of snails of many types, aquatic insects, and shrimplike organisms, are about equally important in their diet.

VOICE: Whistled, purring, and scolding notes have been heard during courtship.

NEST: (I. 23, P.) Generally well hidden in tall grass on dry land, often some distance from the shallow pond, sluggish stream, or marsh channel that provides the pair with feeding ground and loafing spot during the courtship and laying period. When incubation starts, the drake, as in most ducks, deserts the hen and goes off to join other drakes on a large lake where it is safe during the molting period, when it is unable to fly. The nest is a depression in the ground, lined with feathers and grass. An average clutch is 11 dark olive-buff eggs (2.2 x 1.6).

RANGE: (M.) Breeds from n.w. Mackenzie and w. Alaska south to Iowa, Montana, and s.e. British Columbia. Winters from Chesapeake Bay, s. Illinois, n.e. Colorado, and s. British Columbia south to Trinidad and Panama. Occurs on the Atlantic coast from Nova Scotia south in migration.

Goldeneye   *Bucephala clangula*—※9
(Whistler)   L. 18; W. 28½; Wt. 2 lbs.

IDENTIFICATION: The male has a puffy, vertically elongated, somewhat peaked head and a sloping forehead. Its clear white sides and extensively white scapulars and wings make it very white-looking except for its dark head. The well-defined white neck and, in breeding season, the yellow-tipped bill are the female's most conspicuous features.

HABITS: This duck is commonly known as a "whistler" because of the loud, high-pitched whir of its wings, which produce a curiously resonant effect when a flock is on the move. During the non-breeding season this is a bird of large lakes, rivers, and, during midwinter, of coastal waters, where it feeds in small groups in protected harbors and bays or just beyond the ocean surf, flying out to sea at dusk to rest and sleep on the open ocean. Feeding is usually done in water less than 10 feet deep, with 20 feet about the maximum. Under water the bird propels itself with its feet only and obtains much of its food by overturning loose bottom stones. Goldeneyes prefer animal food—crayfish, aquatic insects, and shrimplike crustacea in fresh water, plus many kinds of seeds and tubers and the stems and leaves of pondweeds and wild celery. In salt water, crabs (especially mud crabs), mussels, and many snail-like organisms are eaten.

Most ducks have interesting courtship performances. That of the goldeneye, which is unusually spectacular, starts in February. After puffing up its head feathers the drake thrusts its head forward, then up, and finally throws it back to touch its tail. As the head is returned to its normal position with a quick jerk the bird suddenly spurts forward and reveals its brilliant orange feet.

VOICE: A variety of rather harsh, rasping, or vibrant notes.

NEST: (I. 26, P., D. 60) In a natural cavity in a tree, generally close to, or over, water. An old woodpecker hole, nest box, or open hollow in the top of a broken trunk may be used. The entrance need not exceed 3 x 4½ inches but may be from 5 to 60 feet aboveground. No nest material is used except down. A normal clutch is about 10 clear, pale green eggs (2.4 x 1.7). Like wood duck young, newly hatched goldeneye ducklings climb to the entrance hole, drop to the ground at a call from the female, and follow her to the nearest water.

RANGE: (P. M.) Breeds in the northern coniferous forests of the whole Northern Hemisphere south in North America to c. Maine, the Adirondacks, n. Michigan, n.w. Montana, and c. British Columbia but not on the Pacific coast; in Eurasia to Great Britain, Germany, the Balkans, and c. Siberia. Winters from Maine, the Great Lakes, and the Aleutian Islands south to Florida, the Gulf Coast, s. California, and in Eurasia to the Mediterranean, n. India, and s. China.

Barrow's Goldeneye   *Bucephala islandica*—❋9
L. 18; W. 28½; Wt. 2 lbs.

IDENTIFICATION: The male is much blacker than that of the preceding species. Its sides are broadly margined with black which extends almost to the water line forward of the wing. The scapulars show as a line of distinctly separated white spots, much as they do on a molting goldeneye, which is a much grayer bird. The horizontally elongated, evenly rounded head and the vertical or bulging forehead are safer field marks than the white crescent. The head shape is not so marked in the female, but her head is a darker, richer brown and her bill is all yellow in the breeding season.

HABITS: This duck differs little in habit from the goldeneye. It is not notably migratory, however, most individuals wintering rather close to their breeding grounds, and, where these do not freeze over, it seems to prefer fresh or brackish areas to salt water. Aquatic insects, crayfish, and other shrimplike crustacea and pondweeds are staple fresh-water foods; in salt water it appears to depend largely on mussels, periwinkles, crabs, and sea lettuce. On many salmon streams of the West its chief winter food is waste salmon eggs that float away from the spawning beds and the flesh of salmon that have died after spawning.

VOICE: Hoarse croaks and a vibrant mewing call.

NEST: (P.) In a hollow in a tree, usually near a pond or small lake, but at times up to half a mile from an especially favorable alkaline lake; in treeless country, cavities in or under rocks, in stream banks, or under dense bushy cover. The 10 eggs (2.4 x 1.7) are various shades of pale green.

RANGE: (P. M.) Breeds in Iceland, s.w. Greenland, Labrador, and the mountains of w. North America from s.c. Alaska south to s. Colorado and c. California. Winters in Iceland and Greenland south in the Atlantic to e. Long Island, and in the Pacific from s. Alaska to c. California. Also on open fresh water in the interior near its breeding grounds.

Bufflehead *Bucephala albeola*—♂♀
(Butterball) L. 14; W. 22½; Wt. 1 lb.

IDENTIFICATION: The big head, tiny bill, and small size are diagnostic; in both sexes head markings are unique. Both have a white speculum, and in the male the wing coverts are white.

HABITS: The bufflehead is the smallest of the sea ducks. It is a fast flier, commonly traveling close to the water in small compact groups. In the fall it is generally very fat and is commonly called "butterball." Hunters find it easy to decoy. Although it occurs inland on large bodies of fresh water, in migration and early winter most buffleheads finally reach salt water. Here they feed singly or in small groups in shallow (4 to 15 feet) sandy bays, coming close inshore on a rising tide and often feeding in or just beyond the breaking surf. In fresh water they take shrimplike amphipods, aquatic insects, some snails and fish, and a few plant seeds. In salt water shrimp and other crustacea and shellfish, chiefly snails, are staple foods.

VOICE: The male has a squeaky whistle, the female a hoarse quack.

NEST: In a tree hollow generally close to a pond, usually in the old nest of a flicker or other woodpecker. The entrance may be no more than 3¼ inches in diameter and from 5 to 20 feet up. The 11 eggs (1.9 x 1.4) vary from pale yellow to pale olive-buff.

RANGE: (M.) Breeds from s. Quebec, n. Manitoba, n. Mac-kenzie, and c. Alaska south to s. Manitoba, n. Montana, and n. California. Winters from Maine, the Great Lakes, n.w. Montana, and the Aleutian Islands south to n. Florida, the Gulf Coast, c. Mexico, and Lower California.

Oldsquaw   *Clangula hyemalis*—✳ 10
(Long-tailed Duck)   L. ♂ 21, ♀ 16; W. 28½; Wt. 1½ lbs.

IDENTIFICATION: This brown and extensively white duck is dis-tinctively marked. On water it appears quite chunky, and the male holds its long tail well up in the air. In flight its long, pointed, solid-brown wings are in sharp contrast to the white on the body. The wings appear rather curved, and most of the deep wing stroke is below the horizontal.

HABITS: The oldsquaw is an abundant summer duck in coastal areas throughout the Arctic, where its nests provide Eskimos with eggs and a down almost as fine as eider. Some birds winter in arctic waters, but most come south to salt water in more temperate areas or on large bodies of open fresh water like the Great Lakes. At this season they are quite gregarious. In one area lake fishermen took 27,000 in their gill nets in a single spring. The birds swim under water with their wings like surf and white-winged scoters and have occasionally been caught at the amazing depth of 200 feet. Along the coast they feed in tidal rips and offshore shoals but often resort to sheltered bays to spend the night. Here they are hunted along with other sea ducks despite the fact that they are tough and fishy. As spring nears they become increasingly noisy and active, courting males nearly mobbing certain favored females; from time to time the whole flock may indulge in an upflight that carries it nearly out of sight before it suddenly pitches back to the water. Unlike most ducks, the oldsquaw has distinct nuptial plumage in both sexes. The molt starts in February and in some individuals is completed by May; in others it never fully develops. Staple foods are crustacea like scuds and other amphipods, shrimp, and crabs; shellfish, chiefly blue mussels and snail-like species, and, in fresh water, pill clams; and at times small fish, plus a little plant material. They take aquatic insects to some extent, especially in summer.

VOICE: A noisy duck at all seasons; the distinctive melodious calls can at times be heard at least a mile. The general effect is not unlike the distant baying of a musical pack of hounds or *ow-ow-owdle-ow.*

NEST: (I. 24, P.) The usual site is a depression in a bed of sedge or under a dwarf willow near a shallow tundra pond or near salt water. The remarkably well-concealed nest is made of short bits of leaves which gradually mix with the down that is slowly added as incubation progresses. The 6 eggs (2.1 x 1.5) are olive-buff.

RANGE: (P. M.) Breeds on the Arctic coasts of both hemispheres south to Labrador, s. Hudson Bay, the Aleutians, Kamchatka, and s.c. Norway. Winters from s. Greenland and Bering Strait south to North Carolina, Washington, n. France, the Caspian Sea, and Japan. Occasionally n. Florida, the Gulf Coast, and s. California.

Harlequin Duck

Histrionicus histrionicus—⚔ 10
L. 16¾; W. 25; Wt. 1¼ lbs.

IDENTIFICATION: The pattern of white on the often very dark male, together with the brown flanks, is distinctive. The female can be recognized by its small bill, plain wings, and the 3 light areas on the head.

HABITS: This is a bird of rugged seacoasts, frequenting hidden ledges and reefs just offshore. Most individuals migrate only short distances inland to the turbulent streams where they nest. Here males stay only a few weeks—while the female is laying her eggs—before they return to salt water to go through their eclipse molt and flightless period. Harlequins are usually encountered in groups of 6 or 8 that fly as a compact unit and often swim in regular formations abreast or in line. Occasionally they occur with oldsquaws but more often by themselves, feeding by day and roosting at night on isolated rocks.

On inland streams they move under water in the swift

currents with amazing ease and walk upstream on the bottom like ouzels. In such habitats their chief foods are nymphs of stoneflies, mayflies, and the larvae of caddis flies and other aquatic insects. At sea they feed primarily on the organisms that abound in rocky underwater areas. On sandy coasts they work around breakwaters or sunken wrecks. Staple salt water foods are crabs, isopods, amphipods, and other crustacea, including barnacles and snails, limpets and chitons, which they seem to have no difficulty in dislodging from the rocks to which they cling. They take some sea urchins, starfish, and a few fish, chiefly sculpins.

VOICE: The female's shrill, whistlelike call of from 1 to 4 notes starts high and descends in pitch. That of the drake is lower and hoarser.

NEST: In a cavity among rocks or in a hollow under a bush near a swift flowing stream. The 6 pale buff eggs (2.3 x 1.6) are laid in a sparse bed of grass and down.

RANGE: (P. M.) Breeds in Iceland, Greenland, Baffin Island, and Labrador and from n. Mackenzie, Alaska, and n.e. Siberia south to the mts. of Colorado and c. California, the Kuriles, and Lake Baikal. Winters from the breeding grounds south to e. Long Island, the c. California coast, and Japan.

Labrador Duck   *Camptorhynchus labradorius*—✕ 10
L. 19; W. 30

IDENTIFICATION: The handsome male was unmistakable. Specimens of the rather nondescript female and young show a narrow white speculum and a bill with a leathery spoonlike expansion at the end of the upper mandible and prominent vertical teeth on the lower.

HABITS: Little is known about this now extinct duck. It seems never to have been abundant. Its exact breeding grounds were never established, and its nest and eggs are unknown to science. Only 44 specimens exist in museums, the last having been taken in 1875. The chances of obtaining another in the wild are remote, but a few may still exist in attics or cupboards, the forgotten work of amateur taxidermists of the last century.

Like all ducks, the Labrador (or pied duck) was sold in the markets, but it was not very good eating and was never especially sought after. We do not know how much it suffered from eggers or from the feather-gathering expeditions that visited the Gulf of St. Lawrence region in the mid-eighteenth century. We do know, however, that this type of exploitation during summer, when the birds were flightless, so reduced the bird population of that area that the trips eventually became unprofitable.

The structure of the Labrador's bill shows that it was adapted for sifting out small objects and suggests that the bird's feeding habits may have been unique among sea ducks. It was often called "sand shoal duck" because of its habit of feeding on sand bars and in sandy shallows, but it could also dive for food. The recorded diet is small shellfish, including mussels and small surf clams, but it must have taken seeds and other plant material, since it was reported to frequent brackish ponds of the coastal marsh, along with ducks like the gadwall.

Just what in its life history and behavior made it so vul- nerable to the impact of civilization we do not know, but the conclusion that man played an important role in its rapid disappearance seems inescapable.

RANGE: (M.) Believed to have bred in Labrador. Wintered from Nova Scotia to the Chesapeake but was apparently most frequently seen in the waters off Long Island.

Eider   *Somateria mollissima*—✻ 11
                             L. 24; W. 41; Wt. 4½ lbs.

IDENTIFICATION: The white-backed, black-sided males of this big, heavy duck are unmistakable. The rich brown, heavily barred female has a distinctive canvasback-like sloping pro- file. Young birds are dull brown with a well-defined broad light line over and behind the eye.

HABITS: This is one of the largest and hardiest of ducks. In the North its easily collected eggs are a valuable food that can be kept throughout the winter, while its down is an important article of commerce. One of the best heat-insulating materials known, the down is without equal in the manufacture of lightweight sleeping bags and arctic clothing. Unfortunately, in many regions the killing of both adults and young and the taking of whole clutches of eggs have decimated the popu- lation. As it is too fishy to be very good eating, it seems that it would be wise to give the bird full protection and harvest from a maximum population only the nest down and part of each clutch. There are a few places in Iceland, Norway, and Canada where this is being done with great success. Under protection and encouragement in the form of artificial nest sites, dense populations have been developed near settlements and the birds have become almost as tame as domestic fowl—a splendid example of the wise use of a natural resource; i.e., true conservation.

Most eiders seem not to migrate farther than necessary to find open water and feeding grounds. In flight they travel in long lines low over water with head low and bill tipped downward. The common blue mussel that occurs in dense beds on rocky and pebbly bottoms is a staple food, in many areas almost the only food; 185 have been found in a single stomach. Mussels and other shellfish up to 2 inches long are swallowed whole and broken up by the bird's powerful stomach. Crabs and other crustacea, sea urchins, and occasionally sculpins are common foods. Eiders seem to prefer to feed in fairly shallow water but if necessary can dive 35 feet. They feed by day, often most actively at low tide, and spend the night in rafts at sea or roosting in small groups on isolated rocks.

VOICE: The male's calls vary from pigeonlike coos to harsh, half-human moans. The female has a series of hoarse quacks.
NEST: (I. 28) On the ground in a depression in bare rocks or cliff ledges or hidden in a hollow among grass or shrubs. Generally near salt water and often in dense colonies on favorable rocky islands or headlands; in the Far North, along scattered ponds in low tundra near the coast. The nest has a

foundation of plant material and a thick lining of down, most, if not all, of which can be removed without reducing seriously the hatchability of the eggs. Down from 35 to 40 nests is required to produce 1 pound of commercial down. The 5 eggs (3 x 2) in an average clutch vary from olive to olive-buff.

RANGE: (P. M.) Breeds along the coast from the Kara Sea in n. Russia west through Arctic America to n.e. Siberia and south to Ireland, Maine, James Bay, and Kodiak Island. Winters south to n. France, e. Long Island, and s. Alaska.

King Eider

Somateria spectabilis—✳ 11
L. 22; W. 36; Wt. 4 lbs.

IDENTIFICATION: The black-backed male is unmistakable. The female is a paler and redder brown than in the preceding species; it has a short bill and concave forehead and often a pale buffy chin and throat. Young are grayish-brown, paler below than above, but otherwise like the female. In early winter the throat and breast of the young male begin to turn white, the head uniform dark brown.

HABITS: This is an enormously abundant bird in parts of the Far North. Although it does not winter in great concentrations off the New England coast like the common eider, it occurs there regularly in small numbers. It is a great wanderer and, farther south and inland on fresh water, is by far the commoner of the two. Kings seem partial to reefs and ledges far offshore and can feed in deep water. Specimens have been caught in gill nets in the Great Lakes at depths of 150 feet.

They depend heavily on shellfish and crustacea, but the diet is notable for the sand dollars, sea urchins, sea cucumbers, sea squids, and fish it includes.

VOICE: The call of the male is a soft, dovelike, vibrant cooing, that of the female a grating croak.

NEST: Widely scattered over open tundra well back from the coast and often some distance from water. Five olive-buff eggs (2.7 x 1.8) are a normal clutch.

RANGE: (P. M.) Breeds on the coasts and islands of the entire Arctic Ocean south to s. Greenland, n. Labrador, Bering Strait, and Spitsbergen. Winters from the limit of open water south to New Jersey, the Great Lakes, s. Alaska, and Denmark.

White-winged Scoter　　*Melanitta deglandi*—⚥ 11.
(American Velvet Scoter)　　L. 21; W. 37½; Wt. 3¼ lbs.

IDENTIFICATION: In flight the white speculum identifies this species. The male has a black bill knob, a small white eye patch, and pinkish feet. Some females and most young show 2 white patches on the side of the head. This species and the next are short-necked, heavy-headed birds that habitually carry the bill pointed downward.

HABITS: In summer white-winged scoters breed over a vast area and seem equally at home on a prairie pond, woodland lake, or tundra. They feed on shellfish, crayfish, and other shrimp-like crustacea, aquatic insects, and pondweeds. During courtship in spring they engage in remarkable aerial maneuvers. In migrating overland they fly high in the air, stopping on inland lakes and rivers. A few winter on the Great Lakes, but the chief wintering grounds are along the seacoast, where all 3 species of scoters are commonly known as "sea coots." Here they fly in long lines and loose bunches close to the water just offshore. They feed wherever shellfish beds are available at reasonable depths—15 to 20 feet—in the larger bays and sounds as well as on the offshore shoals and open beaches. Although the blue mussel is their staple food along the Atlantic coast, rock, surf, and razor clams, macomas, oysters, scallops, cockleshells, whelks, moon shells, slipper shells, and crabs of many kinds are taken in appreciable quantities and in sizes up to 2 or 2½ inches in length.

VOICE: The peculiar low, bell-like whistle or tinkling-ice sound attributed to these birds appears to be made with the wings. They also have a hoarse croak.

NEST: (I. 27, P.) In a hollow or crevice among rocks on high ground on an island or near water, generally well hidden under a shrub or in dense vegetation. The 8 eggs (2.6 x 1.8) are pinkish-buff.

RANGE: (M.) Breeds from Ungava and Alaska south to the Gulf of St. Lawrence, c. North Dakota, and n.e. Washington. Winters on the Atlantic coast from Newfoundland to South Carolina; on the Pacific coast from the Aleutian Islands to Lower California. Also sparingly on the Great Lakes and other inland waters.

Surf Scoter

Melanitta perspicillata—❋11
L. 19; W. 32; Wt. 2 lbs

IDENTIFICATION: The male is solid black except for the bold white head markings. The female has a dark crown and an indistinct white patch on the back of the head, but the best field marks for it and for young birds are the two whitish patches on the side of the head and the swollen base to the bill, which makes the profile like an eider's.

HABITS: When great flocks of scoters are passing well offshore it is often impossible to separate this dark-winged species from the next although it is a lighter and often more active bird on the wing. However, upon alighting these have a characteristic habit of holding their wings extended upward until they coast to a stop. If near when they take off or land, a distinctive whistling of the wings can be noted. Although similar in habits to other scoters, these are more frequently observed in the surf close to the beaches where their manner of swimming under water can often be seen through the clear front of a wave just before it breaks. Occasionally they come ashore to root about for food in wet sand. Their summer home is near fresh-water ponds and lakes in the interior, and though they occur in migration on the Great Lakes, they are rare inland at other seasons. They eat pondweeds, eelgrass, and miscellaneous seeds and berries, but aquatic insects are their mainstay in summer. On salt water they draw heavily on mussels, but macoma shells, surf and other clams, periwinkles, and small numbers of many other species, including a few fish, are eaten. Sand and mud crabs, sea urchins, sand dollars, and starfish sometimes furnish an entire meal for an individual bird. When swimming under water both surf and white-winged scoters use the stiffly extended inner wing and alula and carry the primaries folded back over the tail.

VOICE: A low guttural croak or cluck and a deep, clear whistle are the only recorded notes of this very silent bird.

NEST: (P.) In a depression in the ground, lined with grass and down and well hidden in a clump of small trees or shrubs in the vicinity of a lake or, when in a marsh, a cup of dead marsh vegetation. The 7 eggs (2.4 x 1.7) are a very pale buff color.

RANGE: (M.) Breeds from Labrador to n.w. Alaska south to the Gulf of St. Lawrence, James Bay, and n. Alberta. Winters on the Atlantic coast from Nova Scotia to South Carolina and from the Aleutian Islands to Lower California.

Black Scoter   *Oidemia nigra*—⌗11
(Common Scoter)   L. 19; W. 32½; Wt. 2½ lbs.

IDENTIFICATION: On water these birds hold their heads high
with the bills horizontal or slightly elevated; in flight the
undersurfaces of the primaries show a silvery sheen. The
male's distinctive characters are the yellow "butter-bill" and
the black legs and feet. Females and young are dark-capped
and have a more uniformly white face than surf scoters. Also,
this bird has a longer, more pointed tail, which is often
cocked up like a pintail's. Its high forehead and small bill
make it look more like some of the river ducks.

HABITS: On our seacoasts in winter this species (formerly called
the American scoter) is generally the least abundant of the
"sea coots," and it is comparatively rare on inland waters
during migration. It is the first to arrive in fall and often
the last to go north in spring. Like all scoters, it leaves a
few small flocks of non-breeders on the wintering grounds
throughout the summer. A fast, active flier, it rises more
readily from water than other scoters and flies about more.
At times its wings produce a loud whistling sound. In salt
water its staple food is the blue mussel, along with several
species of clams, oysters, and other shellfish. Its high consumption of barnacles and limpets seems to confirm its
reported fondness for feeding over outlying reefs and rocky
ledges. In summer it is abundant in many coastal areas of

the Far North, nesting near salt water as well as inland near tundra ponds, but its habits and distribution at this season are imperfectly known.

VOICE: The male has a melodious, almost bell-like whistle that suggests the call of a curlew, and a twittering call. The female makes only a harsh croak.

NEST: (I. 28, P.) Close to water, generally well hidden in a depression in the ground or in a cleft in rocks. The nest is lined with grasses and other vegetation and is usually under a shrub or in a tall clump of grass. The 6 eggs (2.4 x 1.6) are light buff.

RANGE: (M.) Breeds from Iceland, Newfoundland, Labrador, and James Bay west through Alaska and n. Asia to n. Europe south to Ireland. Winters from Newfoundland to North Carolina, the Aleutian Islands to s. California, and abroad to China and the Mediterranean.

Ruddy Duck   *Oxyura jamaicensis*—⚡10
L. 15; W. 22½; Wt. 1¼ lbs.

IDENTIFICATION: This remarkable duck molts in September and again in April, the male exchanging its finely barred, brownish winter body plumage for a rich reddish-chestnut, and its bill becomes bright blue. In any plumage the black or dark brown cap and white cheeks (crossed by an indistinct horizontal line in the female) are conspicuous. The small size, chunky build, buzzy flight, and the male's habit of cocking up its expanded tail make it an easy duck to identify.

HABITS: The ruddy is grebelike in its ability to sink slowly out of sight under water, its inability to walk upright on land,

and its habit of diving rather than flying to escape pursuit. It takes off only with difficulty after a long run into the wind, travels low over the water with a rather erratic flight, and migrates largely at night. It seldom associates with any other birds except coots and as a rule occurs by ones or twos or in small groups of 8 or 12. The ruddy's tameness or stupidity, which makes it easy to shoot, probably accounts for part of its enormous decline in abundance. This is especially regrettable, as the readiness with which it establishes nesting colonies in suitable habitats far outside its normal breeding range indicates that with encouragement it might become a much more widespread nester on small ponds throughout the country. The male has a striking courtship performance and, unlike other ducks, stays with the female and assists in rearing the precocious young. The food of this little diving duck is three-quarters plant material. It eats a great many seeds, especially of sedges and pondweeds, as well as the leaves, stems, and tubers of sago and clasping-leaf pondweed. Soft-bodied aquatic insects, chiefly midge larvae, plus a few crustacea and shellfish, make up the rest of its diet. In winter ruddys are found on large bodies of fresh water or on shallow brackish bays, where widgeon grass and musk grass are their chief foods. Only rarely are they found on salt water.

VOICE: Silent except for a series of weak clucking notes during courtship.

NEST: (I. 21, P.) A closely woven basket made of leaves from nearby plants and anchored well above the water to the upright stalks of a dense bed of reeds or similar marsh plants growing in water. Ruddys also use old nests of other ducks, muskrat houses, and floating logs as foundations for their own nests, which are often poorly constructed. The 8 or 9 thick-shelled, rough white eggs are enormous (2.4 x 1.8) for so small a bird. It is reported as 2-brooded in southern areas. Many ducks occasionally deposit an egg in a nest other than their own, a habit in which the ruddy indulges quite frequently. A related South American species is completely parasitic.

RANGE: (P. M.) Breeds from Wisconsin, n. Manitoba, s. Mackenzie, and c. British Columbia south to c. Texas, n. Lower California, and throughout the West Indies. Isolated groups breed from Ungava and Cape Cod to s. Mexico and Guatemala. Winters from Chesapeake Bay, s. Illinois, c. Arizona, and n. British Columbia south through the West Indies and to Central America.

Masked Duck   *Oxyura dominica*—✕ 10
                                          L. 13½; W. 20

IDENTIFICATION: The large white wing patch separates this duck
  from its close relative, the ruddy. On water the head markings of both sexes and the male's habit of erecting its tail are
  distinctive.
HABITS: This tropical relative of the ruddy duck makes its
  home in dense reed-grown marshes even when little or no
  open water is present. It also frequents mangrove swamps
  along the coast and makes itself at home in the smallest
  farm ponds. In such habitats it is often impossible to see or
  flush, and its presence is often never suspected, though it
  flies about more than the ruddy, especially in late evening
  and early morning, and seems more at ease on the wing.
  When disturbed it has the grebelike habit of sinking out of
  sight and, like the grebe, it seldom if ever leaves the water
  except for early morning and evening flights. It is somewhat
  migratory and a great wanderer, feeding by day on seeds,
  plants, and insects and traveling at night. The distribution of
  this duck as a breeder is as puzzling and erratic as that of the
  ruddy. It is common as close as Cuba and Jamaica and may
  well occur in our southern marshes more often than the lack
  of records indicate.
VOICE: In response to a loud noise calls back with a clucking
  described as *kirri-kirroo, kirri-kirroo, kirroo, kirrio, kirroo.*
NEST: (P.) In dense beds of reeds close to water. The 4 large
  eggs (2.5 x 1.8) are rough and whitish.
RANGE: (P. M.) Breeds from Cuba and Costa Rica south to n.
  Argentina and c. Chile. Has wandered north as far as Vermont and Wisconsin.

Hooded Merganser   *Lophodytes cucullatus*—✕ 9
                                L. 17½; W. 25; Wt. 1¼ lbs.

IDENTIFICATION: The black-bordered white area on the male's
  head, varying in size as the crest is raised and lowered, is
  distinctive, as are the black chest bars and brown sides. The
  gray females and young are best identified by their soft, loose
  crest of brownish feathers. Both sexes have partially white
  secondaries and inner wing coverts and a fine, round bill.
HABITS: The summer home is timbered stream bottoms, swamp
  forests, and woodland ponds and lakes. At other seasons almost any body of fresh water will serve. Along the coast the

birds frequent marsh ponds and occasionally salt creeks and inlets. On the wing they move fast with a direct flight and commonly travel in small, compact flocks. This duck's tame, unsuspicious character may account for the fact that it is now rather scarce in comparison with its former abundance. Its food is small fish, mostly species of no value to man, crayfish, aquatic insects, and frogs. Although it seems to prefer quiet waters, it is an expert diver and can feed with ease in the swift streams to which it is often driven when other areas freeze over.

VOICE: Low, grunting notes and a chattering sound.

NEST: (I. 31, P.) In a cavity of almost any type, sometimes far from water. Sites vary from holes in trees at any height, the broken top of a tree trunk, or a bird box to the inside of a hollow fallen log or on the ground in a hole under a stump. The 11 eggs (2.1 x 1.8) are pure white.

RANGE: (P. M.) Breeds from New Brunswick, n. Manitoba, s. Mackenzie, and s. Alaska south to c. Florida, Louisiana, Nebraska, Wyoming, and Oregon. Winters from Massachusetts, Michigan, Colorado, and British Columbia south to Cuba and s. Mexico.

Merganser
(Goosander)

Mergus merganser—⚞9
L. 24; W. 36; Wt. 3 lbs.

IDENTIFICATION: The long, slim bill, head, and neck of both large mergansers are distinctive in flight and on water. The male of this species is very white-looking without any noticeable crest. The female has a bright, reddish head and neck with a sharply defined white throat and line of juncture of the reddish neck with the white chest, and a blue-gray body.

HABITS: This merganser is almost exclusively a fresh-water duck, seldom occurring in water saltier than brackish inlets and bays. It shows a definite preference for clear water in which, presumably, it can sight and pursue its prey more readily. Not markedly gregarious, it is usually encountered in flocks of 5 to 20 birds. Unlike the little hooded merganser that can jump into the air, these birds must run over the water quite a distance before they can take off. When feeding they swim with their heads under water to the eyes, diving as they locate food. This is chiefly fish, but on some waters considerable quantities of eels, crayfish, frogs, and aquatic insects are taken. Most of the fish run from 2 to 6 inches, with occasional individuals up to 15 inches.

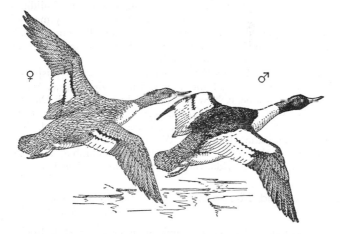

There have been many conflicting opinions concerning the effect of mergansers on game and food fish. Fishery research now indicates that the main reason why fishing is so poor in many ponds and lakes is that the fish population is not being properly thinned. Warm-water fish like bass and perch are so prolific that, in the absence of sufficient predators, overcrowding and growth stagnation soon occur even in newly stocked ponds and reservoirs. In the typical lake from which most fish-eating birds and mammals have been eliminated there are often few "legal-size" fish, even when the over-all fish population in terms of pounds to the acre is very heavy. In contrast, wilderness lakes, especially those known to be fished annually by flocks of migrant mergansers, usually provide excellent fishing, which indicates that the birds are holding the fish population below full carrying capacity, a state of affairs that promotes rapid growth in the survivors. Some kind of thinning is the only known way of producing good sport fishing for warm-water fish. Ordinarily mergansers seem not attracted by the best trout and salmon streams, as they prefer deeper waters with a greater variety of fish, most of which are slow swimmers and easier to catch. Only when the freezing of quiet waters forces the few that do not migrate onto swift streams are many trout taken.

VOICE: A hoarse croak and during courtship a series of purring notes.

NEST: (I. 34, P.) The preferred site is in a cavity in a tree, among rocks, or in a hole in a bank, but ruined buildings have been used. If on the ground the nest is a bulky mass of material placed under dense cover, generally on a small island. Old hawk nests in trees are occasionally used. The 11 or so eggs (2.5 x 1.8) are pale buff.

RANGE: (P. M.) Breeds throughout the Northern Hemisphere, from Newfoundland, James Bay, s. Mackenzie, and s.e. Alaska south to s. Maine, c. New York, c. Michigan, s. South Dakota, n.c. Arizona, and c. California; across Europe and Asia from Iceland, Scandinavia, and n. Siberia to Switzerland, Rumania, and the Himalayas. Winters from the Gulf of St. Lawrence, the Great Lakes, s. British Columbia, and the Aleutians to n. Florida, the Gulf Coast, and n. Mexico.

Red-breasted Merganser   *Mergus serrator*—⚹9
L. 22; W. 32; Wt. 2¼ lbs.

IDENTIFICATION: The conspicuous loose crest, reddish breast, and generally dark-bodied appearance of the male are distinctive. The female is more loose-crested, and the reddish color of its head and neck, paler than in the common merganser, blends into the white of its throat and breast. In flight the white patch on the wing shows a distinct division into 2 halves and the body appears brownish-gray.

HABITS: Most red-breasted mergansers winter on salt water. They are widely distributed, feeding off sandy shores just beyond the breakers, around inlets and river mouths, and in the creeks and channels of salt marshes. Some winter on the Great Lakes; others commonly appear on inland lakes and rivers during migration. More gregarious than the merganser, these birds often occur in flocks of many hundreds, the members of which sometimes co-operate in feeding by forming a long line abreast and driving a school of fish into shallow areas, where they are more readily caught. The diet, although primarily fish, includes more crayfish and marine crustacea than with the preceding species. As the red-breasted always feeds in waters that support large populations of non-game fish, there is little likelihood of its ever taking any large proportion of commercially valuable species.

VOICE: A few hoarse croaks and a double purring note.

NEST: (I. 27, P.) On the ground under dense overhead cover or hidden under a log or in a pile of trash; found inland near rivers and ponds or along the shore, often on small offshore islands. The nest is little more than a down-filled depression. The 9 or so eggs (2.5 x 1.8) are olive-buff.

RANGE: (M.) Breeds north to the shores of the Arctic Ocean in w. North America, Europe, and Asia; occurs from c. Greenland, s. Baffin Island, s. Hudson Bay, n. Mackenzie, and n. Alaska south to Maine, n. New York, c. Michigan, s. Manitoba, and n. British Columbia; in Europe south to n. Germany and c. Russia. Winters from New Brunswick, the Great Lakes, and s.e. Alaska south to s. Florida, the Gulf Coast, and s. Lower California.

BIRDS of PREY
Order Falconiformes

Comparison of Average* Length and Wingspread of Birds of Prey

SPECIES	LENGTH	WINGSPREAD
Sparrow Hawk	10¼	22½
Pigeon Hawk	11½	25½
Sharp-shinned Hawk	12	24
Mississippi Kite	14	35
Broad-winged Hawk	16	36
Aplomado Falcon	16	37
White-tailed Kite	16	40
Cooper's Hawk	17	31
Short-tailed Hawk	17	35
Gray Hawk	17	35
Everglade Kite	17	45
Peregrine Falcon	18	42½
Prairie Falcon	18½	41
Zone-tailed Hawk	20	50
Harris' Hawk	20½	43½
Marsh Hawk	20½	45½
Swainson's Hawk	20½	50½
Red-shouldered Hawk	21	42
Black Hawk	21	48
Rough-legged Hawk	21½	52
Harlan's Hawk	21½	52
Gyrfalcon	22	48
Red-tailed Hawk	22½	50
Goshawk	23	44
Caracara	23	48
White-tailed Hawk	23	50
Osprey	23	68
Swallow-tailed Kite	24	48

*These birds vary widely from average and females are generally much larger than males.

SPECIES	LENGTH	WINGSPREAD
Ferruginous Rough-legged Hawk	24	56
Black Vulture	25	57
Turkey Vulture	29	70
Bald Eagle	35	82
Golden Eagle	35½	83
Sea Eagle	36	88

VULTURES   Family Cathartidae

Turkey Vulture*   *Cathartes aura*—✳45
L. 29; W. 70; Wt. 3½ lbs.

IDENTIFICATION: The small naked head, long narrow tail, and, in a soaring bird, the way the wings are held above the horizontal to form an open V are distinctive. The underwing pattern which is formed by the uniformly grayish flight feathers and the blackish coverts is a good field mark. Nestlings are covered with long white down. Young lack the red head of adults.

HABITS: Few birds are as conspicuous as these scavengers that spend most of the daylight hours patrolling the sky on the lookout for food. Lacking strong talons and therefore practically powerless to cause the death of any creature, they seek what fate provides, but they have amazing powers of sight and little escapes their notice. Each bird operates independently, but by watching one another they learn of every find and gather for miles to share it. The heavy toll of small animal life along highways now provides a steady source of fresh food. Their supposed predilection for well-decayed carcasses appears to be due to their inability to tear up a large animal until decay has softened its tissues. In the South vultures constitute a useful sanitary brigade about city dumps. It has been found that the bacteria of some of the most virulent animal diseases, like hog cholera and anthrax, are destroyed by passing through their digestive system.

The secret of the turkey vulture's success is its ability to search a vast area with minimum effort. This it does by utilizing to the utmost the normal currents of the atmosphere, the most important of which are the thermals—rapidly rising columns of air that has been warmed by contact with the ground. This explains the vulture's practice of not leaving the communal roost (where upward of 100 or more may spend the night) until the sun has set the air in motion, and also its habit of soaring in circles to keep within the limits of a given thermal. Often a bird goes around and around within one of these invisible chimneys until it reaches the point where the cool upper air causes the moist thermal air to condense into a cloud. The vulture's way of holding its wings in an open V is another aid to effortless flight. When the bird tips to either side the lift of the lower wing is increased while that of the upper is decreased. Thus, effortlessly and automatically, it is brought back to normal flying position.

VOICE: A hiss and an occasional raucous grunt or growl.

NEST: (I. 41, A., N. 74) No nest is built, the eggs being laid on the ground in a sheltered and secluded spot. This may be a hollow stump, a crevice in a pile of rocks, a cliff ledge or cave, or an abandoned building. The 2 eggs (2.8 x 1.9) are creamy-white, boldly and often heavily marked with dark browns.

RANGE: (P. M.) Breeds from Connecticut, s. Ontario, n. Minnesota, c. Alberta, and s. British Columbia south through Mexico and South America to the Strait of Magellan and the Falkland Islands.

Black Vulture*   *Coragyps atratus*—#45
                          L. 25; W. 57; Wt. 4½ lbs.

IDENTIFICATION: This vulture is feathered up the back of the neck to the black head. In the air it is much heavier-looking than the preceding and has shorter, broader wings. The short, square tail (feet project to or beyond it) and the large white patches toward the ends of the wings, formed by the white bases to the primaries, are distinctive. Young birds are densely covered with rich buffy down.

ʜᴀʙɪᴛs: The non-migratory black vultures do not range into areas where in winter carcasses remain frozen for long periods. Along the coasts and about cities and slaughterhouses, where they become as tame as domestic fowl, these are more abundant than turkey vultures. They are very gregarious and are generally seen in flocks. At night they gather into large roosts which they sometimes share with turkey vultures. Blacks have not the great soaring ability of these relatives and often seem to depend upon them to locate food for them both. Blacks are heavier and more aggressive, and when a carcass is located they generally force the turkey vultures to wait their turn. Well-decayed carcasses, big enough to allow many birds to share the meal, seem to be the preferred food. Often a few blacks nest in a heron colony, where their normal role seems to be cleaning up the numerous young that fall from the nest or die from other causes, but at times when the adult herons leave eggs and helpless young unguarded the vultures become actual predators. Since vultures' feet are incapable of grasping anything, the birds carry their food by swallowing it and feed the young by regurgitation. In the air this vulture holds its wings almost horizontal and generally soars for only short intervals broken by a series of quick, deep flaps of its heavy broad wings. Other sources of food besides those already mentioned are dead fish along the shore and garbage in city dumps.

voice: Hissing sounds and muffled barking notes.

nest: (I. 40, A., N. 70) The preferred site is a hollowed-out stump or broken-off tree trunk or a shallow cave on a cliff ledge, but often the eggs are laid on the ground in a dense thicket or under the shelter of a fallen tree trunk or in a hollow log. Gregariousness sometimes leads to the formation of a breeding colony at an especially favorable site. The 2 eggs (3.0 x 2.0) are usually gray-green blotched with dark brown.

range: (R.) Occurs from Maryland, s. Indiana, Kansas, w. Texas, and e. Mexico south to s. Argentina and Chile.

HAWKS, BUZZARDS, EAGLES, and ALLIES
Family Accipitriidae

White-tailed Kite*   *Elanus leucurus*—✕39
                                         L. 16; W. 40

identification: The gull-like whiteness of the adult and the black patches at the bend of the wing—a large one above and a small one below—are distinctive. In addition, the rather brownish young have a dark subterminal tail band.

habits: This widely distributed Central and South American bird formerly ranged into 3 areas in the United States, but it is apparently gone now from all but s. Texas and California.

Open, grassy country, especially damp meadows, alfalfa fields, or fresh-water marshes with scattered clumps of trees for roosting and nesting, seems to be the ideal habitat. Here the birds beat slowly back and forth at a moderate height, looking for food. In the air their appearance is very distinctive as the long, pointed wings, although held upward, are so curved that the tips point downward. They also have a habit of dangling their feet in flight, and when prey is sighted they often hover in one spot for some seconds before pouncing or going on. In California, where their feeding habits have been studied, their food seems to be exclusively small mammals, especially the meadow mouse. As this mouse is one of those species whose local populations commonly build up to a peak every 4 years and are then drastically reduced by disease, kites are apt to have to look for new feeding grounds from year to year.

VOICE: Various whistled notes, singly or in series, some drawn out and plaintive, others abrupt and osprey-like.

NEST: (I. 30, A., N. 30) In a tree from 12 to 60 feet aboveground, usually along a stream bank or on the edge of a fresh-water marsh. The nest is a substantial mass of loose twigs with a central cup lined with fine material. The 4 or 5 eggs (1.7 x 1.3) are white, heavily marked with various shades of brown. Two broods are sometimes reared.

RANGE: (R.) Occurred originally from South Carolina south through Florida; s.c. Oklahoma south through c. Texas; and n. California south; through South America to n. Argentina and c. Chile. Now greatly reduced throughout its United States range.

Swallow-tailed Kite*   *Elanoides forficatus*—⚹39
L. 24; W. 48

IDENTIFICATION: This bird could be confused only with a young frigate-bird, from which it differs most strikingly in having white underwing coverts. Young kites can be recognized by the white spots in the dark parts of their plumage.

HABITS: Nothing in all nature is more exquisitely beautiful than the flight of this bird, and its disappearance from its once extensive United States range, except for a few areas on the South Atlantic and Gulf coasts, is a real tragedy. Watching them soaring high in the air one minute with a buoyancy that defies gravity, then swooping to within a few feet of the ground with a power and grace that reveal absolute mastery of the air, one can only marvel at the effortlessness of the whole performance. River bottoms, swamp forests, fresh-water marshes, and the vicinity of ponds and lakes are favorite haunts, but the birds also feed over adjacent open farmlands. The swallow-tail is quite gregarious, often hunting in small groups and migrating in large flocks. Lizards, tree frogs, and snakes plucked from trees or the ground and large insects like dragonflies captured in flight are staple foods. Much of its prey is eaten while the bird is in the air, and it drinks and bathes by skimming the water like a swallow. Probably the drainage of marshes and the cutting of swamp forests have played a large part in its decline in the United States, although wanton shooting as a living target has also been a factor.

VOICE: A series of squealing or whistled notes, sometimes loud and shrill and at other times soft and plaintive.

NEST: (A.) Well out in the upper branches of a very tall tree, seldom lower than 60 feet and usually well over 100 feet. Twigs and small branches to which some kind of tree "moss" is attached seem to be the only acceptable nesting material. The center cup of the rather flat, not too substantial nest is finished off with a lining of moss. The 2 or 3 eggs (1.8 x 1.5) are white blotched with brown.

RANGE: (P. M.) Once bred from North Carolina, s. Ohio, s. Wisconsin, n. Minnesota, and e. Nebraska south to Florida and the Gulf Coast, west to e. Texas, and south through Central and e. South America to n. Argentina. Now seldom found north of c. Florida and a few points along the Gulf Coast. Winters s. of the United States.

Mississippi Kite*   *Ictinia misisippiensis*—※39
L. 14; W. 35

IDENTIFICATION: The pale head and black tail of adults are distinctive, and in flight the way the rear edge of the wing gradually becomes paler toward the body. Young with their brown streaks look very different and show 3 grayish bands on the tail.

HABITS: In the western part of its range this kite feeds over open scrub oak and range land. Here it nests in the few scattered small trees or in the taller groves along creek bottoms. Farther east it nests in tall timber on the borders of lakes and rivers and does most of its feeding over adjacent plantations. It also seems at home in open pine forests, where it nests in the tallest trees. The birds are quite gregarious, gathering in flocks on favorable feeding grounds and during migration, and in some cases forming loose nesting colonies. Like other kites, the Mississippi has a wonderfully buoyant flight and is very active in the air, constantly changing the position of its long, square black tail as it veers hither and thither. With hardly a movement of its wings it suddenly rises high in the sky and as suddenly dips back to earth. One of its characteristic habits is to check its flight abruptly and hang motionless in the sky with wings horizontal and body tipped. Its only known foods are large insects, especially cicadas, grasshoppers, and dragonflies.

VOICE: A thin, high, osprey-like double whistle.

NEST: (I. 30, A.) In the top of a tree, which in some areas means 100 feet or more but in the West may mean only 6 to 12 feet. The nest is generally a flimsy, flat-topped structure made of coarse twigs and is invariably well lined with fresh green leaves. The 2 eggs (1.6 x 1.3) are bluish-white and unmarked.

RANGE: (M.) Breeds from South Carolina, Tennessee, and s. Kansas south to n. Florida, the Gulf Coast, and w. Texas. Winters from s. Florida and s. Texas south. A similar bird, of which this may eventually prove to be a race, occurs from Mexico to n. Argentina.

Everglade Kite   *Rostrhamus sociabilis*—✕ 39
L. 17; W. 45

IDENTIFICATION: This is a broad-winged, square-tailed bird which in all plumages shows much white at the base of the tail, noticeable from below as well as above. The black male, with its long bright red legs and red bill base, is unmistakable. The brown-streaked young birds and females are light about the head and in flight often show considerable white at the base of the primaries as well as on the tip of the tail.

HABITS: This wide-ranging kite has become as highly specialized in its food habits as a bird can be. Today it feeds solely on the big fresh-water snails of the genus *Ampullaria*, which live in fresh-water marshes throughout the Tropics and lay their eggs in conspicuous masses a few inches above the water, on the stems of marsh plants. Most of the kite's feeding is done in the cool early morning or late afternoon, when the snails come up out of the water. Kites hunt by flapping along slowly and rather heavily just over the tops of the marsh grasses. Their bills are pointed downward, their broad tails constantly in use, and when a snail is sighted the bird often hovers for a few seconds before dropping upon it. Once captured, the snail is carried to a regular feeding perch and extracted from the unbroken shell with the long, strongly hooked bill which is so well adapted to this purpose. Soaring seems to be a pastime, and during the heat of the day the birds often ride the thermals for hours.

Once common in Florida, this kite has almost disappeared

with the digging of drainage canals without proper locks to
control the amount of water drawn off. Many marshes now
dry out completely during drought years. This exterminates
the snails, and although the marsh soon looks as flourish-
ing as ever when the rains fill it up again, the snails and
kites are generally gone forever. A few kites still inhabit the
shore of undrainable Lake Okeechobee, but here they are
rapidly falling victims to the type of thoughtless duck hunter
who shoots any hawklike bird that flies past his blind.

VOICE: A rapid series of high-pitched, squeaky notes that produce a weak chatter or cackle.
NEST: (A.) Often in small colonies of a few to a dozen or more
pairs. The usual site is a few feet above the water in an
isolated clump of willows or other marsh trees well out in a
marshy area, but the birds also build directly on a matted
down patch of marsh reeds. The 3 or 4 eggs (1.7 x 1.4) are
white, profusely covered with brown markings.
RANGE: (R.) Occurs from n. Florida and e. Mexico south to
w. Cuba and through Central and South America to n. Argentina.

Goshawk*   *Accipiter gentilis*—✳40
            ♂ L. 21; W. 42; ♀ L. 25; W. 46

IDENTIFICATION: The uniformly slate-gray appearance of adults
is distinctive. Young birds resemble those of the next 2 species

but have a more pronounced light eye stripe and in flight seem proportionately much heavier about the head and neck.

HABITS: This bird of the northern woodlands prefers mixed growths for nesting, usually selecting a remote, secluded stand of heavy timber. Much of its hunting is done about clearings and brushy openings. It seems to migrate only when forced to by lack of food and does not appear south of its breeding grounds in large numbers except during "flight years," which generally occur at regular 9- to 11-year intervals. When hunting, the goshawk flies through the woods below the treetops, often quite close to the ground, first surprising its prey and then catching it in an amazingly swift direct pursuit that may end in a chase on foot into a thicket. Because of this, medieval hawkers trained it to fly from the fist directly at flushed game. For a resting perch it chooses the inside of the top of a well-leafed tree, where it can search the surroundings for prey and see without being seen. At the nest goshawks reveal an utter fearlessness and a savage determination to drive intruders away at any cost. Cackling defiance, they try again and again to strike one on the head with their powerful talons and one cannot help but admire such devotion and courage.

Although members of the genus *Accipiter*—the true hawks —are thought of primarily as bird eaters, the goshawk takes a great many mammals. Often nestlings are fed on nothing else. Chipmunks, red, gray, and ground squirrels, rabbits, and even weasels are common prey; occasionally mice and, in the Far North, lemmings. The goshawk can handle and seems partial to large ground-dwelling birds like grouse, ptarmigan, quail, and ducks but at times will take sparrows. It often learns to avail itself of the tempting food supply offered by a poultry yard or game farm and seldom leaves the owner any choice but to shoot it. Among wild birds its toll appears never to exceed what nature can replace during the following breeding season, since birds like ruffed grouse continue to be common, even abundant, in areas where the goshawk is a regular breeder.

VOICE: A fierce, deep-toned, staccato *ca, ca, ca, ca, ca, ca, ca* uttered as an alarm note about the nest. The normal courtship call is a clear, high-pitched, and rather plaintive *hi-aa, hi-aa* that suggests a red-shouldered hawk's call.

NEST: (I. 37, A., N. 42) The huge, bulky nest, often 3 to 5 feet across, is generally supported by horizontal branches against the main trunk of a deciduous tree some 20 to 60 feet up. It is made of long sticks with a lining of bark and decorated with a few fresh sprigs of evergreen foliage. The 3 or 4 unmarked eggs (2.3 x 1.8) are bluish-white.

RANGE: (P. M.) Breeds through most of Europe and Asia and in North America from Newfoundland, Ungava, n. Manitoba, n.w. Mackenzie, and n.w. Alaska south to n. New England (Maryland in the mts.), n. Michigan, n. Minnesota, and n. Mexico. Winters from s. Canada and Alaska south to Virginia, Illinois, Oklahoma, and n. Mexico.

Sharp-shinned Hawk*   *Accipiter striatus*—#40
♂ L. 11; W. 21½; ♀ L. 13; W. 26

IDENTIFICATION: The sharp-shin and Cooper's are almost identical except for size and the shape of the end of the folded tail —square in this species, rounded in Cooper's. The much larger size of the females, which is characteristic of all hawks, results in a size overlap between large female sharp-shins and small male Cooper's.

HABITS: The little sharp-shin is a woodland species that usually selects a clump of conifers near a road or other opening for nesting. It does not thrive around settled areas and generally becomes scarce as extensive forests disappear. The center of its abundance is now the great woodlands of e. Canada, from which a flood of migrants sweeps south each fall along certain well-defined hawk flyways where hundreds can be seen on favorable days.

This hawk's hunting methods are like those of other Accipiters, but its prey is smaller. Sparrows and warblers supply much of its food, although it can on occasion handle bobwhites, pigeons, and half-grown chickens. Mammals from the size of red squirrels down to mice and shrews are taken, and occasionally a sharp-shin will fill up on large insects.

Years ago ornithologists called this a "harmful" hawk because it preyed on what they called "beneficial" songbirds. Now that ecologists have given us better understanding of the inner workings of wildlife communities we realize that songbirds, like all other living things, produce surpluses that can be harvested without affecting the year-to-year breeding stock. No species can be termed good or bad. Each has its place in one of the many food chains that bind all wildlife together in interdependent communities. Each community can support only so many individuals of a certain kind; the surplus serving as food for other species.

VOICE: The alarm note about the nest is a series of shrill *kik, kik, kik, kik* notes run together into an angry cackle. The call note is a thin, plaintive squeal or whine.

NEST: (A.) A flat, shallow structure of woven twigs so large that the sitting bird is usually hidden from below. Placed from 10 to 60 feet up on horizontal limbs against the trunk of a tree, usually a conifer. Occasionally the nest is in a crevice in a cliff or in a hollow in the trunk of a large tree. Unlike many birds of prey, these normally build a new nest every year, though occasionally they use the old nests of other birds. The 4 eggs (1.5 x 1.2) are white, blotched with browns.

RANGE: (P. M.) Breeds from Newfoundland, c. Quebec, n. Manitoba, s. Mackenzie, and c. Alaska south to n. Florida (and the Greater Antilles), the Gulf Coast, and n. Mexico. Winters from c. New England, Ohio, n. Nebraska, w. Montana, and s.e. Alaska south to Guatemala.

Cooper's Hawk* *Accipiter cooperii*—※40
♂ L. 16; W. 28; ♀ L. 18; W. 33

IDENTIFICATION: Distinguishable from the sharp-shin only by its size and the rounded end of its closed tail. All Accipiters are readily separated from Buteos and falcons by their short, rounded wings and long tails and in flight by their habit of alternately flapping 4 or 5 times and then gliding a few seconds. This they do even on those rare occasions, chiefly during migration or courtship, when they soar high in the air.

HABITS: Apparently Cooper's and sharp-shin hawks occupy niches so similar that they will not tolerate each other's presence in the same area. The cutting up of forests into scattered wood lots interspersed by open farmland has so favored Cooper's that it is today one of the commonest birds of prey. It is seldom seen, however, as it has the Accipiter habit of perching in the dense, leafy crown of a tree and flying close to the ground through woods and thickets. Built for maneuverability, with a long rudderlike tail, it has no trouble following every twist and turn of a fleeing bird or dashing headlong through the thickest woods. It lives on birds of dove, quail, robin, meadowlark, and jay size as well as on smaller ones and small mammals. Many a farmer blames his chicken losses on the larger, more conspicuous Buteos when this hawk is the culprit. However, not every Cooper's is a "chicken hawk." Many reliable accounts of pairs that have nested for years near poultry yards without touching a chicken show that individuals develop highly selective feeding habits from which they seldom deviate. If the habit of raiding chicken yards is acquired the bird is soon shot. The fact that Cooper's continue to be common indicates that many of them never bother chickens.

VOICE: A variety of loud, deep notes uttered in a rapid cackle; also a drawn-out whistled note that sounds like *swee-ew*.

NEST: (A.) When in a conifer it is a broad, flat platform of sticks lined with chips of outer bark and supported by horizontal branches against the main trunk. In deciduous trees it may be in an upright crotch, in which case it is generally deeper. Normal heights run from 20 to 60 feet, but in tree-less country the birds nest in shrubby growths. The 4 eggs (1.9 x 1.5) are dirty white, occasionally spotted with brown.

RANGE: (P. M.) Breeds from Nova Scotia, s. Ontario, c. Alberta, and s. British Columbia south to Florida, the Gulf Coast, and n. Mexico. Winters from s. New England, Ohio, Nebraska, and s.w. British Columbia to Costa Rica.

Red-tailed Hawk*   *Buteo jamaicensis*—⚹42
(Red-tailed Buzzard)
♂ L. 20½; W. 48; Wt. 2 lbs.; ♀ L. 22; W. 53; Wt. 2¾ lbs.

IDENTIFICATION: The broad wings and widely expanded tail of this large, soaring bird are its best field marks. The bright reddish upper tail surface and dark bellyband are usually distinctive, but on pale or dark individuals these are not prominent. The gray-brown tail of the young is finely barred with black while that of adults usually has one or more bars near the tip.

There is so much individual variation in many species of Buteos, including western races of the red-tail, that accurate identification in the field is sometimes difficult. Extreme melanism, rare in some species but quite common in others, produces dark birds that look very much alike, while albinism washes out distinctive colors and markings. The R. T. Peterson "Field Guides" (Eastern and Western), with their excellent flight-pattern drawings and detailed comparisons, are almost essential to the solution of some of these difficult identification problems.

HABITS: (Age 13½ yrs.) Red-tails and other Buteos are very different in habit and appearance from Accipiters or true hawks. This species ranges over most of the continent from the forests of the East to the plains and deserts of the West and from the dwarf subarctic scrub of the North to the Tropics. In the East it is usually found in open woodlands, nesting in mature stands of tall, widely spaced trees or in the occasional large tree in an oak- or pine-barren area. It generally avoids or is soon shot out of well-settled farming country. Once the nesting season is over, the birds wander widely and are found wherever open fields and convenient treetops give perches from which they can watch for prey. A thick, heavy, short-tailed hawk, sitting upright and motionless in the top of a dead tree, is more than likely to be a red-tail. Today it is most abundant in the open country of the West, nesting wherever a cliff ledge, patch of river-bottom timber, or a small tree provides a suitable site.

IMMATURE

ADULT

The red-tail's food varies considerably from one region to another, and individual birds often develop preferences for a certain type of prey. Their extraordinary eyesight enables them to locate prey from a great distance as they soar high overhead or watch from a perch. Once spotted, the animal is pounced upon and caught, often before it realizes its danger. Every kind of small animal from snakes, lizards, and frogs to crayfish and insects have been found in red-tail stomachs. Small mammals, chiefly rodents, such as meadow mice, squirrels (both ground and tree), gophers, rabbits, and shrews, are staple foods. Red-tails are willing to take any bird stupid or sluggish enough to let itself be caught. These generally appear to be old, diseased, or crippled, as most healthy birds are too alert to be taken by surprise and too fast for a Buteo to catch them in flight. Occasionally the discovery that chickens cannot fly and are easy to catch causes an individual of this species to overcome its instinctive fear of man and become a confirmed raider of poultry yards. Such a bird seldom survives long. The habit of eating carrion, which the red-tail shares with a surprising number of other birds of prey, sometimes earns it an undeserved reputation as a chicken or game-bird eater. Until proved otherwise, every red-tail should be regarded as an asset on a farm or ranch where the small rodents on which they prey often take a greater toll of crops than do insects.

DARK PHASE

LIGHT PHASE

VOICE: A long-drawn-out call, halfway between a hiss and a squeal.

NEST: (I. 28, A.) A large, bulky mass of sticks, lined with shredded inner bark and usually kept decorated with a few sprigs of fresh green foliage; generally in the tallest tree near the edge of a clump of big timber, but cliff-ledge nests and nests in low trees are not uncommon in open, treeless country. The same nest is often used many years in succession. The 2 or 3 eggs (2.3 x 1.9) are white, sparingly blotched and spotted with browns.

RANGE: (P. M.) Breeds from Newfoundland, s. Quebec, n. Ontario, c. Mackenzie, and s.c. Alaska south through the United States and Mexico to the Leeward Islands and Panama. Winters from c. New England, s. Michigan, n. Iowa, Wyoming, and s.e. Alaska south.

Harlan's Hawk*
(Harlan's Buzzard)

Buteo harlani—⚡42
♂ L. 20¾; W. 50; Wt. 2¼ lbs.;
♀ L. 22½; W. 55; Wt. 3¼ lbs.

IDENTIFICATION: The dark markings are largely black rather than brown. There seems to be no normal plumage, as individuals vary from very dark to very light. In dark birds the often extensive white spotting above, the heavy dark spots below, the white-flecked dark wing linings, and the boldly barred flight feathers are distinctive. Light adults may be almost white below and about the head. All have the characteristic Harlan tail, grayish or white, blotched and streaked with dark and with a dark terminal band. The similar pale "krideri" race of the red-tail has a more broadly white-tipped tail with dark bars and usually has more reddish color than is ever present on Harlan's. Young in the dark phase are spotted, with white above, and are like adults except for the barred tail, which is like a young red-tail's. In the light phase the young are hardly distinguishable from "krideri" young.

HABITS: Originally described by Audubon as a distinct species, this bird is very possibly a color phase or race of the red-tail. Its very circumscribed breeding and wintering range, however, lend considerable weight to the arguments of those that regard it as a good species. Observers have reported it as more active than the average red-tail and a heavier feeder on small birds, but in general there seem to be no marked differences between it and the red-tail.

VOICE: A sibilant scream or squeal.

NEST: (A.) One was reported as a mass of sticks 60 feet up in a tall spruce tree in an open spruce woodland. The eggs are unknown.

RANGE: (M.) Breeds in e. Alaska, Yukon, and n. British Columbia. Winters in s. Missouri, Arkansas, Oklahoma, and n. Texas.

Red-shouldered Hawk*   *Buteo lineatus*—※42
(Red-shouldered Buzzard)   ♂ L. 20; W. 38; ♀ L. 22; W. 45

IDENTIFICATION: This bird has a longer tail and is not as chunky as a red-tail. The size and shape of the young separate them from the smaller and stockier but otherwise similar young broad-wings. From below this species shows near the ends of the extended wings a light, finely barred area that appears translucent. Young often have a prominent pale band across the upper wing surface just short of the wing tips.

HABITS: (Age 7½ yrs.) This hawk is most abundant about swamps, river bottoms, and other wet woodlands. If not too persistently persecuted it is usually common in well-settled farming country and is often surprisingly tame. Even a small wood lot will provide an acceptable nest site. In many regions the red-shoulder seems to have benefited from the changes brought by civilization while the red-tail and broad-wing have suffered. This is a comparatively sluggish bird which obtains much of its food about wet areas, where it may sit by the hour in the lower branches of a tree, dropping now and then to capture such favorite items as frogs, snakes, and crayfish. When available, grasshoppers, crickets, and large caterpillars are eaten in quantities, also meadow and white-footed mice and shrews. Stomach examinations reveal that red-shoulders take few birds and little poultry, although their scavenging habits occasionally lead to their being blamed for the death of a quail or pheasant that a hunter wounded and never found.

VOICE: Very noisy in spring and early summer, uttering a loud, far-carrying scream that sounds like a long-drawn-out *kee-you*, a call that the blue jay can imitate to perfection.

IMMATURE

ADULT

NEST: (I. 24, A.) A rather deep, flat-topped structure of sticks mixed with such fine material as leaves, moss lichens, and shredded bark and placed from 20 to 60 feet up in a crotch formed by a main limb or branch. Nests of previous years are often used again, occupancy being indicated by sprigs of fresh green leaves with which active nests are kept decorated and the bits of down that are usually in evidence. Later, when eggs are laid, the nest may be kept lined with fresh green leaves. The 2 or 3 eggs (2.2 x 1.7) in a normal clutch are white, marked (often quite heavily) with browns.

RANGE: (P. M.) Breeds from Nova Scotia, s. Quebec, s. Ontario, and c. Manitoba south to s. Florida, the Gulf Coast, and e.c. Mexico and west to the Great Plains; along the Pacific coast from s. British Columbia to n. Lower California and n.w. Mexico. Winters from c. New England, s. Michigan, and Iowa south.

Broad-winged Hawk*   *Buteo platypterus*—⚜42
(Broad-winged Buzzard)   ♂ L. 15; W. 35; ♀ L. 17; W. 37

IDENTIFICATION: This small hawk has a short tail and a chunky build much like a red-tail. The boldly banded tail of adults is distinctive. Young birds have tails like the red-shouldered's but have a whiter, black-bordered underwing.

HABITS: This is a characteristic bird of many extensive tracts of deciduous forest, the shelter of which it seldom leaves except for its long migration to its winter home in South America. In the fall spectacularly large flocks of hundreds or thousands circle high in the air on thermal updrafts or coast along on the updraft over a mountain ridge, using the forces of the atmosphere to carry them on their 4,000- to 5,000-mile flight. Although generally common and rather tame their presence in our summer woodlands often goes undetected. The broad-wing is fond of frogs, toads, and snakes, but its commonest late-summer foods are insects like grasshoppers, katydids, crickets, cicadas, and large caterpillars. The abundant shrews of the forest floor are a staple food, and some mice are taken. Occasionally small birds are eaten, especially the young of forest species like the ovenbird that are easily captured when in the nest or learning to fly.

IMMATURE   ADULT

VOICE: When its nesting woods are invaded this bird protests vigorously with a distinctive shrill, hisslike whistle which sounds like *kwee-e-e-e-e,* plaintive, long-drawn-out, and diminishing in volume.

NEST: (I. 23, A., N. 40) A small, loosely built structure placed in a main crotch or against the trunk of a tree 15 to 50 feet up; made of sticks and twigs with a sparse lining of bark

chips, lichen, etc. Most nests are kept decorated with at least
a few sprigs of fresh green foliage. The 2 or 3 eggs (1.9 x 1.5)
are white with brown and purple markings.

RANGE: (M.) Breeds from New Brunswick, c. Quebec, s. Manitoba, and c. Alberta south to s. Florida and the Gulf Coast
west to e. Texas; and the West Indies. Normally winters from
s. Mexico south to Venezuela, w. Brazil, and n. Peru, but
stragglers occasionally survive as far north as New Jersey and
s. Illinois.

Swainson's Hawk*   *Buteo swainsoni*— ⚹43
(Swainson's Buzzard)   ♂ L. 20; W. 49; ♀ L. 21; W. 52

IDENTIFICATION: For a Buteo, this bird has rather long, pointed
wings and a long tail. In normal adults the dark breast, pale
buffy wing linings (flight feathers are darker), and prominent white lateral tail coverts are distinctive. Young tend to
be most heavily marked on the breast (red-tails across the
belly). In the melanistic phase the wings are uniformly dark
below except for a white wash near the end, but the tail
generally shows a series of pale gray bars.

HABITS: (Age 8 yrs.) Throughout much of the open country
of the West this is the commonest bird of prey. It is quite
gregarious and migrates in flocks that are sometimes of enormous size. Composed of expert soarers and gliders, these
flocks spiral up on rising columns of warm air until they are
almost out of sight. The altitude thus gained is used to glide
north or south until another thermal is picked up and the
process repeated. This labor-saving device must aid them
greatly in their 11,000- to 17,000-mile annual trip to s. South
America. When hunting they often fly quite low with wings
raised in an open V like a marsh harrier.

The almost universal abuse to which our western grazing
lands have been subjected by overstocking has brought about
a great increase in grasshoppers, crickets, and rodents through
the displacement of the overgrazed grasses by weedy growths
—a change that has been favorable to Swainson's hawk.
Ground squirrels of various kinds are their principal mammal
food, plus an occasional gopher, mouse, or rat. Grasshoppers
and crickets are eaten in enormous numbers, more than 200
having been found in a single stomach. The special beds
where grasshoppers gather in great hordes in the fall to lay
eggs sometimes attract these birds by the thousands. Far
fewer young grasshoppers appear following such visits. Swain-

son's hawks commonly frequent highways which afford them opportunities to pick up live animals crossing the road and dead ones. Since they use fence posts and telephone poles as lookouts, they make conspicuous targets for those with a prejudice against all hawks, no matter how useful.

DARK PHASE   LIGHT PHASE

VOICE: A prolonged and rather shrill whistle or squeal, somewhat plaintive in quality.

NEST: (I. 28, A.) The large, bulky nests are of sticks with a lining of finer materials, placed in a tree from about ground level up to considerable heights, depending on the size of the trees locally available. As Swainson's breed where trees are scarce, the nests are generally conspicuous. The 2 eggs (2.2 x 1.7) are dull white, unmarked or sparingly spotted with brown.

RANGE: (M.) Breeds from c.w. Mackenzie and w. Alaska south to n. Mexico and east to Manitoba, Iowa, Oklahoma, and w. Texas. Winters on the Pampas of n. Argentina. A few wander east in the fall and some winter in extreme southern Florida.

Zone-tailed Hawk*   *Buteo albonotatus*—☆44
(Zone-tailed Buzzard)   L. 20; W. 50

IDENTIFICATION: In flight this long-winged, moderately long-tailed Buteo looks rather like a turkey vulture. The 3 tail bands are gray above but clear white below and are progres-sively narrower. The flight feathers are pale below and the wing lining black. Young birds are similar, but the tail is barred with brown above and below shows a single broad dark band near the end and a half dozen narrow ones.

HABITS: River bottoms and the wooded canyons that cut deep into the plateaus and mountains of our Southwest are the home of this Buteo. It is vulture-like even to the angle of the wing and the constant balancing when soaring. Like many tropical birds of prey, it is not as highly specialized in diet as many Temperate Zone species. It seems to take fish, frogs, small mammals, and birds with equal ease. When fishing it is said to hover over the water like an osprey.

VOICE: A series of loud, shrill whistles or screams.

NEST: (A.) In the slender top branches or in the crotch of a very tall woodland tree. The nest is made of sticks with a lining of green-leaved twigs. The 2 white eggs (2.2 x 1.7) are usually unmarked.

RANGE: (P. M.) Breeds from the United States-Mexican border (c.s. Texas to s. California) south to n. South America.

White-tailed Hawk*   *Buteo albicaudatus*—⚹43
(White-tailed Buzzard)   L. 23; W. 50

IDENTIFICATION: Long, rather narrow wings for a Buteo and a short tail are good field marks. Adults are distinctive, but young are quite dark all over. From below they appear to have dark wing linings, but the bases of the primaries and secondaries are whitish and the tail is a hoary gray with in-distinct dark bars.

HABITS: There are indications that this bird is extending its range northward as overgrazing degrades our southwestern grasslands into semi-desert scrub. Released from the competition of the once dominant bunch grasses and largely protected from the prairie fires that killed them out, many thorny, woody plants that provide nest sites and perches for white-tails are invading the grasslands. These birds do most of their feeding in the open areas and seem to be complete opportunists in their feeding habits. Snakes, lizards, and insects are taken as readily as rabbits, gophers, rats, and mice. They consume many small birds and also feed on carrion like vultures. The vicinity of a burning prairie fire is an excellent place to see birds of prey like the white-tail, as fire makes more vulnerable the animals upon which they feed. They seem to come from as far away as the column of smoke can be descried, and hundreds of hawks sometimes gather for the feast.

VOICE: A series of high-pitched rather musical double notes—*kil-la, kil-la*—that have been likened to those of a laughing gull or the bleat of a goat.

IMMATURE

ADULT

NEST: (A.) A loosely built bulky mass of sticks, well lined with clumps of bunch grass and saddled in the crown of a yucca, desert shrub, or scrub oak from 4 to 12 feet (rarely up to 30) above the ground. The 2 eggs (2.3 x 1.8) are white, unmarked or sparingly spotted with faint browns.

RANGE: (P. M.) Breeds from s.e. Texas and n. Mexico south through much of South America to c. Argentina.

Short-tailed Hawk*   *Buteo brachyurus*—⚹45
(Short-tailed Buzzard)   L. 17; W. 35

IDENTIFICATION: This bird has 2 distinct color phases that never
seem to intergrade. The white patch at the base of the bill,
if it can be seen, is distinctive. Light birds have the whole
head and neck hooded with dark gray down to the throat
and the sides of the breast. Dark birds show conspicuous light
bases to the flight feathers and have a pale gray tail with dark
bands.

DARK PHASE   LIGHT PHASE

HABITS: This tropical Buteo has always been considered rare
in Florida and little is known about it. It seems to be a
permanent resident of swamp forests, especially in cypress
stands along streams and lake borders as well as in the Big
Cypress country and the coastal mangrove swamps. Short-tails
seem rather sluggish and evidently do most of their feeding
in swamps, using regular lookout perches from which they
locate and pounce upon their prey. Were it not for their habit
of soaring high on the midday air currents where they are
readily picked out among the many other birds that also seem
to enjoy this form of recreation, short-tails would seldom be
observed. At the rate the trees are being cut, there will be
no more big cypress stands left in Florida within a few years,
so the future of this bird is very doubtful.

VOICE: A high-pitched whistle or squeal not unlike that of an
osprey, also a cackling note.

NEST: (A.) A large, bulky nest of twigs and Spanish moss with a lining of green leaves, always in or near a swamp, frequently in a cypress, generally 60 to 100 feet up and well out on an upper branch. In low coastal mangrove swamps nests are much lower. The 2 eggs (2.1 x 1.7) are white, varying from unmarked to heavily marked with brown.

RANGE: (R.) Occurs from n. Florida and e. Mexico south to n.e. Argentina.

Rough-legged Hawk*   *Buteo lagopus*—※43
(Rough-legged Buzzard)   ♂ L. 20; W. 50; ♀ L. 23; W. 54

IDENTIFICATION: This bird has long, broad wings, a longish tail, and distinctive flight habits. The dark belly, wrist patches, and tail end make a characteristic pattern from below. In very dark melanistic birds the white base of the tail, which is ordinarily such a good field mark, may not be noticeable; but though the under parts and wing linings may be black, the tail and flight feathers are usually pale below and the primaries conspicuously white at their bases. This white shows on the upper surface as a light patch near the end of the wing.

HABITS: When migrating these birds soar high in the air, but when hunting they alternately flap and glide along 50 to 200 feet above the ground. A rough-leg can be identified at almost any distance by its habit of stopping suddenly in mid-air to hover for a few seconds with rapidly beating wings or hanging motionless on an updraft while it looks for prey. Like other Buteos, it uses lookout perches, favoring low ones, like fence posts, in preference to trees. In the North the food of this rather weak-footed hawk is almost wholly composed of lemmings. On wintering grounds mice are the chief food. In some areas these birds feed on ground squirrels, pocket gophers, and shrews as well as on carrion. Southward and northward migrations usually coincide with the fall or thawing of heavy snow, as they do all their hunting over open, grassy areas or in fallow fields. Along the seacoast they are largely confined to extensive open salt marshes and adjacent sand dunes and meadows. They commonly feed in the half-light of early morning or evening, probably because the small mammals on which they prey are more active then than in midday. They are notably gentle and unsuspicious and so easy to shoot that they are sometimes slaughtered at concentration points along their migration routes. If only hawk shooters could be persuaded to open the stomach of every bird they shoot, some at least might in time realize the folly of killing these useful birds.

VOICE: Various sibilant, whistled notes, sometimes very loud, at other times soft, musical, and plaintive.

NEST: (I. 31, A., N. 41) Placed at the high point of a rock outcrop, cliff ledge, stream bank, or boulder, where it commands a good view of the surrounding country, or in the top of the tallest tree, 20 or 30 feet aboveground. The same site is used repeatedly, and a large mass of sticks accumulates; the nest is generally lined with bunches of grass and moss. In normal years 3 or 4 eggs are a clutch, but in peak lemming years 5 or 6 are common. The eggs (2.2 x 1.8) are greenish-white with brown markings.

DARK PHASE   LIGHT PHASE

RANGE: (P. M.) Breeds in the arctic tundra and the northern edge of the Hudsonian forest throughout the Northern Hemisphere. Winters from its breeding grounds south in North America to North Carolina, s. Louisiana, s. New Mexico, and s. California; abroad to Switzerland, Transcaspia, and Japan.

Ferruginous Rough-legged Hawk* *Buteo regalis*—✷43
(Ferruginous Rough-legged Buzzard)   L. 24; W. 56

IDENTIFICATION: The pale head, largely white tail, white patch on the upper wing surface near the tip, and the bright red-

dish-brown of the shoulders, rump, and thighs of a normal
adult are distinctive. Young are less reddish above and rather
uniformly pale buffy below, and the tail is barred with gray
and brown toward the tip. Melanistic birds are dark above
except for a uniformly grayish tail and a white wing patch,
and dark below except for the silvery-white tail and flight
feathers.

LIGHT PHASE

DARK PHASE

HABITS: (Age 20 yrs.) On the High Plains and in the Great
Basin country a big reddish-brown hawk hunting close to the
ground or perched on a fence or knoll is likely to be a ferruginous rough-leg. It is often locally known as squirrel hawk
because of its fondness for the various ground squirrels that
are so abundant in many western areas and often so destructive to cultivated crops. Rabbits, mice, and the host of other
small rodents of vast open grasslands and semi-arid areas are
also utilized for food. Occasionally a bird like a meadowlark
is captured, but birds do not form an appreciable part of the
diet.

Despite the fact that for more than 100 years every ornithologist who has written about this bird has called attention
to its great value as a check on rodents and its complete
harmlessness to poultry, this once abundant species has been
so persecuted that it is now rare in many parts of its former
range. Even today it is not unusual to see carcasses of these

fine birds draped over highway fences—grim reminders of
how much educational work we still have to do.

VOICE: Rather weak, high-pitched screams and squeals, some of
which are quite harsh and gull-like.

NEST: (I. 28, A., N. 60) Either in the tallest available tree
anywhere from 6 to 60 feet up, on a cliff ledge, or on top of
a rocky pinnacle or boulder-strewn elevation. Nests are used
year after year and sometimes reach enormous size. They are
made of large sticks, old bones, and other miscellaneous
material with a lining of bunch grass, shredded bark, and,
invariably, cow or horse dung. The 5 eggs (2.4 x 1.9) are
white, boldly marked with browns.

RANGE: (P. M.) Breeds from s. Manitoba and s. Alberta south
to s. New Mexico, east to w. Nebraska and n.w. Texas, and
west to c. Oregon and Nevada. Winters from s. South Dakota
and e. Oregon south to Hidalgo and s. Lower California and
wanders east to Wisconsin, Illinois, and Louisiana and west
through California.

Gray Hawk*
(Mexican Goshawk)

Buteo nitida—#42
L. 17; W. 35

IDENTIFICATION: The white rump and broadly banded tail are
good field marks. In flight the finely barred wing linings are
the same color as the breast, but flight feathers are white,
tipped with black. Young birds have numerous dark bars on
the tail and much light reddish-brown on the upper parts.

HABITS: This tropical species, which barely reaches our borders, inhabits the mature open woodlands of river valleys in the semi-arid and otherwise rather open country of our Southwest, feeding in the woods and in adjacent grasslands. Although a Buteo, it has a swift, direct flight and captures a wide variety of prey. It seems especially fond of lizards, but snakes, insects, rodents, and birds are also taken.

VOICE: A musical piping note as well as more sibilant calls.

NEST: (A.) Generally in the slender top branches of a very tall tree in a wooded river or creek bottom. Nests are small, rather flat platforms of twigs, most of which are broken off alive and green. The 2 or 3 white eggs (2.0 x 1.6) are unmarked.

RANGE: (P. M.) Breeds from the United States-Mexican border region south to s. Brazil and e. Bolivia. There is a winter withdrawal of the most northerly breeders into n. Mexico.

Harris' Hawk*   *Parabuteo unicinctus*—✕44
(Chestnut-thighed Buzzard)   ♂ L. 19; W. 42; ♀ L. 22; W. 45

IDENTIFICATION: The extensive white area above and below at the base of the long white-tipped tail is a good field mark in any plumage. In the sooty-black adult the chestnut wing linings and thighs are often conspicuous in flight. The less blackish young are more or less streaked with white below; the thighs are paler and finely barred with white and the tail is light brown below without a conspicuous tip.

HABITS: The semi-arid lands of the Southwest, where thickets of mesquite and other thorny shrubs are scattered over flat open grasslands and the watercourses are a tangle of low trees and shrubs, are the home of this heavy, powerfully built, but often sluggish-appearing hawk. Most feeding is done in the early morning or evening, and during much of the midday period the birds sit on a conspicuous perch paying little attention to anything, or soar high in the air. When on the hunt their flight is powerful and fast and they dash through thickets and along stream margins with great speed and control. Apparently they are able to capture rodents and birds with equal ease and are not above eating carrion. Thus their diet is largely a matter of what happens to be locally most abundant and easiest to obtain.

VOICE: A low, harsh cry or a more prolonged scream.

NEST: (A.) Generally low, in the top of a cactus, yucca, mesquite, or other low tree, anywhere from 5 to 30 feet up; of sticks and lined with grass, green twigs, and other soft material; usually small and compact. The 3 or 4 eggs (2.1 x 1.7) are white, some faintly marked with brown.

RANGE: (P. M.) Breeds from s. Texas, s. New Mexico, and s.e. California south to c. Argentina and c. Chile. Winters from breeding areas south. Large flocks are encountered in fall, indicating some migration or wandering at this season.

Black Hawk*   *Buteogallus anthracinus*—⚟45
(Crab Hawk)   L. 21; W. 48

IDENTIFICATION: This is a chunky bird with short, broad wings and a short tail, white at the base and tip and with a broad white central band. The underwing is black with some rusty in the flight feathers and a short diagonal white patch near the end. The brown young have light heads, buffy wing linings, white flight feathers, and a tail that shows about 6 black and white bands.

HABITS: The very broad wings give this bird great buoyancy and a superficial resemblance to the black vulture. It soars with ease and at times indulges in spectacular earthward dives. In flight the long yellow legs frequently dangle in a very distinctive manner. Moist woodlands in the vicinity of water seem to be the normal habitat. The species usually appears rather tame and sluggish, spending much of its time perched on a low branch of a tree overlooking water. Fish, frogs, crayfish, and reptiles are often its chief foods, but in some regions it feeds almost exclusively on land crabs. Small mammals, birds, and insects are also included in its rather broad diet.

VOICE: A loud, harsh, strongly accented call of 4 distinct notes that has been likened to the squawk of a night heron. Other whistled or squeal-like calls have been noted.

NEST: (A.) Commonly 2 to 30 feet up in a small tree, often saddled on a clump of mistletoe; constructed of sticks with a lining of green leaves. New nests are small but are used year after year and may become very large. The 1 or 2 eggs (2.3 x 1.8) are white, sparingly marked with brown.

RANGE: (R.) Occurs from the United States-Mexican border region south to n. South America and the Lesser Antilles.

Golden Eagle* *Aquila chrysaëtos*—✳44
♂ L. 33; W. 79; Wt. 9 lbs.; ♀ L. 38; W. 87; Wt. 12 lbs.

IDENTIFICATION: Eagles have noticeably big heads and necks and powerful bills, and the broad wings of this species give it a robust look. Adults are dark except for the inconspicuous "golden" head and white tail base. Young have white tails with a broad, sharply defined black terminal band and show a white patch on both wing surfaces.

HABITS: (Age 30 yrs.) The range of this splendid bird covers more than half the land in the world, but it breeds and is most commonly encountered in hilly or mountainous country where extensive areas of open land are available for hunting. After the nesting season young and, to some extent, adults wander widely and may turn up almost anywhere. In recent years the golden eagle has been not uncommon during the fall flight of birds of prey down the Appalachian Mountain Range—wintering in its southern half. It also seems likely that a few breed in our eastern mountains. In the more rugged West they are quite uniformly distributed but never common, as studies show that each pair defends a breeding territory of anywhere from 20 to 60 square miles, a township (36 square miles) being about the average. No other golden eagle is allowed to enter this territory, and occasionally, if food is scarce, the presence of red-tails and horned owls is so much resented that they are systematically hunted down and killed.

ADULT   IMMATURE

The golden eagle makes extensive use of air currents. If within the breeding territory there is a hill or cliff that deflects the wind and creates a strong updraft, it serves as a kind of elevator. The bird carries heavy prey into it, then with set wings spirals upward until enough altitude has been gained for a straight glide to the aerie. The food of any wide-ranging species like this is varied. Rabbits, squirrels, woodchucks, and other small mammals are staples, but at times these eagles successfully attack larger prey like raccoons and foxes, and they have been known to kill deer that were weakened by starvation and handicapped by deep snow. They also take skunks and domestic cats. Sometimes they feed heavily on coots, ducks, grouse, and other big birds, including, on occasion, domestic fowl. As they are capable of carrying prey nearly equal to their own weight, it is not surprising that an occasional individual or pair gets into the habit of picking up such domestic stock as young pigs, kids, or lambs. However, studies at hundreds of nests indicate that this is rare and is no justification for persecuting the species as a whole. Like so many birds of prey, the golden eagle also consumes a great deal of carrion, and the fact that it is found eating an animal is no proof that it caused its death.

VOICE: The seldom-heard calls are a series of short, high-pitched squeals and a longer, sibilant whistle.

NEST: (I. 43, A., N. 75) The aerie of this great bird is on a ledge near the top of a cliff commanding a wide expanse of country or, less often, in the top of a large tall tree. Generally a pair has 2 or more nest sites in their territory which they use in alternate years. The nest itself, especially when on a ledge, becomes in time a huge mass of material, ranging from large sticks to all kinds of rubbish and is lined with grass or moss. The 2 or 3 whitish eggs (2.9 x 2.3) vary from finely spotted with brown to virtually unmarked.

RANGE: (P. M.) Breeds throughout parts of the entire Northern Hemisphere. In North America from the edge of the arctic tundra in Ungava, n. Mackenzie, and n. Alaska south to North Carolina (mts.), c. Mexico, and n. Lower California.

Sea Eagle*   *Haliaeetus albicilla*—✳44
(Gray Sea Eagle)   ♂ L. 34; W. 85; ♀ L. 38; W. 92

IDENTIFICATION: Adults are distinguishable from bald eagles by their gray heads. Young are a paler brown than most young balds, and the feather tips and centers are so dark that the upper parts appear spotted and the under parts streaked.

HABITS: This is the Eurasian equivalent of our bald eagle, and the two seem to occupy virtually identical ecological niches in the wildlife communities of the areas where they breed. Young birds are great wanderers and do not nest until they assume adult plumage at about 4 years of age. Undoubtedly an occasional young Greenland bird wanders south to winter on our northern coasts, but its great similarity to a young bald eagle makes sight identification questionable. Like our bird, this white-tailed eagle occurs along seacoasts and inland near large lakes, rivers, and marshes, where it feeds on fish, carrion, water birds, and small mammals.

VOICE: A squeaky, high-pitched chatter.

NEST: (I. 45, A., N. 70) On a sea cliff or in the top of a tall tree. The nests are used year after year and become huge masses of sticks and debris of every description with a lining of soft materials. The 2 eggs (3.0 x 2.3) are white and unmarked.

RANGE: (P. M.) Breeds from c.w. Greenland and Iceland east through n. Europe and Asia to the Commander Islands and south to n. Germany, Greece, Persia, and Japan. Winters south to n. Africa, n. India, and s. China. Has wandered south to Massachusetts and east to the Aleutians.

Bald Eagle*   *Haliaeetus leucocephalus*—✳44
♂ L. 34; W. 80; ♀ L. 36; W. 85; Wt. 13 lbs.

IDENTIFICATION: Adults are unmistakable. Young have longer wings and tails than goldens and bigger bills and seem to have a lot more head and neck. Although the young lack definite white areas until they develop white heads and tails early in their fourth year, the plumage of many is irregularly and often extensively blotched with white. When soaring the eagles keep the wings horizontal.

ADULT   IMMATURE

HABITS: The bald eagle and its relatives, often called sea eagles, are seldom found far from water, but lakes, large rivers, and coastal bays are as acceptable as seacoast. The birds seem to mate for life and occupy the same territory year after year, although they may leave it for a few months after the young have fledged. An eagle's territory is generally at least several square miles in area, and in it a pair frequently has more than one nest ready for use at any time. The great horned owl, the most serious disturber of their peace except man, is apparently able to take over the eagles' nest at will and force them into another site.

Fish are the staple and sometimes the only food of bald eagles. Some they catch by plucking them from the surface of the water; others they steal from ospreys; a great many they find dead, like the spent salmon of the Northwest that die after spawning. In the Far North these eagles often nest near colonies of sea birds like murres and auks on which they feed. Elsewhere they occasionally feed on other birds and mammals.

When not on their breeding grounds bald eagles, especially the dark young, are apt to concentrate in favorable feeding areas—ice-choked rivers, densely populated duck marshes, and even garbage dumps. A healthy duck that can fly is too fast for them, but they quickly spot a crippled, sick, or lead-poisoned duck and keep after it until it is so exhausted that it can be picked up from the water. It has been estimated that one third of all ducks shot are never retrieved and thousands more are known to die of lead poisoning. This gives the eagles plenty of humane and useful scavenging work in fall and winter. The charge that this species eats lambs, pigs, and chickens is generally without foundation unless the animal was already dead when the eagle found it.

In recognition of its status as our national emblem, the bald eagle is now fully protected by federal law, and heavy penalties are imposed for molesting nest, eggs, young, or adults anywhere in the United States at any time.

VOICE: A high-pitched squeaky cackle or chatter.

NEST: (I. 35, A., N. 75) Usually in the main crotch at the top of a large, living tree, rarely in a dead one, but in a few regions cliff-top ledges are common sites. Nests are used again and again and grow in time to enormous size (one record was 20 feet deep and 10 feet across). Sticks are the basic structural material, but all manner of trash is carried to fill in the center, and quantities of any available soft material are used for lining. The 2 eggs (2.8 x 2.1) are dull white.

RANGE: (P. M.) Breeds from Ungava, n. Mackenzie, Alaska, and n.e. Siberia south to s. Florida, the Gulf Coast, n. Mexico, and s. Lower California. There is a southward movement of northern breeders in the fall and a northward one in the late spring from the southern areas where eagles breed in midwinter—Florida-reared young summer in Canada.

Marsh Hawk　　　　　　　　　*Circus cyaneus*—✳39
(Hen-Harrier)　♂ L. 19; W. 42; ♀ L. 22; W. 49; Wt. 1¼ lbs.

IDENTIFICATION: This harrier has long wings, a long tail, and curious owl-like facial disks, but its conspicuous white rump is its best identification mark. The pale gray male with black wing tips is gull-like in appearance and quite different from the brown females and young.

ADULT

IMMATURE

HABITS: (Age 8 yrs.) A large gray or brown bird slowly quartering near the ground, alternating a few deliberate beats of its long wings with glides, is sure to be a marsh hawk. In gliding, the wings are held well above the horizontal in an open V and the body constantly tilts from side to side as the bird alters the direction of flight. In spring males engage in spectacular courtship with a series of dives, each ending in a sharp upturn and stall, followed by another dive. These birds always perch on a low post or snag near the ground, but occasionally during migration, when making use of air currents, they are seen high in the air.

　　Although this hawk has suffered from extensive and none too wise drainage of marshes and from wanton persecution, it has survived better than most birds of prey. In many areas its feeding grounds have expanded as forests have been replaced by low growths. Its habit of nesting on the ground, while exposing it to animal predation, makes it less vulnerable to human disturbance than hawks that build tree nests. Its reproductive rate is nearly twice that of most hawks.

Small mammals up to the size of rabbits are the primary food. In migration and on wintering grounds marsh hawks often gather in large numbers in areas where meadow mice or, in the South, cotton rats have reached high population levels. Though it is not a fast flier, the bird's hunting method, in which it is greatly aided by the long, rudderlike tail, enables it to surprise and catch a good many small birds. Frogs, snakes, crayfish, large insects, carrion, and fish are also taken as occasion offers. At times an individual may make serious inroads on a flock of young chickens if they are allowed to wander too far from the barnyard.

VOICE: A series of short, high-pitched squeals or whistles.

NEST: (I. 31, A., N. 38) On the ground in or adjacent to a low meadow or marshy area and placed where shrubs or tall weedy growths afford concealment. In dry areas it often amounts to little more than a loose cup of weed stems and grasses, but in wet areas it may be a substantial mound of such materials on a stick foundation or saddled on a sedge tussock or willow clump. The 5 eggs (1.8 x 1.4) are white or pale blue, occasionally with a few brown spots.

RANGE: (P. M.) Occurs through most of the Northern Hemisphere. Breeds from Newfoundland, c. Quebec, n. Manitoba, n.w. Mackenzie, and n. Alaska south to s.e. Virginia (rarely Florida), s. Indiana, Arkansas, s. Texas, and n. Lower California. Winters from c. New England, s. Michigan, South Dakota, and s. British Columbia south to the n. West Indies and Colombia. Abroad it breeds in Eurasia from the Arctic Circle south to n. Spain, Italy, Turkestan, and Tibet and winters south to n. Africa, India, and s. China.

OSPREYS   Family Pandioninae

Osprey*   *Pandion haliaetus*—✳44
(Fish Hawk)   L. 23; W. 68; Wt. 3½ lbs.

IDENTIFICATION: These large birds are unmistakable if seen well. In flight the wings appear quite long and the outer half usually has a characteristic backward sweep. Young birds differ only in being flecked with white above and washed with buffy below.

HABITS: (Age 21 yrs.) Provided they are not molested, ospreys will nest wherever reasonably extensive bodies of clear water and some sort of elevated nest sites exist. Seacoasts, bays, large lakes or rivers, and groups of small ponds are all acceptable. The birds have little fear of man and are excellent "watchdogs," cheeping loudly at intruders and driving off crows and other birds of prey. For this reason platforms on tall poles are often erected to encourage them to nest about homes and farmyards.

Their food consists entirely of fish. These they spot from heights of 30 to 100 feet; then after hovering a moment to get into position, they half close their wings and plunge into the water. The fish is seized in their talons, the toes of which are used in pairs, 2 to a side; this and the rough surface of the foot give them a firm grip on the slipperiest prey. After a catch they rise quickly, shake off the water, arrange the fish headfirst, and set out for their nest or feeding perch. If a bald eagle sees the catch from overhead it dives down and forces the osprey to give it up. For successful fishing ospreys must have clear water and fish that feed or swim near the surface. In salt water menhaden, mullet, sea cat, and, in spring, alewives and other herring provide the bulk of their food. In fresh water suckers, perch, and gizzard shad are common prey. Ospreys take some carp when they are spawning in shallow water, but these introduced fish often drastically reduce the bird's potential feeding grounds by roiling the water so badly that it cannot see its prey.

Unfortunately, ospreys are strongly attracted to hatcheries where large numbers of fish are concentrated in a small area. They are so fearless that it is almost impossible to drive them away. To date the none too satisfactory solution has been to shoot them, and in many regions they are becoming scarce as a result. A far better way is to screen the small ponds where cold-water fish like trout are kept. Warm-water pond fish like bass can be protected by keeping the ponds well fertilized. This not only makes the fish grow faster but produces a green algae "bloom" that makes it impossible for the osprey to fish the waters effectively.

VOICE: Distinctive in tone, although the notes vary considerably. Common calls are a long series of loud, sharp, high-pitched whistled notes that vary from a rising *whew, whew* to a rich *cheeap, cheeap*. From a distance they sometimes suggest the liquid notes of a purple martin.

NEST: (I. 38, A., N. 52) Singly or in loose colonies scattered over a considerable area. Nests may be any height above-ground and are built in trees, living or dead, on man-made structures of all kinds, on rocky canyonside pinnacles, and sometimes on the ground along the upper beach. Year after year material is added until the nest becomes an enormous mass of sticks and any other trash the birds can carry, much of it gleaned from the wrack along the upper beach. The 3 eggs (2.4 x 1.8) are white to cinnamon, heavily blotched with browns.

RANGE: (P. M.) Practically world-wide. In the Western Hemisphere breeds from Newfoundland, s. Ungava, n. Manitoba, n.w. Mackenzie, and n.w. Alaska, south to the Bahamas, the Florida Keys, the Gulf Coast to British Honduras, and to w. Mexico. Winters from Florida, the Gulf States, and s. California south to Paraguay, n. Argentina, and Chile. Also breeds in all of Europe, n. Africa, most of Asia, the East Indies, and Australia and migrates to South Africa and India.

SUMMER

Common Loon
p. 3

WINTER

WINTER

SUMMER

Yellow-billed
Loon   p. 4

SUMMER

WINTER

Arctic Loon
p. 5

WINTER

SUMMER

Red-throated
Loon   p. 6

PLATE 1

Pied-billed Grebe p. 12

CHICK SUMMER JUVENILE WINTER

Least Grebe p. 11

SUMMER

WINTER SUMMER

WINTER

Horned Grebe
p. 9

Western Grebe
p. 11

WINTER Eared Grebe
p. 10

SUMMER

WINTER

SUMMER

Red-necked Grebe
p. 7

PLATE 2

Canada Goose
p. 66

LARGE RACE

Brant
p. 68

SMALL RACE

Barnacle
Goose
p. 69

Trumpeter
Swan
p. 65

Whistling Swan
p. 63

ADULT

IMMATURE

ADULT

IMMATURE

Mute Swan
p. 62

PLATE 3

White-fronted Goose
p. 70

ADULT

IMMATURE

Blue Goose
p. 72

IMMATURE

ADULT

Snow x Blue
hybrid
p. 73

Snow Goose
p. 71

ADULT

IMMATURE

Ross' Goose
p. 74

ADULT

IMMATURE

PLATE 4

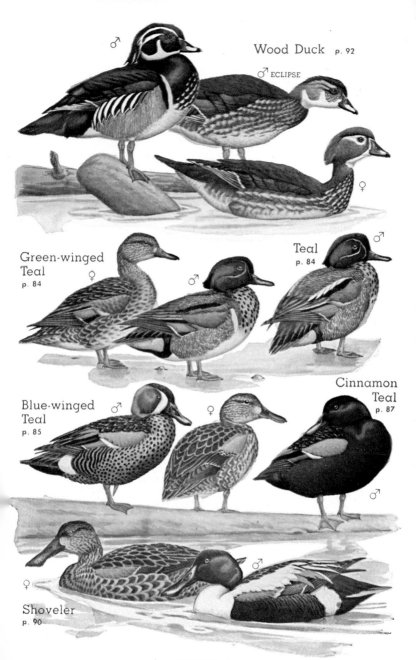

♂

Wood Duck p. 92

♂ ECLIPSE

♀

Green-winged
Teal
♀
p. 84

♂

Teal
p. 84

♂

Blue-winged
Teal
p. 85

♂

♀

Cinnamon
Teal
p. 87

♂

♀

♂

Shoveler
p. 90

PLATE 5

Widgeon
p. 88
♀

♂

♂

American
Widgeon
♀
p. 89

Pintail
p. 82

♂

♀

White-cheeked
Pintail p. 83

Fulvous
Tree Duck
p. 75

Black-bellied
Tree Duck
p. 74

IMMATURE

ADULT

PLATE 6

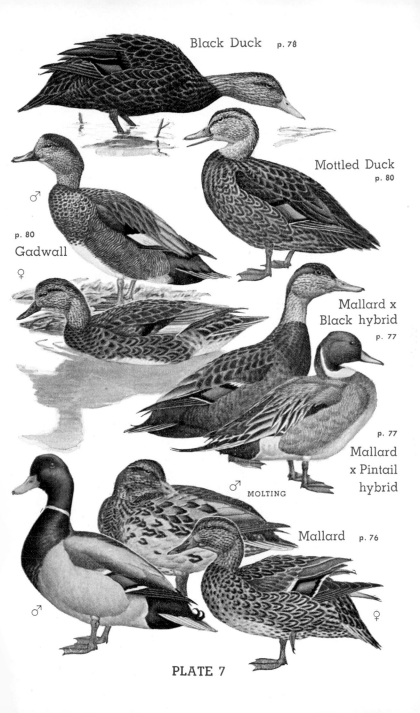

Black Duck p. 78

Mottled Duck p. 80

p. 80
Gadwall
♂
♀

Mallard x
Black hybrid
p. 77

p. 77
Mallard
x Pintail
hybrid

Mallard p. 76

♂ MOLTING

♂

♀

PLATE 7

Canvasback
p. 96

Redhead
p. 93
♂

♀

Ring-necked
Duck p. 95

♂   ♀

Scaup Duck
p. 98   ♂

♀

IMMATURE ♂

♀

Lesser
Scaup Duck ♂
p. 99

PLATE 8

Bufflehead
p. 103
♀
♂

Barrow's
Goldeneye
p. 102

♀

Goldeneye p. 100
♂

Hooded
Merganser
p. 117
♀

♂

Merganser
p 118
♂
♀

Red-breasted
Merganser
p 120
♀
♂

PLATE 9

Harlequin
Duck p. 106

♂

♀

Labrador Duck ♂
p. 107

SUMMER
♀

WINTER
♀

SUMMER ♂

Oldsquaw
p. 104

WINTER
♂

Masked Duck
p. 117

♂

♀

♀

♂ WINTER

♂ SUMMER

Ruddy Duck p. 115

PLATE 10

King Eider
p. 110

♂

♀

Eider
p. 108

IMMATURE

♂

♀

Surf Scoter
p. 112

♂

♀

White
winged
Scoter
p. 111

♀

♂

Black Scoter
p. 114

♂

♀

PLATE 11

Gallinule p. 204
ADULT

CHICK

IMMATURE

IMMATURE

ADULT

Purple Gallinule
p. 204

American Coot p. 205
ADULT   IMMATURE

CHICK

Jaçana
p. 207

IMMATURE   ADULT

WINTER

Corn Crake
p. 203

PLATE 12

Virginia Rail
p. 198

ADULT

IMMATURE

CHICK

Sora   p. 200

ADULT

Black Rail
p. 202

IMMATURE

Yellow
Rail p. 201

. 197
Clapper
Rail

King Rail
p. 196

CHICK

PLATE 13

Reddish Egret
p. 43

DARK PHASE

Little
Blue Heron
p. 45

MOLTING

IMMATURE

WHITE PHASE

ADULT

IMMATURE

Great Blue
Heron
p. 40

ADULT

Snowy
Egret
p. 43

Wurdemann's
Heron
p. 39

Egret
p. 42

Great White
Heron p. 38

PLATE 14

ADULT

IMMATURE

ADULT

IMMATURE

Night Heron p. 47

Yellow-
crowned
Night Heron
p. 48

ADULT

IMMATURE

Tricolored
Heron p. 44

Green
Heron
p. 46

ADULT

IMMATURE

American
Bittern
p. 49

♂

♀

Least Bittern
p. 51

DARK PHASE

PLATE 15

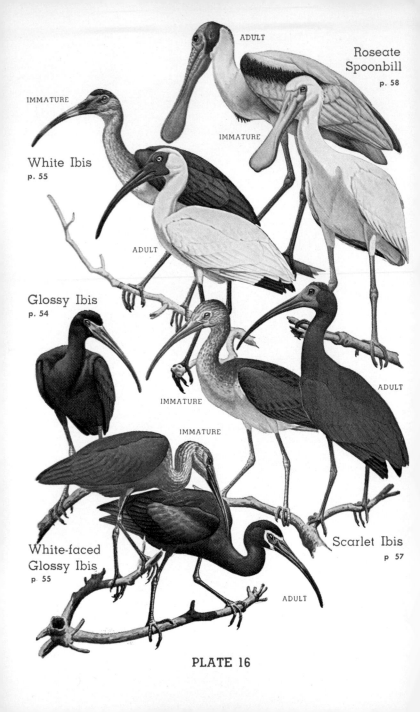

ADULT

Roseate
Spoonbill
p. 58

IMMATURE

White Ibis
p. 55

IMMATURE

ADULT

Glossy Ibis
p. 54

IMMATURE

ADULT

IMMATURE

White-faced
Glossy Ibis
p. 55

Scarlet Ibis
p 57

ADULT

PLATE 16

IMMATURE

American
Flamingo
p. 59

ADULT

Sandhill Crane
p. 192

IMMATURE

IMMATURE

Whooping
Crane

p. 191

ADULT

Wood Ibis
p. 52

Limpkin
p. 194

PLATE 17

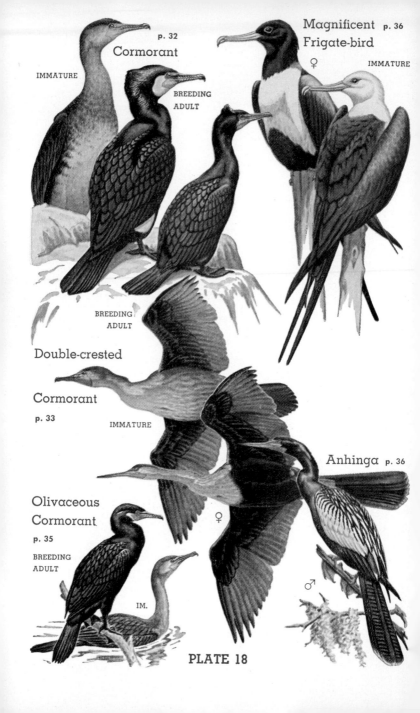

Cormorant p. 32

IMMATURE

BREEDING ADULT

Magnificent p. 36 Frigate-bird

♀

IMMATURE

BREEDING ADULT

Double-crested

Cormorant

p. 33

IMMATURE

Anhinga p. 36

Olivaceous Cormorant

p. 35

BREEDING ADULT

IM.

♀

♂

PLATE 18

Brown Pelican
p. 27

Magnificent
Frigate-
bird
p. 36

IMMATURE

BREEDING ADULT

IMMATURE

♂

ADULT

Blue-faced
Booby p. 28

White
Pelican
p. 25

Gannet
IMMATURE   p. 31

IMMATURE

ADULT

Brown
Booby
p. 29

BROWN
PHASE

WHITE
PHASE

IMMATURE

ADULT

Red-footed
Booby p. 30

PLATE 19

LIGHT PHASE

DARK PHASE

Bermuda Petrel
p. 19

Fulmar
p. 20

Frigate Petrel
p. 23

Storm Petrel
p. 22

Black-capped Petrel
p. 18

Leach's Petrel
p. 21

Wilson's Petrel
p. 22

Common Shearwater
p. 14

Great Shearwater
p. 16

p. 13
Sooty Shearwater

Dusky Shearwater
p. 15

Cinereous Shearwater
p. 17

PLATE 20

Skua
p. 261

LIGHT PHASE

IMMATURE

Long-tailed
Jaeger
p. 260

JUVENILE

IMMATURE

DARK PHASE

LIGHT PHASE

p. 259
Parasitic Jaeger

IMMATURE

DARK PHASE

p. 258
Pomarine Jaeger

LIGHT PHASE

PLATE 21

IMMATURE

Herring Gull p. 268

ADULT
SUMMER

ADULT
WINTER

JUVENILE

JUVENILE

JUVENILE

ADULT
SUMMER

Iceland
Gull p. 265

IMMATURE

ADULT
SUMMER

Glaucous Gull p. 264

PLATE 22

IMMATURE

Ring-billed
Gull p. 271

ADULT
SUMMER

ADULT
SUMMER

Common
Gull
p. 272

IMMATURE

ADULT SUMMER

ADULT
SUMMER

California
Gull
p. 270

ADULT
WINTER

IM.

Ivory Gull
p. 279

ADULT

PLATE 23

IMMATURE

Black-headed Gull p. 273

ADULT WINTER

ADULT SUMMER

IMMATURE

ADULT WINTER

Laughing Gull
p. 275

ADULT
SUMMER

IMMATURE

Franklin's
Gull p. 276

ADULT
WINTER

ADULT SUMMER

IMMATURE

PLATE 24

Kittiwake p. 280

IMMATURE

ADULT
SUMMER

ADULT
WINTER

ADULT WINTER

ADULT
SUMMER

Sabine's
Gull p. 282

IMMATURE

ADULT
WINTER

IMMATURE

ADULT
SUMMER

Bonaparte's Gull
p. 277

PLATE 25

Little Gull
p. 278

ADULT WINTER

IMMATURE

ADULT SUMMER

Ross' Gull p. 281

ADULT SUMMER

IMMATURE

ADULT WINTER

IMMATURE

ADULT SUMMER

Lesser Black-backed
Gull p. 267

IMMATURE

Great Black-backed
Gull p. 266

ADULT SUMMER

PLATE 26

Yellow-billed Tropic-bird

p. 24

IMMATURE

ADULT

ADULT

Bridled Tern

p. 290

ADULT SUMMER

ADULT WINTER

IMMATURE

ADULT MOLTING

ADULT

p. 294

IMMATURE

Black Tern

Sooty Tern

p. 289

IMMATURE

Noddy Tern

p. 295

ADULT

IMMATURE

PLATE 27

Common Tern

JUVENILE

p. 285

SUMMER

WINTER

p. 287

Arctic Tern

SUMMER

SUMMER

Forster's Tern
p. 284

Roseate Tern

p. 288   SUMMER

WINTER

WINTER

Sandwich Tern   p. 292

JUVENILE

SUMMER

PLATE 28

Royal Tern p. 291

WINTER

SUMMER

SUMMER

Caspian Tern
p. 293

WINTER

JUVENILE

JUVENILE

WINTER

Least Tern
p. 290

JUVENILE

Gull-billed Tern
p. 283

SUMMER

PLATE 29

Mountain Plover
p. 215

SPRING

FALL

Killdeer
p. 214

FALL

SPRING

Turnstone
p. 216

FALL

SPRING

Snowy Plover
p. 212

Thick-billed Plover
p. 213

♀   ♂

FALL

SPRING

Piping Plover
p. 212

FALL

SPRING

Ringed Plover
p. 211

PLATE 30

Black-bellied Plover
p. 218

FALL

SPRING

FALL

SPRING

American
Golden
Plover
p. 217

Ruff p. 250

SPRING

Reeve p. 250

FALL

Purple
Sandpiper
p. 234

Lapwing
p. 210

FALL

FALL

SPRING

PLATE 31

Red Phalarope p. 254

FALL

SPRING

♀

♂

Northern Phalarope

p. 256

♀

SPRING

♂

FALL

♀

♂

SPRING

Wilson's
Phalarope

p. 256

FALL

PLATE 32

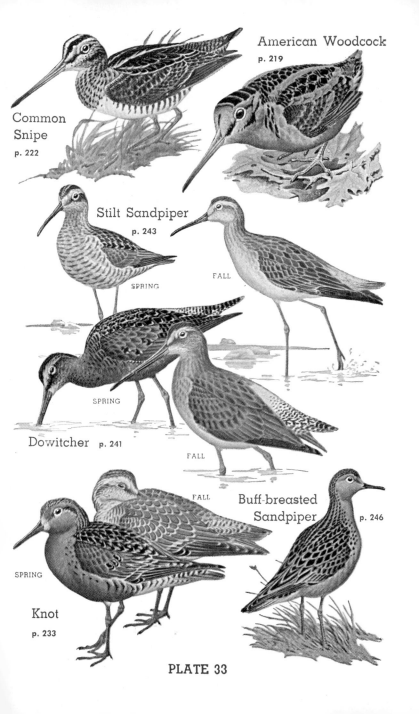

Common
Snipe
p. 222

American Woodcock
p. 219

Stilt Sandpiper
p. 243

SPRING

FALL

SPRING

Dowitcher   p. 241

FALL

FALL

Buff-breasted
Sandpiper   p. 246

SPRING

Knot
p. 233

PLATE 33

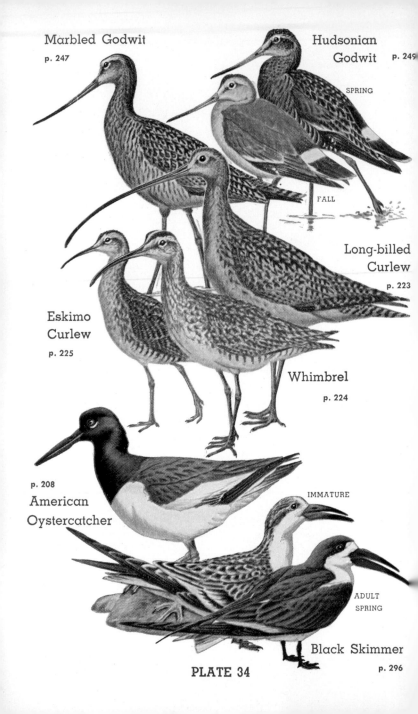

Marbled Godwit
p. 247

Hudsonian Godwit
p. 249

SPRING

FALL

Long-billed Curlew
p. 223

Eskimo Curlew
p. 225

Whimbrel
p. 224

p. 208
American Oystercatcher

IMMATURE

ADULT SPRING

Black Skimmer
p. 296

PLATE 34

Bar-tailed Godwit
p. 248

SPRING

FALL

Willet
p. 229

SPRING

FALL

p. 253

Black-
necked
Stilt

Greater
Yellowlegs
p. 231

American
Avocet
p. 252

Lesser
Yellowlegs
p. 232

Solitary
Sand-
piper
p. 229

Upland
Plover
p. 226

PLATE 35

White-rumped
Sandpiper

p. 236

SPRING

FALL

Baird's
Sandpiper

p. 237

SPRING

FALL

Western
Sandpiper

p. 245

Semipalmated
Sandpiper

p. 243

SPRING

FALL

Least
Sandpiper

p. 238

FALL

SPRING

PLATE 36

Pectoral Sandpiper
p. 235

Curlew Sandpiper
p. 239

FALL

SPRING

SPRING

FALL

Dunlin p. 240

IMMATURE

SPRING

Sanderling
p. 251

FALL

FALL

Spotted Sandpiper p. 227

SPRING

PLATE 37

Puffin
p. 304
SUMMER

SUMMER

Dovekie
p. 302

WINTER

Great Auk
p. 297

WINTER

IMMATURE

SUMMER

Thick-billed Murre

p. 301

IMMATURE

WINTER

ADULT

p. 298

Razor-billed Auk

RINGED PHASE

SUMMER

Murre
p. 300

SUMMER
p. 303

Black Guillemot

WINTER

WINTER

IMMATURE

PLATE 38

Mississippi Kite
p. 129

ADULT

IMMATURE

White-tailed Kite
p. 126

ADULT

♂

♀

IMMATURE

Everglade
Kite
p. 130

Swallow-
tailed
Kite
p. 127

IMMATURE
♀

ADULT
♀

Marsh Hawk p. 159

ADULT
♂

PLATE 39

ADULT   IMMATURE   Goshawk p. 131

IMMATURE

Cooper's
Hawk
p. 135

♂
ADULT   IMMATURE   ♀

Sharp-shinned
Hawk   p. 133

ADULT

BLACK PHASE

Gyrfalcon
p. 164

GRAY
PHASE

WHITE
PHASE

PLATE 40

Prairie
Falcon
p. 165

ADULT

IMMATURE

Peregrine
Falcon
p. 167

♀

Sparrow
Hawk

p. 171

♂

IMMATURE

ADULT

p. 169

Aplomado
Falcon

IMMATURE

ADULT

Pigeon
Hawk

p. 169

PLATE 41

DARK PHASE

Red-tailed   Hawk p. 136

IMMATURE

Harlan's
Hawk

p. 139

DARK PHASE

NORMAL
PHASE

LIGHT PHASE

IMMATURE

Gray Hawk

p. 151

ADULT

ADULT

IMMATURE

IMMATURE

Red-shouldered
Hawk p. 140

ADULT

Broad-winged
Hawk p. 141

PLATE 42

NORMAL
PHASE

Swainson's
Hawk p. 143

IMMATURE

DARK
PHASE

Rough-
legged
Hawk
p. 148

DARK
PHASE

DARK PHASE

NORMAL PHASE

DARK
PHASE

IMMATURE

Ferruginous
Rough-legged
Hawk p. 149

ADULT

White-tailed
Hawk p. 145

NORMAL
PHASE

PLATE 43

IMMATURE

Bald Eagle

p. 157

p. 154

ADULT

Golden Eagle

ADULT

IMMATURE

Zone-tailed
Hawk

p. 144

ADULT

IMMATURE

Sea
Eagle p. 156

IMMATURE

Osprey p. 160

ADULT

p. 152

PLATE 44

Harris' Haw

ADULT

Turkey Vulture
p. 123

IMMATURE

IMMATURE

Black Vulture
p. 124

ADULT

Caracara
p. 163

IMMATURE

ADULT

Black
Hawk
p. 153

DARK PHASE

LIGHT PHASE

Short-tailed Hawk
p. 147

IMMATURE

PLATE 45

Pheasant p. 186

♂

♀

Chachalaca p. 173

Turkey p. 188

Sharp-tailed Grouse p. 181

Prairie Chicken p. 179

Ruffed Grouse p. 175

♂ Spruce Grouse p. 174

♀

PLATE 46

Willow Ptarmigan
p. 177

SPRING ♀

WINTER

FALL ♂

SPRING ♀

WINTER

Rock Ptarmigan
p. 178

FALL ♂

Bobwhite
p. 184

♂

♀

Scaled Quail
p. 185

Partridge
p. 182

PLATE 47

Red-billed Pigeon p. 306

White-crowned Pigeon p. 305

p. 307

Rock Dove

White-fronted Dove p. 314

Passenger Pigeon p. 311

Mourning Dove p. 309

Zenaida Dove p. 308

Key West Quail Dove p. 315

White-winged Dove

Inca Dove p. 314

p. 313

Ground Dove

p. 30

PLATE 48

FALCONS and ALLIES   Family Falconidae

Caracara*   *Polyborus cheriway—* ✕45
(Mexican Eagle)   L. 23; W. 48

IDENTIFICATION: This bird has a big, long neck, remarkably
long legs, and a long tail. In any plumage the centrally pale
primaries and pale tail with a dark terminal band are distinctive.

HABITS: This handsome bird is the national emblem of our
neighbor, the Republic of Mexico, and appears on its seal
with a rattlesnake in its mouth. As its long legs suggest, it is
largely terrestrial, but it has a fast, direct flight, deep wingbeats alternating with short sails. Generally it flies close to the
ground, but there are times when it circles and soars like a
vulture. Caracaras are usually seen in pairs and are seldom
found far from open country, where they feed on a variety of
animal life as well as on carrion—their staple food when it
is available. The bird is in fact known in some places as
"king of the vultures," as it will keep vultures away from a
carcass until it has had its fill. Along the coast caracaras
sometimes force brown pelicans to disgorge their food, which
they then eat themselves. Snakes, lizards, frogs, turtles, small
mammals, insects, and fish are important, depending upon
availability. Birds are seldom caught, and the charge that
this species bothers domestic animals seems groundless and
is probably based on seeing them eat animals that have died
from other causes.

VOICE: Early and late in the day it utters the strange, harsh cackling call from which its name is derived.

NEST: (I. 28, A.) In some areas the nest site is the head of a palm, yucca, or cactus; in others, the crown of a tall tree or, rarely, a cliff ledge, at heights varying from 8 to 80 feet. The bulky, deeply cupped nest to which material is added year after year is made of locally abundant material such as palm-fruit stalks, small bushes, briars, or weed stalks. The 2 eggs (2.3 x 1.8) are white with a brownish wash and heavy brown markings.

RANGE: (R.) Occurs from c. Florida and Cuba, c. Texas, s.w. Arizona, and n. Lower California south to the Guianas and Peru.

Gyrfalcon*
Falco rusticolus— ✕40
L. 22; W. 48; Wt. 4 lbs.

IDENTIFICATION: These falcons are heavily built with a long tail tapering to a point and broad-based wings more triangular than a peregrine's. In flight they have a slow, powerful, short wingbeat, often interrupted by a short glide. Gyrs generally alight on a rise in open ground, but they also use tall poles. They commonly fly close to the ground, stopping suddenly to hover for a few seconds if something of interest is sighted. In both light and dark plumages they are rather uniformly colored above and below. In the gray phase there is more variation, but they lack the heavy mustache marks of the peregrine. Young are streaked instead of barred and spotted below and generally have more uniformly dark under parts.

HABITS: These falcons vary from virtually white to solid black; almost every color between the two extremes may be encountered. In n. Greenland the white phase seems dominant, but across the American Arctic a dark phase predominates, although a great many intermediates occur. The gyr is a versatile bird of prey, quite willing to subsist almost wholly on the small mouselike lemming or the large arctic hare if abundant, but when these animals become scarce, as they do periodically, it shifts to a bird diet, chiefly ptarmigan. When these prolific northern grouse gather into flocks and move to their wintering grounds gyrfalcons commonly follow them and winter in the same area. The teeming sea-bird colonies of the Arctic are another important source of food, the falcons often nesting near them and living on murres, dovekies, and kittiwakes. Shore birds and ducks are taken in summer, and when the gyrs wander down to our coasts in winter they are usually seen near the great gull concentrations.

VOICE: A staccato series of high-pitched notes producing a shrill chatter or rattling scream.

NEST: (I. 29, A.) These birds nest on almost any kind of rock ledge, the same site being used year after year. The nest consists of a few sticks, some moss and grass, but there is often an enormous accumulation of excrement and food waste. The 4 eggs (2.3 x 1.8) are white washed with reddish-brown and heavily spotted with browns.

RANGE: (P. M.) Breeds around the world in the open, treeless tundra of the Arctic south to the northern limit of tree growth. Some migrate south in winter, a few occasionally reaching Long Island, New York, e. Pennsylvania, Ohio, Minnesota, Montana, and Washington. Abroad they reach Great Britain, the Baltic, and c. Russia.

Prairie Falcon* *Falco mexicanus*—♯41
♂ L. 17½; W. 40; ♀ L. 19½; W. 42; Wt. 2 lbs.

IDENTIFICATION: The pale clay-colored upper parts and, in flight, the black areas where the wings join the pale under-body are distinctive. Young are more heavily marked below and have lead-colored feet and legs.

HABITS: (Age 9 yrs.) This splendid falcon is typically a bird of the dry, open country of our West. Although generally confined to lower elevations and foothills, nesting in badlands, canyons, and other rough areas, it ranges widely over adjacent grasslands and wanders into the high mountains and well-wooded country, where it is known to have occasionally nested. The bird is lighter and more agile than the peregrine and can outfly it at high altitudes; it uses short, powerful wing strokes, and there is little that it cannot overtake. Sparrows, horned larks, blackbirds, and meadowlarks provide much of its food, but it can handle magpies, doves, quail, partridge, and grouse. When hunting it often travels only 20 or 30 feet above the ground, hovering now and then to look for prey. Usually it captures and binds to its prey in the air, then carries it to a feeding perch in a tree or on a post. Such mammals as ground squirrels, pocket gophers, mice, young rabbits, and prairie dogs and, at times, grasshoppers are important in the diet. These falcons seem to enjoy diving at and annoying large hawks, great blue herons, and owls, but they often live in peace on the same cliff with ravens. Limited in numbers by their dependence on cliffs for nesting and by their territorial jealousy (16 miles of ideal cliff was found to support only 23 pairs), they are a rather rare bird in most areas.

VOICE: Sometimes a rapid series of high-pitched rather musical whistled notes; at others, a harsh series of cackles.

NEST: (I. 32, A., N. 35) The typical site is a ledge protected by an overhang, or a shallow cave or pothole near the top of a cliff. The birds build no nest but occasionally scrape out a niche in a dirt bank or use the nests of such cliff-nesting birds as ravens, red-tailed hawks, and golden eagles. The 5 eggs (2.1 x 1.6) are white with small dots and larger spots of brown.

RANGE: (P. M.) Breeds from North Dakota, s. Alberta, and s. British Columbia south to Lower California and s. Mexico and east to w. Nebraska and w. Texas. Some birds winter throughout the breeding area, but there is definite migration and a few wander as far east as Minnesota and Illinois.

Peregrine Falcon* *Falco peregrinus*—✕41
(Duck Hawk) ♂ L. 17; W. 40; ♀ L. 19; W. 45

IDENTIFICATION: In flight the long, pointed wings and compressed tail mark this as a falcon. Its size, bold head pattern, and fast, powerful flight distinguish the species.

HABITS: (Age 15 yrs.) The breeding distribution of these cliff dwellers is largely controlled by the availability of suitable nest sites. They favor seacoast areas, and while they occur throughout the Far West they are far less numerous than the prairie falcon in the more arid regions and higher altitudes. Many migrate south along the outer beaches, flying long distances over the water and often perching on the masts of coastwise vessels. Sometimes they stay with a boat for a day or two, feeding on petrels, terns, and small gulls. Incredibly swift and agile, these falcons seem able to take any prey they wish with the greatest ease. Frequently they indulge in spectacular aerial evolutions in what seems to be a spirit of play, harrying flocks of small birds, badgering other hawks, or forcing herons and other large birds to earth without any apparent attempt to do more than scare them. When not in a hurry they fly with a few short strokes followed by a glide and at times soar up out of sight on a mountain updraft.

Most of their prey is killed in the air. Sometimes the victim is sent spinning to the ground by a terrific blow from the big, powerful feet, delivered at the end of a dive from above, and is retrieved later. At other times the prey is simply plucked out of the air. In wooded regions high-flying birds like jays, flickers, robins, nighthawks, and many of the black-birds are the most frequent casualties. In open country many sparrows and meadowlarks are taken, and in some regions, especially in the Far North, small mammals are eaten. Plov-ers and sandpipers are the chief food of the peregrine in many northern areas and of migrant and wintering peregrines along the seacoast.

The skyscrapers of our big modern cities provide the pere-grine with everything it requires—artificial cliffs on which to perch, ledges on which to nest, and an abundant supply of feral rock doves (city pigeons) for food. These falcons are almost the only natural enemy of the hordes of pigeons that frequent our public buildings and parks and are usually welcomed by city authorities.

VOICE: Seldom heard except about the aerie in protest against intruders, a series of harsh, cackling notes, those of the "ter-cel" (male) being higher-pitched than the falcon's. The conversational calls are shrill, whining, or wailing sounds. A common call—*weeeé-chew, weeeé-chew*—suggests the notes of a flicker or grackle.

NEST: (I. 34, A., N. 34) On a cliff ledge, usually well sheltered by an overhang, and near the top, where it commands a wide view of the surrounding country. Occasionally the aerie is hidden below the level of the tops of the trees growing at the base of the cliff, or it may be in a comparatively low rock wall. In some areas a cavity in the broken top of a giant tree or an old tree nest of a large bird is used. Little or no nest is built, the eggs being laid in a "scrape" in whatever dirt and debris are already on the ledge. The 3 or 4 eggs (2.0 x 1.6) are creamy-white, heavily marked with rich reddish-browns.

RANGE: (P. M.) Widely distributed as a breeder on every conti-nent and in many island areas. In North America it breeds

from Greenland, the Arctic Islands, and n. Alaska south to
n. Georgia, n. Louisiana, c.w. Texas, and c. Lower California. Winters from Massachusetts, Indiana, Colorado, and
s. British Columbia south through the West Indies and
Mexico to n. South America.

Aplomato Falcon*   *Falco femoralis*—※41
(Orange-chested Hobby)   ♂ L. 15; W. 35; ♀ L. 17½; W. 40

IDENTIFICATION: The striking head markings and black lower
breast and flanks are distinctive. Young birds are similar in
pattern but brownish, with solid black instead of barred
wing linings.

HABITS: This widely distributed South American falcon reaches
the extreme northern limit of its range in our Southwest,
where it has become increasingly rare within recent years.
Insects are apparently one of its chief foods, but it takes
small birds, snakes, and lizards. Much of its time is spent
searching for prey from a vantage point, which may be the
top of a tall tree or a desert shrub. From here it makes quick
dashes after flying insects or animals whose motion has attracted its attention, returning to the perch to eat the captive. These falcons are quickly drawn to a grass fire, over
which they hover to catch the grasshoppers and other insects
and small animals driven out by the flames. There are reports
that they fly along over trains to catch the birds flushed into
the open by the locomotive.

VOICE: Said to be a loud scream.

NEST: (A.) In our Southwest, a platform of sticks with a grass
lining, placed 7 to 15 feet up in the top of a yucca, mesquite,
or other low tree in dry, open country. Often it is simply
the old nest of some bird like the white-necked raven. The
3 eggs (1.8 x 1.4) are white, well marked with pale or russet
browns.

RANGE: (P. M.) Breeds from s. Texas, s. New Mexico, and s.
Arizona south through most of South America to Tierra del
Fuego. Withdraws southward from its United States range
in winter.

Pigeon Hawk   *Falco columbarius*—※41
(Merlin)   ♂ L. 10; W. 25; Wt. 6 oz.;
                ♀ L. 13; W. 26; Wt. 8 oz.

IDENTIFICATION: This stocky little bird, which has the typical
pointed wings and rowing flight of a falcon, resembles a

pigeon in the air; hence its name. The white-tipped, barred
tail and the heavy dark streaking below are good field marks.
Regional color variation is pronounced. Northern Great Plains
males are pearl gray above while humid coastal British
Columbia specimens are almost black, the brown-backed
females and young showing comparable variations.

HABITS: Woodland openings and borders of lakes, ponds, and
marshes are favorite hunting grounds of the merlin when
it nests in wooded areas. Many nest in open, shrubby barrens,
bogs, or parklike grasslands with scattered trees. Much of
their time is spent on lookout perches on a dead snag or rock,
from which they make swift forays after such prey as may be
sighted. At times they hunt on the wing, soaring or hovering,
and occasionally consume their prey in the air. The merlin
often shows great curiosity about man and little fear of him.
It is a great badgerer of larger birds like gulls, crows, and
kingfishers. Migrations usually coincide with heavy movements of the small birds on which it feeds. Pigeon hawks
seldom appear in numbers except along the marshes and
beaches of the seacoasts or large lakes. Small birds and big
insects are staple foods. Warblers, sparrows, and thrushes
are most often taken, but chimney swifts and swallows are
caught and occasionally birds as large as meadowlarks, flickers, or black-bellied plovers. Dragonflies are a favorite food
(one pigeon hawk had eaten 34), and many butterflies,
grasshoppers, katydids, and cicadas are taken.

VOICE: A rapid series of harsh, cackling notes, seldom heard except at the nest.

NEST: (I. 30, A.) The merlin is not much of a nest builder but is extremely adaptable in the matter of sites, using old crow, magpie, and other nests in deciduous or coniferous trees. A hollow in the ground on a small dune, hill, or other rise will do. Cliff ledges, holes in cut banks, cavities high in tree trunks, including old woodpecker holes, are occasionally used. The 4 or 5 creamy-white eggs (1.6 x 1.2) are washed with reddish-brown and finely or boldly spotted with browns.

RANGE: (P. M.) Breeds throughout the boreal spruce-fir forests of the whole Northern Hemisphere north to the limit of trees. In North America from n. Labrador, n. Manitoba, n.w. Mackenzie, and n.w. Alaska south to Nova Scotia, s. Quebec, n. Michigan, Wyoming, and s. Oregon. Winters from n. Florida and the Gulf Coast, Colorado, and s. British Columbia south through the West Indies and Central America to n. South America. An occasional bird may be encountered almost anywhere in the United States in winter, and it regularly reaches Bermuda.

Sparrow Hawk
(American Kestrel)

Falco sparverius—✕41
♂ L. 9½; W. 21; Wt. 3 oz;
♀ L. 11; W. 24; Wt. 4 oz.

IDENTIFICATION: This little red-tailed falcon has a very distinctive color pattern, and its slender, pointed wings give it a crescentlike silhouette. It hovers a great deal as it hunts. Young are very similar to adults.

HABITS: Like all birds of prey, this falcon has remarkable eyesight and commonly spends much of its time searching for prey from a lookout perch on top of a tall object. It frequents open lands and has therefore greatly increased in the East as forests have been replaced by pastures and croplands with scattered trees. Farther west in the once treeless grasslands this species has benefited from the planting of trees and the setting up of public utility poles, poles and wires being among their favorite perching places. An abundant and easily caught supply of English sparrows, plenty of lookouts, and many convenient crevices for nests make cities good sparrow hawk habitats, and in recent years it has become a common city resident.

This species lives almost exclusively on insects when they are available in quantity. Grasshoppers are of major importance, followed by crickets, large beetles, caterpillars, dragon-flies, spiders, and even ants. Meadow and white-footed mice and other small mammals and small birds, chiefly sparrows, are common foods at other seasons. Many lizards and small snakes are eaten. Remarkable concentrations of these falcons often occur in areas suffering from a plague of grasshoppers, locusts, or Mormon crickets.

VOICE: A series of 6 or 8 clear, high-pitched staccato notes, *kee-kee-kee,* etc., with a rising inflection.

NEST: (I. 29, A.) In a natural cavity or woodpecker hole in a tree or cactus in or near open land, in holes in cliff walls, burrows in banks, and rarely in the open nest of other birds. It uses man-made sites, such as apartment-house gutters and rainspouts, and will occupy an 8-x-8-inch bird box about a foot deep with a 3-inch entrance hole, placed fairly high. The 4 or 5 eggs (1.4 x 1.1) are white with small brown dots.

RANGE: (P. M.) Breeds from Newfoundland, s. Quebec, n. Ontario, s. Keewatin, n.w. Mackenzie, and s.e. Alaska south through the West Indies and South America to Tierra del Fuego. Winters from c. New England, s. Ontario, c. Illinois, Kansas, Utah, and s. British Columbia south.

GALLINACEOUS BIRDS
and ALLIES
Order Galliformes

CURASSOWS and GUANS   Family Cracidae

Chachalaca*   *Ortalis vetula*—✳46
                                              L. 22

IDENTIFICATION: The long, white-tipped tail and orange throat
    skin are distinctive. Juvenile birds are more extensively
    cinnamon-buff than adults and have a barred back, wing
    coverts, and tail tip of this color.

HABITS: In s. Texas this is a bird of dense thickets of small,
    thorny, drought-resistant trees known as chaparral. A perma-
    nent source of fresh water within a mile or so of their terri-
    tory seems to be necessary if they are to occupy an area
    permanently. Chachalacas seem most at home well up in this
    thick growth, although they often feed on the ground. The
    flight is swift and generally above the treetops. They fly
    readily and usually come to rest in the top branches of a tree.
    Berries, tender leaves, and buds seem to be their chief foods.
    The precocial young are apparently carried to the ground
    from the nest until they are able to fly and carried up to a
    tree at night. This is said to be done by the female, who
    allows them to cling to her legs as she flies. The chachalaca
    becomes very tame when kept as a pet, and it takes so readily
    to barnyard life that it could undoubtedly be domesticated.
    Unfortunately, it is rapidly disappearing from the Rio
    Grande Valley as the brushland is cleared for fruit and vege-
    table farms.

VOICE: A loud, resonant, 3-syllable call from which it derives its
    name, that of the male deeper and more resonant than the
    female's. It is delivered over and over from a treetop perch
    in the half-light of early morning or evening and occasionally
    on cloudy days. After one bird starts all those in the neigh-
    borhood join in.

NEST: (I. 22, P.) The small, sturdily built nest is woven out

174 FAMILY TETRAONIDAE

of twigs and lined with leaves. It is usually out on the limb
of a small tree, where it is well hidden by dense foliage. The
height varies from a few feet to 25, and a common site is in
the border of a tree clump not far from water. The 3 eggs
(2.3 x 1.6) are white and rough.

RANGE: (R.) Occurs from extreme s. Texas through e. and s.
Mexico to n. Nicaragua and, as an introduced bird, on Sapelo
Island, Georgia.

GROUSE   Family Tetraonidae

Spruce Grouse   *Canachites canadensis*—✕46
L. 16

IDENTIFICATION: The strikingly white-spotted and jet-black
under parts of the male are distinctive, as is the fine black
barring of the neck and upper back of the female. Young
are like females when in juvenile plumage but molt into virtually adult plumage in August and September. Females
from southern areas are much browner than those from
farther north.

HABITS: This grouse does not display any fear of man and is
quite aptly termed "fool hen." Although generally not good
eating, it is soon exterminated even in sparsely settled areas
by thoughtless persons who kill the birds just for fun. Normally the spruce grouse is common in the whole northern
spruce, fir, cedar, larch, and pine forest community from the
southern edge of the tundra south. Generally it survives the
inroads of civilization longest in the vicinity of lowland
swamps and bogs. It is a solitary species, and the small flocks
encountered are usually a family group. Each male has its
own display ground in a forest opening, where it endlessly
repeats a circuit from the ground to a series of tree perches
and back, during which it noisily whirs its wings, struts, and
inflates the red tissue over its eyes. Staple foods of these
markedly arboreal grouse are the needles and buds of the
various conifers among which they live and, in summer,
berries, seeds, mushrooms, tender leaves of herbaceous plants,
and insects, of which the young seem especially fond. A
plentiful supply of coarse gravel is important, and the major
excursions of these sedentary birds seem to be trips to stream
or lakeside sources of this material.

VOICE: Clucking sounds when disturbed and a low rolling note are the only vocal accomplishments. The male makes a loud whirring noise with its wings as part of a regular display performance which is indulged in to some extent throughout the year.

NEST: (I. 17, P.) On the ground in a hollow in moss, lined with grass and leaves and sheltered by a spruce branch or fallen trunk. The 11 or so buffy eggs (1.7 x 1.25) are spotted and blotched with rich browns.

RANGE: (R.) Occurs from n. Quebec, n. Manitoba, n. Mackenzie, and c. Alaska south to n. New England, n. Michigan, s. Saskatchewan, and n. Washington.

Ruffed Grouse* *Bonasa umbellus*—✳46
L. 18

IDENTIFICATION: A large bird that roars away from almost underfoot, showing a finely barred fan-shaped tail with a black terminal band, is a ruffed grouse. The general color of the upper parts and especially the tail may be reddish-brown or gray as the bird has two distinct color phases. These bear no relation to age or sex, but the proportion of each varies regionally—gray predominating in the North and West, brown in the South. The dark neck ruffs and tail are longer in the male.

HABITS: (Age 6 yrs.) An extensive area of dense woodland of any type is not good ruffed grouse habitat, and the cutting of timber and the establishment of scattered farms in the once virtually unbroken forest greatly benefited this species. Grouse are not gregarious and at most seasons widely dispersed, so an ideal habitat must be able to supply all the bird's seasonal needs within an area of about 25 acres. These needs are conifers for winter roosting cover, a not too dense hardwood stand for nesting and food, brushy land for escape cover and as a source of berries, and sunny openings for dust baths and insect food for the young. Abandoned farms and orchards that are going back to forest provide nearly ideal grouse habitats until the plant succession finally reaches a stage where the invading trees have killed out the shrubs and closed all the openings.

Until the ruffed grouse of an area have had some years of experience with man they display the same lack of fear as the spruce grouse, but, unlike the latter, they have been able to adapt themselves to hunting and are now one of our sportiest game birds—springing into the air from almost underfoot and roaring off on an erratic course through the woods. Each male has a definite territory with one or more sheltered logs, mounds, or rocks on which it stands when "drumming" the air with quick beats of its wings. In spring females are attracted to the males' territory, but there is no pairing since, like many grouse, this species is promiscuous. The male drums sporadically all year and may do so quite actively for a few weeks in the fall.

Grouse populations are subject to wide fluctuations in any given area. The reason is not known and the fluctuations are not as regular as the well-marked cycles in rodent populations. Under wise management the birds are hunted only during periods of abundance, when seasons can be fairly long and the bag limit liberal. When the decline occurs survivors are carefully safeguarded to preserve as large a breeding stock as possible through the critical low. In good habitats a spring population of 1 bird per 10 acres represents a near peak; in the fall, after the dispersal of the young, it may reach 1 bird per 3 or 4 acres.

Young grouse are precocial, leaving the nest as soon as they dry off; they can fly about 25 feet by the time they are 12 days old. In fall broods break up and young wander, often for miles, until they locate suitable habitats where no other grouse are in residence to drive them away. It is during this dispersal flight that young birds occasionally fly through windows or strike buildings and are said to go crazy. In winter this grouse grows comblike snowshoes on its toes and seeks dense evergreen cover for night roosting. Here territoriality breaks down sufficiently for it to share its roost with several others of its kind. During periods of bitter cold and high winds grouse leave the tree roost and bury themselves in the snow for the night or for the duration of the storm.

Ruffed grouse start life on an insect diet but soon add fruit, seeds, and leaves and, as fall comes, buds. Buds of yellow, black, and paper birch, aspens, apple, cherry, and blueberry are staples for fall and winter, supplemented by fruits of dogwood, hawthorn, grape, and greenbrier, acorns, beechnuts, and leaves of sheep sorrel, wintergreen, and laurel. In spring and summer the main food of adults consists of a variety of seasonal fruits and the leaves of plants like sedges, strawberries, blackberries, and jewelweed, plus a few insects.

VOICE: Notes vary from a short *quit-quit* of alarm to a loud squeal or whine uttered by the female when she is surprised with young. At a distance the male's famous drumming gives more the effect of a pulsation or throb in the air than a distinct sound. When one is closer it is heard to start slowly with widely spaced beats that increase in frequency until they become a muffled roar that fades out as it ends.

NEST: (I. 24, P.) A hollow in the ground, lined with leaves and placed at the base of a tree, stump, or rock and concealed by low shrubs or branches or occasionally hidden under a fallen log. A common site is near the edge of a patch of a predominantly deciduous, medium-age, second-growth woodland not far from a road, clearing, slashing, or swamp. The 11 or so eggs (1.5 x 1.2) are creamy- to pinkish-buff, sometimes finely spotted with dull brown.

RANGE: (R.) Occurs from s. Quebec, n. Ontario, s. Mackenzie, and c. Alaska south to Virginia (in mts. to Georgia), Tennessee, s. Missouri, n. Colorado, and n. California.

Willow Ptarmigan
(Willow Grouse)

Lagopus lagopus—✻47
L. 15; Wt. 1 lb. 2 oz.

IDENTIFICATION: This species is larger and has a heavier bill than the other black-tailed ptarmigan—the rock. In the yellow-tinged white winter plumage the face is clear white and sexes look alike. In spring the male has a distinctly reddish neck and breast while the yellow-brown barred female is virtually indistinguishable from a rock ptarmigan. In autumn females become more reddish and the sexes are again similar.

HABITS: Low, open tundra near the coast, grassy arctic prairies, marshy flats, willow-grown river bottoms, and hillsides grown up to dwarf willows are the usual summer habitats. In more southern areas the birds occur at higher elevations wherever patches of stunted spruce and dwarf willow are found in sheltered spots. Pairs are formed after a vigorous courtship period, and the male defends the nest and the female and her brood by flying at intruders. These abundant and prolific birds are a staple food for Eskimos, and the eggs, young, and adults are at times the chief food of many arctic predators such as gulls, jaegers, various hawks and owls, foxes and other mammals.

In fall the birds move out of areas where snow buries their food too deeply, into river-bottom thickets or wind-swept coastal areas where willow, alder, and birch twigs and buds are available. The shift may be only a few miles or it may involve a long flight and many thousands of birds. In summer the diet is varied with tender leaves, berries, grass and sedges, seeds and leaves, and some insects and spiders—the two last being the principal food of very young chicks.

VOICE: An intruder is scolded with a sharp rattling call, said to sound like a nail run over a comb. Courting males utter a peculiar cackling gobble as they settle to earth on quivering wings after a jump into the air. Various other clucking and cackling notes are also heard.

NEST: (I. 22, P.) On the ground in the open, usually in tundra but also on marsh borders, beaches, and river bars. A hollow in the lee of a rock, grass clump, moss hummock, or dwarf willow is lined with grass and leaves. The 7 or 8 eggs (1.7 x 1.2) are pale yellowish, heavily and boldly marked with blackish-brown.

RANGE: (P. M.) Occurs throughout the Arctic Zone of both hemispheres south in Europe to about Lat. 60°, and to Lat. 45° in Asia. In North America breeds from the Arctic Ocean and Greenland south to Newfoundland, c. Quebec, n. Ontario, n. Manitoba, and c. British Columbia. In winter migrates south as far as s. Quebec, c. Ontario, and s. Alberta.

Rock Ptarmigan   *Lagopus mutus*—⚹47
                                                 L. 13

IDENTIFICATION: Males and some females have a black streak from the bill through the eye when in the pink-tinged white winter plumage, which, in parts of the Far North, the adult males wear well into midsummer. The summer plumage is coarsely barred with blackish and buff—darker in males, yellower in females. A finely vermiculated, pepper-and-salt fall body plumage follows in which males are quite gray, females somewhat browner. The flight feathers are always white and the tail, which is concealed except in flight, is black except in juveniles.

HABITS: The barest, rockiest arctic uplands and barrens are the usual summer home of the rock ptarmigan. One of the hardiest of all birds, it ranges south only to exposed mountaintops. In winter some remain on the breeding grounds to feed in wind-swept areas or dig through the snow with their heavily feathered, sharp-clawed, rabbitlike feet. Others move to lower altitudes but never seek real shelter like the willow ptarmigan. Birds of the extreme North gather into flocks and move south out of the region of continuous darkness, often crossing wide bodies of water. They are usually accompanied by gyrfalcons, for whom they are a staple winter food. Eskimos also eat them, luring them into traps by darkening an area to make it look free of snow. The flight of this species is fast but rolling and close to the ground, the birds rising and falling with the contour of the land. Twigs, buds, berries, tender leaves, moss, insects, and spiders are normal foods.

VOICE: A rolling, snorelike, 2-part call and a loud series of pheasantlike cackling notes are given by disturbed birds. At other times clucking, purring, growl-like, and whining notes are heard.

NEST: A hollow in the open ground of the tundra, sheltered only by a rock or hummock and lined with grass, moss, and feathers. The 6 or 7 eggs (1.7 x 1.2) are pale buff, spotted with dark blackish-brown.

RANGE: (P. M.) This circumpolar species ranges from the Arctic Ocean and its islands south in Eurasia, to the mountains of Scotland, n. Spain, c. Austria, s. Siberia, and n. Japan. In North America they breed south to Newfoundland, Ungava, s. Keewatin, c. Mackenzie, and n. British Columbia. There is some withdrawal in winter from the most northern parts of the range.

Prairie Chicken *Tympanuchus cupido*—⚹46
(Pinnated Grouse) L. 17¼; W. 28; Wt. 2 lbs.

IDENTIFICATION: The strongly barred appearance, especially of the under parts, is distinctive, as is the short, rounded tail when the bird is in flight. The blackish neck tufts are conspicuous in the male but much shorter in the female. The female has a barred instead of solid tail and has no air sacs on the neck.

HABITS: The range and abundance of this grouse have undergone many changes since colonial days. When the first settlers arrived they found it abundant where fire or sandy, rocky soil had prevented normal forest growth. In open pine or oak barrens and blueberry heaths the birds fed on acorns, buds, tender leaves, insects, and wild fruits and were called "heath hens." Easy to shoot, they gradually succumbed to over-hunting and disappeared from one part after another of their eastern range. In the West they were originally limited to the eastern part of the natural grasslands or prairies and were not notably abundant until agriculture began to provide large quantities of very acceptable foods. Then they increased tremendously and with the gradual spread of grain raising moved north and west through the Great Plains up into the Prairie Provinces of Canada, gaining in the West, at least temporarily, more range than they lost when they vanished from the East.

Although it was once heavily hunted for the market and is often shot illegally today, the prairie chicken's disappearance from most regions is usually a result of the plowing of too high a proportion of the native grassland, a process which is currently wiping out the Attwater's race that once occupied the coastal prairies of Louisiana and Texas. In these areas utilization of land for rice planting and other intensive forms of agriculture is now approaching 100 per cent. Recent studies show that the birds cannot maintain themselves unless at least 20 to 40 per cent of the land is in permanent wild or cultivated grass which is not overgrazed, mowed too late, or burned—a minimum vegetation height of 6 inches being necessary for roosting cover in winter and nesting in spring. Worn-out croplands, now returning to grass, may help restore some of the lost habitats. Thus, like the ruffed grouse of the abandoned New England farms, this species stands to benefit from our destructive land-use practices.

The prairie chicken has communal courtship grounds where up to 30 or 40 males gather at sunrise and sundown to display, boom, fight, and mate with any females they attract. The grounds are used from January to June and sometimes from September to November. No pairs are formed, and 1 or 2 dominant males do most, if not all, of the mating. After the females have reared the young the birds gather into flocks, each flock all of one sex. At times there is a southward movement, but it seems to involve only flocks of females. Food in summer includes insects, chiefly grasshoppers and locusts, but the staple diet is tender leaves of clover, lespedeza, etc., and seeds of grasses, sedges, and weeds. Later such fruits as coral berry and rose hips are eaten, but as soon as available and as long as it lasts, waste corn, oats, wheat, rye, and sorghum are the birds' chief foods. Heavy snows in late winter send the birds to sumacs and elms, but these supply only emergency foods.

VOICE: A variety of chickenlike cackles and cluckings. In spring, males, with the aid of inflatable air sacs, make a drawn-out hollow cooing sound which carries for a mile or more. It can be approximated by blowing across the top of an empty beer bottle.

NEST: (I. 23, P.) In a slight hollow in the ground, lined with a few grass and weed stems. The site is usually in the open or among brush and scrub trees. The nest is extraordinarily hard to find as it is generally well concealed in a dense stand of last year's grass or weed stalks. The 11 or so eggs (1.8 x 1.3) are olive with fine dots and a few larger pale brown spots.

RANGE: (P. M.) Has occurred at one time or another from s. Maine, s. Ontario, s. Michigan, s. Manitoba, and w.c. Alberta, south to Virginia, Kentucky, s. Louisiana, and coastal Texas, and west to e. Wyoming and n.w. Texas. Now not found east of Indiana.

Sharp-tailed Grouse*   *Pedioecetes phasianellus*—✻46
L. 19; W. 27; Wt. 2 lbs.

IDENTIFICATION: The pale color and dark V-shaped breast markings are distinctive. In flight the wings are noticeably spotted with white and the 2 elongated brownish feathers in the center of the white tail are conspicuous. Juvenile birds are finely penciled with white above and lack the white tail. In winter the species is buffier and more rufous than in summer.

HABITS: The sharp-tail is essentially a brushland grouse and is found on the prairie only in summer and in the vicinity of timber. With the coming of agriculture to the prairies and the increase of the prairie chicken that followed in its wake, the sharp-tail has largely abandoned this habitat in the southern part of its range. It has, however, greatly benefited at the expense of the spruce grouse from the cutting and burning of the northern spruce forest, which has created vast areas of brushland and deciduous second growth well suited to its needs. The sharp-tail is so tame and easy to shoot that despite its high reproductive rate it is not able to maintain itself near civilization, even in good habitats, except under careful management. In spring local males gather in an open area to fight and go through their courtship performance, which is marked by a rapid stamping of the feet, a rustling of the feathers, and cooing noises made with the aid of inflatable purplish air sacs on the sides of the neck.

When grasshoppers and locusts are available, sharp-tails eat large numbers of them and the young feed almost wholly on insects. In the main, the species is herbaceous, feeding on tender leaves, buds, and especially on flowers of both herbaceous and woody plants. Waste wheat and weed seeds are taken and, in the fall, acorns and such wild fruit as hawthorn and rose hips, cornus, coral berry, and juniper berries. In the winter the birds are more or less arboreal and feed in treetops on the twigs and buds of bog and paper birch, willow, poplar, alder, larch, and juniper. However, like prairie chickens, they roost at night on the ground under the snow.

VOICE: Chickenlike cacklings and a gobbling note. During courtship males utter pairs of short, deep *coos* not unlike a mourning dove's.

NEST: (I. 21, P.) On open prairie in a scantily lined hollow in the ground under a thick tuft of bunch grass; in a brushy area often near water and well hidden under a bush or thick weeds; or on a dry knoll in a swamp. The 12 or so eggs (1.7 x 1.3) are brownish-olive, usually finely dotted with dark brown.

RANGE: (P. M.) Occurs from n. Quebec, n. Manitoba, n.w. Mackenzie, and c. Alaska south to n.e. Illinois, c. Kansas, n. New Mexico, s. Utah, and n. California.

PHEASANTS, PARTRIDGES, and QUAILS
Family Phasianidae

Partridge*
(Hungarian Partridge)

Perdix perdix—⚡47
L. 12½; Wt. 13 oz.

IDENTIFICATION: The barred flanks, gray breast, and the chestnut patch on the lower breast are distinctive. In flight the short dark chestnut-brown tail is prominent. Juveniles are buffy-brown, paler below and white on throat and belly, and have a terminal tail band.

HABITS: In the vast grain-raising area of the n. Great Plains land tends to become so intensively cultivated that no native gallinaceous bird can survive, yet it provides an ecological niche for a bird that can utilize waste grain (2 to 5 bushels to the acre), weed seeds, green foods, and insects, and can nest and winter in the scant, largely herbaceous cover that exists in and around the fields. Furthermore, the bird must be so alert and wary that hunters can take only a fraction of its fall population. The Hun has proved to be such a bird, and from a few small releases some 40 years ago it has so increased and spread that it is now abundant over much of the Northwest. In only 2 other areas, in the northern corn belt, has it shown a similar ability to survive, and the money spent to liberate some 300,000 birds in various other parts of the United States has been wasted. Either the climate or habitat was unsuitable or the area was already occupied by a species with which these partridges were unable to compete.

Even where it is established, the Hun often holds its ground only because of its exceedingly high reproductive rate. It suffers heavy nest mortality from spring plowing, the burning of stubble, and from the early mowing of hay and alfalfa and the harvesting of early grains. Predators take a serious toll of those that nest in narrow fence rows where the nests are easily found, and on wet clayey croplands the young often get such balls of mud on their feet that they perish. Heavy snows are hard on the birds unless there is standing corn, as they cannot dig down through more than a few inches of snow to the green food they need to tide them over such emergencies.

VOICE: When flushed, a rapid cackle that slows down as the bird flies away. The male's crow, most commonly heard at dusk, is a hoarse, guinealike *kee-ah*. Both sexes use a similar sound as a rally call.

NEST: (I. 23, P.) The preferred site for early nests is in undisturbed wild grass in wasteland and along roadsides, fence rows, or ditchbanks, but later in the spring many are in hay-, alfalfa-, or grainfields. A scrape in the ground is lined first with coarse stems and then with fine, soft grass. The 16 eggs (1.4 x 1.0) are uniform olive color.

RANGE: (R.) Native to Eurasia from c. Sweden and n. Russia

south to n. Spain, Greece, and n. Persia and east to c. Siberia. Established in s. Michigan, s. Wisconsin, n.w. Ohio, n. Indiana, and n.e. Illinois; also from Montana and British Columbia south to Iowa, s. Montana, and Oregon.

Bobwhite *Colinus virginianus*—#47
(Common Quail) L. 10; Wt. 7 oz.

IDENTIFICATION: This is a small, chunky, reddish-brown bird with a distinctive head pattern and a dark, grayish tail. Head markings are black and white only on the adult male.

HABITS: The bobwhite is usually most abundant about cultivated land, fallow fields, or recently abandoned farmland grown up to weeds and briar patches, but it also occurs in open pinelands, brushy pastures, prairies, and semi-arid grasslands with scattered mesquite, cactus, or other thorny cover. Dense woodlands and areas devoid of occasional patches of dense brush are avoided. Thus the clearing of forested areas and the planting of roadside and fence-row hedges across the prairies have greatly expanded its habitat. In the South the late-winter burning of open pine woodlands stimulates the growth of the wild legumes that are one of its chief foods in this region and produces heavy populations even in the absence of agriculture. The cultivation of corn made possible a northward spread into the region of heavy winter snows where corn shocks or standing stalks with a few unharvested ears provide an always accessible food supply. Here, however, the bird's foothold has remained precarious, occasional hard winters almost wiping them out, and in this region they can seldom stand a very heavy hunting toll. Survival of the fittest through many generations has produced a hardy, heavy, well-feathered strain in these northern areas, but it seems now to have been destroyed in many sections through hybridization with southern birds that were shipped in and liberated in misguided attempts to bolster the overshot local population. In fact, artificial stocking of this prolific bird is seldom justified. If it is not abundant something is wrong with the environment or it has been grossly overshot, in which case all it needs is protection. Usually the trouble is in lack of sufficient well-distributed escape and roosting cover in the form of dense briar thickets and vine tangles, broad, thickly brushed fence rows, and good stands of undisturbed roadside vegetation. Predator-proof cover of this type within 150 feet of a good food supply is an essential winter requirement.

Unfortunately, this species has suffered a serious decline in many farming areas owing to the tendency to keep things too clean. Roadside vegetation is cut close or burned; fields are plowed to the fence or made so large that most of the food in the center is too far from cover for quail to use it. Fall plowing of weeds, stubble, or fallow fields and the breaking down of old cornstalks seriously affect food supplies. Often the most adverse factor is the destruction of nesting and brushy cover by heavy grazing. In the West this has eliminated the bobwhite in many areas, while in the South the fire-exclusion program of recent years has greatly reduced their numbers in the long-leaf pine forests by permitting the development of broom-sedge roughs and deciduous brush.

Food is seldom a problem except in winter as quail are omnivorous, eating seeds, insects, fruit, greens, and buds. In summer they pair to rear their young, but at other times they are in coveys of up to 30 birds. Each group makes its headquarters and roosts at night in good cover, ranging out to feed along brushy travel lanes for 300 to 400 yards and scattering in all directions when flushed. No covey allows others to trespass, nor does any covey accept additional members once the quota of 25 to 30 has been reached.

VOICE: The *bobwhite* or *bob bob-white* call of unmated males in the spring and the *a-loie-a-hee* answering call of the female proclaim their presence far and wide. Members of a scattered covey use a human-sounding *quoi-hee* whistle to locate one another. These form only part of the extensive vocabulary.

NEST: (I. 23, P.) Preferred sites are thick clumps of last year's bunch grass, brushy woodland borders, or tangles of vines and shrubs along fence rows, but any dense, grassy cover may be used. The nest is a hollow scooped out by the birds and lined with grass. The eggs are concealed by a well-woven arch of vegetation. The 15 or so eggs (1.2 x .95) are dull white.

RANGE: (R.) Occurs from s.w. Maine, s. Ontario, and s. Minnesota south to Cuba, along the Gulf Coast, and through Mexico to w. Guatemala and west to South Dakota, e. Colorado, s. Arizona, and formerly Jalisco.

Scaled Quail*   *Callipepla squamata*—✳47
L. 11

IDENTIFICATION: The dull gray appearance of this bird, together with the white-tipped crest and "scaled" under parts, is distinctive. Young are quite rufous.

HABITS: This is a bird of the dry, arid Upper Sonoran Zone, often occurring in areas far from water. It seldom flies but runs from one to another of the dense patches of thorny shrubs, yuccas, and cactus plants that dot such landscapes. Scaled quail are most abundant among the weeds and grasses of dry washes and river valleys, as they like to make daily visits to water. Rather trusting by nature, they quickly become tame about the isolated farms and ranches to which they are attracted by the presence of water. Their numbers have always had a tendency to fluctuate widely, as both heavy rains and drought effect them adversely. Recently in many areas they have been reduced by overgrazing, which has destroyed the brushy thickets which are so essential to their habitat. Insects are important foods, but seeds are staple, along with tender buds and other vegetation.

VOICE: A low, nasal whistle, *pay-cos, pay-cos,* and a loud barking *kuck-yur.*

NEST: (I. 21, P.) In a slight hollow, lined with a little grass, under a low bush or in a dense clump of grass in dry country, occasionally in a hay- or grainfield. The 13 or so eggs (1.3 x 1.0) are pale buff, evenly dotted with red-brown.

RANGE: (R.) Occurs from c. Texas, s.w. Kansas, s. Colorado, and c. Arizona south to c. Mexico.

Pheasant   *Phasianus colchicus*—✻46
(Ring-necked Pheasant)
     ♂ L. 35; T. 18; ♀ L. 20½; T. 11½; Wt. 2½–4½ lbs.

IDENTIFICATION: The white ring on the neck of the male is a variable character, but this striking bird is unmistakable. The protectively colored hen can best be distinguished from a grouse by its long, tapering brownish tail.

HABITS: (Age 8 yrs.) The pheasants in North America are hybrids of several races but are generally closest in appearance to the ring-necked pheasant of e. China. In suitable environments the birds have increased rapidly from small initial introductions and, like so many introduced species, have often reached higher initial population levels than they seem able to maintain permanently. Pheasants generally do best where grains are raised and standing corn or soybean stalks can be gleaned for winter food. Good winter cover is important, but they are wide-ranging and gregarious at this season and can seek it out. The dense, matted vegetation of marsh and bog borders is ideal, but dense young oaks or conifers on recently cutover land and ungrazed wood lots are good. Sometimes unmowed meadows or the weedy growth in fallow fields suffice. Buds and green vegetation such as grass, clover, alfalfa, dandelion, and dock are eaten and in winter serve as emergency food, but seeds are the pheasants' mainstay, especially the seeds of cultivated grain. Fruits such as wild grape, panicled dogwood, wolfberry, Virginia creeper, and Russian olive are often important in the winter diet. Seeds of ragweed, hog peanut, foxtail grasses, skunk cabbage, wild sunflower, knotweed, jewelweed, and smartweeds are among those most extensively utilized. When available, insects are taken, especially larval forms like cutworms, also grasshoppers and beetles. Snails are eaten with relish at times.

In spring the large winter flocks break up, the cocks scattering out to take up individual crowing territories. These are well separated and must include a good patch of brushy cover near herbaceous nesting cover. The cocks mate with one or more females who build their nests nearby. The common habit of nesting in hay-, alfalfa, and grainfields subjects the species to heavy losses when mowing is done before July 10. Not only are eggs and chicks destroyed, but the hens often lose both legs. At first the young live largely on insects picked up in croplands. In fall pheasants return to the hedgerows, which they use as travel lanes, and escape cover while gleaning waste grain and weed seeds from the bare fields.

In good environment cocks can stand heavy hunting pressure since they are polygamous and only 1 is needed for every 5 to 10 females. Pheasants would be far more abundant in many parts of their range if farmers would leave fencerows, ditchbanks, and roadside growths undisturbed; fence cattle out of wood lots, waste corners, and gullies; avoid burning; give dense marshy growths especial protection; do their first mowing as late as possible and the last early enough to permit a little further growth; and keep farm cats and dogs at home during the nesting season. The planting of multiflora rose or other thick hedges, scattered windbreaks, or clumps of conifers will help, as will the leaving of a row or two of unharvested corn, grain, or soybeans along the border of the fields.

VOICE: The male has a loud, bantamlike crow—*kok-cack*— followed by a drumming of the wings and, when flushed, utters a very loud, harsh, almost machinelike clatter. The far less noisy hens have shriller notes.

NEST: (I. 24, P.) A slight hollow in the ground, lined with a little grass. The preferred site is a dense stand of hay, alfalfa, or grain, but many nests are hidden in dense clumps of grass or weeds along fences, drainage ditches, roadside or woodland edges. The 11 or so olive-brown eggs (1.6 x 1.3) are laid over about a 14-day period.

RANGE: (R.) Occurs from the Ukraine across c. Asia to n.e. Manchuria and s. China. Introduced and established in the wild over most of Europe and in North America from c. Maine, s. Ontario, c. Wisconsin, s. Manitoba, c. Alberta, and s. British Columbia south to n. Maryland, n. Kentucky, n. Oklahoma, s. Utah, and c. California.

TURKEYS   Family Meleagrididae

Turkey   *Meleagris gallopavo*—✕46
♂ L. 48; W. 60; Wt. 15–20 lbs.; ♀ L. 36; Wt. 9 lbs.

IDENTIFICATION: The turkey was domesticated in s. Mexico, where the local race has white-tipped upper tail coverts and tail feathers. In northern races these feathers are tipped with brown. A wild turkey is a very trim-looking bird—its legs and neck long, head small, and body slender. The body feathers of the hen have a buffy tip instead of a black bar, which makes her much paler than the cock.

HABITS: (Age 12 yrs.) This splendid game bird has disappeared from roughly 70 per cent of its original range in the United States. Although it is a forest dweller, it likes rather open woodland or woods with frequent clearings, and the turkey's apparent abundance in the East in pre-colonial days indicates that the forests were not as dense as many have supposed. Not only did the Indians' cornfields provide openings, but the fires set by nature or by Indians made for open woodlands of the best mast-producing trees—oaks, hickories, and chestnuts—with an understory of fruit-producing small trees and shrubs and a rich, leguminous flora. With the coming of civilization the turkey at first benefited from the clearings in the forest, but as the forests disappeared and hunting became heavier, a decline set in. Today the bird survives in greatest numbers where only 10 to 25 per cent of the land is cleared. After this it begins to decrease and usually disappears when the amount of cleared and cultivated land rises to 50 per cent.

This was originally not a shy species, but the arrival of men with guns soon made it the alertest, wariest, and most difficult to bag of all our game birds. This has enabled it to survive in favorable habitat, even where it is subjected to year-round hunting, including the deadly water-hole hunting of late summer. It has gone, however, from many areas which, under proper management, could support from 2 to 5 birds to the square mile (under ideal conditions a square mile can support 15 to 20 birds). Proper timber cutting generally improves turkey habitat, once the lumbering operation is over. Removal of trees more than 12 to 16 inches in diameter opens the canopy and stimulates the understory and ground cover, yet leaves plenty of middle-aged trees as mast producers. Extensive clear cutting, by contrast, destroys an area as turkey habitat for many years to come, as the dense, even stand that follows is of little use to the birds except for roosting. In some places within recent years deer have been allowed to increase to such disastrously high levels that they not only compete seriously for mast but so damage the food plants of the forest floor that the area becomes unsuitable for either turkey or grouse. Free-ranging hogs also give serious competition for acorns and mast, and cattle, if allowed in the woods, destroy many important food plants. In some areas in the Southwest new turkey habitat has been created by overgrazing, which has caused much once fine grassland to grow up to scrub oak, juniper, and other turkey-food-bearing plants. A fine change for turkeys, but calamitous in terms of human economy.

In the East the loss of the chestnut was a heavy blow to turkeys and other mast feeders. Beechnuts are produced in large quantities only once in every few years, and today the staple food of the wild turkey is acorns. Fruits of the dogwood, grape, smilax, and sumac families are important, and grasses are widely eaten, the birds stripping the seed heads in summer and fall and taking the new blades in late winter and early spring when other foods are scarce. Actually there is little that turkeys miss as they range through woods and clearings, eating flower heads and leaves of herbaceous plants, picking up grasshoppers and other insects, and scratching for tubers and roots. In a group of turkey stomachs that were studied 354 species of plants and 313 kinds of insects and small animals were found. Turkeys like corn and will also make intensive use of small woodland-clearing plantings of a mixture of cowpeas, soybeans, millet, and buckwheat. A fall planting of wheat, oats, or rye provides valuable green food, and chufa plantings furnish small tubers that the birds can scratch out during winter.

Although they do not have a fixed gobbling territory, turkey cocks drive other mature males from their vicinity and mate with as many females as they can attract. Not until late summer do they lose their belligerency and gather into small gobbler flocks for the fall and winter. Hens stay with their broods until spring, several families joining to form a flock. The precocial young develop rapidly and are able to fly well enough at 4 weeks to start roosting in trees. For roosting, turkey flocks prefer a sheltered stand of fairly large dense pines, where they scatter out and perch near the trunk well up in the tops of the trees. The roost is, in a sense, their home. From it the average flock ranges over some 4 or 5 square miles in the daily search for food and water. During exceptionally bad winter weather turkeys may remain in the roost a week or more, virtually without food except for an occasional visit to a nearby honeysuckle tangle for a few leaves and berries. Turkeys much prefer running to flying and can attain speeds of 15 or more miles per hour when on the ground. But they are strong fliers and, when necessary, can rise to the treetops at a 30-degree angle and then sail off with only an occasional wingbeat for a quarter to a full mile. In this they are greatly aided if the country is rough enough to permit them to sail from one side of a valley to another, as several flights in rapid succession in more or less flat country completely exhaust them.

VOICE: The cock's gobble is most often heard just after sunrise in spring and serves to guide females to him. He answers

distant gobbles or imitations and often gobbles in response
to other loud noises like the calls of crows or great horned
owls. The birds of a scattered flock use a low, quavering yelp
—*keow, keow, keow*—to locate one another when reassem-
bling.

NEST: (I. 28, P.) A slight depression in the ground, lined with
a few leaves which are pulled over the eggs when the hen
leaves the nest. The site is usually near a woodland opening
or woods road in a place where the nest is well concealed by
low growths. Occasionally it is under a small tree or thicket
in an abandoned field. The 11 or so eggs (2.7 x 1.8) are pale
buff, evenly spotted with purplish-gray.

RANGE: (R.) Occurred at one time from s. Maine, s. Ontario,
s. Wisconsin, and South Dakota; south to s. Florida, the Gulf
Coast, and c.w. Mexico; west to Colorado, Arizona, Sonora,
and Colima. Now extirpated or present only as small remnants or recent reintroductions in many parts of the original
range.

CRANES, RAILS and ALLIES

Order Gruiformes

CRANES   Family Gruidae

Whooping Crane*   *Grus americana*—⚹ 17
                                          L. 50, W. 90

IDENTIFICATION: When the pure-white adults take flight the
jet-black primaries are very conspicuous and the fully outstretched head and neck distinguish them from herons. Young
are similar, but the white plumage is irregularly washed with
reddish-brown.

HABITS: These big white birds with calls that can be heard for
several miles were always conspicuous in the flat open
marshes and prairies that were their normal habitats. As
civilization moved west and north over the Great Plains they
found it increasingly difficult to find sufficiently secluded

places for nesting and gradually disappeared. Whooping cranes travel about a marsh largely on foot, their long stride enabling them to cover ground at amazing speed. When disturbed they rise only a few feet and move off with a slow, deep downstroke and a quick upstroke. In migration they travel at great heights in long lines and V's, from which their clamorous notes descend to earth. Family ties seem to be strong, as the adult pair and their 1 or 2 young remain together through the winter. Little is known of their feeding habits, but they appear to eat many kinds of marsh animals—such as frogs, snakes, crabs, and crayfish—as well as roots and tubers of marsh plants. They also visit fields to eat waste grains and browse on the new leaves of winter wheat.

VOICE: Sonorous trumpeting notes varying in pitch but always with a strong, vibrant overtone or roll.

NEST: (P.) A mass of marsh vegetation forming a flat mound with a slight depression in the center and located well out in an extensive open marsh, usually in the center of an area of open water from which the birds have removed the plants in building the nest. The 2 buffy-colored eggs (3.9 x 2.5) are blotched with various shades of brown.

RANGE: (P. M.) Once bred from Hudson Bay and n. Mackenzie south through the Great Plains to Iowa and Nebraska and in the coastal marshes of Louisiana. Wintered in the Gulf Coast States from Florida to Texas and south to c. Mexico. In migration occurred regularly on the Atlantic coast from New England south. Now reduced to a single remnant wintering in the Aransas National Wildlife Refuge on the Texas coast and migrating north through Nebraska, s. Manitoba, and Saskatchewan to unknown northern breeding grounds.

Sandhill Crane*   *Grus canadensis*—✕ 17
                                    L. 44; W. 80

IDENTIFICATION: Adults are uniformly gray except for the red color of the bare skin of the head, a marking which the brown young lack. The heavy body, long curved tertiaries, striding walk, and, in flight, the outstretched neck and flick of the wing on the upstroke are good identification marks.

HABITS: Although essentially a bird of open country, the sandhill crane occurs at times in relatively small marshes and patches of prairie in forested country. In the South, where it is a permanent resident, it also inhabits open pine woodlands interspersed with grassy openings and ponds. A small northern race is still common in parts of the Arctic, where it ranges from the low-lying grass tundra well up into rolling hill and mountain country. Good to eat and long regarded as a game bird, these splendid cranes have decreased or disappeared as breeders from the more settled parts of their once vast grassland range. Except when nesting they are very gregarious. They migrate in great flocks, often, like hawks, making use of thermal updrafts. At night they roost on the ground in a safe place like a sand bar or secluded pond. Like all cranes, the sandhill has a remarkable courtship dance. The birds bow to each other, jump into the air with wings held out loosely and feet thrown forward, then turn, bow again, and repeat. They walk long distances while feeding and eat chiefly roots and tubers, waste grains and other seeds, berries and tender vegetation. Mice, lemmings, crayfish, frogs, snakes, and insects appear to be taken in small quantities as opportunity offers.

VOICE: A loud, deep, rolling croak or vibrant honking that sounds like *gur-roo* or *gar-oo-oo-oo*.

NEST: (P.) A flat mound of marsh vegetation, much of it whole plants pulled up by the roots, in very open and usually moist country. Extensive marshlands, grass-covered tundra, or small ponds in open prairies are common sites. The shallow depression for the eggs is often only a few inches above water, but the nest may be 4 or 5 feet across and is invariably surrounded by open water. The 2 buffy eggs (3.6 x 2.3) are marked with browns.

RANGE: (P. M.) Breeds from Baffin Island, n. Mackenzie, n. Alaska, and n.e. Siberia south to s. Florida and Cuba, s.

Mississippi, Nebraska, Arizona, and n. California. Winters from s. Georgia, the Gulf Coast, and California south to c. Mexico.

LIMPKINS   Family Aramidae

Limpkin*
                 Aramus guarauna—✳ 17
                        L. 26; W. 42

IDENTIFICATION: The white spots on head, neck, and upper body are distinctive, as is the cranelike flick of the wings in flight.

HABITS: These largely nocturnal birds frequent fresh-water marshes and marshy riverbanks, where they feed along the edges of the denser clumps of marsh vegetation in the manner of rails. Nearby trees and shrubs are commonly used as resting and lookout perches, and the birds sometimes feed in the shallow water of swamp forests. When flushed they rise with dangling legs, high enough to clear the vegetation, leisurely fly off a short distance, and drop back into the marsh. Their favorite food appears to be the same big fresh-water snails that the Everglade kite feeds on, but they also eat many of the other small forms of animal life that occur in the marshes.

VOICE: The loud, ringing *kr-ows* of the limpkin usually commence at sundown and continue through the night. There is some variation, but they all sound surprisingly like human wails or howls and give rise to many local names, such as "crying bird."

NEST: (P.) A large, loosely woven mass of leaves and stems of emergent marsh plants, anchored just above the water to growing stalks and located on the open water edge of a dense clump of vegetation. Limpkins also build rather fragile platformlike nests 1 to 15 feet above the ground in thick tangles of vines growing over shrubs on marsh or stream banks. The 5 or 6 buffy eggs (2.3 x 1.7) are boldly marked with dull browns.

RANGE: (R.) Occurs from s. Georgia and s. Mexico south through Florida and the Greater Antilles to e. Argentina.

Comparative Average Lengths of Waders

SPECIES	OVER-ALL LENGTH	BILL	LEGS
Black Rail	5½	½	⅞
Least Sandpiper	6	¾	¾
Semipalmated Sandpiper	6¼	¾	¾
Snowy Plover	6¼	⅝	1
Western Sandpiper	6½	1	⅞
Red-necked Phalarope	7	1	¾
Ringed Plover	7	½	⅞
Piping Plover	7	½	⅞
Yellow Rail	7	½	⅞
Spotted Sandpiper	7½	⅞	1
White-rumped Sandpiper	7½	1	1
Baird's Sandpiper	7½	⅞	1
Thick-billed Plover	7½	⅞	1⅛
Curlew Sandpiper	8	1½	1¼
Sanderling	8	1	1
Buff-breasted Sandpiper	8	⅝	1¼
Stilt Sandpiper	8½	1⅜	2¾
Solitary Sandpiper	8½	1¼	1⅛
Red Phalarope	8½	⅞	⅞
Dunlin	8½	1½	1
Turnstone	8½	⅞	1
Jaçana	8½	1¼	2⅛
Sora	8¾	¾	1¼
Wilson Phalarope	9	1¼	1¼
Pectoral Sandpiper	9	1⅛	1⅛
Purple Sandpiper	9	1¼	⅞
Mountain Plover	9¼	⅞	1⅝
Virginia Rail	9½	1½	1⅜

SPECIES	OVER-ALL LENGTH	BILL	LEGS
Ruff	10	$1\frac{1}{4}$	$1\frac{3}{4}$
Killdeer	10	$\frac{3}{4}$	$1\frac{1}{2}$
Lesser Yellowlegs	$10\frac{1}{2}$	$1\frac{3}{8}$	2
Knot	$10\frac{1}{2}$	$1\frac{3}{8}$	$1\frac{1}{4}$
American Golden Plover	$10\frac{1}{2}$	$\frac{7}{8}$	$1\frac{3}{4}$
Corn Crake	$10\frac{1}{2}$	$\frac{7}{8}$	$1\frac{1}{2}$
Woodcock	11	$2\frac{3}{4}$	$1\frac{1}{4}$
Common Snipe	$11\frac{1}{4}$	$2\frac{5}{8}$	$1\frac{1}{4}$
Black-bellied Plover	$11\frac{1}{2}$	$1\frac{1}{8}$	$1\frac{3}{4}$
Dowitcher	12	$2\frac{1}{2}$	$1\frac{3}{8}$
Lapwing	12	1	2
Upland Plover	12	$1\frac{1}{8}$	$1\frac{7}{8}$
Purple Gallinule	13	$1\frac{1}{4}$	$2\frac{3}{8}$
Eskimo Curlew	$13\frac{1}{2}$	$2\frac{1}{4}$	$1\frac{3}{4}$
Gallinule	$13\frac{1}{2}$	$1\frac{3}{8}$	$2\frac{1}{8}$
Greater Yellowlegs	14	$2\frac{1}{8}$	$2\frac{1}{2}$
Black-necked Stilt	$14\frac{1}{2}$	$2\frac{3}{8}$	$7\frac{1}{2}$
Hudsonian Godwit	15	3	$2\frac{1}{4}$
Willet	15	$2\frac{1}{8}$	$2\frac{1}{4}$
Clapper Rail	15	$2\frac{1}{4}$	2
Coot	15	$1\frac{3}{8}$	$2\frac{1}{8}$
Bar-tailed Godwit	16	$3\frac{1}{4}$	2
Whimbrel	17	$3\frac{1}{2}$	$2\frac{1}{2}$
King Rail	17	$2\frac{1}{2}$	$2\frac{1}{2}$
Avocet	18	$3\frac{1}{2}$	6
Marbled Godwit	18	$4\frac{1}{2}$	$2\frac{3}{4}$
American Oyster-catcher	19	$3\frac{1}{2}$	$2\frac{1}{4}$
Long-billed Curlew	23	6	$3\frac{1}{4}$
Limpkin	26	$4\frac{1}{2}$	$4\frac{1}{2}$

RAILS, GALLINULES and COOTS
Family Rallidae

King Rail*   *Rallus elegans*—⌗13
                      L. 17; W. 24; Wt. $\frac{3}{4}$ lb.

IDENTIFICATION: The distinctly brownish color, bright reddish-
brown breast, and large size are distinctive. The downy chicks
are black with pale bills. Immature birds are darker above
than adults but only faintly buffy below.

'HABITS: Although not quite as secretive as most rails, these birds are seldom seen and usually have to be identified by their calls. Fortunately they are often quite noisy just before dawn and after sundown. When flushed they afford little more than a glimpse as, with dangling legs, they flutter off. If pressed this species can swim and dive, but it prefers to escape by running. It is generally a fresh-water marsh rail, widely distributed wherever rank growths occur in damp ground and commonly ranging into adjacent hay- and grainfields for grasshoppers and waste grain. In the marsh its food consists of the seeds of marsh plants and aquatic animal life. Year after year the king rail, along with a host of other fresh-water marsh species, is becoming scarcer as more and more of its habitat is destroyed by mosquito control or agricultural drainage, or flooded by the construction of power and irrigation reservoirs. We can, however, help these birds to some extent by fencing off the borders of such ponds and marshes as do survive so that cattle cannot beat down and destroy the nesting cover.

VOICE: The calls vary from a series of deep, grunting *umph, umph* notes and clucks that sound like a farmer urging on a horse to a series of *kick, kick, kick* sounds. They are quite deep in tone, all on the same pitch, and are uttered slowly and deliberately except when occasionally they are run together into a rapid jumble that ends with a few slower notes.

NEST: (I. 21, P.) A grass-lined depression in damp ground near a marsh, or a well-built, deeply hollowed cup of leaves and stalks supported above the water on a sedge tussock, bush, or dense patch of marsh plants. When possible the surrounding vegetation is pulled and woven into an arch over the nest. The 10 or so pale buffy eggs (1.6 x 1.2) are sparingly marked with browns.

RANGE: (P. M.) Breeds from Massachusetts, c. New York, s. Ontario, s. Minnesota, and Nebraska south to s. Florida, Cuba, and the Gulf Coast to Texas. Winters in the South Atlantic and Gulf States.

Clapper Rail*

Rallus longirostris—⚹13
L. 15; W. 20

IDENTIFICATION: The generally pale, grayish appearance and only slightly brown under parts are distinctive. Young birds are similar to young king rails.

HABITS: The harsh, vociferous clatter of these rails is one of the commonest salt-marsh sounds. The birds are at their noisiest just before a storm and at dusk, but any loud sound may start a chorus of calls, the first bird being answered by others. Clapper rails live and nest at the mercy of high spring and storm tides that destroy nests, float the eggs into windrows along the beaches, or set the hen and her brood of chicks afloat. Although they can swim well for a short time, rails soon perish unless they can reach high ground or climb on a floating log. In the fall these same conditions make them excessively vulnerable to hunters, who often take a heavy toll. They feed largely at low tide on the mud flats and along the banks of the marsh creeks, where their large, chickenlike tracks (some 10 inches apart) are conspicuous. When walking they bob their heads and twitch their tails, which are held almost vertical, revealing white under coverts. Fiddlers and other crabs and crustacea, mussels, snails, and worms are their chief foods.

As all crustacean animals, such as crabs and shrimps, are very susceptible to D.D.T. poisoning, the rails and many shore birds that use them for food are serious sufferers when the public demand for mosquito control results in the whole-sale use of this deadly poison on our coastal marshes and beaches.

VOICE: A rough, grating series of staccato *cac cac cac* notes that often diminish in volume and pitch toward the end. Also more abrupt single or widely spaced *keck* notes and grunts.

NEST: (P.) On the ground in a dense clump of vegetation on the highest place available in the open salt marsh. The nest, which is hidden by an arch of nearby vegetation, varies from a simple grass-lined depression to a well-cupped mass of grass and stems rising as much as a foot above the ground. Usually a well-defined runway leads to it. The 9 to 12 eggs (1.7 x 1.2) are buffy with brown spots.

RANGE: (P. M.) Breeds in the salt marshes of both coasts from Connecticut to s. Florida, the West Indies, Mexico, and Central America to s. Brazil, and from c. California to n.w. Peru. Winters from Virginia and c. California south.

Virginia Rail*   *Rallus limicola*—✕13
L. 9½; W. 14; Wt. 2½ oz.

IDENTIFICATION: Adults are like king rails except for their small size and gray cheeks. Juveniles are largely blackish. The downy black chick has a yellowish bill with a black band across the middle. In flight the reddish forewing is conspicuous in all plumages.

HABITS: Although active by day, these rails stick so close to the dense vegetation of the fresh or semi-brackish marshes in which they live that they are hard to find. The Virginia's calls, however, reveal its presence, and while most frequent at dawn and dusk, they are heard at all hours. If flushed, which is difficult, as they prefer to escape by running, the birds flutter away with feet dangling for only a few yards before dropping back into the marsh. It is hard to realize that they migrate long distances, flying always at night. The food of this species is drawn from the small animal life of the marsh, ranging from small fish to insects. It also eats seeds and berries, climbing about the plants to get them, and it visits weed-grown fields after the harvest.

VOICE: The courtship call is a vibrant, metallic *kid-ick, kid-ick, kid-ick,* often likened to the sound of a telegraph instrument or a hammer bouncing off an anvil. A descending series of piglike grunts is common, and there are also rough, shrill, discordant squeals and other equally odd calls.

NEST: (I. 19, P.) In a fresh or occasionally slightly brackish cattail or sedge marsh. The nest is a loosely woven structure of grass and stems anchored to the stalks of a clump of vegetation a few inches to a foot above the mud or water. The 8 eggs (1.3 x .91) in an average clutch are pale buff, sparingly spotted with russet-brown.

RANGE: (P. M.) Breeds from Nova Scotia, s. Quebec, s. Ontario,

s. Manitoba, and s. British Columbia south to North Carolina, Kentucky, Missouri, Utah, and n. Lower California. Also c. Mexico and much of South America to the Strait of Magellan. Winters from s. New Jersey, s. Illinois, Colorado, and s. British Columbia south to Cuba and Guatemala.

Sora*   *Porzana carolina*— ✳13
                                             L. 8¾; W. 13½; Wt. 3 oz.

IDENTIFICATION: The heavy, short, chickenlike yellow bill and, in adults, the black face are good field characters. The female is duller, less black about the face, and has more white spots than the male. The downy black chicks have orange throats and yellow bills with enlarged red bases.

HABITS: The sora, our most abundant rail, ranges over most of the continent, nesting in every little fresh-water marsh, bog, or riverside reed patch, even on the outskirts of large cities. A clap of the hands or the splash of a stick or rock will often start a series of calls revealing their presence. They are very curious and can best be observed when one sits still on the edge of a marsh opening toward dusk. Before long these laterally compressed birds—from which the expression "thin as a rail" comes—slip out between the cattails to work along the marsh edge and out on the lily pads and other floating vegetation, picking up insects, mollusks, and other small animals.

Although they flush more readily than some rails, soras seldom do more than flutter off weakly. It is hard to realize that during migration some individuals fly not less than 3,000 miles and that they not only winter throughout the islands of the West Indies but regularly visit Bermuda, often in considerable numbers. Migration flights are performed at night, usually at such low elevations that many birds are killed by striking buildings or other obstructions. The sora's habit of completely evacuating a marsh the night of the first frost often produces great migratory waves. In fall the birds become seedeaters and concentrate in tremendous numbers wherever they find extensive beds of wild rice. The broad marshes along the lower reaches of coastal rivers are much frequented and, to some extent, the salt marshes. Inland they visit corn and grain stubble fields, rank weed growths, and brushy hillsides. Despite heavy hunting and heavy migration losses, these prolific birds, laying clutches up to 14 or 18 eggs, which have to be arranged in 2 or 3 layers for the bird to cover them, remain abundant so long as their habitats are intact.

VOICE: The spring call is a clear, plaintive, quail-like ascending *ker-wee* that in the distance sounds like a spring peeper. This is repeated over and over with monotonous regularity, often during the day as well as at night. The sora's most characteristic call is its "whinny," a rapid series of a dozen or more clear, pleasing notes run together on a descending scale, becoming weaker as it slows down and levels off in pitch at the end. The bird has other short peeping calls, common ones being *ca-weep-eep* or a single *keek*.

NEST: (P.) A cup woven out of dead leaves and anchored to growing cattails or other marsh plants a few inches above water, or a large pile of such material placed on top of a sedge or grass tussock. The usual site is in or near a fairly open place in the marsh, but occasionally the nest is on the ground in low-lying meadowland or crop fields. Often an arch made of the surrounding vegetation hides the eggs. The 11 or more eggs (1.2 x .89) are yellowish-buff with numerous dull brown spots.

RANGE: (P. M.) Breeds from Nova Scotia, s. Quebec, n. Ontario, s. Mackenzie, and c. British Columbia south to Maryland, s. Ohio, s. Illinois, Kansas, Utah, and n. Lower California. Winters from n. Florida, the Gulf Coast, Texas, Arizona, and California south to Venezuela and Peru.

Yellow Rail*   *Coturnicops noveboracensis*—♯13
L. 7; W. 12; Wt. 2¼ oz.

IDENTIFICATION: The small size, yellowish color, and strongly striped upper parts are good field characters, and the conspicuous white patch in the hind wing next to the body is diagnostic if the bird flies.

HABITS: This bird is more of a mystery than any other North American species of comparable distribution. It nests in shallow fresh marshes and wet meadows where grasses a foot or two high predominate, instead of in the taller, denser vegetation like cattails, which most rails prefer. At other than the breeding season they are found in the higher parts of the coastal salt marshes as well as in moist grain- and hayfields. As they are virtually impossible to flush and seem to avoid open places, they are seldom detected except by their notes. So loath are they to fly that a trained dog can often catch them. Most specimens have been obtained with the help of dogs or through mowing or beating down a long lane in the grass and driving the rails across it. This species seems to be hardy and often remains in northern marshes until late fall. The only food they have been recorded as eating is small snails.

VOICE: A series of 5 clicking notes broken by a pause between the second and third—*kuk, kuk—kuk, kuk, kuk;* occasionally a series of 7 or 8 short notes ending with a long, rising *queah.* These notes have been likened to the sound made by hitting 2 stones together, tapping a hollow bone with a piece of iron, or driving a tent peg into hard ground.

NEST: (P.) A well-made cup of fine grass placed just above the shallow water of a grass marsh, on a grass tussock, or in a mat of old dead grass. Occasionally in drier locations the nest is on damp ground. Regardless of the site, it is usually placed so that the eggs are hidden from above by a wisp of old grass. The 8 or 9 eggs (1.1 x .82) are a warm buff with a dense cluster of reddish-brown spots at the large end.

RANGE: (M.) Occurs during the breeding season from Nova Scotia, c. Quebec, n. Manitoba, and s. Mackenzie south to Maryland, Ohio, Missouri, Colorado, and c. California. Winters from South Carolina to s. Florida and across the Gulf States to California.

Black Rail*   *Laterallus jamaicensis*—⚹13
                            L. 5½; W. 11

IDENTIFICATION: This black-billed little rail with its white-spotted back is unmistakable if seen clearly. The downy black chicks of the larger rails are sometimes called "black rails."

HABITS: This still smaller species runs a close second to the yellow rail as a bird of mystery. It is almost as hard to flush except at extreme high tides. The normal glimpse is of a mouselike animal darting away through grass. The salt-hay meadows and Salicornia flats on the highest parts of the coastal marshes, which are reached only by the highest tides, are its home. Where vegetation has gone unburned for several years these areas are covered with a dense mat of old grass under which the birds live. Their only recorded food is isopods—enormously abundant small crustacea that feed on dead or decaying plant material in the salt marsh. Inland, black rails have occurred in the damp, grassy upper borders of marshes.

VOICE: Notes of the female are described as a *croo-croo-croo-o,* like the opening of a yellow-billed cuckoo's song, while those of the male are a *kik, kik, kik, kik.* Another call has been described as *did-ee-dunk* repeated 3 times.

NEST: (P.) A loose cup of fine, soft grass hidden under a tuft of bent-over but not smoothly matted old marsh grass or under a carefully woven arch of growing green grass. The nest is sometimes directly on the damp ground but more often is supported by the mat of last year's grass in which it is built. The 7 or so eggs (1.0 x .78) are buffy-white, evenly dotted with fine brown spots.

RANGE: (P. M.) Breeds from Massachusetts, s. Ontario, and Minnesota south to Florida, Illinois, and Kansas; on the Pacific coast from c. California to n. Lower California, and in South America to Peru and Chile. Winters from s. Florida and the Gulf Coast to the Greater Antilles and Guatemala, and along the Pacific coast from California south.

Corn Crake* — *Crex crex*—⋕12

(Land-rail) L. 10½

IDENTIFICATION: The bright chestnut-brown wings, the large size, and generally yellowish appearance are distinctive.

HABITS: Like our sora, this bird, the common land rail of Europe, is a strong flier and migrates many thousands of miles annually. In view of this it is not too surprising that from time to time individuals stray from their normal migration routes and reach North America. The corn crake is not a marsh bird but a frequenter of grasslands and agricultural croplands, especially clover, and to some extent grainfields. Back in the 1870s an attempt was made to introduce them into this country, but, like most such efforts, it came to nought. The food is chiefly insects, plus a few slugs and earthworms, and some seeds and grain.

VOICE: The spring call is a loud, rasping sound as of a piece of wood being drawn across a comb.

NEST: (I. 17, P.) A cup of grasses on the ground in low-lying meadows, hayfields, or in dense weeds or grainfields. The 10 or so eggs (1.5 x 1.0) are grayish or brownish, splotched with brown.

RANGE: (M.) Breeds from the Faeroes and the Arctic Circle in Norway east to c. Siberia and south to n. Spain, Bulgaria, n. Persia, and the Altai. Winters throughout most of Africa. Has occurred along the Atlantic coast from Greenland to Maryland.

Purple Gallinule*   *Porphyrula martinica*—⚹12
                                      L. 13; W. 22

IDENTIFICATION: The yellow legs, blue frontal plate, and solid
    white under tail area are distinctive. The black down of the
    chicks is mixed with white hairs about the head, and the bill
    is yellow with a black outer end.
HABITS: This gem of the marshlands is a rather fearless bird,
    likely to be seen walking over the floating plants in the
    deeper areas of the marsh or along roadside ditches. Here it
    picks up frogs, small snails and other mollusks, aquatic in-
    sects and seeds from lily pads, spatterdock, and water lettuce.
    The purple gallinule flies quite readily with its long yellow
    legs dangling like a rail's, and as it walks it constantly and
    rapidly flicks its tail. It can alight readily on branches and
    frequently climbs about in shrubbery over water. In fall in
    some areas it visits rice and other grainfields, where it climbs
    up stalks to feed on the seed heads.
VOICE: This noisy bird utters henlike cackles as it flies, and it
    has many other guttural notes. The commonest call has been
    described as a "harsh, shrill, rapid, laughing *hiddy-hiddy-
    hiddy, hit-up, hit-up, hit-up,*" the latter part of slow delivery.
NEST: (P.) Usually in islandlike patches of tall, dense marsh
    vegetation surrounded by open water-lily marsh. In some
    areas clumps of wampee are the preferred site. The nest is a
    saucer-shaped platform of grass and stalks, supported a foot
    or more above the water by surrounding vegetation. In addi-
    tion to the active nest, several dummy nests are built. The
    6 or so eggs (1.5 x 1.1) are pinkish-buff, finely dotted with
    brown.
RANGE: (P. M.) Breeds from South Carolina and the Gulf
    States west to s.c. Texas and south through Mexico and the
    West Indies to Peru and n. Argentina. Winters from c.
    Florida and s. Texas south.

Gallinule*   *Gallinula chloropus*—⚹12
(Moorhen)   L. 13½; W. 21; Wt. 14 oz.

IDENTIFICATION: A ducklike bird, without a duck's bill, which
    continually bobs its head as it swims. The red bill, the white
    lines along the sides (in adults), and the divided white under
    tail coverts are distinctive. The downy black chicks have a
    few white-tipped hairs and show bare reddish skin on top of
    the head and at the base of the black-tipped red bill.

HABITS: (Age 5½ yrs.) Fresh-water marshes with frequent openings where cattails or other emergent vegetation grows in a foot or more of water are the typical habitat of this rather slender, long-necked bird that swims with stern high and tail up, revealing its white underside. The marsh need not be large; often a small bed of cattails on the edge of a lake or river is sufficient. The birds are not particularly shy and are often seen prowling about in the open near the margins of denser clumps of reeds. Civilization seldom disturbs them so long as their habitat remains intact. The "water hen" feeds both on land, where it walks with frequent jerks of its tail and flashing its under tail coverts, and in water, where it walks on floating vegetation or swims, dives, and tips up like a duck. Food includes snails, insects, and other small animals and many seeds and berries but vegetation seems to be their staple, as the birds regularly consume quantities of under-water plants, duckweed, and leaves of grass and herbs.

VOICE: These noisy birds have a variety of often chickenlike notes, and they seem constantly to be conversing with one another. Most calls are loud, rather harsh, and often complaining. Usually 4 or 5 squawks are followed by a series of clucks or abrupt froglike *kups*.

NEST: (I. 21, P.) A shallow cup of old dead rushes, cattails, and stems of marsh plants, usually over water, anchored a few inches from the surface in a clump of vegetation or semi-floating, with a sloping entrance ramp on the side. Occasionally in shrubbery near water. The site is usually near open water on an islandlike tussock or in the edge of a large reed bed. Several nestlike platforms are usually built and may be used for brooding the young. The 11 or so eggs (1.7 x 1.2) in an average clutch are buffy, irregularly splashed with brown.

RANGE: (P. M.) Occurs virtually all over the world, except in Australia, including practically every island, even to Bermuda, Hawaii, and the Azores. In the Western Hemisphere breeds from s. Maine, s. Ontario, s. Minnesota, Nebraska, Arizona, and c. California south and winters from South Carolina, the Gulf Coast, and s. California south.

American Coot*   *Fulica americana*—⚹12
L. 15; W. 26; Wt. 1¼ lbs.

IDENTIFICATION: The white bill, outer under tail coverts, and the rear edge of the inner wing are distinctive. Young are considerably whiter below and have a duller bill. The black down of the chicks is mixed with conspicuous tawny-reddish, curly hairs around the head and neck.

HABITS: The coot is the most aquatic member of its family. Its toes have developed expanded pads to aid in swimming, and it is as much at home in the water as a duck. It swims buoyantly on even keel, nodding its head as it goes. In feeding it tips up like a duck and if necessary dives like a grebe. When taking wing it has to run over the surface for quite a distance. When fighting or defending itself it relies mainly upon its powerful, sharp-clawed feet. During breeding season the birds largely confine themselves to shallow marsh-fringed ponds or open fresh-water marshes, but at other times they associate freely with ducks on all types of water, including, on occasion, brackish and salt bays. Underwater plants are staple foods, but the coot's great fondness for chara or musk grass and other algae usually keeps competition with ducks at a minimum. Coots also feed on land, eating grass, sprouting grains, and, in fall, waste grain. Small aquatic animals are taken as occasion offers.

VOICE: Coots seem to be almost constantly giving vent to a babble of indescribable sounds, accompanied by much splashing and fussing. The notes have been variously described as croaks, toots, grunts, cackles, coughs, quacks, coos, whistles, squawks, chuckles, clucks, wails, and froglike plunks and grating sounds.

NEST: (I. 22, P.) A cup woven out of the dried leaves and stems of marsh plants, usually resting on a floating foundation of the same material and anchored to growing plants. Sometimes well concealed in a dense bed or clump of reeds but often in the open, resting on a matted mass of old reeds with little or no concealment. The 10 or so eggs (1.9 x 1.3) are pinkish-buff, thickly and finely spotted with blackish-brown.

RANGE: (P. M.) Breeds from New Brunswick, s. Quebec, Ontario, c. Saskatchewan, s.w. Mackenzie, and c. British Columbia south to New Jersey, Ohio, w. Tennessee, Arkansas, n.e. Mexico, and s. Lower California. Over parts of this range it breeds only sporadically. It also breeds in c. Florida, the West Indies, s. Mexico, Central America, the Hawaiian Islands, and the n. Andes of South America. Winters from Virginia, s. Illinois, Texas, Arizona, and s. British Columbia south to the West Indies and Panama; a few winter as far north as s. New England and Colorado.

SHORE BIRDS, GULLS, AUKS and ALLIES
Order Charadriiformes

JAÇANAS   Family Jacanidae

Jaçana*   *Jacana spinosa*—✳︎12
                                                        L. 8½

IDENTIFICATION: The long toes, pale yellow-green primaries and secondaries, and, in adults, the yellow frontal plate are distinctive.

HABITS: These curious birds live and nest on the open blanket of water lettuce and other floating plants that often completely cover small ponds, lakes, and old river channels through the American tropics. Their extraordinarily long toes enable them to run over the leaves to catch the insects and other small animals that appear to be their chief food. The birds have the habit of frequently raising and opening their wings, revealing the conspicuously yellow flight feathers. The bend of the wing is armed with a long sharp spur that is evidently used in fighting. Young birds are the ones most likely to wander north to Florida from Cuba or to s. Texas from Mexico, as happens from time to time.

VOICE: A noisy cackle as they fly, also a plaintive whistle.

NEST: (P.) A fragile cup of leaves of water plants, supported by a lily pad or other floating vegetation, out on the overgrown surface of a pond. The 4 eggs (1.2 x .91) are pale brown, evenly and thickly covered with black scrawls.

RANGE: (R.) Occurs from the Greater Antilles, Tamaulipas, and Sinaloa south to n. Argentina.

OYSTER-CATCHERS   Family Haematopodidae

American Oyster-catcher* *Haematopus palliatus*—✳ 34
L. 19; W. 33

IDENTIFICATION: The large size, red bill, and, in flight, the white upper tail coverts and secondaries make this an easy bird to identify. Young have brownish bills surrounded by whitish feathers, and their feet are grayish.

HABITS: Big, noisy, and conspicuous, the oyster-catcher does not long survive near civilization unless given complete protection. Once reported by Audubon as breeding as far north as s. Labrador, it is now scarce or absent from many parts of our coast. That it may again become more abundant is indicated by the recent history of the closely related European oyster-catcher which still ranges as far north as Iceland and the White Sea. Under protection the European bird is becoming increasingly common in many parts of Great Britain and in some areas is nesting a considerable distance inland along rivers running back through open country. Our bird is today seldom found far from the wilder, outer beaches and the nearby flats, where it feeds on the falling and rising tide. "Coon oysters," mussels, clams, cockles, limpets, snails, marine worms, crabs, and other crustacea are eaten. The bird is expert at opening shellfish by inserting its bill into the partly open shell and cutting the adductor muscle before the animal can close up. It is also at home on rocky coasts and islands, where it feeds on the barnacles and mollusks below the high-tide line. Widely scattered when breeding, oyster-catchers gather into large flocks during winter, when some southward migration occurs.

VOICE: When disturbed, a loud, distinctive, scolding *wheep, wheep, wheep* call that has an insistent, penetrating quality. Also a short, sharp *pie* whistle and a more musical double, ploverlike trill that seems to be the equivalent of a song.

NEST: (I. 22, P.) A simple depression, sometimes with a few bits of shell for a lining, at the top of a slight elevation on the upper beach, on a shell bank, or occasionally on a rock ledge just above water, where the bird commands a good view of its surroundings. The normal clutch is 3 buffy eggs (2.2 x 1.5), irregularly blotched with blackish-brown.

RANGE: (P. M.) Breeds from New Jersey south along the Atlantic, Gulf, and Caribbean coasts to c. Argentina, including parts of the West Indies, and from Lower California along the Pacific and Gulf coasts to s. Chile, including the Galápagos Islands.

PLOVERS and TURNSTONES
Family Charadriidae

Lapwing*			*Vanellus vanellus*—✳31
						L. 12

IDENTIFICATION: The color pattern is unlike that of any
American shore bird, and the black crest of adults is unique.
The flight is rather unsteady, and the broad rounded wings
are flapped rather slowly. The wing lining is white, upper
and under tail coverts reddish-brown.

HABITS: Occupying in the Old World a niche rather similar to
that of our killdeer, the lapwing has gained vastly in habitat
through the spread of agriculture. Though it is the source of
the gourmet's "plover's eggs," it remains abundant in the Old
World in nearly all reasonably moist farming areas. Plowed
croplands, fallow land, and closely grazed pastures in flat,
open country, especially if there are occasional marshy
spots, provide ideal conditions. Food consists largely of insects picked up in crop fields, but lapwings also take worms
and other small animal organisms as well as weed seeds and
grain. After nesting they gather in large flocks and roam the
country, visiting mud flats, marshes, flooded fields, and other
typical shore-bird haunts. Occasional stragglers reach our
shores. On the night of December 18–19, 1927, a large flight
left Scotland and northern England for their wintering
grounds in Ireland but, evidently owing to a strong tailwind
and a dense fog, overshot their destination. Persisting on
their course, they reached various points in Labrador, Newfoundland, and Nova Scotia, where they perished from the
cold in a few days.

VOICE: A loud, wheezy *pee-wee* or *pee-wit* is the common call,
uttered in flight.

NEST: (I. 25, P.) A depression in the ground with a grass
lining. The normal site is a high spot in a pasture, crop field,
or marshy meadow. The 4 pale brown eggs (1.9 x 1.3) are
blotched with black.

RANGE: (P. M.) Breeds across n. Europe and Asia from n.
Norway to e. Siberia and south to n. Spain, Transcaspia, and
n. China. Winters from Great Britain, s. Europe, and China
south to n. Africa, n. India, and Japan. An occasional
straggler to the e. coast of North America.

Ringed Plover*   *Charadrius hiaticula—* ✳30
(Semipalmated Plover)   L. 7; W. 15

IDENTIFICATION: The single complete chest band, short bicolored
bill, and bright orange-yellow legs are distinctive. Fall birds
have brownish chest bands, and the young have a solid black
bill and pale yellow legs.

HABITS: This is a common migrant throughout the United
States. It travels in flocks but, like all plovers, scatters out to
feed. Mud flats are favorite feeding grounds, and often the
backs of the birds so match their surroundings that they are
almost invisible until they run. Inland they seek out freshly
drained lakes or freshly plowed fields that have been made
muddy by heavy rains. Along the coast they are attracted by
tidal flats, retiring at high tide to rest in small, compact
bunches on the upper beach. They also feed in salt marshes
wherever there is a shallow pond, an open mud flat, or an
area of short grass such as that produced by mowing or a
fire. Inland they occur along the shore line of lakes and rivers,
and on the coast they sometimes feed with sandpipers on the
edge of the water. Small mollusks, crustacea, and marine
worms are staple salt-water foods, while inland aquatic insects and earthworms are taken. When feeding they run about
very actively, stopping suddenly from time to time to listen,
look, or quickly reach down and grab some small animal.

VOICE: The common call when flushed is a clear, somewhat
plaintive double whistle, *chee-wee*. The song, occasionally
heard in migration, is a series of short notes uttered faster
and faster until they become a whinny or chuckle.

NEST: (I. 23, P.) A depression in sand or on the ground or in
moss or lichens near a beach. Like most plovers, these birds
sometimes give their nests a slight lining of shells, pebbles,
or grass. The site is often near a landmark, like a piece of
driftwood. The 4 buffy eggs (1.3 x .93) are boldly to finely
marked with blackish-browns.

RANGE: (M.) A circumpolar species, breeding from the shores
of the Arctic Ocean south to Nova Scotia, the n. Gulf of St.
Lawrence, James Bay, n. Manitoba, and c. British Columbia,
and in Europe to the Mediterranean. Winters from South
Carolina, the Gulf Coast, and c. California south to Argentina and Chile; from the Mediterranean to c. Africa and n.
India.

Piping Plover*   *Charadrius melodus*—✳30
                                 L. 7; W. 15

IDENTIFICATION: The pale gray, sand-colored upper parts, together with the orange-yellow legs, are distinctive. The black ring at the base of the neck is variable in completeness, and in winter adults or young birds this and the black forehead mark may be indistinct or absent.

HABITS: These little birds match the dry sand so perfectly as to be almost invisible, and they often escape by running or crouching motionless in the sand. During summer they prefer beaches with broad, open sandy flats above the high tide line or between dunes. They quickly take advantage of areas where recent grading and filling or disposal of dredging wastes have created sandy flats. Here they nest until the areas grow up too thickly to grass or other vegetation. Much of their feeding is done on wet sands, where they work the edge of the incoming waves along with sandpipers, or, to some extent, on mud flats exposed at low tide. Marine worms, crustacea, and insects appear to be their chief foods. They are early migrants in spring and leave very early in fall to winter in small flocks along southern beaches.

VOICE: A clear, melodious, and rather ventriloquial bell-like *peep-lo,* the first note rather low, the second higher. Also a series of a dozen or so short, clear whistles, often on a descending scale.

NEST: (I. 28, P., N. 33) A depression lined with stones or shells in the loose dry sand of a flat, open upper beach or a recent fill where little or no vegetation has become established. The 4 eggs (1.2 x .95) are pale buff, lightly but evenly dotted with blackish.

RANGE: (M.) Breeds from Newfoundland, s. Quebec, s. Ontario, s. Manitoba, and s. Alberta south on the Atlantic coast to North Carolina, west along the Great Lakes to n. Ohio and n. Illinois and to c. Nebraska. Winters south from South Carolina along the coast to n. Mexico and in small numbers to the n. West Indies.

Snowy Plover*   *Charadrius alexandrinus*—✳30
(Kentish Plover)   L. 6¼; W. 13½

IDENTIFICATION: A smaller, whiter plover than the piping, with a longer, slenderer bill, slate-gray legs, and a dark ear patch. Young and winter adults lack most or all of the dark markings and can best be distinguished by bill shape and leg color.

HABITS: Ideal habitat is extensive, dry, flat, barren areas near water where little or no vegetation grows. This the snowy plover finds on the broad expanse of upper beach and nearby sandy flats where occasional storm tides keep vegetation from developing. Inland similar conditions exist where saline or alkaline waters and rapid evaporation have created vast areas of exposed and largely barren flats that are submerged only after very heavy rains. In both these sharply and usually widely separated habitats the snowy plover is often associated with the least tern. The snowy's food is obtained along the water's edge or on the flats. At times it follows the waves on the beach like a sandpiper; at other times it forages for crustacea and flies about dead fish and other material in the sea wrack along the edge of the upper beach. These, plus marine worms and smaller mollusks, must be its chief foods. Saltworks where commercial sea salt is obtained by evaporation are quickly adopted by these birds, who use the low dikes between the ponds for nest sites.

VOICE: The common call is a series of 3 rather low, mellow, whistled notes, the second louder than the others. In flight the bird often utters a low, rapid trill.

NEST: (I. 24, P.) A hollow in the ground on as elevated a site as is available on a broad, open beach or salt flat. There is often a lining of shell, stones, or bits of vegetation. The 3 sandy-buff eggs (1.2 x .88) are dotted or scrawled with black.

RANGE: (P. M.) This species breeds in widely separated areas all over the world, occurring on every continent and in many island groups. In the Western Hemisphere it breeds on the coasts of the Gulf States from Florida to Texas, also Yucatan, the Bahamas, the Greater Antilles, and n. Venezuela; on the Pacific coast from Washington to s. Lower California and in Peru and Chile; inland from n. Utah and Kansas south to New Mexico and n. Texas. Winters from the Gulf Coast and c. California south to Paraguay.

Thick-billed Plover   *Charadrius wilsonia*—✳30
(Wilson's Plover)   L. 7½

IDENTIFICATION: The long, heavy, solid-black bill, the white line over the eye, and the dusky-pinkish legs are distinctive. Winter males, females, and young have grayish markings in place of the breeding male's black ones. Some males show considerable rusty-brown on the sides of head and nape.

HABITS: The thick-billed plover makes its home along broad stretches of open sand between the dunes and the lower beach. Inlets with extensive bars, mud flats, and storm-washed points often support small, loose colonies. The birds feed on small seashore animals, including small crabs, shrimp, and other crustacea, insects, and small mollusks.

VOICE: Call notes are a single abrupt *wheet* or a deeper double whistle. Also other higher-pitched runs of whistled notes.

NEST: (I. 24, P.) A depression on the open, sandy beach just above the tides or a similar open flat near water. Occasionally in a hollow among sand dunes. The 3 eggs (1.4 x 1.0) are pale buff, evenly marked with small black dots and scrawls.

RANGE: (P. M.) Breeds from Virginia south to Florida and along the shores and islands of the entire Gulf of Mexico-Caribbean basin. Also on the Pacific coast from c. Lower California to Peru. Winters from the Gulf Coast southward.

Killdeer*

Charadrius vociferus—✳30
L. 10; W. 20; Wt. 3 oz.

IDENTIFICATION: The double breast band and orange-brown lower back, rump, and upper tail coverts are distinctive. Young birds are similar but paler and browner above and have grayish breast bands.

HABITS: Heavily grazed meadows and borders of pasture ponds, plowed cropland, and waste places created by grading and filling for roads and railroads are preferred habitats. Few birds appear to have benefited more from the changes incident to the settlement of the country. Although killdeer often feed about wet places they are largely independent of water during the nesting season. Many species do a "broken-wing" act when their nest or young are approached, but few put on as good a show as the killdeer. Alert and noisy, the birds warn the neighborhood when an intruder sets foot in their domain. They are hardy and even in areas where they have to go south for the winter they are gone only a few months, returning with robins as harbingers of spring. In winter they move about in loose flocks, often in association with other shore birds, but seldom in saline coastal areas. Beetles, grasshoppers, and other insects are their most important foods. The balance consists of other small animals.

VOICE: The alarm note is a loud, vociferous *kill-dee* call. A long trill is often heard about the breeding grounds.

NEST: (I. 25, P.) This bird likes an open location for its nest, which is only a slight depression in the ground, lined with grass. Barren, open spots, plowed cropland, closely grazed pastures, and gravel bars are common sites. The 4 eggs (1.4 x 1.1) are pale buff, blotched and scrawled with blackish. Two broods are sometimes reared.

RANGE: (P. M.) Breeds from s. New England, s. Quebec, n. Ontario, s. Mackenzie, and n. British Columbia south to the Greater Antilles, c. Mexico, and s. Lower California. Also on the coast of Peru. Winters from Bermuda, New Jersey, Ohio, Missouri, Colorado, and s. British Columbia south to n. Venezuela and n.w. Peru.

Mountain Plover*   *Eupoda montana*—※30
                                                L. 9¼

IDENTIFICATION: The black forehead and lores, the white line over the eye, and the diffuse buff-gray wash on the breast, together with the uniform coloring of the back, are distinctive. Winter adults lack black markings and are best told by their nondescriptness and, in flight, by the pure white of their axillars and wing linings, which contrasts with the gray of their flight feathers. The tail is tipped with white and has a blackish subterminal band.

HABITS: During summer this is a bird of dry, short-grass prairie, miles from water, where the sparse clumps of bunch grass are only a few inches high. From here it ranges into sandy, semi-arid areas with scattered sagebrush and cactus. Open ground seems attractive to the species, as winter flocks are often found on plowed land or on sprouting grainfields, alkaline flats, or closely cropped pastures. Long-legged and very fast afoot, this plover prefers to escape by running. When forced to fly it stays close to the ground, alternately flapping and sailing on decurved wings. Upon alighting it may crouch down and become almost invisible. Its food is largely insects, chiefly grasshoppers, crickets, beetles, and flies.

VOICE: The whistled notes are short and vary in tone from musical and plaintive to shrill, harsh, and lisping. They have been likened to the croaking of a frog.

NEST: A slight depression with little or no lining on bare ground between tufts of short prairie grass. The 3 eggs (1.5 x 1.1) are olive-buff, spotted and scrawled with black about the larger end.

RANGE: (M.) Breeds from w. Nebraska and n. Montana south to n.w. Texas and New Mexico. Winters from s. Texas, s.

Arizona, and n. California south to c. Mexico and s. Lower California, rarely east along the Gulf Coast to Florida.

Turnstone*

Arenaria interpres—✱30
L. 8½; W. 18

IDENTIFICATION: Spring adults are so striking as to be unmistakable. Winter adults and young are best told by their orange legs and dark breast patch. At all times turnstones reveal a striking pattern of white and dark when they fly.

HABITS: Stockily built, pugnacious shore birds waddling about on short orange legs, overturning shells, pebbles, and lumps of seaweed or digging holes in the sand as large as themselves, can only be turnstones. They occur in greatest numbers along seacoasts, but some migrate through the interior, where they frequent the shores and beaches of larger lakes. Sandy beaches and pebbly shingle are favorite feeding grounds. Here the birds root like little pigs among the sea wrack along the upper beach and fight vigorously over choice finds. At low tide when seaweed- and barnacle-covered rocks and beds of mussels and oysters are exposed, they seem to find an abundance of food. Although small mollusks, crustacea, and insects are staples, turnstones are quick to take advantage of a variety of items. In various places, especially in the Arctic, they eat quantities of berries, climbing about in the bushes to get them. Horseshoe-crab eggs are taken from the spawning beds, and on Laysan Island turnstones were found systematically breaking and eating tern eggs at every opportunity. Although generally encountered in small groups when feeding, the birds often migrate in large flocks, either by themselves or with their common associate, the black-bellied plover. At times they can be identified by their un-shore-bird-like habit of perching on vantage points up off the ground.

VOICE: When they take flight turnstones utter a metallic rattle or low chatter, often recorded as *cut-i-cut* or *kek*. They also have a more musical ploverlike whistle.

NEST: A depression in the ground, usually in the open tundra or among dunes near the coast or along rivers or occasionally tucked into a sheltered cavity. The 4 eggs (1.5 x 1.1) are olive-buff, boldly marked with brown.

RANGE: (M.) Breeds on the islands and coasts of the Arctic Ocean south to Southampton Island, the Yukon delta, Iceland, islands in the s. Baltic Sea, lakes in the Kirghiz Steppes, and Kamchatka. Winters from Bermuda, North Carolina, the Gulf Coast, and c. California to s. Brazil and c. Chile; also from Great Britain, the Mediterranean, s. China, and Hawaii south to s. South Africa, Australia, and New Zealand.

American Golden Plover*   *Pluvialis dominica*—✳31
L. 10½; W. 22; Wt. 6½ oz.

IDENTIFICATION: In breeding plumage this species is black below to the tail and uniformly dusky, flecked with yellowish spots above. The tail is dark. In fall plumage this is a fairly dark brownish-looking bird without conspicuous black or white markings. Young are often very yellowish in the early fall. Compared with a black-bellied, this plover is smaller and slenderer, with a smaller bill and head and longer, more pointed wings that are uniformly grayish below. It also has the habit of holding its wings up over its back for a moment after alighting and of bobbing its head frequently.

HABITS: This is one of the champion long-distance migrants. Once an abundant bird, it is only beginning to recover from the market hunting that almost wiped it out 60 years ago. In spring these plovers all go north through the central part of the country, frequenting freshly plowed fields and the short grass of prairie and pasture. They are especially attracted to recently burned areas. In fall stragglers from the offshore flight turn up along the North Atlantic coast, where they occur in the above types of habitat and with other shore birds on the coastal mud flats. There is also an inland flight in the fall made up predominantly of young birds that show more preference for wet and muddy areas about marshy places. During most of the year the food is largely insects and other small forms of animal life, but in the North these plovers also eat quantities of fruits like the abundant crowberry.

VOICE: The many calls are harsher than the black-bellied's, more killdeer-like, and usually with a chucklelike roll. The commonest is of two syllables, the first ending with a quaver, the second falling in pitch. It is sometimes rendered as *quee-e-e-e-a*. Other variations are a short *que* and longer calls like *quee-del-eee*.

NEST: (P.) A slight depression, usually in reindeer moss, with a lining of moss and other lichens. The usual site is a ridg' top in open tundra. The 4 buffy eggs (1.9 x 1.3) are boldly and heavily marked with brownish-black.

RANGE: (M.) Breeds from Devon and Melville islands, n. Alaska, and all n. Siberia south to the southern limit of the tundra, reaching n. Manitoba, the c. Alaska coast, and Kamchatka. Winters on the plains of s. South America from Bolivia to e. Argentina and in e. India, s. China, Australia, and the islands of the Pacific south to New Zealand. The main migration moves north up the Mississippi Valley region in spring and southeast off the Atlantic coast from Nova Scotia to n.e. South America in fall, large flights passing over Bermuda and Barbados at times.

Black-bellied Plover*   *Squatarola squatarola*—✳31
(Grey Plover)   L. 11½; W. 23; Wt. 8 oz.

IDENTIFICATION: The light grayish back and largely white head and belly are distinctive. Most fall birds are all gray, paler below, with streaked, rather finely barred flanks as in the golden. Juveniles are spotted with yellow above, especially on the rump, but this generally fades to gray in the fall. In any plumage the black axillars, white rump, black-barred white tail, and white line in the wing are conspicuous.

HABITS: This wild, wary bird, largest of our plovers, is stockily built, with a big head and a distinctive, erect carriage. Although it has an extensive breeding range in the North, it is widely scattered and seldom abundant; in migration it never travels in vast flocks as did the once far more abundant golden plover. Black-bellies come south in small numbers clear across the country, but the largest concentrations occur on coastal tide flats, sand bars, and salt-marsh meadows, where the birds are likely to be seen with knots, their commonest associates. Inland they prefer lake shores, mud flats, and marshy pastures but are also found at times on freshly plowed land and rain-flooded fields. They take whatever forms of small animal life are most accessible, including crabs and other crustacea, small mollusks, worms, and insects.

VOICE: The calls are rich, melodious, and somewhat plaintive whistles, the commonest a series of 3 notes, a drawled *pee-u-wee*. It is easy to imitate, and the birds decoy to it readily.

NEST: (I. 23, P.) A slight hollow in the ground or tundra moss, lined with lichens or grass. It is usually on a ridge and often on the edge of a river bluff, where it commands a good view. The 4 eggs (2.1 x 1.4) vary from pale buff or grayish to greenish or pinkish, lightly spotted with blackish.

RANGE: (M.) Breeds in the Arctic on the islands off and around the coasts of the Arctic Ocean from w. Greenland west to Siberia and the Kanin Peninsula of Russia and south in North America to Southampton Island and the Yukon delta. Winters from North Carolina, the Gulf Coast, and s. British Columbia south to Brazil and n. Chile and from the Mediterranean and India to South Africa and Australia.

SNIPE and SANDPIPERS   Family Scolopacidae

American Woodcock*   *Philohela minor*—✕ 33
                                 L. 11; W. 18; Wt. 6 oz.

IDENTIFICATION: A big, heavy-bodied, rich brown bird with broad, rounded wings and a very short neck and tail. Seldom seen until it suddenly zigzags off from underfoot with a twittering whistle.

HABITS: Although the woodcock is not uncommon few people are familiar with it except those who have sought it out. During the day the birds remain on the ground in moist alder thickets, spring-fed hillside runs, or rich, moist bottom land, where their protective coloring renders them practically invisible. The spectacular spring courtship flights in which the male spirals up to a considerable height, circles a few times, and then descends in a series of abrupt side-slips and sudden upswoops seldom begin until half an hour after sunset. They continue until dark, or off and on all night if the moon is out. In the morning the song is given during about the same period of light intensity, the time varying with season and weather.

Their staple food is earthworms, which they can extract from depths up to 3 inches down in the soil by means of their highly specialized bills. The flexible outer end of the upper mandible can be moved away from the end of the ridged lower mandible when the bill is closed at the base and inserted full length into the ground. Woodcocks apparently locate worms through their sense of hearing or by the sense of feeling in their feet, as they often catch them on the first try. The round holes left in damp earth by the birds' bill serve as excellent signs of the birds' presence in an area. Insect larvae, chiefly those of flies and beetles, are taken, but woodcocks never stay long unless there is an abundant supply of earthworms. Of these they can eat more than their own weight in a 24-hour period. Occasionally seeds, berries, and tender leaves are added to the diet.

There is no real pairing, as each sex has its own territory and males may mate with females from more than one adjacent area. The male's territory must include a small, flat, open space grown up to grass, weeds, or brush for use when he is singing, and a patch of moist, second-growth woodland for feeding and daytime roosting. The female prefers a rather open stand of young trees near a boggy feeding place. Young birds grow rapidly and are able to fly a little when they are 2 weeks old. They are practically full grown when they are 25 days old. When they are too small to fly the female is said to be able to carry them on flights, one at a time, by holding them between her legs or pressing them against her body with her legs. In fall woodcocks often do not migrate until they have to, and many winter as far north as they can find unfrozen ground. In spring they press north as soon as the ground thaws. Migration takes place at night, and the birds seem to travel as individuals, not as part of a flock, as is the case with most shore birds. They often fly close to the ground, and many are killed by hitting wires or other obstructions.

The clear cutting and burning of the woodlands of eastern North America by the early settlers created a great deal of woodcock habitat where the land was not cultivated but allowed to grow up again to trees. Fire, in destroying the very acid, humus layer on top of the soil made conditions much more favorable for earthworms and encouraged the growth of deciduous birches, alders, and aspens in place of the original stand of conifers. In addition, widely scattered small ownerships, divergent practices on adjacent tracts, and, within recent years, the increased abandonment of agricultural land have created an interspersion of cover that is ideal for woodcocks.

As most of these not-too-wise land use practices have continued right up to the present day, we still have an abundance of woodcock habitat. It seems likely, however, that under the pressure of an increasing human population our land-use practices will be radically altered in the near future. The abandonment of agricultural land will soon have to stop and our woodlands will no longer be periodically degraded to the birch-aspen stage by clear cutting and fire. Instead the forest continuity will remain relatively undisturbed except for the occasional harvesting of a few of the more mature trees. How much woodcock habitat will still remain under such conditions is questionable. Very possibly the woodcock's days as a game bird are numbered.

VOICE: Between its courtship flights, at about 2-second intervals, the woodcock utters an explosive, harsh, nasal sound not unlike a nighthawk's *peent* call. It is always preceded by a much weaker, muffled, gurgling, coo-like *took-oo,* which is sometimes given alone. As the bird starts up in the air it produces short whistled notes which, as they get faster and faster, become a shrill twitter; some ornithologists believe that these are made, at least in part, by the curiously narrowed outer primaries. At the peak of its ascent and as it zigzags back to earth, the bird utters groups of clear, melodious chipping notes that so fill the air that they seem to come from all directions.

NEST: (I. 21, P.) A sparsely lined depression in the ground, commonly near a moist thicket but often in the open, in a young, not too dense second growth of mixed hardwoods

and conifers, or in brushy cover. Occasionally in open brushland or weedy fields. The 4 eggs (1.5 x 1.1) are buffy with a
light sprinkling of small brown spots.

RANGE: (P. M.) Breeds from s. Newfoundland, s. Quebec, n.
Michigan, and s.e. Manitoba south to c. Florida and e. Texas
and west to w. Missouri. Winters from s. New Jersey, the
Ohio Valley, and s. Missouri south to c. Florida and s.e.
Texas.

Common Snipe*   *Capella gallinago*—⚹33
(Wilson's Snipe)   L. 11¼; W. 15; Wt. 4 oz.

IDENTIFICATION: The strongly striped head and back, the whitish
belly, and the long bill are diagnostic. In flight the bird has
long pointed wings and a short, conspicuous orange tail.
Young are like adults but rustier about the head, neck, and
breast.

HABITS: The hardy and once abundant snipe is a bird of
tussock-filled wet meadows, grassy marshes, and bogs. Its
protective coloration and its habit of "freezing" until it i
almost stepped on makes it hard to see on the ground. When
flushed it zigzags off with startling suddenness. Snipe come
north as soon as the ground thaws, migrating at night, apparently in small flocks, and scattering widely during the day
to feed. Closely grazed wet pastures with shallow, temporary
rain pools in low spots or in the hoofprints of cattle attract
them as do hog wallows. They also feed on burnt-over,
mowed, or plowed wet land and in the more normal shore-
bird habitat of high salt marsh and the grassy edges of lakes,
ponds, and ditches.

Insects, chiefly those with aquatic larval stages, supply about
half their food. Small crustacea, earthworms, and snails are
also important, and at times seeds of marsh plants. Snipe do
most of their feeding early or late in the day and seem more
active on cloudy days. It is at these times that their unusual
flight song is most often heard. This is produced as the bird
circles high in the air and takes sudden swoops that cause
either its wings or its narrow outer tail feathers to vibrate
and produce a noise not unlike the whistle of a duck's wings.

VOICE: When flushed snipe give one or more distinctive, abrupt,
rasping notes that identify it at once. On the breeding ground
it scolds intruders with a loud, whistled *wheat, wheat* repeated a number of times. During courtship flights it produces a high-pitched, pulsating hum or whistle with its

feathers. This carries a long distance; usually the source is hard to locate and the whole effect is rather eerie.

NEST: (I. 20, P.) A shallow depression lined with grass in the center of a sedge tussock or fern clump in a boggy marsh or under a small shrub on the edge of a marsh. The 4 eggs (1.5 x 1.1) are pale brown, boldly blotched with dark brown.

RANGE: (P. M.) Breeds throughout much of Europe, Asia, and North America from Newfoundland, Ungava, n. Manitoba, n. Mackenzie, and n.c. Alaska south to c. New England, n.w. Pennsylvania, n. Indiana, e. South Dakota, s. Colorado, and s. California. Winters from s. Virginia, Arkansas, s. New Mexico, and s. British Columbia south to s. Brazil and Colombia. A regular migrant in Bermuda.

Long-billed Curlew*   *Numenius americanus*—✳34
L. 23; W. 38; B. 2.3–9; Wt. 2 lbs.

IDENTIFICATION: Bill length is not always a reliable character, but the unstriped head, large size, warm brown body color, and the clear pinkish-cinnamon of the wings are diagnostic.

HABITS: This splendid species, which once bred abundantly throughout the western grasslands as far east as the prairies of Illinois, was often common on the coasts of Massachusetts in migration. Now the birds are restricted to the plains region, nesting usually near moist, low meadows and in the more luxuriant grass of river-valley slopes. When migrating they also frequent lake shores, river bars, and seacoast salt marshes, mud flats, and sandy beaches. Insects, especially grasshoppers, locusts, and crickets, are staple foods, but crayfish, crabs, mollusks, and, at times, berries are also taken. When not nesting they generally gather into roosts at night but scatter out during the day in twos or threes to feed. They migrate, however, in large, often noisy, V-shaped flocks. A whistle will decoy them, and their habit of returning again and again to a wounded member of the flock enabled hunters to slaughter them in great numbers in the days when they were classified as game birds.

VOICE: The loud calls are mostly clear and melodious, usually of 1 or 2 notes but sometimes prolonged into a roll or rattle. The notes suggest at times those of the upland plover, the willet, and the rally call of the bobwhite.

NEST: (P.) A slight hollow in the ground in an open grassland, lined with grass. The 4 eggs (2.6 x 1.8) are olive-buff, evenly spotted with brown.

RANGE: (M.) Breeds from Manitoba and e. British Columbia south to w. Kansas, n. New Mexico, and n.e. California. Winters from South Carolina (once abundant, now rare), the Gulf Coast, s. Arizona, and c. California south to the West Indies and Guatemala.

Whimbrel*   *Numenius phaeopus*—✕34
(Hudsonian Curlew)
        L. 17; W. 32; B. 2¾–4 (1½ in some young birds)

IDENTIFICATION: The downcurved bill identifies a curlew. This bird has a striped head and is grayish-brown in body color.

HABITS: Originally this curlew was not as abundant in North America as the long-billed or the Eskimo, with which many early American ornithologists confused it. Today it is relatively common along our coasts and is apparently increasing. It seems possible that the 3 curlews occupied similar enough niches, at least at certain seasons, for the abundance of the other 2 to have held down the population of the whimbrel until, with the coming of the white man, its greater wildness gave it an advantage. Although whimbrels breed in open tundra, the present nesting grounds are concentrated in certain relatively restricted areas. The birds seem to prefer coastal areas near fresh water and often near the scattered stands of small trees that occur in favorable spots along the southern edge of the Barren Grounds. In migration they travel in long lines and V's, calling with 4 short whistles and often sailing for short periods on set wings. Inland they are rare, occurring usually in flooded fields, on the edges of shallow lakes, and on river bars. Their main flights are coastal and apparently offshore for long stretches, as these curlews occur regularly in Bermuda in the fall and are abundant at certain points along the coast, though scarce at others. They feed in mud flats, high salt marshes and coastal beaches, gathering at night into large roosts on isolated marsh islands or sand bars. Their food varies from fiddler crabs and other crustacea, mollusks, and worms to insects and such fruits as the common crowberry of the Arctic.

VOICE: When flushed, a series of loud, rather harsh, whistled *pip, pip, pip* notes. When calling to one another, sweet, liquid, tremulous notes, often in a long rolling series.

NEST: (P.) In a depression in the ground or in a clump of moss or sedge on open tundra. The 4 eggs (2.3 x 1.6) are olive-buff to green, heavily marked with brown.

RANGE: (M.) Breeds locally throughout the northern part of the Northern Hemisphere; in North America from s. Greenland, Southampton Island, and the w. shore of Hudson Bay and n. Mackenzie to w. Alaska south to Fort Churchill, Mount McKinley, and the mouth of the Yukon; in Eurasia south to n. Scotland and c. Russia. The main wintering grounds appear to be from British Guiana to the mouth of the Amazon and from Lower California to s. Chile. Since there are always some individuals that fail to complete the migration, the species is often present the year round along its migration routes. Abroad it winters south to s. Africa, Tasmania, and the islands of the South Pacific.

Eskimo Curlew*   *Numenius borealis*—⚡34
L. 13½; W. 28; B. 2–2½; Wt. 1 lb.

IDENTIFICATION: This bird is so hard to separate in the field from the whimbrel that sight records are always open to question, yet it is so rare that a record is not worth the sacrifice of a single individual. The only absolutely diagnostic point of difference is the unbarred primaries. This species has generally a shorter, slenderer, straighter bill, a much smaller body, and is more buffy-brown in color, often quite blackish above with stronger contrast between upper and under parts. As a rule the dark crown shows no clear-cut light median stripe and the underwing is darker, more of a reddish-brown instead of pinkish-buff.

HABITS: The shooting of this bird in the fall on the North Atlantic coast, on the Pampas of Argentina, and from Texas to the Prairie Provinces of Canada in the spring changed the status of the Eskimo curlew from one of fabulous abundance to one of dismaying scarcity during the period from 1870 to 1890. The birds' lack of suspicion and fear and their extreme gregariousness made them especially vulnerable to hunters, and in spring, when they gathered in vast flocks on freshly burned prairie and newly plowed fields to feed on insects, they were shot, often by the wagonload, and shipped to market in New York and Boston. In fall they fed largely on crowberries and other fruit and became very fat before making their long ocean flight. It was only when storms diverted them from their route that they appeared in numbers along the coast south of Nova Scotia. Undoubtedly a few of the birds survive, as there continue to be sight records. A specimen was shot in Labrador in 1932. Probably the best place to look for them is with flocks of golden plover, Hudsonian god-wit, or whimbrel, as their extreme gregariousness should draw them into association with flocks of the more abundant species. Every record of this rare bird is worth publishing.

VOICE: In flight the members of a flock utter soft, melodious, and rather tremulous whistles suggesting those of a bluebird. Often these notes are so constant that the flock produces a twittery sort of chatter that carries a long distance. A thin squeak like one note of the common tern, as well as soft, Bartramian sandpiper-like whistles have been noted.

NEST: (P.) Out in open tundra in a depression in the ground. The 4 eggs (2.0 x 1.4) are brown to olive, spotted and blotched with dark browns.

RANGE: (M.) Apparently bred on the Barren Grounds of n. Mackenzie west into Alaska and wintered in Chile and Argentina south to Patagonia. The main migration route south lay across the ocean from the Newfoundland area to Brazil and came north across the Great Plains in spring, roughly paralleling that of the golden plover and Hudsonian godwit.

Upland Plover*   *Bartramia longicauda*—✳35
(Bartramian Sandpiper)   L. 12; W. 22; Wt. 7 oz.

IDENTIFICATION: The short, slender bill; small head and slender neck; very dark rump; large, white-bordered, finely black-barred, pinkish-buff tail, and strongly black-and-white under-wing area are helpful aids to identification. Young are similar but darker-backed, more strongly buffy, and less streaked on neck and breast. Once learned, its calls will identify the bird, even when it is passing overhead at night during migration.

HABITS: On its nesting grounds this sandpiper often flies with a slight flutter of the tips of its stiffly held, downcurved wings after the fashion of a spotted sandpiper. Its normal flight, however, is very buoyant and swift, as its long pointed wings and tail are large for its weight. The "quailie," as it is often designated because of its call, inhabits open grassy areas ranging from sandy, sparsely vegetated flats to open grassy bogs, but it is most often found in rich pastureland and hay-fields. Although originally a bird of western prairies and plains, it became common through the entire Northeast as farms replaced forest. Then, with the market hunting of the '80s and '90s, it almost vanished from both regions. Now with complete protection on its breeding grounds it is increasing, but with a breeding potential of only 4 young a year, a long and hazardous migration route, and a hunting toll on its wintering grounds, its recovery will be slow. How foolish it now seems to have permitted these almost wholly insectivorous birds to be shot off to supply a few tons of food. Not only were they an attractive, animated part of our landscape, but they and the other migrant, upland game birds must have once played an important role in checking serious outbreaks of grassland insects. Even today they concentrate in areas where grasshoppers, crickets, and weevils are most abundant. Fortunately, the upland plover continues to show itself adaptable, as at times it feeds and nests in open croplands as well as in alfalfa fields and has recently adopted airports as regular feeding grounds and stopping places during migration.

VOICE: The various calls of this sandpiper are among the most beautiful sounds in nature—some infinitely rich, mellow, and liquid; others strangely windlike and mournful. The alarm note is a rapid *quip-ip-ip-ip*, but as the bird flies about it utters a rich, rolling trill. The 2-part song, often given from high in the air, carries for great distances. It starts as a rapid, almost tree-toad-like trill which, after rising in pitch, changes to a clear, mournful whistle that swells and fades in volume.

NEST: (I. 21., P.) A hollow in the ground, lined with a little grass, sometimes in the open but generally hidden in a tuft of grass or a small clump of brush. The 4 eggs (1.8 x 1.3) are pinkish- to greenish-buff, evenly covered with small brown spots.

RANGE: (M.) Breeds from c. Maine, s. Ontario, c. Wisconsin, s. Mackenzie, and n.w. Alaska south to Virginia, s. Illinois, s. Oklahoma, n.e. Utah, and s. Oregon. Winters from s. Brazil to c. Argentina.

Spotted Sandpiper*   *Actitis macularia*—✕37
L. 7½; W. 13½; Wt. 1½ oz.

IDENTIFICATION: Summer adults with their round, black spots are unique. In fall adults and young are similar and can best be told by their olive-brown backs, the white stripes through and along the rear edge of the inner wing, the narrow, blackish-white border to the dark tail, and the pale base of the lower mandible. Sometimes the folded wing does not fully cover the white side, which shows as a conspicuous white spot just above the bend of the wing.

HABITS: The spotted is more uniformly distributed across the country than any other sandpiper. There is hardly a body of fresh water, running or still, in open country from sea level to mountain timber line that may not harbor a breeding pair of "teeter-tails." Sometimes the nest is only a few feet from water but more often is at some distance away in a grassy field, wasteland, or cultivated area. Rocky as well as muddy or sandy shores are frequented, and the birds reach their greatest concentration on especially favorable islands where, despite their normally unsociable nature, they sometimes form loose colonies. They seem to avoid the seacoast in some regions, but in New England they nest on coastal islands and along beaches, where they show special fondness for pebbly shingles. All manner of small animals are acceptable as food, from crustacea and small fish to grasshoppers and other upland insects.

The "spottie's" habits of constantly waving its tail up and down and of fluttering off across the water on vibrating, stiffly held downcurved wings for only a short distance before returning to the shore are distinctive. The birds are so inconspicuous that often the first indication of their presence is their loud *peet-weet* call. They like to walk up and down logs or rocks near water, teetering all the while. Unlike most shore birds, they can perch on small twigs or wires. Not only do the precocial young swim well, but the adults readily take to the water to escape danger and swim under water with half-extended wings or walk on the bottom like dippers.

VOICE: When flushed or disturbed, a series of *peet-weet* calls or a long run of *weet* notes. A soft, low, rolling call to the young and a single loud, intermittent whistle not unlike a spring peeper's are heard in summer.

NEST: (I. 21, P.) A depression in the ground, sparsely lined with grass, or, in more northern areas, a deep cup of moss, seaweed, and grasses. The site may be in the open, well hidden in a dense bed of vegetation, or under a bush, log, rock, or bank. The 4 buffy eggs (1.3 x .91) are spotted and heavily blotched with browns.

RANGE: (P. M.) Breeds from Newfoundland, n. Ungava, n. Manitoba, n. Mackenzie, and n.w. Alaska south to South Carolina, c. Alabama, s. Louisiana, c. Texas, s. New Mexico, and s. California. Winters from Bermuda, South Carolina, the Gulf States, and s. British Columbia south to s. Brazil, Bolivia, and c. Peru.

Solitary Sandpiper* $\qquad$ *Tringa solitaria*—✳35
L. 8½; W. 16; Wt. 1¾ oz.

IDENTIFICATION: The tail, which is conspicuously white with dark bars, except for 2 dark center feathers, and the uniformly dark wings and upper parts are distinctive. Young birds in summer are paler, more olive-colored above, thickly spotted with white or buff, and grayer on the head and neck.

HABITS: During migration this dainty, graceful bird occurs singly or in small groups about all sorts of fresh-water areas. Secluded woodland streams, ponds, bogs, and stagnant rain pools are favorite haunts, but it also frequents pasture ponds and even stagnant barnyard mud puddles as well as lake and river edges. Few nests or downy young have ever been found, but it is believed that the solitary generally nests about the ponds, bogs, and swamp-like borders of the northern coniferous woodlands. Its habit of starting its southward migration in early July has probably been responsible for some of the reports of its breeding farther south. The birds are easily approached as they wade about in the shallow water, bobbing their heads from time to time. When flushed they fly off with deep strokes of their dark pointed wings, which are momentarily held extended over the back after the bird alights. The flight is buoyant but often erratic—quite unlike a spotted sandpiper's. Little is known about their food, which must be largely crustacea and aquatic insects.

VOICE: When flushed, a series of *weep* notes similar to a spottie's, but more abrupt, higher-pitched, and thinner. Also shorter *pit* or *pip* notes, singly or in a series.

NEST: (P.) The 4 eggs (1.4 x 1.0) are laid in the old nest of such birds as the robin, grackle, or rusty blackbird from 4 to 20 feet above ground. They are pale green or creamy-buff, thickly spotted and blotched with purplish-grays and brown.

RANGE: (M.) Probably breeds from Newfoundland, n. Ungava, n. Manitoba, n. Mackenzie, and c. Alaska south to about the northern border of the United States. Winters from the West Indies and s. Mexico south to Argentina. There is an offshore as well as inland migration, as it is regular in Bermuda.

Willet* $\qquad$ *Catoptrophorus semipalmatus*—✳35
L. 15; W. 27; Wt. 8 oz.

IDENTIFICATION: The bold black-and-white wing pattern created by the white bases of the primaries and almost wholly white secondaries and tail is distinctive. On the ground it is a heavy, rather uniformly colored grayish bird with bluish legs and a heavy bill. Fall adults and young are paler and largely unstreaked.

HABITS: East of the Mississippi the willet breeds only on the coastal salt marshes and beaches, but in the West it is exclusively an inland breeder, widely scattered about the lakes and sloughs of the open grasslands. Only small remnants survived the shore-bird shooting days of the past, but within recent years it has become locally abundant in some areas. From these it seems to be slowly spreading back into its former haunts as population pressures force the young outside the limits of their natal region. This is so slow a process that some ornithologists have suggested speeding it up by transferring eggs or newly hatched and as yet unoriented young to suitable refuge areas within the bird's original range.

In fall there is a marked east and west migration that carries western willets to the Pacific and to the Atlantic coast as far north as New England. Nova Scotia birds seldom appear in the New England area in fall and only occasionally in spring, which must mean that their migrations are largely across the ocean to the West Indies or South America. Willets sometimes feed on sandy beaches but seem to prefer the shallows and mud flats of marshes, where they eat small mollusks, fiddler and other crabs, crayfish, small fish, insects, and other small animals.

VOICE: The loud, clamorous cries are highly varied. The most common is a series of *whee wee wee wee* notes. The song is a more musical *pill-o-will-o-willet.*

NEST: (P.) Along the seacoast the nests are on the upper beaches and dune edges, in brushy or open land adjacent to the inland edge of the salt marsh, on ditchbanks and other high spots in the marsh itself. In the West the birds nest on prairies or alkaline flats about shallow, marshy lakes. The nests are either on the open ground or hidden in a clump of grass or under a bush and vary from slightly lined depressions to bulky cups of grass and weeds. The 4 eggs (2.1 x 1.5) are olive-buff, spotted and blotched with browns.

RANGE: (M.) Breeds in Nova Scotia and from s. New Jersey to Florida, the n. West Indies, and Texas; also from s. Manitoba, s. Alberta, and c. Oregon south to n. Iowa, c. Colorado, and n.e. California. Winters from North Carolina, the Gulf Coast, and n. California south to Brazil and Peru.

Greater Yellowlegs*   *Totanus melanoleucus*—✳35
(Greater Yellowshank)   L. 14; W. 25; B. 2–2.3; Wt. 7 oz.

IDENTIFICATION: The bright leg color of a yellowleg is diagnostic. In flight the bird shows a dark back and wings and a largely white rump and tail. This larger species has a proportionately longer neck and legs; a longer, heavier, slightly upturned-appearing bill; distinctive call notes; and often seems to have more orange-yellow legs and darker, more strongly marked upper parts than the lesser yellowlegs.

HABITS: The big yellowlegs is an alert, wary, and very noisy bird that prefers to feed in shallow water, often wading in up to its breast and occasionally even swimming. Little is known about its summer haunts in the muskeg and marshes of the northern forest. Few nests have been found. It is an early migrant both in spring and fall and occurs more or less regularly in nearly every area suitable for shore birds in the Western Hemisphere, except the Arctic. In fall, when some birds use a transoceanic route, the species is often less common in the interior. Although flying high, passing flocks are readily identified by their long legs and frequent calls, to an imitation of which they readily decoy. The "tattler" or "tell-tale," as hunters call it because of its habit of sounding an alarm at their approach, frequents rain pools in fields as well as shallows along the shores of ponds and sluggish streams. On the coast it prefers the small pools of the high salt marsh and half-covered tidal flats to the ocean beach. When feeding the birds seldom probe in the mud but run here and there in shallow water chasing fish, tadpoles, and the various crustacea and aquatic insects that are their main foods.

VOICE: A loud, clear, forceful *wheu,* most frequently uttered in groups of 3 or 4 but occasionally as a double note or series of single notes. Also a rolling, yodel-like, rapid series of mellow, rather musical notes.

NEST: (P.) A depression or scrape in the ground on a hummock in or near a wet, boggy stretch of open tundra or marsh or on a low, timbered ridge in muskeg country. The 4 eggs (1.9 x 1.3) are orange-brown, heavily and boldly marked with reddish-browns.

RANGE: (M.) Breeds sporadically from Labrador, s. Ungava, s. Mackenzie, and s. Alaska south to Newfoundland, s. Manitoba, and s. British Columbia. Winters from South Carolina, the Gulf Coast, s. Arizona, and c. California through the West Indies, Mexico, and all Central and South America to the Strait of Magellan.

Lesser Yellowlegs*
(Lesser Yellowshank)

Totanus flavipes—⌗35
L. 10½; W. 20; Wt. 3 oz.

IDENTIFICATION: The marked size difference between the otherwise almost identical yellowlegs is of little value in identification unless a direct comparison can be made with other nearby shore birds whose size is known. The lesser is a more delicate and compactly built bird with a finer, shorter bill; shorter neck and legs, the latter usually appearing more lemon-yellow; and upper parts that often appear to be a softer, lighter, more uniform gray.

HABITS: As a breeder this bird stays south of the treeless tundra, preferring the grassy meadows and bogs between the thin strands of timber. In the more heavily wooded areas farther south it seems to benefit from forest fires, as it avoids densely timbered areas and nests quite commonly in burnt-over forest and in the open poplar-aspen stands that follow fire. The spring migration is largely inland, but in fall the birds are also common on the coasts. Some of them must fly south over the ocean to South America, as in fall they occur quite regularly in Bermuda and Barbados. These "summer yellowlegs" come north later and go south earlier than the greater, or "winter yellowlegs." Both species feed in shallow water, rain pools, wet grassy areas, and brackish salt-marsh ponds, picking their prey out of the water or from the surface rather than probing for it. The normal diet consists largely of crustacea and insects, including land forms which inhabit grassy areas and mowed fields. The lesser seems a bit more gregarious and more inclined to flock up than the greater, and though the birds scatter out for feeding, they are often associated with other shore birds. Both species are active feeders that chase prey through the water, and both have the curious habit of abruptly raising and lowering the head as they pause to look around.

VOICE: The common call is a single or double *wheu,* softer and more nasal, as a rule, than the greater's. It has a yodeling roll similar to the greater's, and the members of a flock use a variety of soft, conversational notes.

NEST: (P.) In a depression in the ground on a slope, ridge, or high ground, often quite far from a pond or boggy marshland, and more or less in the open or in a burnt-over, thinly wooded area. The 4 eggs (1.7 x 1.1) are buffy, blotched with browns.

RANGE: (M.) Breeds from n. Ungava, n. Manitoba, n. Mackenzie, and n.c. Alaska south to c. Quebec, s. Manitoba, and n. British Columbia. Winters from Florida, the Gulf Coast, and Mexico south to the Strait of Magellan.

Knot* *Calidris canutus*—✳33
L. 10½; W. 20½; Wt. 5 oz.

IDENTIFICATION: There is no other short-billed shore bird with a brick-red breast in spring. In fall its large size (nearly that of a black-bellied plover), short legs, and stocky build are good clues. In flight it shows a narrow white line in the wing and a pale grayish rump and tail.

HABITS: Some individuals of this sturdy species probably make an annual trip of some 19,000 miles from the most northern to virtually the most southern land in the Western Hemisphere. Although in the Arctic it nests inland and feeds about the fresh-water marshes of the tundra, the knot is largely a bird of the immediate seacoast and a rare migrant in the interior. "Robin snipe" are very gregarious, feeding and flying in densely massed flocks which change color in spectacular fashion as they wheel in the air in perfect unison, showing gray backs one moment and red breasts the next. Sandy beaches and, to a lesser extent, sandy flats, especially near inlets, are favorite feeding grounds. Here the birds pick food from the surface after the manner of the black-bellied plover, which is generally their commonest associate, though they are also frequently seen with turnstones. Pebbly shores and eroding outcrops of marsh deposits attract them, and on rocky coasts they feed on seaweed-covered rocks at low tide. Year after year they return in migration to certain favored spots where they may be abundant although seldom seen a few miles away. The knot's principal food is small snails and clamlike mollusks, plus insects, crustacea, and the seeds of marsh plants like widgeon grass.

voice: A very low-pitched, hoarse, single *knut* note, variously described as a honk, croak, or grunt; also a low, double, whistled *wah-quoit,* ending in a slight roll.

NEST: (P.) A hollow in the ground, often lined with lichens and placed among the rocks and sparse vegetation of ridges and hills, often well above and away from feeding grounds. The 4 eggs (1.7 x 1.2) are olive-buff, spotted and blotched with brown.

RANGE: (M.) Breeds in n. Greenland, the Taimyr Peninsula, and many of the islands of the Arctic Ocean south to the Melville Peninsula and Victoria Island. Winters from Buenos Aires to Tierra del Fuego on the east coast and south to Peru on the west coast of South America; also to the Mediterranean and Black Sea region, w. Africa, Australia, and New Zealand.

Purple Sandpiper*

Erolia maritima—✷31
L. 9; W. 15; Wt. 3 oz.

IDENTIFICATION: This short-legged, rotund rock dweller is the darkest of our sandpipers and has yellowish legs and bill.

HABITS: Outside the breeding season this bird occupies a highly specialized niche and is seldom seen away from seaweed-covered offshore rocks. Occasionally a weedy reef or a fresh deposit of sea wrack along an upper beach holds a wandering individual for a time, but this is rare. Until the coming of civilization purple sandpiper habitat was virtually non-existent south of n. Massachusetts. Now with the building of many long stone jetties and breakwaters up and down the coast the bird is extending its winter range.

At low tide these sandpipers are almost invisible from shore except as they momentarily flutter into the air to avoid a wave and so reveal their white bellies and wing linings. At high tide, when they are forced up to the tops of bare rocks, they are more conspicuous. Purples are quite gregarious and, although they scatter to feed, they usually flush as a group. They seldom fly far but curve back to land in the manner of, and often with a flight that suggests that of, the spotted sandpiper. Little is known about their food, which seems to be largely small mollusks and crustacea. Inland in the Far North during the breeding season they sometimes eat buds and leaves.

VOICE: A low, swallowlike single or double *twit*. Also high-pitched, twittery trills.

NEST: (P.) A hollow in the ground, well lined with grass and leaves, on a barren hillside or mountaintop, often far from the sea, but in the Far North in tundra not far from shore. The 4 eggs (1.5 x 1.0) are light green or buff, spotted and blotched with brown.

RANGE: (P. M.) Breeds from Melville Island, n. Greenland, Spitsbergen and the Taimyr Peninsula south to Southampton Island, Iceland, and n. Scandinavia. Winters from s. Greenland to New England and casually south to South Carolina; also to Great Britain and the Baltic coasts.

Pectoral Sandpiper*   *Erolia melanotos*—※37
L. 9; W. 17; Wt. 2 oz.

IDENTIFICATION: The dark crown; a longer neck than that of other small sandpipers; a rather dark, reddish-brown back with fine light stripes; a sharp line of separation between the dark, buffy upper breast and the white under parts; and the greenish-yellow legs are distinctive. In flight the wings lack a white stripe and the tail is pale gray-brown except for the dark center feathers. Unlike so many sandpipers, this species commonly carries its neck well extended with the head high.

HABITS: This bird is well termed "grass snipe," as wet meadows, rain pools in grasslands, and even fairly dry, rough pastures are its favorite haunts. Along the coast dense beds of salt hay (black rush) back in the farthest reaches of the salt marsh next to the upland are its chief feeding grounds. Pectorals seem to prefer short grass, and mowing always improves an area's attractiveness for them. The small flocks of 10 to 30 birds scatter out to feed, freezing and crouching to avoid observation, and only flushing one by one when about to be stepped on. Then they zigzag away in snipelike fashion with a few very distinctive grating notes. Grassy shores of lakes, marsh ponds, and rivers are good places to look for scattered birds. Occasionally they feed on open mud flats with other shore birds, where their habit of stopping at intervals in erect and watchful attitude, with head extended, can be observed. In flight the flocks are compact and maneuver in unison. The great difference in size between the largest females and the smallest males is quite noticeable. On the grassy tundra breeding ground the male inflates its neck and upper breast, thrusts forward its buffy pectoral pads, and, with wings askew, utters a tremulous, hollow, and yet resonant and musical song which sounds like someone blowing across the top of a bottle. Insects form a large part of the food of this species, plus worms, crustacea, and other small animals.

VOICE: When flushed, a sharp, abrupt, grating *crrrik,* hoarser and more snipelike than the notes of other small shore birds. The call notes of a flock are low, rather reedy chips.

NEST: (I. 22, P.) Usually a well-made cup of grass and leaves in a depression in a dry, generally grassy area up on a ridge or on the rolling tundra upland, but occasionally in the reedy grass of a pond border. The 4 eggs (1.4 x .98) are white to buff, blotched with browns.

RANGE: (M.) Breeds in Southampton Island; along the extreme west shore of Hudson Bay and the Arctic coast and from here to n. Alaska and n.e. Siberia; south in Alaska to the n. Yukon delta. Winters from Bolivia and Peru to c. Patagonia and s.c. Chile. Migrates north between the Appalachians and the Rockies but moves south in fall across the continent from coast to coast with a marked offshore flight that regularly takes it to Bermuda and the Lesser Antilles.

White-rumped Sandpiper*   *Erolia fuscicollis*—✕36
(Bonaparte's Sandpiper)   L. 7½

IDENTIFICATION: In flight the white upper tail coverts are set off by a very dark tail, but in so small a bird the contrast is often none too conspicuous. In spring the back has a striped appearance and the crown and especially the scapulars are more or less pinkish-buff. In fall the color is uniformly pale gray with an occasional rusty feather. The streaking on the head and neck is usually fine and crisp and so extensive that no white shows in the bend of the wing as in a semipalmated. This bird is also slimmer than a semi and appears proportionately longer from legs to end of tail.

HABITS: This is a puzzling bird. Over much of Argentina it is said to be the commonest wintering shore bird, and accounts from the Arctic speak of it as occurring in tremendous numbers in migration, and in breeding areas like Southampton Island it is second only to the semipalmated sandpiper in abundance. Yet in most of the United States it is a rarity, and only in the Great Plains and on the North Atlantic coast is it seen in flocks of any size. It commonly occurs in a wide variety of shore bird habitats, from beaches and sandy river bars to pasture rain pools, wet meadows, and stubble fields, and is usually associated with other small waders, but favorite haunts are muddy shores of shallow lakes and the tidal sounds along the coast. The white-rumps' actions are inclined to be slow and deliberate. When feeding they probe deeply and repeatedly in one spot, often standing up to their bellies in water with the whole head under when feeding. They are frequently so tame that they fly only a few feet when disturbed and immediately go back to feeding.

VOICE: The squeaky call when flushed is so distinctive that it at once reveals the presence of a white-rump in a flock of "peep" (small sandpipers). The call is an abrupt, sharp *tzeet* that sounds batlike or like the click of 2 marbles struck together. The twitter of a spring flock is quite swallowlike.

NEST: (P.) A thinly lined depression on a dry rise or hummock in a low, grassy swale or near a lake or pond. The 4 eggs (1.3 x .95) are olive-green with a few heavy brown blotches.

RANGE: (M.) Breeds from s. Baffin Island and the s. Arctic Islands west along the coast to n.e. Alaska. Winters from Paraguay south to the Strait of Magellan and the Falkland Islands. The migration route is east of the Rockies and in fall is partly, if not largely, transoceanic, as the birds occur regularly in Bermuda.

Baird's Sandpiper*   *Erolia bairdi*—✳36
L. 7½; W. 16

IDENTIFICATION: The bright clay-colored appearance is distinctive. The sides of the head and neck, and the breast especially, are very buffy. The back feathers, particularly in young, are so broadly edged with light buffy that the birds have a scaled appearance. The legs are brownish- or greenish-black and rather short. The comparatively short, slender bill and the dark primaries, which extend an inch or more beyond the tertials, give the bird a long slim look. In flight it shows a broad, indistinct white line through the wing.

HABITS: This nondescript little bird is usually found in association with other "peep." Although it flies in the same flock with others, it leaves them upon landing and feeds by itself, alternately running and abruptly stopping as it picks up food from the mud. It does not like to probe in shallow water or very wet mud, and even on the beach it stays along the upper edge of the wave-washed area. The damp ground along the inside edge of coastal ponds back of the beach and the sparse or cutover marsh-grass areas are also good places to look for them. Inland they may be found far from water in grasslands, but river bars, shores of receding lakes, and irrigated or rain-soaked fields are the most common habitats. Baird's seems to be something of a mountain sandpiper. In Chile, where most of them appear to winter, they occur up to elevations of 13,000 feet, and in Colorado they have been noted about lakes at comparable elevations. Crustacea and insects seem to supply most of their food.

VOICE: A fairly loud, yet rather mellow, rolling trill similar to that of other species.

NEST: (P.) A shallow depression in moss or grass on a ridge or knoll in the tundra or well up on a rock-strewn mountain slope. The 4 eggs (1.3 x .9) are buff, ranging from pinkish to olive, with generally small brown spots.

RANGE: (M.) Breeds from Baffin Island (or Greenland) along the Arctic Islands and coast west to n.e. Siberia and south to Southampton Island, c. Mackenzie, and c.w. Alaska. Winters in Chile and s. Argentina. The main migration route is across the Great Plains. Stragglers occur from coast to coast, especially in the fall, and more commonly on the West Coast than the East.

Least Sandpiper*
(American Stint)

Erolia minutilla—✳36
L. 6; W. 11½

IDENTIFICATION: This smallest of our sandpipers has dusky yellow legs, a thin, short bill, a fairly dark, well-streaked breast, and a distinctly brownish appearance. In flight the white wing stripe is easily noted.

HABITS: Breeding grounds are the open bogs and marshes of the northern spruce-fir forest. Courtship, however, gets under way as the birds move north, the male circling in the air on quivering wings while uttering short bursts of song—clear, tremulous trills rising in pitch and given in a sweet, minor key. Most leasts do not reach their breeding grounds until late May, yet early July sees small flocks already moving south through the northern states. On migration the birds are very tame and quite gregarious, occurring alone in small flocks or in association with other shore birds in mixed flocks. Their favorite haunts are wet or muddy areas, sparsely grown up in grass or recently cut over. When flushed they zigzag off like miniature snipe or pectoral sandpipers, of which they often seem to be a small edition. Occasionally, especially in spring, they visit sandy ocean beaches, but muddy shores of grass-fringed marsh creeks or the more open flats where glasswort grows are the best places to look for them. Inland they frequent river bars and beaches, pond and lake shores, rain pools, and, at times, dry pastures. When feeding they pick from the surface or probe in mud or shallow water, their diet being the normal shore-bird selection of insects, crustacea, worms, and small mollusks.

VOICE: When flushed the first call is a soft, slightly grating *scrēē-ēē-ēē,* followed by shorter *greet* calls. Also many other short notes and a little whinny.

NEST: (P.) A depression in the grass or moss of a hummock or knoll in an open marshy place or bog in the subarctic forest zone south of the open Barren Grounds. Sometimes the nest is in brushy upland near a pond or the seacoast. The 4 eggs (1.1 x .83) vary from pinkish- to greenish-buff, boldly blotched or finely spotted with browns.

RANGE: (M.) Breeds from n. Labrador, n. Manitoba, n. Mackenzie, and s.w. Alaska south to Newfoundland, n. Ontario, s. Mackenzie, and s. Alaska. Winters from North Carolina, the Gulf Coast, and s. California south to e. Brazil, Peru, and the Galápagos Islands. Well distributed from coast to coast on both migrations, some taking an offshore route in fall, when they occur regularly in Bermuda.

Curlew Sandpiper* *Erolia ferruginea*—✳37
L. 8; W. 15½

IDENTIFICATION: The long, slim bill is a good but not diagnostic field character, as in some individuals it is identical with a dunlin's. The white upper tail coverts are always diagnostic, and the long legs, upright carriage, slim body, and pale, indistinctly streaked, often buffy, breast are good clues. Spring birds are unmistakable.

HABITS: This Asiatic species is occasionally encountered in North America in both spring and fall, usually in association with the dunlin. It seems to share the habits of the latter and occurs both on mud flats and sand beaches. In intensively watched areas like those around New York City it is recorded with considerable regularity (*Birds around New York City*—Cruickshank).

VOICE: A soft, musical *chirrup* is the common flight call.

NEST: (P.) A depression on south-facing slopes of the tundra where snow melts first. The 4 eggs (1.4 x 1.0) are pale yellowish with blackish spots.

RANGE: (M.) Breeds on the coast and islands of n.c. Siberia. Winters in Africa, India, and Australia. There is a regular westward migration to the coast of Europe which apparently carries a few birds across the Atlantic and down the east coast of North America, through the West Indies to Patagonia.

Dunlin*
(Red-backed Sandpiper)

Erolia alpina—⚹ 37
L. 8½; W. 15

IDENTIFICATION: Red-backed, black-bellied breeding adults are unmistakable. In fall the long, heavy, curved bill; uniformly dull, rather dark grayish upper parts; dusky breast, and hunched-up appearance are distinctive. In flight the wings show a distinct, narrow white line.

HABITS: (Age 5 yrs.) In the United States the dunlin is a hardy, late fall migrant and winter bird. In dense flocks or associated with other shore birds, especially sanderling, dunlins frequent the ocean beaches, sandy bars and flats near inlets, or mud flats on tidal bays. Inland they occur as spring migrants on the muddy borders of rain pools in fields or on recently flooded river bottom land, and in fall on muddy bottoms of dried-up shallow ponds and lakes. They are very tame and, as a rule, rather sluggish, moving slowly and methodically as they probe and dig for food—chiefly crustacea, worms, small mollusks, and insects.

Once abundant, this little shore bird had become a rarity by the end of the nineteenth century, as it spent the better part of the year on our coasts, where it was subjected to merciless hunting. Now it is again common and still increasing, but neither it nor any of our other shore birds can ever again be game birds. Their rate of reproduction is too low, their highly specialized habitat requirements concentrate them too much, and their habit of flying in dense, closely bunched flocks that return again and again to wounded members make them too vulnerable. Now that our seacoasts have become so densely settled as resorts that every part of them is easily accessible by road or boat, a single open season on shore birds could undo all that has been accomplished by many years of protection.

VOICE: An abrupt *chu* is given as the bird flushes. The flight call is a loud *purre,* melodious and often rather plaintive. The song, delivered as the bird hovers in air, is a rapid tinkling trill that drops in pitch and increases in tempo as it progresses.

NEST: (P.) On a hummock or dry knoll, usually near a pond in low, moist grass-tundra, coastal marsh, or, in Europe, in highland moors. The nest is a grass- and leaf-lined depression, well hidden under a tuft of old grass. The 4 eggs (1.4 x 1.0) are pale green to olive-buff, spotted or blotched with brown.

RANGE: (M.) Breeds around the world, south from the shores of the Arctic Ocean, in Europe to Great Britain and the Baltic countries. In North America occurs from Southampton Island to w. Alaska and south to n. Manitoba, s. Mackenzie, and the Yukon delta. Winters from New Jersey and s. British Columbia south along the coast to c. Florida, Texas, and s. Lower California. East of the Mississippi, is of regular occurrence inland, especially around the Great Lakes. Farther west, becomes increasingly rare until the Pacific coastal area is reached, where it again becomes common.

Dowitcher*   *Limnodromus griseus*—✳33
L. 12; W. 19; Wt. 4 oz.

IDENTIFICATION: A fat, chunky, dark body and a long bill on a shore bird of the open mud flats, together with a finely barred white tail and a pale gray rump patch that tapers to a point up on the lower back, mark the dowitcher.

HABITS: Little is known about the breeding grounds of this snipelike bird, but migrant flocks are commonly seen on their way south through our northern states by the last week of June. Dowitchers show preference for mud and sand flats of coastal bays, and both here and inland they frequent reedy marsh borders and marsh creeks. Inland they also occur about rain

pools and the muddy shores of lakes and ponds. The compact
flocks often stay well bunched, even after they alight to feed.
Tame, rather sluggish, and methodical, they wade about in
shallow water, probing with vertical up-and-down thrusts
of their long bills. Marine worms, particularly clam worms,
are the most important food along the coast. Aquatic insects
are everywhere important in the diet, larvae of midges
coming first, followed by those of crane, soldier, horse, brine,
and dance flies. Small snails and other mollusks are taken,
also crustacea and small quantities of seeds of pondweeds,
bulrushes, and other marsh plants. The so-called long-billed
and short-billed dowitchers, though usually classified as races,
differ considerably in appearance and ecology and may prove
to be distinct species.

VOICE: The call in flight is composed of 2 or 3 whistled *pheu*
notes in a rising series, generally softer and more rapid than
the similar notes of the lesser yellowlegs. The song in flight
is a short, clear, liquid gurgle or twitter.

NEST: (P.) A grass-moss-lined depression in a hummock in
open, wet grass-tundra or, farther south, in the spruce-
tamarack-dotted tundralike muskeg of the Canadian forest.
The 4 eggs (1.6 x 1.1) are greenish- to olive-buff, spotted
with browns.

RANGE: (M.) Breeds from the west side of Hudson Bay west
to w. Alaska and from the shores of the Arctic Ocean south
to n. Manitoba, c. Alberta, and c. Alaska. Winters from South
Carolina, the Gulf Coast, and c. California south to c. Brazil
and Peru. Migrates along both coasts, where it is abundant,
and in the interior, where it is generally far less common

Stilt Sandpiper*   *Micropalama himantopus—*✳33
                          L. 8½; W. 16½; Wt. 2½ oz.

IDENTIFICATION: The rusty head stripes and finely barred under parts of spring birds are unmistakable. In fall the white eye stripe, scaled back, strongly greenish-yellow legs, and the long, heavy, tapered bill make these birds quite unlike the lesser yellowlegs, with which they are often confused. Actually the stilt sandpiper looks and acts more like a short-billed, long-legged, pale-breasted dowitcher. In flight its wings are without stripes and only the upper tail coverts are white.

HABITS: Away from its regular migration route across the Great Plains the stilt sandpiper is of irregular occurrence, varying greatly in numbers from one year to the next. Its favorite haunts are quiet, shallow pools where it can wade about up to its breast as it plunges its bill into the mud with a vertical, dowitcher-like motion or sweeps it from side to side along the bottom. The small flocks usually stay bunched together as they walk about feeding in a slow, methodical manner, often working for several seconds with their bills under water. Low water in ponds and lakes of the interior or tidal changes along the coast produce the type of shallows in which they like to feed. Sometimes, however, they are seen on open beach or in dry upland pastures. The small, wormlike larvae of various flies and other insects, small mollusks, crustacea, and seeds are the chief foods.

VOICE: A low, hoarse *whu* or a longer *whrru* ending with a sort of chatter.

NEST: (P.) On the ground in tundra country near water. The 4 eggs (1.4 x 1.0) are pale buffy with large brown blotches.

RANGE: (M.) Breeds from n. Manitoba and the west shore of Hudson Bay west across Keewatin and Mackenzie to n.e. Alaska. Winters in South America south to c. Argentina and Chile. The main migration route is across the short-grass plains between the Rockies and the tall-grass prairie. In fall it occurs east to the coast and occasionally offshore in Bermuda and the West Indies.

Semipalmated Sandpiper*   *Ereunetes pusillus—*✳36
                                L. 6¼; W. 12; B. .5–.9; Wt. 1 oz.

IDENTIFICATION: The fairly short bill, black legs, grayish general appearance, and the white of the sides showing in front of the bend of the wing help identify this sturdy little sandpiper. The buffy edges of the feathers of the upper parts give juveniles a somewhat scaled appearance in early fall. They also have unstreaked, faintly buffy breasts and dusky, slightly olive legs.

HABITS: Over much of North America this is the most abundant shore bird. Along the coast, where it is seen by the thousands, it follows the waves in and out along the beach and feeds everywhere over the wet sand and mud flats at low tide. Many also work back along the marsh creeks and visit the shallow pools of the high salt-hay meadows. At high tide those that have been feeding near the water huddle in compact flocks on the dry sand of the upper beach to rest until the tide ebbs. Here they balance on one foot with their bills tucked into their back feathers, sleepily hopping away from an intruder until forced to put down the other foot and run. When feeding, these little birds are very active, picking and dabbling here and there, seldom taking time to probe deeply or persistently in one place. Inland they frequent muddy lake shores, river bars, and rain pools in plowed land. Mid-July sees adults coming south, as they leave the young to fend for themselves when 10 days to 2 weeks old and just learning to fly. Not until a month later do the young birds begin to follow, still in their buffy juvenile plumage, which sometimes causes them to be mistaken for the larger Baird's sandpiper.

VOICE: The flight call is a hoarse, shrill *cherk*. When flushed the bird utters an abrupt *ki-i-ip*. Various other chipping, twittering, and rolling notes are heard from a flock. The song uttered as the bird hovers on quivering wings at a height of 30 to 50 feet is an uneven quavering trill or cicada-like buzz ending with a few sweet goldfinch-like notes. Posturing birds also give a little whinny as they run about on the sand. Most of our shore birds go through at least part of their courtship display and occasionally give their interesting songs as they pass through the United States on their northward migration; these should be carefully watched for, especially in May and early June.

NEST: (I. 18, P.) A depression lined with willow leaves and grass on a ridge or knoll in low, wet, grass-tundra, often near a pool or along the coast in grassy dunes. The 4 eggs (1.2 x .84) are pale white to olive-buff with reddish-brown blotches.

RANGE: (M.) Breeds from n. Labrador, s.w. Baffin Island, n. Keewatin, n. Mackenzie, and n. Alaska to n.e. Siberia and south to James Bay, n. Manitoba, and the Yukon delta. Win-

ters from South Carolina and the Gulf Coast south to s. Brazil
and Peru. In spring it occurs from the Atlantic coast to the
Rockies. In fall it moves south on an even broader front
from interior of British Columbia to well off the Atlantic
coast, where it is a common fall visitor to Bermuda and the
West Indies.

Western Sandpiper*

Ereunetes mauri—⚹36
L. 6½; B. .83–1.25

IDENTIFICATION: The long bill, tapering from a heavy base and
slightly decurved at the tip, and in spring the rusty crown
and back and more heavily streaked breast are helpful characters. Fall birds are hard to identify, but they often have
rusty scapulars and are quite pale about the head. As in the
preceding species, the feet are partly webbed; i.e., semipalmated.

HABITS: This bird is so much like the semipalmated sandpiper
that the two species were not separated until 1864. Audubon,
Wilson, and other early ornithologists failed to distinguish
them, and it takes an expert to separate them in the field
except for particularly long-billed or very strongly marked
individuals. Because of the difficulty in telling them apart
we know little about the western's migration routes to and
from its southeastern wintering grounds. There are few
records of the birds from the interior. Apparently their numbers along the North Atlantic coast vary greatly from year to
year, depending, presumably, upon where the flights hit the
coast as they come in from the Northwest. The habits of this
species seem to be identical with those of the semipalmated,
though one observer has suggested that westerns often seem
to work in deeper water, where they have to feed with the
head completely immersed.

VOICE: The flight call is a *kreep* note, coarser than the similar
note of the semipalmated and more plaintive or querulous.
The other notes and the song are similar to the semi's.

NEST: (I. 21, P.) A grass-lined depression in the ground in a
wide variety of sites from low, moist areas where it is hidden
by grass to dry, upland tundra and the moss-covered lower
slopes of mountains. The birds are remarkably tame and
fearless about the nest. The 4 eggs (1.2 x .86) are cream-
colored, heavily blotched with rich browns.

RANGE: (M.) Breeds in n.w. Alaska from Point Barrow south
to the Yukon delta. Winters from North Carolina, the Gulf

Coast, and Washington south to Venezuela and Peru. The main migration route is up and down the Pacific coast, birds wintering in the Southeast apparently returning directly northwest across the interior. In fall they move east on a wide front, some striking the c. New England coast, the numbers increasing southward toward the Carolinas and Florida, where they are abundant.

Buff-breasted Sandpiper* *Tryngites subruficollis*—⚹33
L. 8; W. 16½; Wt. 2¼ oz.

IDENTIFICATION: The uniformly buffy under parts, including under tail coverts, and the yellowish legs are diagnostic. In flight the wings show a light center area on the upper surface and are largely pure white below. There is a narrow line of dark down the center of the rump and tail. Its long neck, round head, chunky body, and small, weak bill give the bird a ploverlike appearance, which is accentuated by its alert, head-high carriage.

HABITS: These little shore birds are found in short-grass prairie, rough or sparse pasture, or burnt-over grassland, where their dry-grass color renders them almost invisible. They are very gregarious and if not in a small flock of their own are with other shore birds, common associates being golden plovers, upland plovers, and (years ago) Eskimo curlews, but, rather than be alone, buff-breasts will join other shore birds in habitats wetter than they normally frequent. To avoid detection they freeze at alert with head high and often remain behind when their companions fly. Frequently they are tame to the point of stupidity, trying to escape by running, not rising until almost stepped on, and then, often as not, flying only a few feet. In flight even a single bird twists and turns, showing its yellowish body and dark-bordered white underwing surfaces. Whole flocks often perform such evolutions only a few feet off the ground. The buff-breast's courtship posturing, in which one wing (or sometimes both) is extended and held at an unusual angle or raised as high as possible over the head while the bird stands upright, is most remarkable. The food of the species is largely insects—beetles and their larvae and the larvae and pupae of flies. Like the Eskimo curlew, these birds were usually reported to be excessively fat. Most occurrences along the Atlantic coast are in September and suggest individuals blown in by strong easterly winds from an offshore migration route.

voice: The spring call is a sharp, thin *tik* or series of such notes that recalls the sound made by striking two small stones together. When flushed, young birds in fall utter an abrupt, harsh *crik,* not unlike the pectoral's note.

NEST: (P.) A thinly lined depression in the high, dry reindeer-moss tundra of the Barren Grounds. The 4 eggs (1.5 x 1.0) are pale buff, boldly blotched with browns.

RANGE: (M.) Breeds in n. Alaska and n.w. Mackenzie and winters in s. Argentina. In spring these birds seem to come across the Gulf of Mexico to the coastal prairies of w. Louisiana and e. Texas and then fly northwest across the Great Plains, going north through Canada just east of the Rockies. Some, largely young birds, return by the same route, but there are many indications of a considerable movement to the east coast of Canada and an offshore flight to South America similar to that of the golden plover and Eskimo curlew, birds that have much in common with this species.

Marbled Godwit* *Limosa fedoa*—※34
L. 18; W. 32; B. 4¼; Wt. 12 oz.

IDENTIFICATION: The buff-brown appearance, mottled above, including the tail, and finely barred below, is distinctive, in connection with the long, pink-based, upturned bill and blue-gray legs. In flight the upper wing shows a narrow black border along the front edge and a patch of pinkish-cinnamon. Below, the whole wing lining is pinkish-cinnamon, set off by a black patch near the bend and by the black tips to the primaries. In winter the birds lose most or all of the barring on the breast and sides.

HABITS: One hundred years ago Audubon reported these big godwits as abundant in migration from Massachusetts to Florida. Apparently in those days the godwit population split after the breeding season into 3 groups. One moved almost due east to the North Atlantic coast, another south down the Mississippi Valley, and a third went west to the California coast. Today only the migrants to California have recovered anything like their original abundance, the other 2 units being so small that the birds are hardly more than rare stragglers to their old haunts.

The breeding grounds are in extensive grassy areas, where the birds feed largely on insects, but as they gather into flocks in July they move to the muddy shores of lakes. Along the Pacific coast they feed on the sandy outer beaches and the flats of the bays, but along the Atlantic coast they seem to like the high salt marsh and its ponds and the tidal flats near inlets. In all these places they probe in the soft ground for food, often inserting the bill to its full length to obtain worms, crustacea, and small mollusks.

VOICE: These noisy birds have a variety of loud calls ranging from a harsh *kerk* to 2- or 3-syllable calls accented on the second or middle syllable. Depending on the bird's mood, these are slow and even, at times musical, or rapid and harsh.

NEST: (P.) A slight hollow in short grass out in open grassland. The 4 eggs (2.2 x 1.5) are olive-buff, lightly and irregularly blotched with dull brown.

RANGE: (M.) Breeds from s. Manitoba and s. Alberta east to Minnesota and south to South Dakota and Montana. Winters from South Carolina, the Gulf Coast, and s. California south to Peru. Occurs during the fall migration from s. New England south along the Atlantic coast and the entire California coast as well as inland. Moves north in spring up the California coast and the Mississippi Valley.

Bar-tailed Godwit
(Pacific Godwit)

Limosa lapponica—✳35
L. 16; Wt. 11 oz.

IDENTIFICATION: The spring male is a solid, rich pinkish-cinnamon over the entire under parts from the tail clear up onto the head. The female is much paler, often only slightly pinkish below with a streaked breast. In winter the under parts are white except for the breast and lower neck, which are gray and narrowly streaked in adults and buff and heavily streaked in young birds. In flight the long wings are pale below, uniformly colored above, and the lower back, rump, and tail area is white, increasingly barred with brown toward the rear.

HABITS: This is one of the abundant shore birds of the Old World, flocks of thousands occurring in the British Isles during migration and in winter. It is a strong flier that regularly covers many miles of ocean to reach practically all the islands of the Southwest Pacific. Since it nests at high latitudes around the Polar Sea where the hemispheres come together, it is surprising that we have so few records of it from North America. The bar-tailed should be looked for along our coasts in September on mud flats and sand bars. Here it wades, deeply probing at times to the full length of its bill for worms, crustacea, and mollusks. In flight it pulls its head back onto its shoulders, which, with its rather short legs, gives it a heavy appearance.

VOICE: The flight call is a low, barking *terrek, terrek.*

NEST: (P.) In a depression hidden by grass on a dry ridge in rolling upland tundra or on the lower mountain slopes. The 4 eggs (2.2 x 1.5) are greenish or brownish with a few brown markings.

RANGE: (M.) Breeds from n. Scandinavia east along the Arctic coast to n.c. Alaska and south to the Yukon delta. Winters south to c. Africa, India, Australia, and from Hawaii to New Zealand. Accidental on the Atlantic coast.

Hudsonian Godwit*   *Limosa haemastica*—✳34
L. 15; W. 26; Wt. 11 oz.

IDENTIFICATION: In spring the finely black-barred, reddish under parts fading to white about the head and broadly barred with white toward the tail are distinctive. Fall birds look like sedate greater yellowlegs or slender, short-billed willets, but in flight they show clear white upper tail coverts in strong contrast to the sooty-black tail with its narrow white tip. The upper wing surface shows only a narrow white line; underneath, the axillars and linings are a very dark sooty-brown.

HABITS: Although years ago this godwit is reported to have occurred in flocks of thousands in Argentina, Audubon never saw a live one. Since it followed the same migration route as the once incredibly abundant Eskimo curlew, it is a wonder that it survived the hunting period that brought the latter to virtual extinction. Today, however, it seems to be increasing rapidly, as it is regularly noted in some numbers within the limits of its restricted range. On the Atlantic coast the birds are seen after strong easterly winds in late August or September. Like the closely related black-tailed godwit of Europe and Asia, this species frequents muddy shores and shallows. Inland they are found on lake and pond shores and marsh openings. Along the coast they are attracted by broad tidal flats and sandy shores about inlets and river mouths. The long bill probes with a rapid thrusting action, and the birds often feed in water so deep that the head is completely submerged.

VOICE: Rather silent. The flight call a low, double *ta-it.*

NEST: (P.) On the ground in open tundra, often near water. The 4 eggs (2.2 x 1.5) are olive-buff, lightly marked with dark spots of the same color.

RANGE: (M.) Breeds locally from Southampton Island west to n.w. Mackenzie and south to n. Manitoba. Winters in extreme s. Argentina, Chile, and the Falkland Islands. The spring migration route is north up the w. Mississippi Valley and Great Plains, and while some birds return in fall over the same route, most of them fly eastward to the Gulf of St. Lawrence region and then offshore to South America, stopping at times at Bermuda and Barbados.

Ruff   *Philomachus pugnax*— ✳31
(♀ Reeve)   ♂ L. 11; ♀ L. 9

IDENTIFICATION: Breeding males are extraordinary-looking birds with elongated ear tufts and breast feathers that vary in color from white to black through browns of many shades and may be plain or coarsely or finely barred. In winter sexes look alike. In spring the female's breast feathers become dark brown with white or buff edges, but otherwise there is little change. In flight ruffs have a narrow white line in the wing and always show 2 conspicuous, long, oval white patches on either side of the dark, central lower back, rump, and tail-covert area. The legs are rather short and vary from orange or yellow through greens or browns to grayish or flesh color.

HABITS: The ruff carries individuality in plumage coloration to the limit. Seldom do 2 males look exactly alike. In spring the species does not pair, but the males (ruffs), like male prairie chickens, have a display ground on which each bird has a fixed station. To this the females (reeves) come from the nearby nesting meadow or marsh to mate, often with several males in succession. The brilliance or unusualness of a ruff's adornments seems to influence the reeves in their choice. The species in general appears to prefer the muddy shores of fresh-water ponds or marshes and wet short-grass meadow- or marshland, but most American records are from along the coast, where it often occurs about salt marshes and the banks of narrow, winding channels. It moves rather deliberately, probing the mud for food and seldom wading into the water. The food is chiefly insects (especially beetles), worms, crustacea, and mollusks and, in fall, seeds, including grains.

VOICE: These silent birds when flushed occasionally utter a low *tu-whit* or, in flight, a louder *teuuuu-i-toi*.

NEST: (I. 21, P.) A grass-lined depression in a meadow, marsh or grass clump on more open tundra. The 4 eggs (1.7 x 1.2) are pale gray, green, or buff, boldly spotted with sepia.

RANGE: (M.) Breeds from n. Scandinavia along the Arctic Islands and coast to e. Siberia south to w. France, Hungary, s. Russia, and n. Manchuria. Winters south to s. Africa, Ceylon, and Borneo. Within recent years usually at least one fall record for the Atlantic coast of North America, Barbados, or n. South America.

Sanderling*   *Crocethia alba*—✳37
L. 8; W. 15; Wt. 2½ oz.

IDENTIFICATION: A very pale-backed, white-breasted sandpiper in winter, the only dark area being a small patch at the bend of the wing. In flight the wings appear quite dark with a conspicuous long white line down the center. The legs and bill are always black. Adults may show more or less of the rusty-brown that suffuses the head, chest, and back in the breeding season, even in winter. In early fall young have dark, mottled backs and streaked and barred rumps, the latter being retained all winter.

HABITS: These big-headed, active, chunky little sandpipers, always in a hurry, are common on almost every ocean beach in the world at one season or another. Wherever they are, they nimbly follow the advancing and receding water's edge, probing vigorously for small crustacea and mollusks, often leaving a long line of holes and tossed-out sand in their wake. Occasionally at low tide they visit the sand flats and bars of bays near inlets or seaweed-covered rocks. Inland they are usually far less common, frequenting chiefly lake beaches and river bars and only occasionally mud flats. On dark mud the birds must recognize their conspicuousness, as one observer tells of a pair leaving such a spot to sit in a snowbank when attacked by a Cooper's hawk. Along the beach they rest on dry white sand, where they are almost invisible. Inland, as in the Arctic, insects are their chief food. Sanderling are not especially gregarious, and single birds feed by themselves as contentedly as in the small flocks in which they usually travel. Other birds join these flocks, but seldom is the reverse true.

VOICE: A shrill *twick, twick* is given as the birds flush, and a soft twitter is heard from feeding flocks.

NEST: (P.) A leaf-filled hollow near or in a small clump of vegetation growing on a barren open or stony place on a low ridge or terrace of the dry upland tundra. The 4 eggs (1.4 x .97) are olive with small brown spots.

RANGE: (M.) Breeds on the islands of the Arctic Ocean, n.

Greenland, and the coast of the Taimyr Peninsula region of Siberia. In North America breeds south through the many islands to Southampton Island. Winters from Virginia, the Gulf Coast, and c. California south to s. Chile and s. Argentina; also s. Africa, Australia, Hawaii, and the n. South Pacific islands.

AVOCETS and STILTS   Family Recurvirostridae

American Avocet*   *Recurvirostra americana*—✻35
L. 18; W. 33; B. 3¼–4; Wt. 12 oz.

IDENTIFICATION: This big shore bird is unmistakable. Various shades of gray replace the cinnamon of the head, neck, and breast in winter. In flight the back and tail are white, the outer wing black, its inner side white with a diagonal black band. Underneath, the flight feathers are dark in contrast with the pure-white wing lining.

HABITS: The present home of these tame and inquisitive birds is around the borders of the broad, shallow alkaline lakes and sinks of the Great Basin country and the more sparsely vegetated shallow marshes of the plains. When migrating they are also attracted to flooded meadowland and occasionally visit the shallow tide pools of the coastal marshes. Avocets feed like roseate spoonbills, walking rapidly or running in fairly deep water, swinging the bill from side to side on the muddy bottom. Often a large group feeds shoulder to shoulder in a long, evenly advancing line; at other times they swim with their webbed feet and feed by tipping up like puddle ducks. They take numbers of shrimp and other small crustacea, aquatic insects, and many seeds of aquatic and marsh plants. Insects are also frequently picked or "skimmed" from the surface. This species flies with the neck extended, and at times flocks indulge in elaborate maneuvers. Few American birds are handsomer than the avocet, and an attempt to restore it as a breeding species to the marshes of the Atlantic seaboard would be a fascinating wildlife-management project.

VOICE: The protest note is a loud, yelping *wheep*.

NEST: (P.) A depression, often with only a slight lining, on the bare, open ground of a mud flat. In times of high water the nest is added to in order to keep the eggs dry, and it may eventually become a mass of sticks, grass, and other debris a

foot or more high. Loose colonies are established. The usual
site is the sun-dried mud of an inland slough or alkaline flat
on ground that is often under water earlier in the spring. The
nest depression is in the open without concealment, although
rank weeds may later come up and hide it. The 4 eggs (2.0
x 1.3) are olive-buff, spotted and blotched with blackish-
brown.

RANGE: (P. M.) Breeds from s. Manitoba, s. Alberta, and e.
Washington south to s. Texas and s. California. Winters from
s. Texas and c. California to Guatemala. Once bred eastward
to the Atlantic coast, at least in s. New Jersey, where now it
is only a casual visitor in the fall.

Black-necked Stilt*   *Himantopus mexicanus*—✳35
                            L. 14½; W. 28; B. 2–2¾

IDENTIFICATION: In flight, solid black above except for a white
rump and upper tail coverts and a gray tail. Females, and
especially young, are less black and more brownish on the
back and have paler legs.

HABITS: The noisy, aggressive stilt breeds in small, loose colonies about shallow bodies of water. Although it is often most
abundant around fresh water and is quickly attracted to irrigated or flooded fields and pastures, it also breeds near stagnant, alkaline, or brackish ponds. In many areas, especially
about alkaline bodies of water, the avocet and stilt are closely
associated. Along the coast stilts breed about the brackish
ponds and flats of the upper salt marsh back against the upland and in the brackish to fresh ponds back of the beaches
or in the center of coastal islands. This bird is a very active
feeder, running about picking objects from the surface of the
water or mud, plowing the water with its bill, and occasionally probing deeply into the mud. Considering the length of
its legs (8 to 10 inches), it seems to feed most of the time in
rather shallow water. Aquatic beetles, bug and fly larvae are
staple foods. Snails and crustacea, although eaten, are not
generally important. It has been about 100 years since these
birds nested on the coast as far north as New Jersey, where
today even stragglers are rare. Since hunting rather than
habitat destruction was the cause of their disappearance,
stilts, even more readily than avocets, could probably be re-
established as breeders by egg transfers to nests of other shore
birds like willets.

VOICE: The alarm call is a sharp, yelping *pep, pep,* which rises in pitch to a frantic *yip, yip, yip*. Many of the notes suggest the call of a tern.

NEST: (P.) On the ground in the open or hidden by vegetation on or near the shore, or on a small island or hummock in a shallow body of water. The nest is usually a grass- or shell-lined scrape, but as incubation progresses these, like so many shore birds, often keep adding material, and if a flood comes they may engage in a frantic race to build it high enough to keep the eggs above water. The 4 eggs (1.7 x 1.2) are buffy, spotted with brownish-black.

RANGE: (P. M.) Breeds from South Carolina (formerly s. New Jersey), the Gulf Coast, Nebraska, n. Utah, and c. Oregon south through the West Indies and Mexico to n. Brazil, Peru, and the Galápagos Islands. Winters south from the West Indies and Mexico. Very similar birds occur all over the warmer parts of the world, and many ornithologists call them all one species, making our birds simply a race.

PHALAROPES   Family Phalaropodidae

Red Phalarope   *Phalaropus fulicarius*—⚔32
(Grey Phalarope)   L. 8½; W. 15

IDENTIFICATION: The extensively reddish breeding females are unmistakable. Males are paler red, with less white on the cheek, and are streaked instead of solid black on top of the head and neck. In winter the white forehead, pale blue-gray back (often brownish on rump and upper tail coverts), and the pale gray wings on which the broad white wing stripe and white tips to the secondaries are not too conspicuous are the best field marks. Compared with the red-necked, or northern, this is a larger, stockier, thicker-necked bird with a short, stout, broad-based bill. The bill and legs are more or less yellowish or brown. In winter the red phalarope is paler than the northern in all respects.

HABITS: In the two pelagic phalaropes we have shore birds, the numbers of which have not been appreciably reduced by civilization. They are still abundant over a vast breeding range in the Arctic. Only the virtual extermination of the whales of the Northern Hemisphere more than a century ago and the recent increasing pollution of the seas by oil from ships' bilges are likely to have affected their welfare. To what extent the deadly fuel-oil droplets that so mat a bird's feathers that they can no longer insulate its body from the cold sea water have taken toll no one knows, but, like all sea birds, these must at times suffer from this modern scourge of oceanic bird life.

Fishermen call phalaropes "whale" or "mackerel" birds and watch to see where flocks settle, believing that they depend upon feeding schools of crustacea-eating whales, mackerel, or other fish to help them locate abundant supplies of the small reddish copepods, commonly known as brit, that are one of the phalarope's chief foods at sea.

The red is the more pelagic of the two. Only small numbers occur on or near land outside the Arctic except in the early morning after a very foggy night or during a severe storm with an onshore wind. At such times phalaropes may swim erratically about in small ponds behind the beaches or in the surf. Here they bob their stiffly held heads and dab in all directions for food. At other times these buoyant little ducklike birds spin around in one spot in characteristic fashion or tip up and feed off the bottom. Very rarely one is observed feeding on a mud flat or on a beach near the water's edge. Food in the North consists largely of gnats and their larvae and other insects. When feeding, this species is reported to make twice as many dabs in a second (5) as the red-necked. In fall, adults are early and rapid migrants. They have been reported off Buenos Aires by August 12, although young birds linger in the Arctic until the end of September. In these fall flocks a few birds, as a rule, retain enough reddish breast plumage to indicate the species.

VOICE: The common note is a sharp, whistled *weet*. There are other notes, some wheezy or grating, others extremely thin and high-pitched.

NEST: (P.) The site is usually near the coast in low, marshy tundra with scattered ponds where the birds can feed. The nest is generally a depression in the ground on a high spot in or near the marsh. It may be in the top of a sedge tussock in the marsh proper or it may be a well-made cup of grass supported in the vegetation over water. The 4 eggs (1.2 x .85) are olive-buff with bold, irregular brown spots.

RANGE: (M.) Breeds on the islands and coasts of the entire Arctic Ocean south to the Yukon delta, Southampton Island, and Iceland. Winters at sea south to Lat. 50° S. Migration wholly pelagic.

Wilson's Phalarope   *Steganopus tricolor—✕32*
                                                    L. 9

IDENTIFICATION: Richly colored breeding female is unique, but
male's only distinctive markings are a white spot on the hind
neck, a pale chestnut wash on the side of the neck, and a long
black needlelike bill. Juveniles are quite cinnamon on the
upper parts and mottled and buff below. In winter the long
black legs change to pale or greenish-yellow. In flight the bird
has uniformly dark wings and a white rump and tail like a
yellowlegs, but neither the largely white under parts nor the
pale gray, scaled upper parts show streaking or spotting.

HABITS: This bird, the most beautiful of shore birds, is the only
"landlubber" in its family. Although it rides on water as buoyantly as the others and has been recorded to have made as
many as 247 consecutive spins, it does a large part of its feeding on foot in wet meadows, mud flats, and in shallow water
where it can wade. Here it picks insects from the surface,
probes vigorously in the mud, head under water like an
avocet, and swings its bill from side to side along the muddy
bottom. Rain pools in meadows and pastures attract it, as it
eats large numbers of land, as well as aquatic, insects. This
phalarope, which breeds in loose colonies about suitable
shallow ponds and marshy land, once occurred throughout the
entire northern prairie region east to northwestern Indiana.

VOICE: A distinctive, soft honking or trumpeting, also shriller
and more nasal notes.

NEST: (P.) A grass-lined depression in damp meadowland and
near a shallow body of water, in the open in a mowed area or
hidden in the taller grass of an unmowed one. The 4 eggs
(1.3 x .92) are pale buff, well spotted with blackish-brown.

RANGE: (M.) Breeds from s. Ontario, s. Manitoba, c. Alberta,
and s. British Columbia south to n. Indiana, c. Iowa, Nebraska, Colorado, Utah, and c. California. Winters inland
from c. Argentina and c. Chile south to the Falkland Islands.
In migration rare east of the plains and does not reach the
Pacific coast north of s. California. On the Atlantic coast,
although rare, it is seen with some regularity in fall.

Northern Phalarope   *Lobipes lobatus—✕32*
(Red-necked Phalarope)   L. 7; W. 14

IDENTIFICATION: The color pattern of the breeding plumage is
distinctive, although in the male it is duller and less bold.

being extensively flecked with white, gray, or brown. This species has a smaller head and a slimmer neck than the red phalarope, a much finer, almost needlelike bill, and legs that are blue-gray to blackish. In winter the darker gray, conspicuously streaked back and darker wings, on which the white wing stripe is more noticeable, are good field marks. The dark eye-to-ear patch generally separates a phalarope from a sanderling.

HABITS: This graceful, dainty bird is a common associate of the red phalarope at sea, but it also migrates north and south across the n. Great Plains in considerable numbers. Although seldom seen along the Atlantic coast south of New Jersey, and then only after storms, this species is not uncommon on the Pacific coast along the ocean front, on bays or on inland waters near the shore, or, especially in fall, on lakes in the interior. Like all phalaropes, this species has lobed toes and semipalmated feet and prefers to feed and rest afloat. It is very gregarious, nesting in loose colonies and gathering at sea in large flocks that maneuver in typical shore-bird fashion. On land small flocks up to 30 birds are the rule. Like the red, these phalaropes seek out feeding bowhead whales and plankton-feeding fish or gather in tide rips and among patches of drifting seaweed. Few birds are so fearless, individuals occasionally allowing themselves to be picked right out of the water.

Phalaropes are notable as one of the few cases among birds where the ordinary roles of the sexes are reversed. The female wears the bright plumage, arrives first at the breeding ground, advertises for a mate with display flights and calls, competes with other females for the male's attention, and permits, or makes, him do most or all of the incubating of the eggs. The pair remain together, however, and seem to share the care of the precocial downy young until they leave the nest shortly after hatching and go to a nearby pond. On land these phalaropes seem dependent upon mosquito larvae, water bugs and beetles found in fresh water, and on the brine shrimp and alkali flies found in the saline and alkaline waters of the Great Basin country.

VOICE: Similar to but lower-pitched than the red's.

NEST: (I. 20, P.) A hollow in a mound or sedge tussock in a marshy area with scattered ponds, or in a lakeside marsh. The 4 eggs (1.2 x .83) are olive-buff, boldly spotted with brown.

RANGE: (M.) Breeds from the Arctic Ocean south to about

Lat. 55° N.; i.e., from c. Greenland, Melville Island, and Alaska south to Labrador, James Bay, n. Manitoba, the Upper Yukon Valley, and the Aleutian Islands; also in Iceland, Spitsbergen, and the Arctic coast of Eurasia south to the British Isles, Baltic States, c. Russia, and Sakhalin. Winters at sea probably from just north of the equator to Lat. 60° S., at least off South America.

SKUAS   Family Stercorariidae

Pomarine Jaeger*   *Stercorarius pomarinus*—⚡21
(Pomatorhine Skua)   L. 22; W. 48; Wt. 27 oz.

IDENTIFICATION: This species has a more extensive pale area in the center of the upper wing (produced by the white shafts and bases of the primaries) and below (produced by white bases to primaries) and is a larger, broader-winged bird than other jaegers. In adults the projecting ends of the elongated central tail feathers, twisted through 90 degrees so that the web is vertical, produce from the side a distinctive dark blob beyond the tail. The 2 color phases vary in proportion from one breeding area to another, with the light phase running 80 to 95 per cent. In the light phase the pomarine generally has a more pronounced breast band than other jaegers and dusky barring on the flanks. Young lack the elongated tail feathers and can only be told by their larger size and much heavier bill.

HABITS: Jaegers are the most abundant birds of prey in the Arctic. There this species feeds on lemmings, eggs, small birds and young of all bird species, as well as on carrion and what food they can steal from other sea birds. Later, when they go to sea for the winter, they are attracted by gatherings of feeding terns, gulls, or shearwaters, all of which they rob. Jaegers can, however, catch their own food and often follow ships like gulls. The pomarines' flight is steady, deliberate, and powerful, but they seem less active and aggressive than the other jaegers. They move north off our coasts from mid-April to late May and come south in late August and September, their numbers varying greatly from year to year. Few are ever seen from shore, and to become acquainted with these and the many other interesting birds of the open ocean

that a landlubber seldom sees, it is necessary to visit the offshore fishing banks.

VOICE: Varied single- or double-noted squealing, hawklike
whistles.

NEST: Widely scattered over low, swampy tundra, a grassy
cup on dry mounds, occasionally on cliff ledges. The 2 eggs
(2.4 x 1.7) are olive or brown, sparingly spotted with brown.

RANGE: (M.) Breeds on the islands and coasts of the entire
Arctic Ocean, south in the Western Hemisphere to Iceland,
Southampton Island, and the Yukon delta. Winters at sea
from Virginia and probably from Lower California to the
waters off Peru, w. Africa, and e. Australia. Of rare but occasional occurrence on large bodies of inland water like the
Great Lakes and the Caspian Sea.

Parasitic Jaeger*   *Stercorarius parasiticus*—⚡21
(Arctic Skua)   L. 17; Wt. 18 oz.

IDENTIFICATION: This bird has long, pointed, slender wings with
a very sharp angle at the bend and a smaller, more tapered
bill than the preceding species. Below, the outer flight
feathers, though paler than the wing lining, do not form a
sharply defined white patch. On the upper wing surface the
light area is mainly due to the white quills of the primaries.
The elongated (2–3½ inches longer) pair of central tail
feathers are diagnostic, though lacking in young birds. There
are 2 color phases: the young of both are similar. It takes 3
years for the young to mature, becoming progressively less
barred with dark or white, depending upon the phase.

HABITS: This is the jaeger that commonly harries flocks of feeding terns and attaches itself to migrating flocks of arctic terns
and travels with them across the ocean. Swift and agile beyond belief, the parasitic jaeger follows every twist and
plunge of a tern until the desperate bird gives up its prey,
which the jaeger catches before it hits the water. In the North
this jaeger feeds to some extent on lemmings, but it is the
scourge of longspurs, horned larks, redpolls, and snow bunt-
ings, as well as of the smaller shore birds and young ducks.
It catches and carries its prey in its bill and commonly swallows it whole, feathers and all. These jaegers move north in
April and May and go south from the last week in July to
early October. In migration the light phase seems dominant
along our coasts, but on the breeding grounds the proportion
of dark to light birds varies from 0 to 95 per cent from one

region to another. In southern areas and near the coast dark birds predominate, but inland and in the Far North the lighter phase is commoner.

VOICE: A dry *tick a tick-tick* or *tuk-tuk;* also other wailing or squeaking notes and a mewing *ka-aaow.*

NEST: A depression, often well lined, in flat, grassy tundra or open stony ground near the coast, or at higher elevations inland near lakes and, in the South, in open moorland. The 2 eggs (2.2 x 1.6) are usually olive with brown markings.

RANGE: (M.) Breeds on the islands and coasts of the Arctic Ocean south to Scotland, n. Labrador, Southampton Island, n. Manitoba, s. Mackenzie, s.w. Alaska, and Kamchatka. Winters from Florida and c. California south to the fringes of the Antarctic Ocean. Its migration is largely pelagic, but in fall it is the jaeger most often seen along our coasts and on our inland waters, where it is at all times rare.

Long-tailed Jaeger*   *Stercorarius longicaudus*—⚡21
(Long-tailed Skua)   L. 21; Wt. 12 oz.

IDENTIFICATION: Although longer over-all, this bird has a shorter body than the preceding and slimmer wings. A dark phase is virtually unknown, and the normal bird is grayer-backed and cleaner-breasted than the parasitic. It shows little white on the underwing and generally only the 2 outer quills of the primaries are white above. In adults the central pair of tail feathers are 5 to 8 inches longer than the rest and are quite distinctive. The legs are blue-gray rather than black. Young are barred and grayer, with less white on the wing than in the other species.

HABITS: This little jaeger has the grace and buoyancy in the air of a swallow-tailed kite or frigate-bird. It hovers like a tern and sails, soars, and engages in wild chases through the sky, apparently in a spirit of play. In years of lemming abundance it is a common breeding bird in most parts of the Arctic. So dependent is it upon those small mouselike animals that when they periodically become scarce in a given locality, as they do every 4 years, the long-tails move on to breed, or at least to summer, elsewhere. This species spends little time harrying gulls or terns, but rounds out its summer diet with insects, many of them captured in mid-air, and with fish and, rarely, small birds. In fall, before it goes south, it is reported to fatten up on that arctic staple, the crowberry. Although the bird is common in the Arctic and in some parts of the

Southern Hemisphere, its migration route between these two points has long been a mystery. Evidently the migration is performed rapidly at considerable elevations, with few, if any, feeding stops, since the birds in spring are on the breeding ground ahead of similar migrants and already mated when others arrive. In fall they depart in what appear to be family groups. May and September records from Bermuda and others from shipboard indicate a mid-ocean rather than a non-stop overland route.

VOICE: A shrill, harsh *cree-oo* with a roll, plus other similarly hard single and double notes.

NEST: (A.) A depression on a knoll or ridge in the tundra, often on the dry, rolling uplands or lower mountain slopes. The 2 eggs (2.2 x 1.5) are brownish-olive, irregularly marked with brown.

RANGE: (M) Breeds on the islands and coasts of the entire Arctic Ocean south in North America to c. Greenland, n. Labrador, n. Mackenzie, and the Yukon delta. Little is known of its wintering grounds, which appear to be well south in the oceans of the Southern Hemisphere. In the Northern Hemisphere it migrates through the central ocean areas and is seldom seen either along the coast or inland.

Skua*   *Catharacta skua*— ✉ 21
(Great Skua)   L. 21; W. 59; Wt. 2½ lbs.

IDENTIFICATION: The extensively white bases of the primaries form a large pure-white patch in the wing that is distinctive. Young birds lack the pale yellow streaking on the neck of summer adults, while the light spotting on the back and the white wing patch may be so reduced that it shows only on the under side of the wing.

HABITS: This is the world's only bipolar breeding bird, although its role in the Northern Hemisphere is minor compared with its abundance and dominance in the Southern Hemisphere. There it is a gull-like scavenger on carrion and other refuse both on land and at sea, a catcher of fish, shrimp, and surface-swimming plankton animals, a robber of other sea birds, and an aggressive predator, catching and eating small sea birds like petrels and the weaklings of any species. During the breeding season it usually nests near penguin or petrel colonies, preying on both eggs and young. Its rapacity extends even to its own young, one of which generally strays too far from the nest to be recognized and is eaten, but the one that survives is defended against man and beast with unequaled ferocity and fearlessness. In the Northern Hemisphere this species has been increasing rapidly in recent years, and there seems to be no reason why it cannot eventually colonize the whole Arctic.

In the air the skua is a massive-looking bird with a short, upcocked tail. It soars well and flies with deep, rapid strokes of its broad, powerful wings that propel it with unsuspected speed. It looks more like a miniature eagle or hawk than a gull and has a strongly hooked bill and long, sharp, curved claws which are used in holding and tearing up prey but not for carrying food. Food is either swallowed at once or carried in the bill. Away from its breeding grounds, the skua is usually solitary, ranging widely over coastal waters and on the high seas, though in our region it is seldom seen from shore. At sea it often follows ships and, unlike the jaegers, often alights on water. Curious and always hungry, these birds at times crowd around a man skinning game or cleaning fish, accept food from his hand, and ignore all attempts to drive them away.

VOICE: Sharp, shrill, gull-like screams and at times a ducklike quacking note.

NEST: Loose colonies are often formed near breeding colonies of other sea birds. The site is on open ground or a rocky slope near the sea, generally on a high place like a cliff top or headland. The 2 brown or olive to grayish eggs (2.8 x 1.9) with dark brown spots are laid in a grass-lined scrape on the ground.

RANGE: (P. M.) Breeds on the shores of the Antarctic Continent, the islands of the antarctic and subarctic seas, and on the coast of South America north to c. Chile on the west. In the Northern Hemisphere it is a subarctic species, occurring in summer across the North Atlantic from s.e. Baffin Island, Greenland, and Iceland to the Faeroes and Orkneys, although only known to breed from Iceland east. Winters from Lat. 60° N. to the Sargasso Sea but is encountered south at least to the Gulf Stream all summer. Birds undoubtedly from the Southern Hemisphere range north in summer in the Pacific Ocean to the latitude of British Columbia and Japan, and the occurrence of skuas in greatest numbers in July, August, and September on the fishing banks off Newfoundland and Massachusetts suggests that the same thing may be true in the Atlantic.

Comparison of Average Length and Wingspread of Sea Birds usually seen in Flight

SPECIES	LENGTH	WINGSPREAD
Storm Petrel	6	—
Wilson's Petrel	7	$15\frac{1}{2}$
Leach's Petrel	8	—
Frigate Petrel	8	—
Least Tern	9	20
Black Tern	$9\frac{1}{2}$	—
Little Gull	11	—
Dusky Shearwater	$11\frac{1}{2}$	—
Long-tailed Jaeger (immature)	13	—
Bonaparte's Gull	13	32
Ross' Gull	$13\frac{1}{2}$	—
Sabine's Gull	$13\frac{1}{2}$	—
Common Shearwater	14	—
Franklin's Gull	14	—
Gull-billed Tern	14	34
Bridled Tern	$14\frac{1}{2}$	—
Forster's Tern	$14\frac{1}{2}$	30
Black-headed Gull	15	—
Noddy Tern	15	—
Parasitic Jaeger (immature)	15	—
Common Tern	15	31
Bermuda Petrel	15	35
Black-capped Petrel	15	38
Arctic Tern	$15\frac{1}{2}$	—
Roseate Tern	$15\frac{1}{2}$	—
Sandwich Tern	16	—
Yellow-billed Tropic-bird (female)	16	37
Sooty Tern	$16\frac{1}{2}$	—
Laughing Gull	$16\frac{1}{2}$	—
Ivory Gull	17	—
Common Gull	17	—
Kittiwake	17	36
Sooty Shearwater	17	42
Parasitic Jaeger	18	—
Black Skimmer	18	46
Fulmar	$18\frac{1}{2}$	41
Ring-billed Gull	$18\frac{1}{2}$	48
Royal Tern	19	43
Great Shearwater	19	43

SPECIES	LENGTH	WINGSPREAD
Long-tailed Jaeger	21	—
Cinereous Shearwater	21	45
Caspian Tern	21	53
Skua	21	59
California Gull	21½	—
Pomarine Jaeger	22	48
Lesser Black-backed Gull	23	—
Iceland Gull	24	55
Herring Gull	24	56
Glaucous Gull	28	60
Brown Booby	29	57
Red-footed Booby	29	60
Great Black-backed Gull	29	65
Yellow-billed Tropic-bird (male)	32	37
Blue-faced Booby	32	63
Gannet	36	72
Magnificent Frigate-bird	40	90
Brown Pelican	50	80
White Pelican	60	100

GULLS and TERNS   Family Laridae

Glaucous Gull*   *Larus hyperboreus*—✕22
L. 28; W. 60

IDENTIFICATION: The outstanding characteristics of this species and the next are their very pale gray upper parts and pure-white primaries. The glaucous is not only larger than the Iceland, as a rule, but it has a heavier head, a yellow eye ring, and a longer, stouter bill (even larger than a herring gull's). Juveniles are creamy-buff and brown, uniformly pale, with flight feathers as pale as, or paler than, the rest of the wing. In their second and third years the young birds gradually become uniformly creamy-white all over. The young start out with a whitish bill with a dark tip that fades as the bird matures, then becomes yellow with red spots.

HABITS: This huge, powerful gull with its broad, heavy wings and steady soaring flight has little of the bend in the wing seen in most gulls and often looks very much like a soaring hawk. To a large extent it is a bird of prey, living during the summer chiefly on the young of murres and other alcids, ducks, and gulls. Even the adults of species as large as dovekies and plovers are captured, often in the air, and swallowed whole, feathers and all. At other seasons it robs gulls and diving ducks of their catches, searches far and wide for carrion and refuse of any sort, and also appears to do some hunting for sea food on its own. In winter it ranges along the edges of any open water and often gets quite far out to sea in favorable areas like fishing banks. To residents of the Far North the glaucous gull is the harbinger of spring, arriving about mid-April as the first migrant from the South.

VOICE: Very hoarse, loud, drawn-out, almost ravenlike croaks; also shriller, more typically gull-like screams.

NEST: On ledges near the tops of cliffs or on isolated high areas, generally near colonies of murres and the other sea birds on which they prey, also on small islets in tundra lakes or in coastal dunes. The nest is a substantial cup of grass, moss, and seaweed. The 3 eggs (3.0 x 2.1) are clay color to brown, irregularly marked with chocolate-brown.

RANGE: (P. M.) Breeds on the islands and coast of the Arctic Ocean south in North America to Newfoundland, James Bay, n. Mackenzie, and the Pribilof Islands. Winters from the edge of open water south to Long Island, the Great Lakes, and c. California and abroad to the Mediterranean and Caspian seas and Japan.

Iceland Gull*   *Larus leucopterus*—✄ 22
L. 24; W. 55

IDENTIFICATION: Coloring similar to the preceding except that the eye ring is red and in one race (kumlieni) there are grayish markings near the tips of the primaries. The Iceland is smaller but proportionately longer-winged, the folded wings extending well beyond the tail. Its shorter, weaker bill and small head (smaller than a herring gull's) give it a much more gentle look. Juveniles are darker than young glaucous gulls, but the species matures faster. The bill is at first uniformly blackish but becomes light greenish by the second year.

HABITS: In the air this longer-winged white gull seems more graceful and buoyant than the glaucous. It also appears to be less predatory, depending more on fish caught through its own efforts and refuse of all kinds. Young in their first fall eat crowberries until they develop fishing skill. In winter, like so many gulls, this species is best looked for about piers where fish are being cleaned or around garbage dumps and sewer outlets.

VOICE: Like the herring gull, but shriller.

NEST: In colonies, often large ones on ledges near the top of cliffs, usually those frequented by nesting kittiwakes and other sea birds. Occasionally it nests lower down, on or close to a sandy shore. The 2 or 3 eggs (2.7 x 1.9) laid in a grass, moss, and seaweed nest are like those of the glaucous.

RANGE: (P. M.) Breeds on the Arctic Islands of North America, Greenland, and Jan Mayen Island. Winters from the edge of open water south to n. New Jersey, the Great Lakes, and Great Britain.

Great Black-backed Gull*   *Larus marinus*—✕ 26
L. 29; W. 65

IDENTIFICATION: The blackish mantle and great size distinguish adults. Young are notably light-headed and paler below than the young of herring gulls.

HABITS: This gull, largest of its kind, occupies much the same niche in the wildlife community as its more northern relative, the glaucous. A majestic bird, fond of soaring and wheeling on high, it usurps the most elevated nest sites on an island and when with other gulls insits upon having the most com‑ manding perch available. In summer it preys on the eggs and young of eider ducks, cormorants, terns, and other gulls and takes adults of smaller species like Leach's petrel and guille-mot. At other seasons it makes its living by robbing other gulls, eating carrion and hunting sea food on the flats at low tide. In winter it becomes gregarious, associating freely with herring gulls, although as a rule continuing to assert its dominance.

In recent years the species has extended its breeding and wintering range southward and has become more abundant on both sides of the Atlantic. On our coast this has followed the increase and spread of the herring gull and the double-crested cormorant, which has been so great and rapid as to lead to demands for artificial checks on their numbers. But, as invariably happens if man does not interfere, nature pro-vides checks. In this case it seems likely that the presence of the highly predatory black-back will tend to keep down the populations of the herring gulls and cormorants.

VOICE: A variety of harsh barking calls or croaks and screams, in general lower-pitched and more guttural than those of other gulls.

NEST: (I. 27) Solitary or in small colonies, rarely large ones, on small coastal islands or isolated headlands, also occasionally on an island in a lake a mile or two inland. The nest is a mass of debris in a hollow in the ground or among rocks on the highest available open area. The 3 eggs (3.1 x 2.1) are buffy-brown to olive, spotted and blotched with dark brown.

RANGE: (P. M.) Breeds on the coasts of the North Atlantic and adjacent parts of the Arctic Ocean from n. Labrador, c. Greenland, Iceland, n. Scandinavia, and n.w. Russia south to Long Island and Brittany. Winters from s. Greenland south to the Great Lakes, North Carolina, the Canary Islands, and the Mediterranean and Caspian seas.

Lesser Black-backed Gull* *Larus fuscus*—✕26
L. 23

IDENTIFICATION: The mantle in this species varies from slate-black to slate-gray, but the yellow feet are distinctive and the dusky streaking on the head and neck in the winter plumage is more extensive than in the great black-backed. Juvenile birds may be darker than those of a herring gull but are often indistinguishable, as the trend toward yellow legs is not apparent until the second or third year.

HABITS: This gull, an occasional wanderer from Europe to our side of the Atlantic, and the herring gull apparently stem from a common ancestral gull population which originated somewhere in northeastern Siberia. As this Siberian species pushed out east and west to colonize nearby regions the new populations tended to vary a little from the original stock. These units begat others until finally the two divergent lines met halfway around the world, that represented by the lesser black-back having apparently come from the east, that of the herring gull from the west across North America. Beginning with the present Siberian population (the Vega herring gull) and following each of the lines, one discovers that each group is so similar to its neighbors (often interbreeding with them) that they all appear to be merely races or subspecies of a single species, and yet when the lines meet the end groups breed side by side without interbreeding. This, the surest test of a valid species, poses a problem in nomenclature which some ornithologists have solved by putting all the birds in one superspecies. Why the herrings and the lesser black-backs did not interbreed when they met is hard to determine, but the acquisition by the former of a 2-week-earlier breeding season may have had something to do with it. In behavior and habits the two remain almost identical, though at times the lesser black-back seems to be a bolder and more aggressive bird.

VOICE: Similar to the herring gull's, but generally somewhat lower-pitched.

NEST: (I. 27) In colonies of from a few to many pairs on rocky islets or headlands or, more usually, on open grassy, weedy, or brush-grown land, the nest itself varying from a sparsely lined scrape to a large pile of debris. The 3 eggs (2.7 x 1.8) vary from pale blue-green to brown, spotted with blackish-brown.

RANGE: (P. M.) Breeds from Iceland and the n. Russian-Scandinavian peninsula south to Brittany and the Baltic Sea. Winters from the British Isles, e. Mediterranean, and Persian Gulf south to the coasts and lakes of c. Africa.

Herring Gull*

Larus argentatus—❌22
L. 24; W. 56; Wt. 2½ lbs.

IDENTIFICATION: An adult gull with a pale gray mantle, pinkish or flesh-colored legs and feet, and white-spotted black wing tips is in North America always a herring gull. Some Old World races have yellow feet like a lesser black-back. The only seasonal change is a brown streaking on the head and neck which the birds acquire in winter. There is much individual variation in the rate at which young mature. Generally speaking, the first plumage change occurs in their second winter, when gray begins to appear in the mantle and the head becomes lighter. In the third winter the upper tail coverts become at least partly white, and by the fourth winter only a trace of dark remains in the tails of some individuals.

HABITS: (Age 17 yrs., 49 in captivity.) This species, the common gull of the Northeast, has been increasing rapidly in recent years and has extended its breeding range from e. Maine south to New Jersey. Whether this is a reoccupation of former breeding areas from which the bird disappeared when it was persecuted by eggers, plume hunters, and fishermen, or a real extension, no one knows. We do know, though, that the dumping of garbage, fishing wastes, and sewage into our coastal waters has expanded the food supply for all scavengers. It seems likely that this is permitting more gulls to survive the winter, when starvation normally eliminates that fraction of a population which is in excess of the environment's carrying capacity. If so, we are witnessing the typical response of any wild animal to an expansion of the food supply during that period of the year when food is normally at a minimum and the amount available is critical in determining the population for the entire year. The most interesting question now is: At what level will the herring gull population stabilize itself under these new conditions? Much as we may hope that it will not go much higher because of the adverse effect it is having on tern colonies along the coast, the point at which it levels off will be controlled by nature's law of supply and demand, and possibly to some extent by great black-backed gull predation. The fact that herring gull populations are undergoing a similar rapid increase and expansion into new range in parts of Europe is probably more than coincidence.

Although most abundant along the seacoast, there is hardly a body of inland water too small to be visited occasionally by migrating herring gulls, and on all our larger rivers and lakes it is at times common. The farther south one goes, the higher the proportion of young birds to old, as first-year birds make the longest migration, mature adults the shortest. This gull's food, aside from that inadvertently provided by man, consists of fish, crustacea, marine worms, shellfish, sea urchins, insects, eggs (especially of sea birds, small birds, and mammals), and occasionally fruit like crowberries and blueberries. Some fish are caught by shallow plunges and some are stolen from more expert avian fishermen, but most are picked up at low tide in shallow pools on the mud flats or are found washed up dead. Worms, crustacea, and shellfish are often obtained by a rapid treading of wet mud or sand, which liquefies it and reveals these marine animals. Hard-bodied shellfish are carried aloft and dropped on a hard surface to break them open. Quite gregarious, herring gulls gather into large roosts at night on sheltered inland waters, islands, the upper reaches of a beach, or in secluded open fields or marshes. This is usually the commonest of the ship-following gulls, often balancing over the stern updraft and gliding along without a wingbeat. Seldom, though, do they follow a ship much beyond the continental shelf. Like many gulls, they seem to like to visit fresh water from time to time and are commonly seen flying back from the coast to some nearby body of fresh water, where they drink, bathe, and rest.

voice: The calls vary greatly in pitch, quality, and loudness. The common note is a series of dry *kak-kak-kak* sounds, but when aroused the bird has a loud, trumpeting *kyow-kyow-kyow* in which the notes run together at the end.

nest: (I. 26) Occasionally solitary but usually in colonies, often of considerable size, and frequently closely associated with colonies of other sea birds like the arctic tern or double-crested cormorant. Generally the birds nest on the ground, but they will resort to tree nesting if disturbed too much. The usual site is an open rocky or weed-grown island off the seacoast or in a lake, also on sand dunes or headlands. The nest is a rough pile of seaweed and other rubbish with a shallow cup for the 3 bluish, greenish, or brownish eggs (2.8 x 2.0), irregularly spotted with browns.

range: (P. M.) As explained under the preceding bird, it is hard in the case of the herring gull to determine what is a race and what a species. Gull populations currently regarded as belonging to this species breed around the whole Northern Hemisphere from the shores of the Arctic Ocean south to n. New Jersey, the Great Lakes, s. Manitoba, and n. British Columbia and abroad to s.c. Asia, the Mediterranean, and the Canary Islands. Winters south to the West Indies, Panama, c.w. Africa, and Indo-China.

California Gull*   *Larus californicus*—✕23
L. 21½

identification: Regarded by some ornithologists as just an inland-nesting race of the herring gull, from which it differs only in its smaller size, the larger white area at the very tip of the black primaries, the greenish-gray or greenish-yellow legs, the pure-gray rather than blue-gray mantle, the black in addition to the red on the bill, and—the best field mark of all—the abruptly black ends to the wings when seen from below. First-year birds, although not quite as dark—i.e., streaked with more white, and with a more extensively flesh-colored bill, dark only at the tip—are doubtfully distinguishable. Second-year birds are even closer to herring gulls, although the legs may begin to show a greenish cast.

habits: In winter most of these gulls are found along the Pacific coast following ships offshore and feeding about harbors and bays with other gulls. Inland, especially during the breeding season, this gull obtains its food in the marshes and lakes where it nests and in the adjacent uplands over which it ranges for many miles. Fish (like carp), crayfish, and other aquatic animals of shallow water are taken as available and occasionally birds' eggs are eaten, but grass-hoppers, insect larvae and adult insects from freshly plowed fields, and at times mice and ground squirrels make up the bulk of the diet.

Gulls, because they range widely and are able to concen-trate in enormous flocks, can be uniquely effective in bringing destructive outbreaks of insects or rodents under control. A dramatic instance of this was the sudden descent of thou-sands of California gulls on the fields of the early Mormon settlers in Utah when a species of long-horned grasshopper (the Mormon cricket) was destroying their crops. The birds were regarded as heaven-sent, and a monument was later erected to commemorate the occasion. Yet in spite of this and other proofs of their value, little has been done to preserve the colonies of these gulls or to establish them throughout the West within feeding range of agricultural land. We have not yet realized that the biological control of insects and rodents through wildlife management is far safer and cheaper in the long run than to continue year after year to load our soils with ever-increasing quantities of poisonous chemicals.

VOICE: Similar to that of the herring gull.

NEST: In colonies, generally large ones that are often shared with ring-billed gulls, on islands in fresh or alkaline lakes or marshes. The nests are often scrapes in the bare ground or among sparse vegetation, more or less lined with any sort of debris the gull can find, but occasionally a pile of material a foot or more high is collected. The 3 eggs (2.7 x 1.8) are olive-buff to buffy-brown, evenly spotted with brown.

RANGE: (P. M.) Breeds from e. North Dakota and s. Mackenzie south to Wyoming, n. Utah, and c.e. California. Winters on the coast of Texas in small numbers and from n. Utah and s. British Columbia south both inland and on the coast to s.w. Mexico.

Ring-billed Gull*   *Larus delawarensis*—✳ 23
L. 18½; W. 48

IDENTIFICATION: The ring on the bill is the best field mark, but the clear yellow legs, black under sides to the wing tips, and the more delicate appearance of the whole bird separate it from an adult herring gull. Even first-winter birds are very light and spotted in appearance above and largely white below and have a pinkish-flesh color on the legs and on the bill which is abruptly dark-tipped. Until fully adult the tail has a sharply defined narrow black band of even width across the end. (Second-year herring gulls, because of the light upper tail coverts, appear to have such a band but not of *even* width.)

HABITS: Regarded by Audubon as the commonest of American gulls, the ring-bill once bred on hundreds of inland lakes and marshes and in some coastal localities. It is rather intolerant of disturbance and with the encroachment of civilization gradually disappeared from many areas. However, ring-bills still breed virtually from coast to coast and have so increased in recent years that at one season or another they are fairly common in every part of the country. Inland they are often plow followers. Feeding habits are similar to those of the California gull. Many insects like grasshoppers are captured on the wing, as the ring-bill is very agile in the air and a graceful, buoyant flier. Along the coast it seems particularly fond of feeding on the beaches along the wave edge, where it captures crustacea in the wet sand, after the manner of a shore bird. It also follows ships and scavenges like any other gull and is often common about garbage and refuse dumps and wharves.

VOICE: Higher-pitched and generally more subdued than that of similar gulls.

NEST: In colonies, often associated with other gulls, terns, and cormorants. On the ground in the open or among rocks and bushes on islands, rocky reefs, or matted marsh vegetation. The nests of grass, weeds, and trash are usually up on high ground and have been reported occasionally in low trees. The 3 eggs (2.3 x 1.7) are buffy or olive-buffy, irregularly spotted and blotched with darker browns.

RANGE: (P. M.) Breeds from s. Labrador, James Bay, n. Manitoba, s. Mackenzie, and s. Alaska south to the Great Lakes, s. Colorado, n. Utah, and n. California. Winters from s. New England, the Great Lakes, Montana, and British Columbia south to Cuba and s. Mexico.

Common Gull*   *Larus canus*—※23
(Mew Gull)   L. 17

IDENTIFICATION: The small, almost ploverlike head and bill and the long wings that give the body a slim, tapered appearance are very noticeable. The greenish legs, unmarked yellow-green bill, large white spots on the wing tips, and the slightly darker-than-herring-gull mantle are useful field characters. First-year birds are very dark and brownish. In the second year they lack the sharply defined tail band of the ring-bill.

HABITS: From its range it would appear that this Eurasian gull is a relative newcomer which, after crossing Bering Strait, is still in process of colonizing North America. In winter it migrates to coastal areas and has habits similar to those of other gulls, scavenging about harbors, dropping shellfish to break them, and treading the mud to detect worms and other animals. It is very active when feeding, often dropping repeatedly into the water from some height or dipping to the surface as it flutters along with dangling legs. At times it works the wave edge along the beach. It frequently occurs in flocks which, unlike those of larger gulls, exhibit much of the co-ordinated flock action of shore birds on the wing. Inland it is a plow follower and often frequents cultivated fields and grasslands for insects as well as feeding in lakes and marshes. The accuracy of Audubon's many records of this species along the Atlantic coast is now questioned, but in view of the regular occurrence of several other European gulls on our coast in recent years this one should be looked for carefully, especially among flocks of ring-billed gulls.

VOICE: The varied calls are shriller and often shorter than those of the larger gulls.

NEST: (I. 23) This species is flexible in its breeding habits. It nests inland about lakes or on islets in ponds in low, marshy country, but it also nests on cliffs or hillsides near the sea, on coastal islands and pebble beaches. Usually the colonies are small and solitary nesting pairs are not uncommon. The nest may be on the ground, on rocks, or in the tops of low trees. The 3 eggs (2.2 x 1.6) are buffy with brown markings.

RANGE: (P. M.) Breeds from n.w. Mackenzie and n.w. Alaska south to n. Saskatchewan and c. British Columbia and across Europe and Asia from the Faeroes, n. Scandinavia, n. Russia, and n. Siberia south to the Baltic and Caspian seas, Mongolia, and Kamchatka. Winters from s.e. Alaska to s. California and south to the Mediterranean and s. China coast.

Black-headed Gull*   *Larus ridibundus*—⚹ 24
(Brown-headed Gull)   L. 15

IDENTIFICATION: This chocolate-brown-headed gull with its crimson bill and legs is 1 of 6 dark-headed gulls occurring in

North America. From August on, the head is white except
for a dark patch over the ear and in front of the eye and
often some brownish-gray on the crown. The white outer
primaries above and the blue-gray wing lining and dark gray
to blackish primaries below (except for a white outer one)
are distinctive. Young have yellowish to flesh-colored legs and
bills, the latter with a black tip; a black-tipped tail, and
wings that show 4 bands of color along their upper surface—
white, dark brown, pale gray, and finally dark gray along the
rear edge.

HABITS: (Age 25 yrs.) In Europe this bird has adapted itself to
civilization more completely than any other gull and is at
home both along low-lying coasts and nearby harbors and
estuaries and far inland on rivers, lakes, and marshes. It feeds
in grasslands and crop fields, as well as in marshes, taking
insects, earthworms, some weed seeds and waste grain, and
other crop residues—often roosting at night in flocks in secluded, open fields. The black-head's flight is buoyant and
almost ternlike in the way the body rises and falls, but it is
heavier than the similar Bonaparte's gull and has more
rounded wing tips. Like the Bonaparte's, it feeds by dipping
to the surface with dangling legs but not alighting. Occasionally, however, it plunges into the water. It also hawks about
high in the air after flying insects, tramples the mud for
worms, and harasses ducks, coots, and other divers when they
are feeding.

The scavenging opportunities offered by cities have been
increasingly exploited in recent years by this species, which
is now one of the commonest wild birds of many densely
settled European areas; e.g., London. Black-heads feed around
the docks and in harbors and inland on dumps, in parks,
and wherever refuse is thrown. At night they gather in rafts
on nearby reservoirs to bathe and sleep. In the past 50 years
they have increased greatly, probably because of their ability
to adapt themselves to man-made environments, and have
spread to and established breeding colonies in Iceland. Every
winter they occur in small numbers along our Atlantic coast,
especially about harbors and inlets. Several birds banded in
Europe have been taken on this side, and it seems possible that
the species may eventually establish itself as a breeder on the
western shores of the Atlantic.

VOICE: Harsh, often abrupt, crowlike, single *kwup*, frequently
prolonged into *kwur-ir-ip*.

NEST: (I. 21) Along the seacoast on upper beaches and dunes, as well as on open flats and marshes. Most of the colonies are inland on small islets and tussocks in marshes, bays, and reed-grown lake borders. Large colonies are the rule. The nests are a loose mass of material, varying considerably in size and placed on the ground, on matted-down vegetation or occasionally on rocks or even in bushes or trees. The 3 eggs (2.0 x 1.5) are buffy-brown with blackish markings.

RANGE: (P. M.) Breeds across Eurasia from Iceland, c. Scandinavia, n. Russia, and n.c. Siberia south to s. France, Sardinia, Albania, s. Russia, and Mongolia. Winters south to the Canaries, n.c. Africa, India, and the Philippines. It now occurs regularly in small numbers on our Atlantic coast, where it has been recorded from Greenland south to s. Mexico and the s. Lesser Antilles.

Laughing Gull*   *Larus atricilla*—✳ 24
                                              L. 16½

IDENTIFICATION: The dark lead-gray wings with solid, blackish ends and a white rear edge are distinctive. In winter the head is largely white and the bill tip and legs less red. Young are very dark above and on the breast; have white upper tail coverts, a gray tail with a black subterminal band and white tip, and a blackish bill and legs.

HABITS: The laughing gull, the only breeding gull of the South Atlantic and Gulf-Caribbean area, is essentially a warm-water bird that seldom ranges into cold water at any season of the year. This probably accounts for the precariousness of its hold on the region north of Cape Cod where, with the recent increase of the herring gull, it seems likely to disappear as a breeding bird. It is less of a scavenger than most gulls and catches fish and shrimp in the shallows and crabs on the mud flats when the tide is out. It is, however, quite willing to steal what it can from pelicans and other hard-working fishermen. The laughing is definitely a coastal bird, although at times it ranges inland for fresh water on which to sit while it drinks, preens, and bathes. It likes to soar on thermal updrafts and often hawks about in the air like a swallow in pursuit of such insects as dragonflies. It is a common plow follower and after heavy rains visits fields to get earthworms. Away from the coast it is most frequently encountered along some of the larger rivers.

VOICE: The common call is a *ha-ha-ha,* given in flight, which at times sounds rather gooselike. The "laugh" is a long series of such notes, the last ones prolonged, higher-pitched, and clearer.

NEST: Large colonies are the rule and they are usually on an island. The nest sites vary from sand dunes densely grown up to beach grass, weed and shrub areas, and high salt marshes to bare sand bars. The nest is often a well-woven, well-lined structure of grass and weed stems that raises the eggs above the tides. The 3 eggs (2.1 x 1.5) are brownish-olive, irregularly marked with brown.

RANGE: (P. M.) Breeds from Maine to the Lesser Antilles, Central America, and probably n. South America, and from Lower California to Central America on the Pacific coast. Winters from South Carolina to n. Brazil and s. Mexico to Ecuador.

Franklin's Gull*

Larus pipixcan—✳24
L. 14

IDENTIFICATION: The narrow white areas separating the black wing tips from the gray mantle are distinctive in adults even in fall, when the dark of the head is reduced to a dusky area from eye to eye across the back of the head and neck. Young have similar heads (very white on the forehead), but their wings are uniformly dark, the under parts clear white, the legs blackish.

HABITS: This gentle, trusting bird, rosiest-breasted of the dark-headed gulls, is often called "prairie dove" by the farmers whose plows it follows when it first comes north, just as the ice is going out of the lakes. Although these gulls eat many aquatic insects in both larval and adult forms, they get most of their food from crop fields, where they feed among stalks of growing grain. Throughout the breeding season the small bands of foraging gulls that travel out from the colony for many miles can be seen coming and going from dawn to dusk. Later, when the young are on the wing, the birds roam far and wide over the grasslands in great flocks, which in early fall are augmented by many Bonaparte's gulls. These flocks take an especially heavy toll of mature, egg-laying grass-hoppers at the time most effective in reducing the next year's supply of grasshoppers. Yet instead of making into wildlife refuges the relatively small marsh acreage that the birds require for nesting, we have allowed these areas to be drained to produce small additional crops which may amount to little more than a fraction of the yield lost on neighboring farms as a result of the higher insect population which inevitably comes when the gulls are absent.

Few gulls are as graceful on the wing as these birds that frequently hawk like swallows for flying insects. At times they whirl in the air in small flocks or soar to great heights, dive earthward, and repeat the performance like wood ibis. A teeming rookery of these birds is a never-to-be-forgotten sight. Unlike other gulls, Franklin's often take care of one another's offspring instead of killing them, and they live in harmony with eared grebes, ducks, terns, and blackbirds, seldom, if ever, succumbing to the egg-stealing tendencies of the rest of the gull family.

VOICE: This species has many soft clucking or mewing notes, but the most characteristic calls are shrill, clear, and rather mournful *week-a* or *po-lee* sounds.

NEST: The sites of the large breeding colonies these gulls usually form are very apt to shift from year to year. The location, however, is always among bulrushes or other reed-like plants growing in from 1 to 6 feet of water in a marsh or along a shallow lake shore. The nest is a large floating mass of old stalks, anchored among new or old growths and finished off with a dry, well-made cup for the 3 eggs (2.0 x 1.4). These are pale buff to olive-brown, variously marked with darker browns.

RANGE: (M.) Breeds from s.c. Manitoba and s. Alberta south to s.w. Minnesota, South Dakota, and Utah. Winters from the Gulf Coast of Louisiana and Texas south to the west coast of South America as far as c. Chile. A few individuals wander east every fall, at least as far as Lake Ontario.

Bonaparte's Gull*   *Larus philadelphia*—✻25
L. 13; W. 32

IDENTIFICATION: In summer this is a dark, slate-gray-headed gull with a very small black bill and bright orange-red legs and feet. The outer primaries are largely white, both above and below, and black only on the tip in adults. In young birds the whole wing has a dark-bordered appearance, the bill a light base, and the legs a dusky flesh color. This species is paler-winged than the Franklin's, and the primary coverts are white in all plumages.

HABITS: This plump, small-billed gull is very pigeonlike in appearance and very active on the wing. Its buoyant, somewhat bounding flight and habit of holding its bill pointed

downward suggest a tern. It occurs at one season or another
in practically every part of the country, but the exact limits
of its breeding range are not known. At one time it apparently bred south to the Great Lakes. Inland, where it is
commonest in spring, it migrates along river valleys but prefers lakes, including the strongly alkaline lakes of the Great
Basin, for feeding. Along the coast, where it is more abundant
in fall, it feeds offshore over tide channels and rips and kelp
beds. It also comes in at times to feed on tide flats, salt
marshes, and ponds, and to scavenge in harbors and about
sewer outlets. The travels of its loose flocks, which often
comprise many thousands, are unpredictable and erratic, but
in general its numbers seem to have declined in recent years.
Bonaparte's feed largely by dipping to the surface of the
water, but occasionally they drop into it. With each bird
taking a few deep strokes, then gliding with dangling legs
to the surface to flutter for a moment in one spot before
bounding off again, a feeding flock has something of the
appearance of a gathering of white butterflies. Small fish,
crustacea, and some snails and marine worms are staple
foods, but inland in summer the birds feed chiefly on insects
which they capture in the air or pick from croplands (often
from behind the plow) or from the surface of lakes or
ponds.

VOICE: A harsh, high-pitched, ternlike *tee-er* or *cheer* and many
weak conversational whistled notes when feeding.

NEST: About lakes and marshes in the spruce-fir forests. The
nest is made of moss, lichen, grass, and twigs and is saddled
on a horizontal branch from a few to 15 or 20 feet up. The
3 eggs (1.9 x 1.4) are pale buff to olive-buff, spotted and
blotched with browns.

RANGE: (M.) Breeds from n. Manitoba, n. Mackenzie, and n.w.
Alaska south to c. Alberta and c. British Columbia. Winters
from s. New England to Florida, the Gulf Coast, and Yucatan, and from s.e. Alaska to the c. Mexico Coast.

Little Gull*   *Larus minutus*—✳26
                                                    L. 11

IDENTIFICATION: The completely blackish underwing surfaces
of adults are distinctive. The wings of young birds in their
first fall are white below and even in the second year are not
as dark as those of adults, but they always show a bold,
blackish, inverted, open V running through the length of the

upper surface, much like that on the wing of a young kitti-wake.

HABITS: In Europe this bird, the smallest of all gulls, frequents inland marshes and marshy-bordered lakes during the nesting period. At other seasons it occurs both inland and along the coasts, especially about harbors, bays, and estuaries. Very active and graceful in flight, it might be confused with a tern were it not for its rounded wings. In feeding habits it resembles the other dark-headed gulls and often associates with them and with terns both on nesting grounds and at sea. It picks small fish and crustacea from the surface, and inland it relies largely on insects for food. Repeated close observation of large flocks of Bonaparte's gulls and common terns along the Atlantic coast and the eastern end of the Great Lakes invariably reveals a few individuals of this species. There is a marked westward movement of these gulls after the breeding season in Europe which may carry a few of them across the Atlantic, but some ornithologists believe that they may nest in North America in small numbers.

VOICE: A *kek-kek-kek* call or a higher-pitched, harsh *ka-ka-ka*.

NEST: In colonies in marshes, the grass and leaf nest being placed in a clump of emergent vegetation or on a floating mass of dead plant material; also occasionally on islands. The 3 eggs (1.6 x 1.2) are pale brownish to olive brown, spotted and blotched with dark brown and ashy.

RANGE: (M.) Breeds from c. Sweden, n.c. Russia, and n.c. Siberia to the Sea of Okhotsk south to Holland, c. Russia, and Lake Baikal. Winters south to n. Africa, the Caspian Sea, and s. China. Rare but regular in e. North America, generally associated with Bonaparte's gulls.

Ivory Gull* *Pagophila eburnea*—✳23
L. 17

IDENTIFICATION: A pure-white gull with black legs and feet and a yellow-green bill becoming bluish at the base can only be an ivory. Young are grayish about the face, spotted with dusky olive, and have a blackish bill.

HABITS: This pure-white gull has long, broad wings and is a powerful flier, accustomed to traveling long distances for food. Although short-legged, the birds run about very actively on land or ice but do not seem to like to alight in water. On their breeding grounds they take lemmings and insects as well as crustacea and mollusks. During much of the year they seem to follow such arctic mammals as seals, whales, and wolves, on whose dung they are known to feed. They also relish flesh and blubber and closely follow the Eskimo hunters.

VOICE: Harsh, shrill, and often ternlike notes.

NEST: In small colonies on bare, open ground or rock, or occasionally on the lower ledges of seaside cliffs. The nest is a pile of moss, lichens, and seaweed on top of which the bird deposits 2 buffish-olive eggs (2.4 x 1.7), marked with dark brown.

RANGE: (M.) Breeds in n. Greenland, the n. Arctic Archipelago north from Melville Island, n. Baffin Island, Spitzbergen, and Franz Josef Land. At other seasons it frequents the edges of the pack ice and adjacent coasts. It reaches our northern states and the coast of France only as a rare straggler.

Kittiwake*

Rissa tridactyla—№ 25
L. 17; W. 36

IDENTIFICATION: The abruptly and completely black tips to the gray wings that pale toward the ends and the black feet are distinctive. The dark collar across the back of the upper neck and the broad, dark band through the wing identify young birds.

HABITS: The kittiwake is a truly pelagic gull that regularly drinks salt water; in fact, seems to prefer it. Probably it is the most abundant member of the gull family, as it breeds in enormous numbers throughout most of the Arctic and along the subarctic coasts. In the non-breeding season it is common over a very large proportion of the ocean area of the Northern Hemisphere. The long wings and long, broad tail give it a very fast and graceful flight. The wingbeats are rapid but not deep; the bird sails a great deal and usually hovers a moment before dropping to the surface to dive for food. Although kittiwakes follow steamers for days and gather about fishing fleets to pick up refuse, they are basically fishers, not scavengers. Their staple foods are small fish and especially the small plankton animals that drift with the ocean currents and also serve as the chief food supply for herring, mackerel, and whales. Of these the small pteropod mollusks known as "clio" and the euphausiid crustacea known as "kril" are among the most important. The kittiwake's ability to dive from the surface and swim under water, which is unique among gulls, enables it to obtain these animals with ease. Lacking the coastal ties of other gulls, this species seems to avoid the immediate shore line and is not encountered until one is several miles out. In stormy weather the birds can often be seen from exposed rocky headlands or capes, but to see them at their best one should go out to the fishing shoals.

VOICE: The bird's name comes from its soft, pleasant *kit-ti-wake* call. When disturbed it utters a rapid series of shrill, harsh notes that vary in tone.

NEST: (I. 22) In large colonies on high cliffs, usually on island cliffs facing the sea but occasionally some miles inland. The nests are cups of moss and seaweeds securely fastened to ledges or mere rock projections on the perpendicular face. Sites where there is an overhang or cave are favored. The 2 eggs (2.2 x 1.6) vary from pinkish-buff to olive-buff or bluish-white, irregularly spotted with brown and blotched with gray.

RANGE: (P. M.) Breeds on the islands and shores of the Arctic Ocean south to the Gulf of St. Lawrence, n.w. France, and the Kurile and Aleutian Islands. Winters from the northern limit of open water south to the Sargasso Sea, the Cape Verde Islands, the Mediterranean and Caspian seas, Japan, and n. Lower California; occasionally the Great Lakes.

Ross' Gull*   *Rhodostethia rosea*—※ 2G
                                              L. 13½

IDENTIFICATION: Winter adults lack the black neck ring, but at any season the pinkish color of the body plumage, although it varies in intensity, is, together with the clear gray of the back and both wing surfaces, quite distinctive. Young birds have the typical wedge-shaped tail of the species, a dark gray, slightly buffy rump, and a bold wing pattern.

HABITS: It is unfortunate that this most beautifully colored of all gulls is seen by fewer people than any other member of its family. After its brief 1½-month visit to its breeding ground it loses itself in the vast wilderness of the Polar Basin. Contrary to popular belief, this area is covered with a relatively thin layer of ice which is constantly in motion owing to the combined action of strong currents and the wind, thus producing leads of open water at all seasons of the year where gulls can readily feed. Only from Point Barrow, Alaska, where thousands are seen migrating to the Northeast in October, and Franz Josef Land, where they have been reported as abundant in August, have any numbers ever been seen. When inland during the nesting season they become insectivorous, but at sea small crustacea-like scud and other plankton animals that occur in arctic waters in such teeming abundance as to form a scum on the water, and some fish, are probably their staple foods.

VOICE: High and quite melodious single and double notes.

NEST: In small colonies on a high place in boggy tundra or on an island in a tundra lake. The substantial nest of grass, twigs, and lichens holds the 3 brown-spotted, olive-green eggs (1.7 x 1.3) a few inches above the water.

RANGE: (M.) Breeds in the valleys and deltas of a number of rivers in n.e. Siberia and possibly elsewhere in the Arctic. It has been recorded from almost every part of the Arctic Ocean and evidently winters about the open leads in the polar ice. South of the Arctic Ocean proper it is the rarest of accidental stragglers.

Sabine's Gull*   *Xema sabini*— ⚹ 2
                                        L. 13½

IDENTIFICATION: The slight fork in the tail is not conspicuous, but the 3 bold triangles of solid color into which the upper wing surface is divided are characteristic of both adults and young.

HABITS: This gull is very abundant in many parts of the Arctic, especially about the coasts of Bering Sea. In the air it is graceful and ternlike, flying with a continuous wingbeat, dipping to the surface for food (never diving or dropping), and occasionally hovering for a moment. On the ground it runs about on mud flats, picking up food much like a plover, which at such times it closely resembles. Its food when nesting is largely insects. Later the birds feed along the beaches on crustacea and other organisms in the plankton scum deposited by the waves. Although lacking the gregarious instincts of most gulls and apt to occur singly or in small groups, favorable feeding conditions may bring them together in vast numbers, and at times they associate with the arctic and other terns in migration. This abundant bird is seldom encountered after it leaves the Arctic, which must mean that it becomes wholly pelagic and scatters out over the relatively untraveled warm oceans of the Tropics.

VOICE: A short, harsh, grating note like that of the arctic tern, also a squeaky, chattering, or chipping sound.

NEST: Singly or in small colonies in low, marshy, pond-strewn tundra in close association with the arctic tern. The 3 brown to olive-buff eggs (1.8 x 1.3), spotted with sepia, are laid in a hollow in the damp ground in the most rudimentary kind of grass nest.

RANGE: (M.) Breeds on islands in and along the coasts of the Arctic Ocean south in North America to n. Hudson Bay and s.w. Alaska. In fall mass flights of many thousand are sometimes encountered off our Pacific coast and the French coast, and a few are seen in spring. Elsewhere it is a rare straggler, as apt to be encountered on the w. Great Plains as anywhere else, but there are records from almost every state. The only winter records come from off the west coast of n. South America.

Gull-billed Tern*   *Gelochelidon nilotica*—※29
                                                                L. 14; W. 34

IDENTIFICATION: The short, heavy black bill, stocky body, slight fork in the tail, and the call notes are distinctive. Young have white heads, generally with a fine blackish streaking behind, as in winter adults, and a brown band on the end of the tail. Juveniles also have buffy edges to the feathers of the upper parts, some dark brown mottling, especially on the scapulars, and an orange-brown bill and reddish-brown legs.

HABITS: These terns were once extremely abundant in the salt marshes of the Atlantic coast from s. New Jersey to Virginia. By the early 1900s they had been practically wiped out by eggers and by the insatiable demands of the New York millinery trade. The species has never recovered, and only a few scattered pairs breed on the outer beaches in close association with other terns. It was originally a marsh nester like the Forster's tern and the laughing gull and was known as the marsh tern. In general its habits are more like those of the dark-headed gulls, and it nests inland in marshes and about lakes as well as along the coast. While gull-bills occasionally dive for fish and other animals in regular tern fashion, they are more inclined to stoop to pick things off the surface. Insects are apparently one of its staple foods, caught in the air or as the bird walks about on its rather long legs in crop fields or behind the plow. Grasshoppers are much sought after, and the birds often hover over a marsh fire to catch them. Next to insects, crustacea such as crabs and sand bugs (*Hippa*) seem to be their choice, but frogs, worms, lizards, and even small mammals are acceptable. The gull-

bill's flight is steady and heavy for a tern, but it stoops
and maneuvers with all the precision of a swallow.

VOICE: The common call is a dry, rasping, insectlike *kay-ty-did*
or *kay-did* and a short, single note repeated several times in
rapid succession.

NEST: (I. 22, N. 30) A shallow, shell-lined depression or occasionally a substantial pile of plant stems and shells on an
open, shell-strewn upper beach. Also on low, grassy marsh
islands where the eggs are laid on the damp ground or on
matted old grasses with little real nest. The 3 eggs (1.8 x 1.3)
are creamy to buff, sparingly spotted with brown.

RANGE: (P. M.) Breeds all over the world in widely scattered
colonies. In North America from the coast of s. New Jersey
south to the Gulf of Mexico, West Indies, and s.e. Brazil;
and from the Salton Sea in s. California south probably to
Peru. Winters from the n. Gulf Coast and n. Mexico south
to Patagonia and Peru. Also breeds from the Baltic Sea, c.
Urals, and s. Mongolia south to n. Africa and Australia.

Forster's Tern*   *Sterna forsteri*—⚹28
                                       L. 14½; W. 30

IDENTIFICATION: The silvery-white primaries (paler than the
mantle), pure-white underbody and wings, pale gray tail
with white outer edges and a dark border inside the fork, and
the rather yellowish-orange bill make adults fairly easy to
identify. In fall both adults and young are unmistakable
because of the black ear patches on an otherwise white head.
Juveniles are quite heavily marked with buff and brown, both
above and below, but this is largely gone by winter.

HABITS: For many years ornithologists failed to recognize this
exclusively American species which, although it closely resembles the common tern, differs from it in many ways; e.g.,
in flight, Forster's moves its wings with a quick, sharp snap
instead of with the slower, deeper strokes of the common.
Forster's is an insect eater as well as a fisherman; it often
hawks over the marshes for dragonflies and other large insects and can swoop gracefully to the water to pluck one
from the surface without wetting a feather.

VOICE: The notes have a distinctive nasal quality, and are very
different from those of other terns. Adults have a soft, even-
pitched, buzzy *snee-e-e-e* that suggests a nighthawk's call, also
a series of shrill *kit, kit, kit* notes, like a man clucking to a
horse. Young make a shrill, squeaking sound.

NEST: (I. 23) Most commonly on the mats of dead canes drifted into the marsh at high tide. A substantial nest and nest cup of finer grass are built. Occasionally the nest is on a small marsh island on almost bare ground among grasses, with a sparse grass lining for the mud cup, or in a sandy place with bits of shell and grass for a lining. Inland the site is on floating mats of rotting reeds in a lakeside marsh or on top of an old muskrat house. The 3 eggs (1.7 x 1.2) are buff to olive-buff with small dark brown spots and lines.

RANGE: (P. M.) Breeds on the Atlantic coast from Maryland south to Texas and from c. Manitoba, c. Alberta, and Washington south to n.e. Illinois, n. Nebraska, c. Colorado, Utah, and s.c. California. Winters from South Carolina, the Gulf Coast, and c. California south to Guatemala. Occurs regularly in migration from the Great Lakes and New England southward.

Common Tern*   *Sterna hirundo*—⚹28
                                        L. 15; W. 31

IDENTIFICATION: The blackish primaries (darker than the mantle), the pure-white tail—dark only along the outer edge —and the orange red bill, which usually has a black tip, are distinctive points. In fall and winter both young and adults are black from eye to eye around the back of the head but not on top, and have a dark band along the front of the inner wing. The bill darkens in winter but retains some red at the base, and the vermilion legs fade to a paler, more orange color.

HABITS: (Age 18 yrs.) This is the most widely distributed and often the most common of the 4 closely related terns that beginners find so hard to separate. When conditions are favorable it establishes huge breeding colonies, but these lead a hazardous existence and are often short-lived. The invasion of a colony by thoughtless humans, even when there is no intent to harm, may keep adults off eggs or young long enough for the hot summer sun to kill them. The presence of cats and dogs or "man's camp follower," the Norway rat, is nearly always disastrous to a colony, as is the presence of such wild animals as foxes, skunks, raccoons, opossums, or weasels. In the daytime terns put up a spirited defense against intruders and actually strike with their bills, causing considerable discomfort to humans and often death to young gulls or other small animals. Another danger is the presence of ants that enter the eggs and kill the hatching young before they get clear of the shell. The greatest hazard of all is high storm tides that in a few hours can destroy thousands of eggs and young. Occasionally a sudden change in conditions at sea causes a complete disappearance of the small fish on which the terns depend for food for their young, and while the adults save themselves by leaving, the young starve to death. To compensate for these losses, the adults usually attempt to renest (either in the same place or elsewhere), until well on toward midsummer. Once on the wing, a young tern must survive 3 years before it is ready to breed and generally does not lay a full clutch of 3 eggs until its fourth year.

Few creatures are more graceful in the air than these fork-tailed birds with their deep wingbeats. They always enliven a water area, and fishermen often find them quite useful. They are attracted to the areas where mackerel or other large fish are forcing small ones to the surface, thus enabling fishermen to tell exactly where to set their nets. Furthermore, the birds' sense of direction is so unerring and the path of their homeward flight with their catch so direct that they often help guide the boats home through dense fog. Their food is small fish like sand launces, pipefish, menhaden, and alewives, plus plankton organisms like crustacea and, at times, insects.

Unless we give some thought to the preservation of suitable nest sites for these and other terns, they face an uncertain future along our coasts. Herring gulls, as they increase, are pushing terns off many islands, and in some areas the only surviving colonies are on "spoil-banks" created in the course of dredging inlets and harbor channels. With proper planning, many more of these artificial sandy islands can be created and kept free of vegetation for terns and other sea birds that require isolated coastal nest sites.

voice: The anger note is a harsh, piercing, rather prolonged *kee-ar-r-r*, with the accent on the first syllable and a drop in pitch at the end. Also a rapid series of short, high-pitched *kik-kik-kik* notes that under excitement become *keerr,* and a robin-like *chip*.

nest: (I. 21, N. 30) Open sites like sandy or pebbly upper beaches or flat rocks on islands are preferred, but long peninsulas and other semi-isolated sites often suffice. Occasionally they nest among grass or weeds and bushes, but this is probably always on an old once bare nest site that the birds have fertilized so heavily that it has induced a heavy weed growth.

Sometimes windrows of drifted trash attract them, both on beaches and in marshes, and they have occasionally built floating nests on masses of dead plants in shallow water. The nest may be a substantial grass cup or little more than a hollow in the sand. The 3 eggs (1.6 x 1.2) are a pale brown, spotted with dark brown.

RANGE: (P. M.) Breeds around the world through much of the Temperate Zone of the Northern Hemisphere. In North America from the east coast of Labrador, c. Ontario, n. Manitoba, and s. Mackenzie south to the West Indies and possibly n. South America along the east coast, but only to s. Alberta, n. North Dakota, s. Wisconsin, and n. Pennsylvania inland. Absent as a breeder from the Pacific coast but a migrant from s. British Columbia south. Winters from Florida and w. Mexico south to the Strait of Magellan.

Arctic Tern*   *Sterna paradisaea*—⚹28
                                                    L. 15½

IDENTIFICATION: The distinctly grayish under parts, becoming white only along a narrow line where they meet the black cap, and the deep blood-red bill without a black tip are fair field characters. Its tail is longer and more deeply forked than that of a common tern, and when perched its body is much closer to the ground. The bill is usually shorter and, in fall and winter, solid black, while the short legs darken to almost blackish.

HABITS: (Age 18 yrs.) This abundant tern of the Far North nests some 500 miles farther south on our East Coast than it does anywhere else in the world. Once the nesting season is over, the birds go to sea and winter in the oceans south of the equator, but it is now known that most of them do not reach the true Antarctic. The 22,000-mile round trip flight from Arctic to Antarctic, formerly attributed to this bird, making it the long-distance migrant champion of the world, is certainly not characteristic of the entire population, though it may well be accomplished by a few individuals. When nesting the arctic tern feeds on insects, fish, and crustacea, the last evidently being its chief source of food at sea.

VOICE: The short *kee-ar-r* anger call is accented on the second syllable and rises in pitch. A high-pitched *kee-kee* is distinctive, as are other shrill squeaks or squeals and a grating *kikka-reek* call.

NEST: (I. 21) In large colonies, scattered groups, or single pairs by themselves or associated with various other terns and gulls. Rocky and sandy coastal islands, beach and dune areas are common sites, but in the Far North they nest on islands in lakes, ponds, and marshes and occasionally in the open tundra. The 2 eggs (1.6 x 1.2) are brownish or greenish, irregularly marked with brown, and are laid in a hollow which sometimes has a grass, shell, or pebble lining.

RANGE: (M.) Breeds on the islands and coasts of the Arctic Ocean south to Massachusetts, n. Manitoba, n. British Columbia, and the Aleutians, and abroad to the British Isles, Baltic Sea, and parts of c. Siberia. Winters in the oceans of the Southern Hemisphere. Migrates at sea and is never seen along the Atlantic coast south of Long Island. There is every indication that many North American birds cross almost to the French coast before turning south. Off the Pacific coast it occurs south to s. California in fall but is seen only occasionally in spring.

Roseate Tern*
$Sterna\ dougallii$—✕28
L. 15½

IDENTIFICATION: This is a slender, nearly white tern with a long, pure-white, deeply forked tail that projects well beyond the wing tips when the bird is perched. Its bill is black except for a little red at the base (occasionally more). The rosy tint on the breast is seldom visible, but the notes are diagnostic and the flight notably buoyant. Young birds have fine brown streaks on the forehead and crown and conspicuously dark spotted under parts.

HABITS: (Age 7 yrs.) This most graceful of all terns is a strictly maritime bird, and the regions in which it breeds are widely separated. The plume hunters in the employ of the New York and Paris milliners nearly exterminated it in many areas during the latter part of the nineteenth century, and it is still a long way from being as abundant as it once was on the New England coast. The roseate feeds in salt water, largely on small fish, and often follows the schools of feeding bluefish that drive spearing and other species to the surface. It never occurs inland and is seldom seen in numbers along the coast except where nesting.

VOICE: The alarm note is a low-pitched, rasping *aaak* that sounds like tearing cloth. It also has a mellow, 2-syllable *chee-wee* whistle that suggests a ringed plover's.

NEST: (I. 21) In colonies on rocky, pebbly, or sandy areas on islands or the shore, often in close association with other terns and gulls. The nests may be in the open or well hidden in long beach grass or weed growths. The scrape or hollow in the ground seldom has more than a sparse lining of dead grass. The 2 eggs (1.7 x 1.2) are pale buff to olive-buff with reddish-brown spots.

RANGE: (P. M.) Breeds in widely scattered coastal and island colonies on both sides of the North Atlantic, the Indian Ocean to s. Africa, and the Southwest Pacific region; in North America from Nova Scotia south to Venezuela and west to Texas and British Honduras. Winters from the Bahamas and the Gulf Coast to Brazil.

Sooty Tern*   *Sterna fuscata*—✕27
L. 16½; W. 34

IDENTIFICATION: The black above and white below pattern is unique among terns, as is the solid-brownish coloration of the young.

HABITS: (Age 18 yrs.) This is an extraordinarily interesting bird about which much is unknown and mysterious. Sootys are the most abundant nesting birds of the equatorial oceans, yet no one has ever encountered them in numbers away from known breeding colonies, out of which they may range as far as 200 miles to feed but from which they disappear after nesting. "Wide-awakes," as they are commonly called, are active 24 hours a day about their breeding colonies, nest relief and feeding usually taking place at dusk and during the night. Frequently they are heard about their breeding grounds at night some weeks before they are seen by day. Near the equator, where there are no marked seasonal changes, they often do not wait a year but return to nest every 9 or 10 months. The strangest thing of all about this largely pelagic sea bird is that it apparently has to avoid getting wet because its feathers are not waterproof. It apparently neither dives for food nor alights in the water, and as it has seldom been seen to use a perch it must remain continually on the wing. When feeding it swoops close to the water or hovers and snatches its prey from the surface or grabs it as it leaps out. Small fish and squids, both of which commonly jump out of the water to escape their enemies, are its only known foods.

VOICE: A harsh, squeaky, quacklike *quanck,* also a high-pitched 3-syllable call, often rendered as *ker-wacky-wack,* and many other barking, squawking, and snarling notes.

NEST: (I. 26) In colonies, often of fabulous size. The single egg
   is laid on flat ground or rocks or occasionally on ledges. Some-
   times a hollow is scraped. The egg (2. x 1.4) is whitish,
   spotted and blotched with reddish-brown.
RANGE: (M.) Breeds on oceanic and coastal islands of the
   Tropics throughout the world. In North America from the
   Bahamas, Dry Tortugas, and formerly the Texas coast through
   the Gulf and Caribbean region, and on islands off the w.
   Mexican coast. Wanders with some regularity to our Gulf
   Coast. Hurricanes from time to time carry stray birds up the
   East Coast as far as Nova Scotia.

Bridled Tern*   *Sterna anaethetus*—⚹27
                                              L. 14½

IDENTIFICATION: The whitish collar across the back of the lower
   neck, the gray-brown (often quite pale) back, and the white
   line over and back of the eye are distinctive. Young birds are
   similar but barred and streaked above with white.
HABITS: Little is known about the habits or annual movements
   of this tern. It seems to prefer to feed well out to sea and is
   known to take small fish and squids. Whether it avoids contact with water like most tropical terns is not known, but its
   habit of perching on flotsam instead of swimming suggests
   this.
VOICE: Said to resemble certain high-pitched notes of the crow.
NEST: In colonies, often with sooty terns and other sea birds.
   The nest site is usually well hidden among broken rocks, in
   an erosion cavity in a rock face, or in a burrow entrance. The
   1 egg (1.8 x 1.3) is white, spotted with shades of brown.
RANGE: (R.) Breeds on the islands of the Tropics throughout
   the world. In North America from the Bahamas to British
   Honduras and Venezuela and apparently off the west coast of
   Mexico. A regular visitor to the offshore waters of the east
   coast of Florida.

Least Tern*   *Sterna albifrons*—⚹29
(Little Tern)   L. 9; W. 20

IDENTIFICATION: The white forehead and yellow bill and legs
   are distinctive. In fall the bill becomes dusky to blackish, the
   legs dull yellow, and only the hind head and a line to the eye
   are black. Young birds are similar, with some sandy-buff
   above, and have quite dark wing coverts and primaries.

HABITS: When nesting this little tern does not require an isolated area like most other terns and is frequently found on
mainland beaches; probably its more scattered colonies are
less vulnerable to predators. Inland its preference for river
sand bars often makes it a late nester, as these are not exposed
until the spring floods recede, which may not happen until
midsummer. In the Gay Nineties a market price of 10 or 12
cents each for their skins, to be used fully mounted on ladies'
hats, was enough to almost exterminate the species, which
was formerly abundant on our Atlantic coast. Enough survived, however, to re-establish it, once the growth of the
Audubon movement relieved it from this type of persecution,
and it is now the most abundant tern of the region, where it
nests on beaches and land fill and other man-made sites. Its
tolerance of disturbance and its ability to adapt itself to
civilization enable it to thrive in regions where island nesters
like the common tern are declining. The least's food, which
seems to be derived entirely from the water, consists of fish
and crustacea, for which it dives, usually after a preliminary
hover.

VOICE: Very shrill and sharp. The protest call is a series of *kip,
kip, kip* notes. It also has a *kit-tic* note and a harsh, rasping
cher-ee-eep.

NEST: (I. 20, N. 18) Broad, open sandy flats that are occasionally washed by high tides and are free of vegetation, new
fill, river sand bars, and inland salt plains are usual nest sites.
Commonest nesting associates are piping, thick-billed, and
snowy plovers. The 2 or 3 buffy to olive-buff, brown-spotted
eggs (1.2 x .93) are laid in an unlined hollow.

RANGE: (P. M.) Breeds throughout temperate Eurasia from the
British Isles, Baltic, and Japan south to c. Africa, India, and
Australia; and in the Western Hemisphere from Massachu-
setts, Iowa, and c. California south to Venezuela, British
Honduras, and on the Pacific coast to s. Mexico. Winters
from the Gulf Coast and Central America south.

Royal Tern*   *Thalasseus maximus*—※29
L. 19; W. 43

IDENTIFICATION: The tail is forked for about half its length and
extends to or beyond the wing tips when perched. The slim
bill is orange or yellowish-orange. The clear white forehead,
contrasting strongly with the black of the crested hind head, is
a good field mark for young and for adults except during the

short prebreeding courtship period, when the cap is solid
black. Young birds sometimes have light orange-yellow legs,
but those of adults are always blackish.

HABITS: (Age 6 yrs.) This large tern is a common sight everywhere along our southern coasts, fishing offshore or about
inlets and bays. It feeds almost wholly on fish up to 4 inches
in length, which are obtained by dives into the water, often
from considerable heights.

VOICE: The ordinary calls are clear, shrill, and generally short.
Some sound like *tsirr* or *kree,* but it also has a longer, melodious, rolling, almost ploverlike whistle.

NEST: Usually in large, densely packed colonies, often mixed
with other species of terns on low, sandy islands along the
seacoast. The 2 white to pale buff eggs (2.5 x 1.8), spotted
with dark brown, are laid in a hollow scraped in the open
sand.

RANGE: (P. M.) Breeds from Virginia to Texas and through
the West Indies and on the Pacific coast of Mexico. Wanders
north to New Jersey and c. California in late summer and
winters from the Gulf Coast and s. California south to Argentina and Peru. It also occurs along the west coast of
Africa from Gibraltar to Angola.

Sandwich Tern*   *Thalasseus sandvicensis*—✳28
(Cabot's Tern)   L. 16

IDENTIFICATION: The long, yellow-tipped black bill is the best
field mark of this long, narrow-winged, pale tern. The completely black cap is assumed before the courtship period, but
the white forehead may return before the eggs are hatched.
Immature birds are similar to winter adults, but earlier in
the juvenile plumage the mantle is spotted with black.

HABITS: (Age 21 yrs.) This is a fast, powerful bird on the wing.
It often feeds well offshore, diving from considerable heights
which carry it well below the surface. Fish, shrimp, marine
worms, and squids are among its known foods. In our region
it is intimately associated with its close relative the royal tern,
especially during the breeding season. On both sides of the
Atlantic the Sandwich tern seems to be spreading northward
in increasing numbers. In Great Britain it now nests among
coastal dunes, on rocks, and occasionally on inland lakes.

VOICE: A very loud *kir-ritt* and a more abrupt *gwit, gwit,* less
harsh and grating than with most terns.

NEST: (I. 23, N. 35) In colonies on bare, sandy islands and

beaches along the coast, usually in small groups among royal and other terns. The 2 eggs (2.0 x 1.4) vary from white to pinkish- or greenish-buff and are variously marked with blackish-brown. They are laid on the open sand with no nest.

RANGE: (P. M.) Breeds from Virginia to Florida, Texas, British Honduras, and the West Indies; and in Europe from the North Sea to the Mediterranean and Caspian seas. Winters from the Gulf Coast south to Colombia and Brazil and on the Pacific Coast of s. Mexico and Guatemala; and abroad to s. Africa and n.w. India.

Caspian Tern* *Hydroprogne caspia*—※29
L. 21; W. 53

IDENTIFICATION: A heavy, broad-winged tern with a short, only moderately forked tail and a stout, coral-red bill. In flight the undersurface of the primaries is almost black. The slightly crested head is solid black until fall, when it becomes streaked with white. Young are barred and spotted with black on back and tail but are otherwise much like fall adults, although the bill is often smaller and more orange and the head is first darker and then later in the season lighter than in adults.

HABITS: (Age 13½ yrs.) The big, ample-winged Caspian, largest of terns, looks very gull-like at a distance and soars readily, often going to great heights. It plunges for fish like most terns, but it also settles on the water to feed like a gull and occasionally robs other birds of their catches and eats eggs and small birds. When fishing it flies rather close to the water with bill down in typical tern fashion, but when migrating it is a high flier and carries the bill pointed forward. Least gregarious of terns, the Caspian moves about singly as a rule or in small groups. Throughout the range of the ring-billed gulls it seems to prefer their company to that of any other bird, not only nesting near them but frequently resting with them on the same sand bar at other seasons. North American Caspians do not seem to differ from those of Europe. A bird reared in Lake Michigan was found dead in England 12 years later, which gives evidence of at least an occasional interchange across the Atlantic.

VOICE: A hoarse, deep, almost croaking *ca-arrrrr ka-ka-ka-kaow*, also a short *kow* or *kowk*.

NEST: (I. 21) In colonies, frequently close to large colonies of other terns and gulls, also singly or in a few pairs by themselves on a small islet. The site is usually a sandy or rocky

island, but the birds also nest on the heavy mat of dead
floating vegetation near the shores of shallow lakes. The eggs
may be laid directly on the ground, but often a fairly substantial lining and rim of grass, seaweed, or moss are provided. The 2 or 3 eggs (2.5 x 1.8) are pinkish-buff, lightly
spotted with dark brown.

RANGE: (P. M.) Breeds in scattered colonies inland and along
the coast of Europe, Asia, Africa, and Australia; and in North
America from s. Labrador, the Great Lakes, and Great Slave
Lake south to the Gulf Coast and c. Lower California. Winters from South Carolina and c. California south to Mexico.

Black Tern*   *Chlidonias niger*— ⚹27
L. 9½

IDENTIFICATION: The small size, short notched tail, and rather
short broad wings, slate-gray above and paler below, are distinctive. The head and body are solid black only in summer,
but at other seasons the head has a characteristic dark hood.

HABITS: The black tern is a bird of inland marshes and shallow
lakes during the breeding season, that often feeds over adjacent grasslands and on occasion follows the plow. Its flight is
buoyant and erratic, in tempo suggesting a nighthawk's, except
for frequent hovering. The limited amount of suitable nesting
habitat usually concentrates these birds into loose colonies,
but until they reach the ocean in fall they are not notably
gregarious. Along the coast they at first feed over salt marshes,
but as they move south they join other terns on the bays and
ocean. Inland grasshoppers, locusts, dragonflies, and many
other insects, caught on the wing or picked from the grass or
surface of the water, are staple summer foods, although a few
fish, crayfish, frogs, and tadpoles are taken from the water in
shallow dives. Once on salt water, the birds feed like other
terns on fish, crustacea, and other marine animals, but they
seldom dive deeply, preferring to pluck their food from the
surface like the sooty tern.

VOICE: The normal call is a sharp, abrupt, somewhat metallic
kik, varying in pitch, length, and intensity with the bird's
mood, often becoming *sheep* or *kleearr.*

NEST: (I. 17) In marshes or shallow lakes on matted canes or
floating masses of vegetation, also on old muskrat houses and
old nests of other species. The nest is either a hollow in dead
plant material or a sparse cup of stems that serves to keep the

eggs out of water. The 3 eggs (1.3 x .95) are olive or buff, heavily marked with dark brown.

RANGE: (M.) Breeds over much of the Northern Hemisphere. In North America from n. Vermont, Ontario, c. Manitoba, s. Mackenzie, and e.c. Alaska south to w. Pennsylvania, Tennessee, Missouri, Colorado, and c. California; in Eurasia from s. Sweden and n.c. Siberia south to s. Spain, the Caspian Sea, and n.w. China. Winters along the northern coasts of South America south to Ecuador, and in Africa south to Angola and Tanganyika. In late summer many fly directly to the nearest seacoast before starting south.

Noddy Tern*
(Brown Noddy)

Anoüs stolidus—✻27
L. 15

IDENTIFICATION: The round tail, brown color, and white crown are distinctive. Young are a paler brown that becomes gray-brown on the crown, which is bordered by a white stripe above the eye.

HABITS: The noddy is strictly confined to ocean areas with high surface temperatures. Near the equator, where there are no seasonal changes, individuals are found nesting in every month of the year. The elaborate nodding ceremony which the birds use as a greeting to one another and as part of their courtship is much in evidence about the colonies. They do their fishing near the colony, capturing their prey by swooping close to the water and seizing it without wetting their feathers. Drinking and bathing are similarly accomplished on the wing. Although they can, and occasionally do, alight and swim in water, they prefer to rest on exposed reefs, floating driftwood, or buoys. Small fish driven to the surface by underwater predators are staple foods.

VOICE: A harsh, crowlike *kar-r-rk* or *kwok-kwok*.

NEST: (I. 34) In colonies on islands where the eggs may be laid on bare rock or ledges or in nests of twigs and seaweeds supported on grass clumps, shrubs, or trees at heights up to 10 feet. The single dull granular egg (2.0 x 1.4) is buff, lightly spotted with lilac and brown.

RANGE: (P. M.) Breeds on islands of the tropical oceans north to the Bahamas, Dry Tortugas, Tres Marias, the Hawaiian and Bonin Islands, and south to Tristan da Cunha, San Felix Island, the Tuamotu Islands, Norfolk Island, and Madagascar.

SKIMMERS   Family Rynchopidae

Black Skimmer*   *Rynchops nigra*—✳34
                                              L. 18; W. 46

IDENTIFICATION: The black-tipped red bill with its elongated
   lower mandible, the long wings, and the black plumage are
   distinctive. Young are brownish, streaked above with white,
   and have more evenly matched mandibles. Their bills are
   dull orange.

HABITS: (Age 10 yrs.) This spectacular species, though it
   maneuvers in compact flocks with all the agility and synchronization usually seen only in shore birds, is not a strong
   flier and is one of the southern sea birds most apt to be carried north by hurricanes. Although confined to coastal regions
   in North America, this and other skimmers commonly frequent large rivers and nest on river and sand bars during
   periods of low water. The black skimmer has the curious
   habit of cutting the surface with the tip of its bill as it flies
   over water, but whether this aids it in obtaining food is a
   matter of dispute. One theory is that the bird creates with
   its immersed mandible a disturbance which brings to the
   surface fish which it picks up on the return trip that it usually
   makes over the same course. Like many other water birds that
   obtain food from near the surface, skimmers feed mostly at
   night or early or late in the day, when their prey rises closer
   to the top of the water. When not pressed for food for their
   young the birds spend much of the day resting in compact
   flocks on exposed sand bars. Along our coasts they are seldom
   found far from quiet bays, marsh channels, inlets, and river
   mouths. Fish and occasionally crustacea, the staple foods, are
   caught by sudden stabs as the skimmers fly over the surface
   or stand still in shallow water.

   As the larger, higher islands along the coast are increasingly occupied by human settlements with accompanying
cats, dogs, and rats, skimmers are forced to use low, sandy
islands and temporary sand bars, where its colonies are continually being washed out by high tides or the whole site cut
away by currents. For this bird particularly, the bare islands
of sandy wastes often made by United States Army engineers
in dredging river and harbor channels or canals through shallow bays have come as a godsend. Many of their present
colonies are now on such sites.

voice: The resonant, throaty, barklike *kaup* and an angry *aaar* are quite unique.

nest: In colonies, usually by themselves but often close to those of some other species of tern or gull. The site is generally a low, open area of broken shells or sand just above the tides, on an island along the coast. The 4 or 5 eggs (1.8 x 1.3) are laid in an open scrape in the sand and vary in color from pale bluish to buff, heavily marked with brown.

range: (P. M.) Breeds from s. New England, Florida, and Texas south to c. Argentina on the East Coast and from Ecuador to Chile on the Pacific coast. Winters from North Carolina and the Gulf Coast southward.

AUKS, MURRES, and PUFFINS
Family Alcidae

Great Auk*   *Pinguinus impennis*—✳38
                                                    L. 29

identification: The upright posture on land was very distinctive, and the bird was often called a penguin.

HABITS: All Alcidae have small wings which they use in swimming under water, but only in the great auk were they so modified for this purpose as to render the bird flightless. Until man appeared the great auk's evolutionary adaptation to ocean life and a diet of fish was highly successful. The bird was abundant and evidently had few enemies, since a single offspring a year was apparently enough to maintain a thriving population. From earliest times its colonies were a valuable food resource for residents of the bleak northern coasts where it bred. Although the colonies were on offshore islands, they were generally well back from the water's edge so that landing parties could easily surround groups of birds and drive them to their boats. In some cases auks were driven aboard over gangplanks to be kept alive until needed. The eggs were also taken and the birds themselves were salted down for bait and food.

When European fishermen began to visit the Grand Banks in the early 1500s the largest American colony, located on Funk Island 35 miles off the east coast of Greenland, became a regular source of food and bait. Nearly 300 years of this type of use did not appreciably reduce the population, until in the late eighteenth century professional hunters also began to exploit the birds for feathers and oil. Parties went ashore for the entire breeding season and killed the birds as fast as the carcasses could be handled. With no one to stop them, though some people realized what was happening and sounded warnings, these looters, for the sake of a few tons of feathers and some oil, exterminated a unique bird and destroyed a valuable natural resource.

VOICE: Said to have been a croak.

NEST: In dense colonies on rocky islands. The single egg (4.9 x 3.0) was deposited on bare rock. It was a dirty white, scrawled and blotched with gray, black, and brown.

RANGE: (P. M.) Once bred on islands across the North Atlantic, probably from s.e. Greenland, Iceland, and Norway south to the Gulf of St. Lawrence and n. Scotland. Wintered south to Cape Cod and the Bay of Biscay, occasionally to Florida and Gibraltar. Last recorded in 1844 in Iceland.

Razor-billed Auk*   *Alca torda*—❄38
(Razorbill)   L. 17; W. 26

IDENTIFICATION: The deep bill of adults, crossed by a white line, and the bird's habit of holding the rather long tail cocked upward when in water are distinctive. Young have a much smaller, unmarked bill and are whiter about the head and neck. In flight the head is held in close to the compact body, with the bill pointed forward and the feet hidden by the tail.

HABITS: Razorbills, although seldom seen from shore except during the breeding season, are birds of coastal waters, concentrating and wintering on fishing banks or other favorable offshore feeding areas. Fish, shrimp, and squids are among their staple foods and are generally obtained close to the surface. Auks have, however, been caught in gill nets of fishermen at depths up to 60 feet. They swim buoyantly, with the head close to the body, and in migration fly in small groups in a single line not far off the water. They show little fear of man and are so curious that they can often be decoyed by loud noises or arm waving.

VOICE: None save a few hoarse, guttural croaks or growls.

NEST: (I. 30) In colonies with other sea birds on cliffs or among rocks and boulders. Individual nest sites are usually in cavities, crevices, or under deep overhangs and rocks. The single bluish- or greenish-white, strongly tapered egg (3.0 x 1.9) is spotted and blotched with brown or black and is laid on bare rock or loose stones.

RANGE: (P. M.) Breeds from s. Greenland, Iceland, and n.e. Russia south to Maine, Brittany, and s. Sweden. Winters south to Long Island and the w. Mediterranean and in small numbers to North Carolina and the Canaries.

Murre*   *Uria aalge*—♯38
(Guillemot B.O.U.)   L. 16½; W. 30

IDENTIFICATION: On water the narrow, sharp-pointed bill,
  smaller head and longer neck than a razorbill's, and the
  stubby tail are distinctive. In flight the head is fully extended
  and held below the horizontal while the feet project beyond
  the tail. The sides of the heads of winter birds are extensively
  white, crossed by a dark line behind the eye. In some individuals this becomes a white line in spring when the heads become dark.

HABITS: In many parts of its range the murre is tremendously
  abundant. It was once much commoner along the North
  Atlantic coast than it is today, records showing that at one
  time it appeared in numbers off New England. Easy to collect
  and good to eat, its eggs for years were an article of commerce, and the birds themselves were relished as food. The
  murre swims under water like other Alcidae, with wings extended, and lives on fish, crustacea, worms, and mollusks.
  Fishermen have caught them in gill nets at depths up to 180
  feet. Like razorbills, murres seem to stay in coastal shelf
  waters throughout the year and are seldom seen in mid-ocean.
  The flight, which is swift but marked by frequent changes in
  direction, takes place close to the water except in migration.

VOICE: A prolonged growl or hoarse purr, varying in tone.

NEST: (I. 30) In close-packed colonies, often enormous, on rocky islands and cliff ledges. The strongly tapered eggs are laid wherever the rock is flat enough to keep them from rolling off. The single egg (3.2 x 2.0) is pale green or blue, variably marked with brown or black.

RANGE: (P. M.) Breeds around the shores of the Northern Hemisphere from s. Greenland, Iceland, Novaya Zemlya, and Bering Strait south to Nova Scotia, c. Portugal, c. California, and n. Japan. Winters south to Maine, occasionally to Long Island, s. California, and the Canaries.

Thick-billed Murre* *Uria lomvia*—※38
(Brünnich's Guillemot) L. 18

IDENTIFICATION: In summer the shorter, stouter bill with a pale line along the gape, a pointed top to the white breast, and the color contrast between the top and sides of the head distinguish this species from the murre. In winter the sides of the head are less extensively white and the neck is not extended as far in flight.

HABITS: The thick-billed murre and its eggs are widely used for food, but owing to its more northerly range and the inaccessibility of many of its colonies, it is today a commoner bird in the western Atlantic than the preceding species. Although many individuals winter in the Far North near the breeding colonies, if water remains open this species regularly migrates south in small numbers and ranges out to sea farther than the murre or razorbill. Occasional eruptive flights have carried birds to the Great Lakes and down the coast to South Carolina. Fish, crustacea, and squids seem to be their chief foods, while the birds themselves are the chief food of the peregrines and gyrfalcons that nest on the same cliffs with them.

VOICE: A sheeplike bleat and other purring and croaking notes.

NEST: (I. 31) In dense colonies on sea cliffs, sometimes in close association with the preceding species. The single eggs (3.1 x 2.0) are laid on bare rock as close together as the birds can sit to incubate them. They are green-blue, heavily blotched and scrawled with browns.

RANGE: (P. M.) Breeds from the islands and coast of the Arctic Ocean south to n. Hudson Bay, the Gulf of St. Lawrence, and the Aleutian Islands. Winters south to s. New England, s. Alaska, and Japan.

Dovekie*
(Little Auk)

Plautus alle—✻38
L. 8

IDENTIFICATION: This tiny, chunky alcid with a little bill, even less neck, and a buzzy flight is unique.

HABITS: The dovekie is one of the tremendously abundant northern sea birds that nest by the millions in favorable spots. Through it some of the bountiful resources of the nutrient-rich arctic waters become available for the support of fox, gull, falcon, and man. Easily caught with long-handled "butterfly nets," dovekies are staple food for many Eskimo tribes, which take them by the thousand. Like so many other arctic species, from fulmars to whales, these auks feed on the crustacea which abound in cold ocean water. Some of these crustacea are very small, but the dovekie has unique cheek pouches to aid it in carrying them back to its young. Except when nesting this species scatters out over most of the North Atlantic and becomes completely pelagic.

VOICE: A high-pitched chatter.

NEST: (I. 24) In congested colonies in the crevices of talus slopes of large broken rock fragments at the foot of cliffs. The single bluish-white egg (1.9 x 1.3) is unmarked and is usually laid several feet back from the entrance used by the birds.

RANGE: (M.) Breeds north of the Arctic Circle from n. Greenland, Franz Josef Land, and Novaya Zemlya south to n. Iceland. Winters chiefly between the southern limit of pack ice and the Gulf Stream to the Virginia capes and the

Faeroes, with occasional irruptive flights carrying them to Cuba and the Canaries.

Black Guillemot* *Cepphus grylle*—⚮38
L. 13

IDENTIFICATION: The large white area on the wing and the red feet are very conspicuous; they always identify summer adults in flight. Winter birds are whitish all over, which reduces the conspicuousness of the wing patch, which in young birds is mottled with dark. Guillemots take flight more readily than most alcids.

IMMATURE

HABITS: This species has none of the gregariousness of other alcids. Although widely distributed, only one to a few pairs are encountered in the vicinity of the average nesting place. This is a hardy bird and not much of a migrant. Often it remains near its breeding place throughout the year, even in the Far North, where it continues to feed under the ice, provided a few holes remain open so it can come up for air. Its attachment for a given feeding place seems to be so great that when it is disturbed by a boat it simply flies off in a circle and comes right back. Crustacea, shellfish, worms, and small fish like sand eels, captured under water or from rocky bottoms, are staple foods. It seems to avoid sandy areas.

VOICE: A weak, high-pitched, wheezy whistle or twitter.

NEST: (I. 24, N. 35) Not especially gregarious, this species nests wherever it can find a sheltered site under a rock or in a crack or crevice among boulder piles, talus slopes, or cliff faces near water. The 2 eggs (2.3 x 1.6) are laid on bare rock or on loose pebbles; they are dull whitish, boldly blotched with various shades of brown.

RANGE: (P. M.) Breeds from the islands and coasts of the Arctic Ocean, except in n.w. North America, south to James Bay, Maine, Iceland, Ireland, and s. Finland. Winters in open leads and air holes of the Arctic Ocean and the North Atlantic south to n. Massachusetts and n. France.

Puffin*   *Fratercula arctica*—⚹38
                                              L. 12½

IDENTIFICATION: In the breeding season the bill acquires a brightly colored sheath which is later shed; in winter it is smaller and duller brown at the base, largely yellow at the tip; its triangular shape is always distinctive. Young have so small a bill that their grayish cheeks become their best field character. The general appearance of the bird is chunky and short-necked.

HABITS: The puffin, though still common in many parts of the North, has declined greatly near settled areas. Tame and often curious, it is easily shot for food, though its eggs are not readily obtained. Like other burrow nesters—e.g., Leach's petrel—it is very vulnerable to mammal predators, and its colonies soon disappear from islands invaded by rats, cats, dogs, or foxes. It feeds largely in the coastal waters near its breeding grounds. Swimming under water with its wings, it readily obtains fish, mollusks, and a great variety of other marine organisms. On land it walks easily in upright position and roosts on rocks and ledges near water when not fishing.

VOICE: A short, single growl or a series of 3 in descending pitch.

NEST: (I. 41, N. 49) In colonies of varying size on small coastal islands with sufficient soil covering to permit the digging of shallow burrows several feet long. The single, generally pure-white egg (2.5 x 1.7) is laid in a cavity lined with a little straw and feathers at the end of the burrow, which is either dug by the puffin or taken over from a petrel. The entrance is usually well concealed under a flat rock, and the burrow is much curved.

RANGE: (P. M.) Breeds from n. Greenland, Spitsbergen, and Franz Josef Land south to Maine, Iceland, Brittany, and Portugal and west to Novaya Zemlya and w. Sweden. Winters as far north as there is open water, usually near its breeding areas, but some birds go to sea and small numbers occur throughout the North Atlantic south to Massachusetts and the w. Mediterranean.

PIGEON-LIKE BIRDS

Order Columbiformes

PIGEONS and DOVES   **Family Columbidae**

White-crowned Pigeon   *Columba leucocephala*—✳48
                                                    L. 13

IDENTIFICATION: The brilliantly white crown on the otherwise dark bird is distinctive. The crown is a pale gray on the some-what duller females and dull sooty on the rather brownish-bodied young.

HABITS: Generally quite gregarious, these handsome pigeons nest and roost in great concentrations. Fast fliers, they often move about the country in large flocks and frequently travel great distances daily in search of food. They feed on the fruit of the abundant berry-producing trees and shrubs which in the

West Indies form dense jungles over vast areas of land unsuitable for agriculture, converting the berries into potential
human food. The birds, however, have been so ruthlessly destroyed, especially about their nesting colonies and roosts on
mangrove-covered islets, that much of the food they once
consumed now goes unharvested. A typical example of man's
thoughtlessness in killing off an animal that represents his only
link to an organic product that is unavailable to him until
it has been gathered and processed into meat by a living
organism.

VOICE: Three short, deep cooing notes repeated several times,
followed by a drawn-out, tremulous closing note, the whole
performance sounding quite owl-like at times.

NEST: In colonies, often very congested ones, on small islands.
The nest is a compact structure of twigs, lined with plant
fibers, placed on top of a cactus, shrub, or tree from a few to
many feet above the ground. Two white eggs (1.5 x 1.1) are
the normal clutch.

RANGE: (P. M.) Breeds from the Bahamas and Florida Keys
south through the West Indies to Dominica and on islands
along the east coast of Central America from Yucatan to
Panama. Largely withdraws in winter from Florida and the
Bahamas.

Red-billed Pigeon   *Columba flavirostris*— ⚡48
                                         L. 14; W. 24

IDENTIFICATION: The 2 deep color tones of this broad-tailed
bird give it a wholly dark appearance at a distance. Its only
distinctive markings are the deep purplish-red middle coverts
on the otherwise slaty wings. Females and young are less
intensely colored and tend toward a dull wine and ashy tone.

HABITS: The red-bill is normally a pigeon of the mature forest,
feeding on fruits and nuts high in the crowns of the taller
trees. It is a solitary nester, but at other seasons it gathers
into small flocks to roam the countryside in search of food.
Like many birds of the tropical forests, these are most readily
observed when they make their daily visits to water to drink
and bathe. In recent years in s. Texas they have learned to
visit the stubble fields to glean waste grain, along with other
members of their family.

VOICE: Loud, clear cooing notes, generally rather abrupt and
high-pitched.

NEST: A fragile structure of sticks, sometimes with a lining of fibers, placed on a horizontal limb in a dense clump of vegetation, generally 6 to 12 feet from the ground but occasionally higher. The single egg (1.5 x 1.1) is white.

RANGE: (R.) Occurs from s. Texas and s. Sonora south to Costa Rica.

Rock Dove* *Columba livia—*✳48
(Domestic Pigeon) L. 13½

IDENTIFICATION: Distinctive markings of this pigeon in its normal wild plumage are the white lower back and wing linings, the 2 black wing bars, and the tail band. Selective breeding in captivity has produced many individual variations in plumage color, but a population of freely interbreeding escapes seems gradually to acquire all the genes necessary to reproduce the normal color. Since normal genes are generally dominant over mutants, the entire group eventually returns to the plumage of the ancestral wild stock.

HABITS: Cliffs near water, especially along the seacoast, are the normal habitat of the rock dove in its native home. Here it is often closely associated with the peregrine falcon, which nests on the same cliffs and often feeds largely upon these pigeons. The rock dove is a ground feeder, frequenting the wrack line of beaches, wastelands, and grain stubble, where it obtains seeds, green food, and animal material.

About cities the bird is quite dependent upon handouts of bread crumbs from pigeon lovers. The generosity of such persons largely determines the size of the local population, since the species is so prolific that it invariably keeps its numbers at the approximate maximum the food supply can support. In a few cities urbanized crows take a toll of the eggs; in others peregrine falcons, nesting on the high ledges of office buildings and hotels, feed upon the birds themselves. But as neither crows nor falcons seem able to reap a harvest that can equal the rate at which pigeons produce young, they can hardly be said to exercise any real control over the population.

VOICE: The soft, often gurgling *coo* is well known.

NEST: (I. 14) A few bits of debris on a cliff or cave ledge. With the growth of cities these birds have utilized window ledges and crevices in ornamental stonework for nesting. They are indifferent to crowding, if not actually colonial, and will accept multiple-compartment birdhouses commonly known as dovecotes. The 2 eggs (1.5 x 1.1) are white and several broods are reared annually, the breeding season continuing almost throughout the year.

RANGE: (R.) Native to the islands of the e. Atlantic from the British Isles to the Cape Verdes and through s. Europe and n. Africa east to China. Introduced throughout the Temperate Zone by the escape of domestic stock.

Zenaida Dove   *Zenaida aurita*—※48
L. 10

IDENTIFICATION: The brownish upper tail coverts and center of the black-banded square tail, the black-spotted inner area of the wing, and the white bar along the rear of the wing are distinctive. Females are generally browner and lack head spots. Young are similar, with a large pale russet area on the wing.

HABITS: This dove avoids dense forests but occurs almost everywhere else, in brushy growths, open woods, grasslands, and old fields—habitats that have greatly increased since the coming of civilization. Frequent visits to water appear necessary, and zenaidas seem especially common in the vicinity of coastal mangrove thickets and inland marshy areas. Most of their feeding is done on the ground, where seeds, green vegetation, and fruits can be picked up. When flushed they generally take off with a loud wing clapping but soon drop out of sight into the nearest dense cover.

VOICE: Cooing notes similar to, but often deeper than, those of a mourning dove.

NEST: On the ground, in reed beds, holes in rocks, and various sites in trees or shrubs. The nest is always a sparse structure of twigs and grass. The 2 eggs (1.2 x .90) are white.

RANGE: (P. M.) The Bahamas, West Indies, the coast of Yucatan, and occasionally s. Florida.

White-winged Dove*   *Zenaida asiatica*—※48
L. 10

IDENTIFICATION: The bold diagonal white bar across the inner wing and the white corners of the rounded tail are distinctive. Young are similar to adults but grayer.

HABITS: These gregarious doves frequently occur in huge concentrations where extensive areas of junglelike thicket composed of tall shrubs and low trees are present to provide nest sites. Water must be available within 10 miles. Wild fruits, nuts, and seeds are normal foods, but huge flocks gather after the harvest to feed in stubble fields on weed seeds and waste grain. Texas's two southernmost counties supported several million white-wings before the extensive agricultural development of the Rio Grande Valley destroyed much of their nesting habitat.

VOICE: The cooing calls are variable in tone and often quite musical, those of a large flock carrying for long distances. A common series of notes is 3 vigorous, abrupt hoots, followed by a prolonged *coo*.

NEST: (I. 18) Although they do nest singly, most nesting is in huge colonies, often many acres in extent. Dense thickets of mesquite, mangrove, or other low trees are the usual site, with the nests from 6 to 15 feet aboveground. A frail platform of loose twigs holds the 2 creamy-buff eggs (1.2 x .87). Two broods are often reared.

RANGE: (P. M.) Occurs from the Bahamas, occasionally Florida and the Gulf Coast, s. Texas, s. New Mexico, and s. California south to the Greater Antilles and Costa Rica. Also on the Pacific coast of South America from s. Ecuador to n. Chile. There is a winter withdrawal from the northernmost part of their range.

Mourning Dove[1]   *Zenaidura macroura*—⊀48
L. 12; Wt. 4 oz.

IDENTIFICATION: The long, pointed tail bordered with white on a slim, brown bird with a small head is distinctive.

HABITS: (Age 9 yrs.) The changes wrought by civilization have been almost wholly favorable to the tame, confiding mourning dove that readily makes itself at home in close proximity to man. The weed seeds and waste grains of crop fields provide an abundant supply of its favorite foods, while shade trees, hedgerows, and wood-lot borders furnish it with cover for nesting and roosting. The planting of trees which serve as nest sites, the close cropping of pastures which leaves the ground rather open and bare—the way doves like it—and the development of ponds for watering livestock have made many areas of once open grassland much more favorable dove habitat. Like a number of other game birds, this one appears at times to benefit from our foolish abuse of land, as overgrazing and soil erosion lead to an increase in weeds (the seeds of which are good dove foods) at the expense of the more valuable but poorer seed producers, the perennial range grasses.

After nesting large numbers of doves concentrate in favorable areas and use a communal roost at night, but there is no close flock organization. Daily mass flights to sources of water and grit are a regular feature of winter concentrations. Only a few doves remain in the northern states in winter, the greater number migrating to our southern states or on down into Mexico and Central America. Although ordinarily ground feeders, these doves occasionally take the seeds of opening pine cones high in the trees. During the breeding season they display a craving for salt and lime, which they often obtain by eating snails.

The mourning dove occurs in every state in the Union, but only in the South is it a game bird. In the North it can maintain itself in moderate numbers only if not shot, as here it suffers higher natural losses and has a lower rate of reproduction. The more severe winters make migration necessary, which shortens the breeding season and cuts the number of broods. Thus there are in the North no large numbers of surplus birds that hunters can draw upon without affecting the breeding population of the following year. Furthermore, in the South the hunting toll is spread between local birds and migrants, while in the North it falls entirely on the local breeding stock.

VOICE: A monotonously repeated series of long and short cooing notes varying considerably in pitch and very doleful in character. Also a rapid series of shrill, squeaky whistles when flushed into flight.

NEST: (I. 14, N. 11) A flimsy, flat platform of sticks lined with finer material. In treeless country doves nest on the ground, but elevated sites are undoubtedly safer and seem to be preferred. Fifteen to 25 feet above the ground is an average height, but sites may range from just off the ground in a bush to the top of a tall tree. A substantial horizontal limb or other solid support is sought, and the old nest of such birds as robins and grackles is often used as a foundation. Most nesting is solitary in isolated trees, but small, loose colonies are not uncommon. Conifers are often favored. The 2 eggs (1.1 x .85) are pure white. Three and occasionally 4 broods are reared, and although the breeding season often starts in February, the last nestlings may not fly until mid-October.

RANGE: (P. M.) Breeds from Nova Scotia, s. Maine, c. New York, s. Ontario, Wisconsin, Minnesota, Manitoba, and c.

British Columbia south to the Bahamas, Greater Antilles, and through most of Mexico. Winters from Massachusetts, s. Michigan, Nebraska, Wyoming, and Oregon south to Panama.

Passenger Pigeon *Ectopistes migratorius*—✳ 48
L. 16; W. 24

IDENTIFICATION: The solid-gray head and the generally blue-gray appearance of the upper parts were distinctive. The male had a very reddish breast, while the under parts of the female were almost wholly pale gray.

HABITS: Probably no other bird has ever occurred in quite such huge concentrations as the passenger pigeon. Most writers who have left firsthand accounts begin with an apology for what they know will sound like exaggeration. John J. Audubon and Alexander Wilson estimated that the numbers they saw in the vast migratory flights that darkened the sky and took hours to pass exceeded either 1 or 2 billion birds. Before we dismiss these figures we must remember that the species had as its original habitat nearly a billion acres of forest, much of which eventually became highly productive farmland. This forest must have yielded vast quantities of such nutritious pigeon foods as beechnuts, acorns, and other tree seeds; fruits of all sorts; buds and such supplementary items as grubs, earthworms, and roots that the birds scratched out of the ground.

Pigeons the world over are largely fruit, seed, and mast eaters and forest dwellers. This species, evolving in the largest and richest of all forests, developed a mobility which enabled it to escape the hardships of winter and of regional crop failures. Home seemed to be where food was found. The birds had no rigid migration pattern but roamed the eastern half of the continent, stopping wherever they found something to eat and remaining until the supply was exhausted. During the breeding season they established nesting colonies miles in extent, in which each tree might have from a few to more than 100 nests. Such concentrations must have been in some way extremely favorable to the rearing of young to compensate for the enormous distances the adults had to travel daily for food. The birds also nested in scattered pairs and small colonies, but there are indications that such nestings were relatively unproductive; which may help explain the pigeon's rapid decline, once the destruction of the forest made the establishment of large colonies impossible.

It is difficult to understand the rapidity of this decline. True, the birds were harried the year round by market hunters, but generally the law of supply and demand makes such hunting impracticable long before a species is exterminated. It may be that the passenger pigeon's extreme gregariousness kept the survivors together almost to the end, or at least until the number was so small that a productive colony could not be formed—and as long as they were together they were, of course, very vulnerable to hunters. Apart from direct killing, there were other forces at work which might in time have doomed them just as surely. Year by year their habitat was shrinking before the ax, and in the South increasing numbers of competitors for their winter food supply—razorback hogs—roamed the woods. Nothing, however, has really explained the swiftness of their disappearance.

One suggestion is that a large segment of the surviving population may have met disaster in crossing one of the Great Lakes in a storm or fog. Other theories involve the outbreak of an epidemic disease, possibly acquired from domestic pigeons or poultry, or the introduction to this country of a new disease or insect that suddenly spoiled vast segments of the mast crop. The chestnut blight which did eliminate the most valuable of all mast producers, the American chestnut, came some years later. Toward the end there were well-meant laws forbidding certain types of pigeon killing, especially in the breeding season, but in the face of the hunter's greed and the insatiable appetites of the great cities, they were seldom enforced.

The last great nesting, some 100,000 acres in extent, from which more than 1½ million birds are known to have been shipped to market by railroad alone, took place in 1878. The last specimen was shot just 20 years later in 1898. The last survivor, a bird hatched and reared in captivity, died in a zoo in 1914 at the age of 29. Now that a chance to see one alive is forever denied us, we must be content with the accounts that have been brought together in such books as those by M. H. Mitchell and W. B. Mershon.

VOICE: The calls were loud and rather harsh chattering, clucking, or croaking notes that bore little resemblance to the cooing of most pigeons.

NEST: (L. 14, N. 18) Often in huge, congested colonies many miles in extent with many nests to a tree. One in 1871 in c. Wisconsin was estimated to have covered 850 square miles and contained 136 million nests. Small colonies, however, were not uncommon, and occasionally solitary pairs nested. The nest was a frail platform of sticks supported in the branches of a tree. A single white egg (1.5 x 1.1) was the normal clutch.

RANGE: (M.) Bred from Nova Scotia, c. Quebec, James Bay, and n. Manitoba south to s. New England, Pennsylvania, West Virginia, Kentucky, Mississippi, and Kansas. Wintered from North Carolina and Arkansas south to n. Florida, the Gulf Coast, and c. Texas. Occasional stragglers or small flocks occurred far beyond these limits, north in summer to the Arctic Circle and south in winter to Cuba and s. Mexico. Now extinct.

Ground Dove   *Columbigallina passerina*—✕48
L. 6¾

IDENTIFICATION: The small size, short tail, and the extensive area of reddish-brown revealed when the bird takes wing are distinctive. Females and young are considerably paler, grayer, and less strongly spotted.

HABITS: This well-named little bird is usually seen on the ground where, with tail high and head nodding at every step, it searches for grass and weed seeds. It prefers open dry ground and has taken kindly to gardens, plowed cropland, overgrazed grasslands, and dirt roads, while still occurring in open pine woodlands, barren stony areas, and on beaches. Seldom fluttering away until almost stepped on, the doves zigzag off for only a short distance before dropping to the ground or perching in a tree. Very abundant in many areas, they have mysteriously disappeared from others where they were once common.

VOICE: A soft, mournful *coo-oo* rising at the end, repeated over and over.

NEST: (I. 13) Either on the ground in a scantily lined depression hidden among weeds or tall grass, or on a flat platform-like structure of fine plant fibers on a stump in a vine tangle or saddled on a low limb of a tree, or occasionally in the old nests of other birds. The 2 eggs (.86 x .64) are white and 2 or more broods are reared during the unusually long breeding season.

RANGE: (R.) Occurs from Bermuda, the Bahamas, South Carolina, the Gulf States, s. New Mexico, and s. California south through the West Indies and Central America to c. Brazil and Ecuador.

Inca Dove*   *Scardafella inca*—❋48
                                              L. 8

IDENTIFICATION: The scaled upper parts and the long white-bordered tail are distinctive. The wings when spread show extensive areas of reddish-brown.

HABITS: The Inca is a ground dove feeding on bare, open ground or under the sparse shrubs and cactus of semi-arid areas. It finds towns and the vicinity of any human habitation much to its liking, and in many regions it has become the most domestic of birds. It is now extending its range northward in response to the creation of these seemingly ideal Inca dove habitats. Gardens, lawns, parks, and chicken yards are favorite feeding grounds, and a source of water (so necessary to all pigeons) is seldom far away. It displays practically no fear of man and seems to prefer to nest close to centers of human activity.

VOICE: A monotonous, abrupt *coo-oo-coo* with a blowing quality.

NEST: (I. 14, N. 12) On a horizontal support some 6 to 15 feet above the ground, usually a tree limb but often a man-made structure. The nest is a flat platform of fine twigs and plant fibers with little or no lining. Not infrequently it is placed on top of the old nest of some other bird. The 2 eggs (.88 x .66) are pure white. As many as 4 or 5 broods may be attempted in a single season.

RANGE: (R.) Occurs from s.c. Texas, s. New Mexico, and Arizona south to n. Costa Rica.

White-fronted Dove*   *Leptotila verreauxi*—❋48
                                              L. 12

IDENTIFICATION: In flight the rounded tail shows a narrow white tip on either side of the dark central feathers, and the wings have conspicuous reddish-brown linings. At other times the pale forehead and under parts are the most distinctive characters.

HABITS: This rather solitary dove frequents dense, moist woodlands, where it ranges from the treetops to the ground in its search for the fruits and seeds that appear to be its sole food. It is best located by its deep note, as it seldom leaves the woods, where it is hard to see in the thick underbrush and dense, leafy tree crowns. When flushed it makes a shrill woodcock-like whistle with its wings.

voice: A very low-pitched, long-drawn-out, soft *coo* or *whooo,* descending in tone.

nest: A platform of sticks and plant fibers, generally from 5 to 10 feet above the ground in a dense shrub, low tree branch, or vine tangle. The 2 eggs (1.2 x .90) are cream-colored.

range: (P. M.) Occurs from s. Texas, s. Chihuahua, and s. Sonora south through Central and South America to c. Argentina. Some withdrawal in winter from extreme northern parts of the range.

Key West Quail Dove*   *Oreopeleia chrysia*—#48
L. 11

identification: Because of its iridescence this species is quite variable in color, but the long white streak below the eye is characteristic. Young are bright cinnamon-rufous above and dull cinnamon on the breast, very unlike adults.

habits: This is the most northerly-ranging species of a large genus of Central American and West Indian ground pigeons. It is a bird of the heavily shaded but open forest floor beneath the dense tangle of low, scrubby trees that cover the dry hillsides and moist lowlands of its island habitats. Here it feeds on fallen fruits and seeds and resorts to secluded, well-shaded pools to drink and bathe. As it probably still occurs as far north in the Bahamas as the latitude of Palm Beach, Audubon's account of it as a summer resident of the Florida Keys that migrated to Cuba in winter seems quite reasonable. If the Bahama birds are at all migratory, this species may still occur from time to time on the Keys, although it has now been many years since it has been recorded in this area.

voice: A series of groaning notes, said to sound like *whoe-whoe-oh-oh-oh.*

nest: Apparently the nest may be a loose collection of leaves and trash in a hollow on the ground or a platform of sticks up to a considerable height in a tree. Two creamy-buff eggs (1.2 x .90) are a normal clutch.

range: (R.) Occurs in the Bahamas, Cuba, and Hispaniola, and at one time appears to have bred on some of the Florida Keys.

INDEX

For kingfishers, water-thrushes, owls, woodpeckers, grackles, crows, ravens, the roadrunner, and all small land birds, consult Index to Audubon Bird Guide. *This companion volume covers every bird of Eastern North America not found in this book.*